E·L·S·A
LANCHESTER
HERSELF

*"Her hair is in the chestnut trees of London
and her feet are in the mud of the Thames."
(Vogue magazine, circa 1920)*

E·L·S·A
LANCHESTER
HERSELF

ST. MARTIN'S PRESS / NEW YORK

Editor: Toni Lopopolo
Assistant Editor: Karen Johnsen
Managing Editor: Carol E. W. Edwards
Book Designer: Manuela Paul
Jacket Designers: Andy Carpenter and Manuela Paul
Production Manager: Chuck Thompson
Copyeditor: Elisa Petrini
Agent: Mike Hamilburg

Sections of photographs follow pages 26, 154, and 268.

Library of Congress Cataloging in Publication Data

Lanchester, Elsa, 1902–
   Elsa Lanchester, herself.

   Includes index.
   1. Lanchester, Elsa, 1902–   2. Actors—Great
Britain—Biography.   I. Title.
PN2598.L16A34   1983   792'.028'0924 [B]   82-16998
ISBN 0-312-24376-6

First Edition
10 9 8 7 6 5 4 3 2 1

E·L·S·A
LANCHESTER
HERSELF

Prologue
The Lanchester Case
My Parents

Edith Lanchester, my mother, was born in 1873 in Brighton, Sussex.
She was the fifth in a family of eight. Her father, Henry J. Lanchester,
was a prosperous architect. They could be said to be comparatively
wealthy. The children all had high-pressure educations and finished up
early with distinguished college and university degrees. By the time my
mother entered school, the oldest, Harry, was already a town planner
for the government and the next brother, Fred, was busy inventing the
Lanchester Car and its fluid flywheel. Even the girls, Mary, Carrie, and
Edith, were extraordinary—though some might say a little odd. It was
unusual for girls to be so well educated, for in the Lanchesters' stratum
of life girls were not expected to want a career. Mary painted flowers,
and Carrie got married to a cousin—rather shocking.

Edith matriculated at the Universities of London and Cambridge
and at the College of Preceptors, and passed her exams with *A*s and
honors in every single subject: Scripture History, Euclid, French, Bot-
any, Political Economy, and so on. She was a teacher for about a year,
then went to Birkbeck College to learn shorthand and typing. Afterward she became secretary to Eleanor Marx, Karl Marx's daughter.

My mother was a good speaker at meetings and rallies. In the fight
for freedom and equality and the division of wealth she was an important personality, backed by the Social Democratic Federation (SDF)
and the Independent Labour Party. At that time the Fabian Society, a
group of upper-class intellectuals buzzing around George Bernard
Shaw, was also growing and flourishing. But Edith Lanchester could
not have expounded her down-to-earth theories in the company of the
Fabians. Her own background probably influenced her choice—to
promote her cause through true working-class socialists. At one small
meeting that made the news, she spoke with scorn of how her mother

collected the used tea leaves from the day's various teapots, strained them, and spread them on newspapers on the kitchen stove until dry, then repacked them and gave them to the poor.

Another personality among the SDF group was James Sullivan, the son of an Irish policeman long settled in London. He had a mop of black curly hair and a large mustache. James Sullivan worked in a black lead factory. He spoke with a cockney accent but he spoke well and was respected. He was intellectually ambitious, studying the dictionary and the encyclopedia, learning shorthand and typing, and developing elegant, scriptlike handwriting. In time Edith Lanchester and James Sullivan fell in love. As they did not believe in marriage and as a declaration of freedom, they let it be known in no uncertain terms that they were going to live together.

They rented two rooms from a certain Mrs. Mary Grey. But one morning, as my mother was having breakfast alone, the door burst open. Her eldest brother, Harry, strode in, soon followed by her father, two other brothers, and Dr. G. Fielding Blandford, a well-known mental specialist. As the men questioned her, she restated her opinions about freedom and marriage. Thereupon they presented a certificate of insanity, an "Urgency Order," already filled out and signed by the doctor and Henry J. Lanchester. The "Supposed Cause" of her insanity, the certificate stated, was "over-education."

When Henry Lanchester told his daughter that they were going to take her away, she fought them off. The landlady, joining in the fray, got a black eye. Then my mother's father and brothers got a rope and pinioned her arms to her sides. A private brougham waited outside and off they went. Although they held her legs, it was reported later that Miss Lanchester kicked out a window of the carriage.

Mrs. Grey, the landlady, rushed out to find James Sullivan at his work. Immediately the two went to the police, who sent them to a judge to obtain a writ of habeas corpus. It took a visit to the Lunacy Commission to find my mother's whereabouts. Her family had taken her to a private house in Roehampton Lane—The Priory, an asylum for the insane.

That night a band of SDF members stood outside the walls of the asylum and sang "The People's Flag." The story broke fast. In *The London Times* of October 30, 1895, the following account appeared.

THE TIMES, WEDNESDAY, OCTOBER 30, 1895
THE CASE OF MISS LANCHESTER

Yesterday afternoon, in consequence of a communication from the Lunacy Commissioners, Miss Edith Lanchester was released from Roehampton Asylum, where she had been detained since Friday last. On Monday Dr. Chambers, the medical superintendent of the asylum, received an order authorizing Miss Lanchester's release on Friday next, but yesterday Dr. Chambers, accompanied by Mr. John Burns, M.P., again saw the Commissioners, with the result that an order was issued for her immediate release. The two gentlemen at once proceeded to Roehampton, where they were joined by Mr. Sullivan, Miss Lanchester's lover. Miss Lanchester then left with her friends. Last night Miss Lanchester was seen at her rooms in Este-road, Battersea, where she has lodged for the past two years, and she spoke of the experiences that she had gone through during the past few days. She said that on Friday morning her eldest brother called to see her before she was up. On coming downstairs she asked him if he had received the letter she sent him the night before, in which she announced her intentions. He replied that he had not, whereupon she handed him a copy which she had kept. She left him a few minutes, and on her return two other brothers, her father, and a doctor entered the house. The doctor discussed the marriage question with her and afterward went away. She then remarked that it was time she started for the office, and her brothers said they would go with her. When she was ready her eldest brother said, "We are going to take you home," to which she replied that she did not intend going home, and she called out to Mrs. Gray, her landlady. One brother then took hold of her round the shoulders and another by the legs, and she was carried out of the house and thrust violently into a brougham. One of her brothers then tied her wrists with a piece of rope. The blinds were pulled, so that she could not see the direction they were going. Eventually she found herself at the asylum at Roehampton, where she was seen on arrival by Dr. Chambers. She then asked to see him alone, and the doctor directed her brothers and her father to retire. She explained matters fully to the doctor, who replied that he had a certificate and was obliged to receive her. She was well treated. On Sunday morning she was given a separate sitting room. On Monday evening two Commissioners in Lunacy called. After talking with her for more than half an hour they had a consultation with Dr. Chambers and his assistant, and then they informed her that they could not honestly detain her, as they considered her perfectly sane, but somewhat foolish. They said they would write an order for her discharge on or before November 1. She appealed to Dr. Chambers to let her go at once, but he said she could go on the following day, and he invited her to consider herself the guest of himself and his wife until then. Yesterday Mr. Burns called and lunched with her, and on Mr. Sullivan calling they left together for Battersea. Referring to her dispute with her parents, Miss Lanchester said that down to Friday last she was willing to study their wishes to a certain extent, and had agreed to go abroad with Mr. Sullivan; but after the treatment to which she had been subjected she should consider them no longer, but should take her own course. Her opinions on the marriage question had undergone no change by her detention in the asylum, but, if anything, she held to them more firmly than before.

The Ladies' Column
by Mrs. Fenwick-Miller

Immense excitement was caused in London by the arrest of Miss Lanchester under the Lunacy Laws. The young lady is twenty-four years old, and, as everybody knows by this time, had made up her mind to "marry" a young artisan without the formalities of either the Church or the Law. She proclaimed her intention—if not exactly from the house-tops, at all events in the ears of her parents. It is quite easy to understand and sympathise with the anguish of Miss Lanchester's parents, who see their daughter about to place herself in a position which will undoubtedly taint and harm her entire future. She is a highly educated girl and is said also to be a good platform speaker, attractive in person, and of hitherto unblemished repute. She was a candidate at the recent School Board elections. For such a girl, if she keep "within the pale," there is nowadays a noble and interesting career possible.

From then on, it became known as "The Lanchester Kidnapping Case," reported in newspapers in India, Germany, America, South Africa—practically worldwide. Editorials discussed the nays and yeas of freedom, and of course letters poured in from hundreds and hundreds of people either praising or vilifying Edith Lanchester and James Sullivan: "What about when the little babies come and he leaves you?" There were even some proposals of marriage. The Marquis of Queensberry, who formulated the Queensberry rules in boxing, wrote to congratulate the couple and to offer them a hundred pounds if they would marry at a big church, then get up on the altar and deny their vows. Edith Lanchester and James Sullivan ignored his proposal.

Still, a great deal of money was needed to fight the kidnapping and Blandford's unwarranted certificate.

Before the kidnapping, my mother had maintained close ties with her family. She still had her own room at her father's house and generally had gone there to visit about once a week. But after her release from the asylum she never saw her father again.

Public meetings were held at more than fifty branches of the SDF "to decide what legal steps are to be taken," but the lawyers concluded that "Miss Lanchester cannot bring an action against her father or against Dr. Blandford with any reasonable success." Eventually all parties were obliged to retire. With the newspaper headline MISS LANCHESTER WILL NOT MAKE A PLATFORM OF HER KIDNAPPING CASE the issue finally seemed closed.

The SDF fought hard to have Dr. Blandford censured by the Lunacy Commission, but he was elusive and powerful, and the medical press—*The British Medical Journal* and *The Lancet*—honored his status, although they criticized his procedure in the kidnapping, particularly his questionable medical certificate.

The Lanchester storm in a teacup contributed in its way to reform of the sanity laws. Edith Lanchester and James Sullivan—Biddy and Shamus, as they called each other—continued being active socialists, and their work in the movement helped to advance the cause of trade unionism.

On May 6, 1897, they had a son, Waldo Sullivan Lanchester. I, Elsa Sullivan Lanchester, was born October 28, 1902.

My father's red tie was kept in the top left-hand drawer of a big mahogany chest of drawers. It was rolled up round two mothballs and wrapped in tissue paper. This tie must have been bought before I was born, and it was only after I was able to move a chair over to the chest that I could sometimes take a look at it during the year. It was made of knitted, very shiny silk and was a bright rich scarlet. It was worn on May Day, the socialists' own day. That morning we started off early from the outer suburbs—Lewisham or Norwood or Clapham Common—and took the bus to Charing Cross Embankment. There the breaks were lined up, with the restless cart horses already snorting to get going or get out of harness—very dangerous-looking beasts, strong enough to overturn a breakful of people. My mother and father and brother and I stood around for ages, meeting stalwart old socialists and their children. The children grew bored and itchy as mothers and fathers with overeager eyes talked about the old days and the early socialist movement and the progress of socialism. My father with his red tie and his glittering teeth, tobacco-stained under his black walrus mustache, was a pumping handshaker with fellow comrades. My mother got particular attention and many more "Hullo, comrade's" than the others. At the time I wondered why.

Vendors sold colored paper windmills on sticks, boiled sweets, and sherbet. The sherbet was a fruity powder that came sealed in a triangular bag with a licorice tube sticking out of it. You sucked up the sherbet and it fizzed violently in your mouth. Very exciting and quite worth the long day ahead.

Around ten o'clock the decorated breaks started off, streamers flying, and made their way along the Charing Cross Embankment, up Whitehall, across Trafalgar Square, up Regent Street, then a turn to the left on Oxford Street and so to Hyde Park—everyone singing all the way but not in unison. Here and there an outburst of "Hark the Battle Cry Is Ringing" and "Arise, Ye Starvelings from Your Slumbers." And of course "The People's Flag," sung to the tune of "O Tannenbaum."

> The people's flag is deepest red,
> It shrouded oft our martyred dead,
> And ere their limbs grew stiff and cold,
> Their hearts' blood dyed its ev'ry fold.
>
> Then raise the scarlet standard high!
> Within its shade we'll live or die,
> Tho' cowards flinch and traitors sneer,
> We'll keep the red flag flying here.

By the late afternoon, sticky with sherbet, bored, tired, and sick of the Labour leaders droning on about freedom, we children slumped around on the grass or in the flapping tent. The grass squashed by humanity had a very soporific effect, and grown-ups and children slept all over the place, not caring what they looked like. Perhaps someday that haunting smell will prove to be some sort of drug. In the tent my mother and father and other parents swilled tea and had a good old grizzle about the capitalists and the system. And then home, by break and bus.

Home—wherever we were living at the time. Besides Norwood, Lewisham, and Clapham, there were also Catford, Battersea, and various other places we moved from and to. We were always moving away from something that had overtones of legal involvement, however harmless. My mother always seemed to have the law on her side. She knew every loophole in dozens of bylaws. Vaccination, census night, landladies who would not make repairs, and corrupt sanitary inspectors. My parents moved six times to avoid having me vaccinated because my brother Waldo had "taken" very badly six years before. Such government interference with individual freedom of choice was not to be tolerated again. My mother tried to claim that Waldo's vaccination certificate was mine, but the difference in our ages and sex made the stupid officials doubt her, so we moved again. The local greengrocer, a socialist, would move our few possessions in the night, which was called "shooting the moon."

On census night the head of the house has to sign a statement about who was under the roof on the given night. My father would remain under the roof and perform this function, so that day, brother, mother, and I took off for the Surrey woods, carrying blankets, a tarpaulin, and some old pillowcases to fill with twigs and bracken. We went by bus and tram and then walked. The day was cold, and the clouds were deep gray and very low. We hung our tarp between the branches of two young oaks in a young wood and took out our bread and butter and a bottle of water. At first it seemed fun, but then it started to pour. During the night we awoke deep in a pool of water. We moved up a few feet to higher ground, but of course we could no longer sleep. It had just begun to get light and the rain had stopped, yet there was the strangest pattering sound around us. When I went out to survey the terrain, I soon found my hair full of creeping crawling clicking ticking life, which turned out to be minute green caterpillars fallen from the oak saplings. We were all three brushing them off when a loud, unfriendly man's voice said, "What are you doing here? You're trespassing." "I don't think so," answered my mother. "It is not yet sunrise." She was right, legally. We quietly folded our soaking blankets, said good-bye to the gamekeeper, and walked through the caterpillars off the private property and finally to the tram. We had not been counted.

We often went out camping overnight and felt more secure on private property, taking advantage of the protection provided by the law that you could not be turned off after sunset or before sunrise. Gypsies, who might otherwise settle in, were thus kept on the move.

My mother, Biddy, found it irresistible to get the better of the upper classes. She felt almost sorry if there was no confrontation with a gamekeeper or an owner. I learned to enjoy despising property owners, but I didn't admire Biddy very much either. Often we camped out in Sussex or Surrey on some farmland and had our meals at farmhouses—mostly eggs, bread, butter and jam, and milk. It would be too early for apples, but we would have lots of raspberries and cream. Every day we wandered into the fields and woods for a picnic. Once I strayed into a copse of spindly trees, where I thought I could smell my brother's bicycle lamp. I ran back to the family, and the more I ran, the stronger the smell got. I had been racing through wild garlic. Just try putting a drop of water on a lump of carbide (used to create gas for old bicycle lamps) and you'll see what I mean. I think my earliest memories remain as a vision and a smell. Come to think of it, most early memories seem to include only one or two of the senses. In later years memories get more complicated, but that scent of garlic came to stay.

On one of our camping trips, my father, Shamus, got an earwig in his ear. With only the light of one candle to tempt it out, we passed a scary night. Apparently, crawling inside his ear, the earwig sounded like the crack of lightning with thunder, and we were also afraid it would nip his eardrum. At last, toward morning, it just walked out— very glad, I'm sure, to get out of a hairy ear. No more camping out for Shamus.

When Biddy met Shamus, he was working in a black lead factory and would come home quite black. He was and would remain a self-improver. Later, after long study, he became a shorthand typist and bookkeeper—quite a step up for the son of an Irish policeman and his wife from Cork. There were eight children in that family. Biddy also came from a family of eight children. And *her* mother, *Octavia,* also was the last of eight. A witching number, it seems.

The London County Council ruled that all children had to attend school at age five. Waldo was safely enrolled in a boys' school at Clapham, run by a most wonderful and distinguished socialist, a Mr. Frederick Kettle. My highly educated mother wanted to teach me at home. Through our continual moving, I managed to avoid school for about a year. We were finally caught in a flat in Rudloe Road at Clapham Common. Waving her master's degree at a County Council inspector, my mother insisted that she would teach me at home. The officious inspector said no, it was illegal—a parent, however well edu-cated, could not take over a teacher's duties. Why, a parent might teach the child about sex and leave out grammar or French, or omit history! Tch, tch! So I did go to Council school at the age of six and a half. At Biddy's request, I was kept outside during morning prayers. When I went home in the evening I thought it advisable to stand on my head in case there was a God—you never know. To do anything difficult would serve, I thought. I had no idea what classes were all about and was treated like an idiot by the teachers and children alike. In the playground I was left alone. "That's the kid who looks through the glass door when we're at prayers!" I knew about where babies came from, how to draw grasses and some flowers, with some geometric forms thrown in, some French. But when the teacher asked me how many pennies there were in a pound, I walked out of the class and ran home. In tears, of course. When the inspector came to investigate, I lay on the floor, rigid and straight and silent.

A week later I was the only girl at my brother's school. Mr. Kettle's school was "advanced." Madge, his attractive daughter, who was quite a flirt, taught French when she felt like it—which was fairly often. A Mr. Hamilton taught mathematics in a very practical kind of way. He had a cupboardful of instruments—telescopes, theodolites, and so on, and I was soon busy with logarithms and parabolas. First thing in the morning we read the newspapers. We more or less chose the day's work for ourselves and did as we liked, as long as we did *something.* I grew into an antipower child, opposed to any power, including Biddy's and Shamus's. My brother Waldo probably had similar feelings but he was an inactivist, and many a punch in the stomach I gave him for being that way.

A child in London develops a sense of self-preservation rather like a gutter rat—dodging traffic, walking a long way alone on dark evenings, jumping on and off moving buses and trams. Biddy very often said, "If you can't look after yourself now, you never will." She and Shamus also insisted that they did not have children as insurance for their old age, as some mothers and fathers do.

Wherever we lived we had The Kitchen and not much more—with luck, two bedrooms or a front room with two camp beds. The bathroom and w.c. we shared with the people above us or below us. Most of our neighbors were stuffy, respectable people to us, but to them we were always Miss Edith Lanchester and Mr. Sullivan and the two Lanchester children. A vague scent of notoriety seemed to be in the air we breathed, but I was unaware that we were different. The recognition grew with me gradually so I had no dramatic jolt.

Our Kitchen was a meeting place for socialist comrades. All evening people drifted in and out, talking of meetings and rallies and thumping our table. The comrades usually finished up comparing socialism to Marxism and communism, and it often got quite rowdy, but by that time I'd usually gone to bed. I was quite used to sleeping through all kinds of noise. That big, oblong deal table was well marked by the life of that kitchen. Besides table-thumping there was eating, homework, and shoe cleaning.

On Saturday mornings I cleaned all the knives with burnt cork and cleaned the tap over the sink with Brasso, for which I got one penny a week. Then I cleaned my own hands with Monkey Brand, a very abrasive pumicelike tablet. Our vegetarian food—Biddy's version—cooked on the coal- or coke-burning iron stove, was tasteless and miserable. Poor Shamus craved meat and fish, particularly pork or bloaters (salted smoked fish). He thought that pork cured his rheumatism, and it did seem to. It was agreed that he could occasionally have half a pig's head, just plain boiled with vinegar, which was really about all we could afford. Sometimes he had a bloater or two. The smell of those fish was like a clarion call to my brother and me. We would rush in and sit opposite him as he ate, staring in wonderment that he could eat anything with eyes in it. My mother would make it her business to drift by during the show, to say in a sarcastic tone, "Hope you're enjoying your corpse." Then Shamus would sit in front of the grate with his boots too near the fire and read the encyclopedia to improve himself and wish they'd got married and been done with it—that's what I thought, anyway.

Despite the pig's heads, Shamus got rheumatic fever and was confined in St. George's Hospital for weeks. We visited him all the time. Waldo was inspired to invent a money-collecting device that was fixed to the hospital's iron gates. At the top it had a framed picture of a winding rustic road which led to down a model of St. George's. You put a penny in a slot at the top and saw it roll down the road into the hospital. At the top it said, "See Your Money Roll into St. George's Hospital." After seeing Shamus, we used to visit Waldo's invention, too.

After so much bread, margarine, cheese, potherbs, and apples I began to crave meat, too. The smell of frying bacon coming from houses on the way to school made me start to think that maybe my mother was a bit evil. I believed the famous advertisements. Bovril was advertised at every railway station across England, so much so that foreign travelers often asked, "Why is every small town in England called Bovril?" Added to that there was and probably still is that tremendous billboard in Piccadilly Circus with a picture of a brawny great bull snorting away and apparently saying "Bovril Puts BEEF Into You." I saw this advertisement twice a week at least as I walked through the West End with my violin case on the way to Dr. York Trotter's School of Music. Well, damn my mother and her vegetables! I wanted meat. I decided that I needed it to survive, and I began to spend my penny a week on Oxo or Bovril cubes. I cut them into four pieces and chewed one quarter at a time. They were delicious!

I was deprived of meat; also I was deprived of a God. After all, who *was* this Christ person? Justice is justice, so I decided to punish Biddy by embarrassing her with questions about what men and women actually did to have children. Biddy was very confused in her effort to be honest and gave me a description in terms that a plumber would use to describe a difficult job. Of course, I knew the whole works already and had a lovely secret satisfaction, like the Mona Lisa seems to be feeling. Children may be cruel but so are grown-ups.

Once on a wet day the boys and I were playing a game, racing around the tops of the school desks, and I fell between two of them, breaking a china inkpot with my chin. I was hurried to a clinic and Biddy was fetched. She forbade the doctors to stitch me up. She said, "Strap it up," but they said that would leave a bad scar. I said, "Then put a stitch in," and they did. It certainly hurt and Biddy fainted. I felt rather like a piece of meat, and I expect that's what made the vegetarian Biddy pass out. Her daughter a beefsteak.

We moved round the Clapham Common area for a few years—Cavendish Road, Rudloe Road, Leathwaite Road—because Mr. Kettle's school was at Clapham Common. The school was behind a beautiful Queen Anne house facing the Common where Mr. Kettle lived with his family. The playground at the back beyond the high wall was tree-shaded and inside there were a lovely pear tree and a fig tree growing straight out of the asphalt. We spent a lot of time out there with Mr. Hamilton, measuring distances and heights and marking out lengths in whitewash for games of cricket, football, or rounders. Mr. Hamilton bristled with energy and whitewash. There were usually about twenty boys of all ages and me. For a period of about four months we took in two Greek girls, Queenie and Cora Gingell, daughters of a visiting diplomat. They were my age, rather beautiful, with long hair that they could sit on and fuzz on their upper lips. While they were there, I gave up football and rough games, as there were other things to do. I visited their upholstered lodgings and they came to Rudloe Road, although I was very ashamed of our house and didn't want them to come. The Rudloe Road place had that cabbage smell that goes with no money. The girls loved our gray African parrot, Jock. He was part of the Kitchen and he talked endlessly, suiting every action we made with the right sound. Go near the tap, and you'd hear water running before you got there. Open a door—"Good morning." Touch a hat—"Good night." For food he would say "Please," and then "Thank you." *Thank you* was difficult to teach him, but I shook the cage before he could eat the food until he would say it. After a time I didn't have to shake the cage. Queenie and Cora had never seen anything like him; nor had anyone else. We taught him the whole song "Pop Goes the Weasel." No *Polly wants a cracker* for old Jock.

I played my own secret pranks on the boys at Mr. Kettle's school. In my search for new words in the dictionary I came across the word *fecundate.* Early one morning, or maybe during a playtime break, I marked that word in pencil in all their dictionaries. It took a long time for any of them to notice, but finally I did hear some whispering among them, and I giggled to myself. Another time I took an expensive Stylo pen from an empty desk that had been vacated by a very rich boy. I loved that pen, but taking it caused me a lot of sorrow and fear. Like a guilty animal, I was forever hiding it in different places at home. I never wanted to take anything that wasn't mine after that.

When I discovered books, I discovered Darwin and Haeckel. With my first paintbox, I colored the pictures in *The Origin of the Species* and *The Riddle of the Universe*—pink for a fetus, mauve for colons and livers and other "offal." Biddy the vegetarian inspired the use of this word. That's what meat was to her. When I could read well enough, I started to look through a box of early photos and cuttings from newspapers and letters that Biddy had saved. I usually did this when everyone was out—not that Biddy and Shamus kept the box hidden. They left it around in a kitchen cupboard for me to read. It was definitely educational, too. That's how I learned about the grimmer details of Biddy's "kidnapping case."

There was a cutting from *The Japan Gazette:*

One Miss Lanchester, aged 24, daughter of people in good circumstances, has decided to live with a man named Sullivan, of inferior station . . .

And one from *The Scrutator* . . .

Miss Lanchester will have to take her fate, whatever it may be. Should she have children she will learn the disgrace which she deliberately assigns to them.

There were lots of Letters to the Editor . . .

THE BRITISH FATHER
Sir,—I think Mr. Lanchester has acted towards his daughter as every British father should do—more especially when he thinks his daughter is on the road to ruin . . .

The supply of clippings was endless. *The Daily Telegraph,* in a long editorial, called Biddy "shameful" and "obstinately bent on disgracing herself," with a "starving vanity," "a morbid craze for notoriety," and a "conceit condemned to obscurity."

Another piece:

. . . as for her children being "bastards," the name is obsolete for evil. Some of the "best born" families in the land bear it proudly.

So that's why one or two boys at school asked, "Why is your father's name Mr. Sullivan and your mother's name Miss Lanchester?" and children on our street sometimes asked the same question. Grown-ups, if they remembered the case, thought that an illegitimate child was doomed, as another one of the cuttings said, to "inevitable degradation," and were silent.

As the result of monogamy in England children born out of wedlock become the despised and rejected of men, so that Miss Lanchester in deliberately refusing to submit to the restrictions

of marriage may be bequesting to innocent persons a fearful
legacy of ignominy and shame.

Actually, in a few years, I found it rather glamorous to be a bastard.
Among their comrades Biddy went on being a courageous woman for
many years. Shamus didn't seem to get much credit.

Shamus was more of a sound-and-fury socialist than many of his
comrades, repeating slogans against capitalists rather than inventing
slogans of his own. As far as I could make out, he seemed to have been
active along these lines even before he met Biddy, serving as a secretary for candidates and promoting the elections of socialists such as
"the well-tried and popular comrade, H. B. Rogers." Shamus wrote
letters asking for speakers from the Fabian Society, and representing
the Battersea branch of the Social Democratic Federation, he often
held forth at meetings at the drop of a hat. I never heard Shamus speak
in public but I often heard him say, in a loud voice, "Hear, hear!" to
other speakers. I began to think that indoor meetings were more like
lectures followed by questions and answers, whereas outdoor speaking
was more of a harangue, with people shouting back. Soapbox speakers
and tub thumpers. I suppose Shamus was one of them. Biddy used to
describe him to us as being a persuasive speaker in Hyde Park and at
other outdoor meetings. Anyway, Biddy must have seen something
fine about him. Even I could see that he was a firebrand. Although
Biddy was an extremist in her opinions about the marriage laws, I got
the feeling that if it hadn't been for Shamus she might have become
a Fabian. She might have functioned better in that group since the
Fabians spawned so many intellectuals. I certainly would have liked to
have met some of the Fabians because they were calm and mostly
aristocratic and thought that reforms in the social system should be
gradual. But Shamus and Biddy and the comrades wanted action, as
their songs proclaimed:

> Workers of England, why crouch ye like cravens?
> Why clutch an existence of insult and want?
> Why stand to be plucked by an army of ravens?
> Or hoodwinked forever by twaddle and cant?

Another one by Herbert Burrows, the old friend who aided Biddy and
Shamus during the kidnapping case:

> Not words but acts we need to-day,
> Your rulers long have held the sway!
> 'Tis time their power you swept away,
> For Freedom then unite!

Although Shamus never seemed to be a leader in the Cause, he was always an enthusiastic worker. With Biddy's prodding, he went on expounding socialist theories until the first World War, still serving as secretary and promoting speakers when needed. Hear, hear.

In spite of all the arguments I heard in favor of equality, I didn't want any part of it. I saw alert and clever people leaving others behind and rising to the top. Biddy and the Kitchen comrades would have said, "like scum," I suppose. But from an early age I never liked dull people and didn't see how equality would work for long since some people were so bright and others were so dull. Of course, the rich were too rich and the poor were too poor, but I still didn't see that screaming in Trafalgar Square or rioting in the streets would do any good. But eventually I understood that it did help. Cooperatives and unions were beginning to develop, the workers were beginning to have their say. Shamus became more subdued and he sat by the fire more and more.

With all the Kitchen talk about socialism and communism and the proletariat, the name Karl Marx became as familiar to me as a song like "Yes, We Have No Bananas!" So I was caught up at once when Biddy mentioned Eleanor Marx, Karl Marx's daughter. Biddy had been her secretary before Waldo was born. Eleanor Marx had been living with or married to or in love with a man called Aveling. When Aveling left her, Eleanor Marx committed suicide. "If a person must commit suicide," Biddy said, "Eleanor Marx did it very well. She had a bath and cleaned herself thoroughly inside and out, wrapped herself in a sheet, and took prussic acid." Biddy thought this very fine—"not at all messy."

Along with the other causes that surfaced in our Kitchen was the fight for the emancipation of women. Women's suffrage. The creator of the movement was Mrs. Emmeline Pankhurst, a rather aristocratic woman from a well-to-do background. I don't think Biddy cared much for Emmeline Pankhurst's fashionable hats and all that went with them. Her daughters Sylvia and Cristabel were more Biddy's cup of tea.

The processions and the meetings in Trafalgar Square were exciting and still frightening. Instead of waving red flags and wearing buttons saying *SDF*, we waved green, white, and purple flags and wore clothes of those colors, with buttons saying *WSPU* (Women's Social and Political Union). There was one awful rally when, encircled by the police in chain formation, the vast crowd became a jellified mass moving as one. Biddy shouted to me, below her waist level, "Keep your arms down!" "Yes," screamed Shamus, "keep your arms down, girlie, don't reach up, they might get broken." Another time when I was with Biddy at a suffragette rally I was pushed into a doorway in Scotland Yard. The police all had truncheons and were banging women on the head. I screamed a lot, I think, but the whole thing is now oddly a still picture with no sound at all. Shock, I suppose—a blank in time memory.

Early in the women's suffrage movement, Biddy was arrested in a riot and spent one night and a day in prison. She had to pick oakum and got very sore fingers, so they changed her duty to pulling rags apart to make "shoddy"—fibers that would be pressed together into cheap felt. Mrs. Pankhurst and many other suffragettes who got themselves arrested went on hunger strikes if they were in prison long enough. There was a constant furor over forcible feeding, and the Home Office was attacked by the press for its brutal methods. The Home Secretary then was McKenna, and the well-known song "Nellie Bly" was given new words to make fun of what was called the "Cat and Mouse Act":

> Nellie Bly caught a fly,
> Tied it to a string;
> Let it out to run about,
> Then she pulled it in.

This was his policy of arresting the suffragettes, sending them to the Holloway Women's Prison, where they would refuse food, then letting them out when they were too ill. Once they recovered, they would break another window or slash another painting, then be arrested again.

Emily Wilding Davison was one of the martyrs to the cause of women's suffrage. As *The London Times* reported on June 5, 1913:

DESPERATE ACT OF A SUFFRAGIST
FALL OF THE KING'S HORSE
DISQUALIFICATION OF THE FAVOURITE

The race for the Derby yesterday was marked by two incidents for which it will be long remembered. The King's horse was brought to the ground by a woman suffragist, who rushed from the crowd at Tattenham Corner, apparently with the object of seizing the reins. The horse fell and rolled on the jockey, who, however, was not severely hurt. The woman was knocked down and received such serious injuries that it was reported at first that she had been killed. The incident had a disconcerting effect on the other jockeys, who turned round in their saddles at the untoward occurrence. It appears that immediately after the woman fell a placard bearing the words "Votes for Women" was raised by somebody in the crowd, suggesting that the whole thing had been prearranged.

The second incident—there has been no parallel to it for about 70 years—was the disqualification of the favourite, Craganour. The King and Queen were present. There were the usual vast good-natured crowds on all parts of the course. The weather was bright and the air clear, though the sun was hidden for long intervals behind clouds which now and then gave rise to a degree of anxiety. Immediately after the accident, the King ordered inquiries to be made as to the nature of his jockey's injuries.

Then four days later:

THE SUFFRAGIST OUTRAGE AT EPSOM
DEATH OF MISS E. W. DAVISON

Miss Emily Wilding Davison, the suffragist who interfered with the King's horse during the race for the Derby, died in hospital at Epsom at 4:50 yesterday afternoon. A number of lady friends called at the Epsom Cottage Hospital on Saturday afternoon to inquire as to the condition of Miss Davison. Two visitors draped the screen round the bed with the W.S.P.U. colours and tied the W.S.P.U. badge to the head of the bed. Only members of the staff of the hospital, however, were present when the end actually came.

I was taken to her funeral and we walked for miles, it seemed. Each segment of the endless procession wore one or two of the colors. I think our section was purple and white, but I was so tired I was just dragged along by Biddy and Shamus and didn't care. All I could see were shiny steel nuts and bolts and screws that had fallen from cars and horse buses embedded in the tar road surface. A pretty mosaic. The *Times* noted our demonstration at the funeral and concluded the article by citing the inscription on Emily Davison's coffin:

Emily Wilding Davison. Born 11th October, 1872. Died 8th June, 1913. Fight on. God will give the victory.

I must have been about nine or ten—it's not easy to pinpoint the time, but it was summer—when Biddy took up with Raymond Duncan and his group who started free classes at Crosby Hall in Chelsea. He taught hand-weaving, spinning on a spinning wheel (also a distaff), sandal-making, Greek gymnastics, and folk songs.

Adding to the usual wear and tear on our kitchen table, Biddy and I used it to make Greek sandals for ourselves. We started them from scratch, making the soles from thick leather that we first had to soak in water, then cutting it with a sharp knife and also cutting the straps from a large piece of thinner hide.

Duncan was thin, sensual-lipped (quite like Hugh Hefner), attractive, and tough—an American businessman in a hand-woven gown with a Greek fillet binding his long hair. I was willingly swept along on this new tide, especially by the songs and movements. The system of movement created by Raymond Duncan was based on Greek figures on vases and friezes. Raymond Duncan thought I was talented, and Biddy was delighted—every mother during those years hoped her daughter would be another Pavlova. Like other little girls, I had been taken to see Pavlova dance "The Dying Swan." I shall never forget her and I was never quite the same after that. I rumbled with ambition.

At the local music hall at Clapham Junction I fell for the great comedians like George Robey, Marie Lloyd, and the "male impersonators" Vesta Tilley, Ella Shields, and that school. And then at bigger music halls such as the Palladium and the Colliseum I saw Loie Fuller and Maude Allen and other top-of-the-bill artists. I very much enjoyed the scandal about Miss Allen, a famous classical dancer who had orgies and was called a pervert in the newspapers. It all seemed to be mixed up with another scandal about Loie Fuller. She and Maude Allen both danced in bare feet and wafted about the stage with yards of flying chiffon. Loie Fuller and her company used the most chiffon, sometimes covering the whole stage and her corps de ballet with a kind of transparent tarpaulin. Isadora Duncan and Maude Allen used much less chiffon and openly despised Loie Fuller for her mode of salesmanship. And those two dancers despised each other, too.

At the Rudloe Road flat, Clapham Common, where we lived for what seemed so long to me, the wallpaper (at least six layers pasted on top of each other) had become filthy, the w.c. didn't work properly, and the penny meter for hot water was stuck. We asked the landlady to do some repairs, but she took the rent and avoided us. We thought she had bribed the sanitary inspector as well. Eventually she tried to put yet another layer of wallpaper over one side of the kitchen, but the wet paste was too heavy and the whole thing fell off, bringing decayed old plaster down with it. My brother Waldo and I examined the smelly debris through our microscope and found minute bugs in the old layers of paste. Biddy sent a report to the sanitary authorities and we stopped paying the rent.

Legally, after six weeks' nonpayment of rent, a bailiff can be hired to enter the property and must be given access. He must be put in a room in the house for ten days, but there was no requirement to provide him with food, water, or even a chair. We did give ours a chair. After the bailiff has been in residence for ten days, the landlady can distrain—that is, seize the furniture *not in use* and auction it to recover the back rent. Our bailiff was changed many times during the ten days because we turned his room into a kind of hell. I remember rushing around the room with a red-hot poker. I also let my pet mice out.

On the Saturday they came to distrain—the tenth day—we jumped into the beds. Legally a bed could not be taken from under a person. Part of Biddy's legal program was to have all the furniture *in use,* so we had also put some sort of food on the table and even on a few chairs. Socialist neighbors of ours stored several things that we rather liked. The landlady took what was left not in use and that supposedly paid the rent up to date. A socialist friend went to the auction and bought back an old mahogany and brass coal scuttle that had belonged to Shamus's mother and father.

Biddy's next legal twist was masterly. The landlady had got her pound of flesh with the furniture sold at auction. We stored our remaining furniture with other friends and immediately nailed up old curtains at every window to make the place seem inhabited. If the landlady had tried to get in, she would therefore have been trespassing. She would have to wait for another six weeks before she could put the bailiff in again, so we added the first six weeks' rent that we saved to the second six weeks' rent (well, it was all very clear to Biddy), and off we went on a holiday to Clacton-on-Sea.

The holiday at Clacton-on-Sea was simply splendid. The weather was sunny and hot. At Clacton-on-Sea, as in nearly all English seaside towns, there was a little wooden stage on the beach, with the usual Pierrot shows, the usual red-nosed comics, and a "lead" who wore a tilted straw hat and had the brightest blue eyes. It looked to me as if the sea was showing right through him from the background. He made lots of smutty jokes that made the grown-ups laugh and that were supposed to be above the children's heads.

He pushed me into the parlour,
Pushed the parlour door.
Pushed himself upon my knee,
Pushed his face in front of me.
He pushed me round to the jeweler
Near the Hippodrome,
Then he pushed me in front of the clergyman
And then he pushed me home.

After the regular show, children got up on the stage and competed for prizes by singing and dancing and imitating members of the troupe. Sometimes they sang while trying to balance on a barrel, winning better prizes and louder applause if they didn't fall off. I felt that performing was beneath me, or perhaps it was because I was shy to the point of paralysis, but anyway I did learn most of the songs and at home afterward I sang them to myself.

The best landlady you can find
Is a nice little wife of your own.
She won't take your sugar or your tea,
Won't be afraid to sit upon your knee.
Find a nice little sweetheart
And change her name to Brown,
Then with your landlady just settle up
And then settle down.

At a charity fair in aid of a big local orphanage I won a competition for shoe-cleaning. There I also saw and adored a tiny girl performer, Netty Diggs, who wore a Scottish outfit with a swinging kilt and a tiny sporran. She sang Harry Lauder songs in a penetrating nasal voice and also played on a pair of tiny bagpipes. She paraded up and down the open-air stage and, wonder of wonders, broke into a rapid tap dance now and then. She got louder and longer applause than any I had ever heard. How could such a tiny little girl be so clever? I thought a lot about Netty Diggs and asked Biddy if I could go back to see her where she was appearing again for the orphanage. "Oh, you don't want to see her," said Biddy. "She's a midget." This was a great blow, and I became very silent, very silent.

Shamus returned to London before us and found us a new place to live on the other side of Clapham Common. It had the same kind of setup—kitchen, front room, and two small attic rooms above. But this flat was different because it backed on the Common and had a leads (a flat roof) over the back room. The back room was let to a nice middle-aged dressmaker. On the front gate she had a big brass plate that I got tuppence a week for polishing. In flourishing script it said *Miss Valler. Robes et Modes*. It was a lovely piece of brass and a pleasure to clean. We grew a lot of things in boxes on the leads—mustard and cress and radishes. I also built a Japanese garden with a stream running through it. Waldo constructed a pump that worked for a few minutes at a time. I thought that I might discover perpetual motion on the principle that a piece of cloth will siphon water upward if the other end is lower. I gave that project up reluctantly.

This new flat was at Leathwaite Road and the same distance as the one on Rudloe Road from Mr. Kettle's school—about a mile and a half, a nice walk along the side of the Common. On the way to school I passed a pretty red brick house that stood on a square well-kept garden, with a high green hedge round it. Sometimes a gentleman leaned over the gate. He was gentle-looking, with a beard and a mustache, and once he said good morning. He was John Burns, Member of Parliament, the man who had helped Biddy and Shamus in their fight for freedom in 1895. I don't expect he knew who I was, but if he did perhaps he didn't want to get involved again.

This daily journey was my very own private panorama. I was then first stirred by the changing seasons and, unawares, had changing moods with the weather. Walking through the snow in sandaled feet, wiping the fresh snow off the iron railings. (I always got chilblains in winter.) In the summer, dressing up as a boy, I lurked with street friends in the bushes to try to smoke a cigarette. Then the sad autumn days . . . I was born in October and thought that my sorrows must have started then, just before I was born. The first green sprouts in spring drove me to the other extreme—I would run the whole way to school sometimes.

When people in big houses were ill they could afford to put straw on the streets to deaden the sound of passing horses' hooves and of the few motorcars. The smell of the straw would grow overpowering, then suddenly the mixture would all be shoveled up and taken away. (It must have made wonderful compost.) Then you knew that the sick person had died. With luck, I would see the funeral with carriages and hearse. The banks of white flowers on the coffin and the shiny black horses were like a real theatre show against misty, gray old London.

In all the seven years I walked to school, no dirty old man ever stopped me for a chat. I wonder why.

I used to go to school on roller skates, but after the Duncan influence I wore sandals summer and winter and walked because the skates, of course, would only fit on shoes or boots. One winter I did put on boots to go skating on one of the ponds on Clapham Common.

The ice skates had to be screwed on, and Shamus did this as I sat on a bench by the pond. The screw went right through my boot, but my feet were so cold that I didn't even know it until my boot was half full of blood. Shamus felt terrible. Well, so did I.

We always put Jock the parrot by an open window at election time, and he canvassed for different Labour leaders and also screamed "Votes for women" from his perch. He lived to a very old age, probably fifty. When he was about twenty, he laid an egg but was still called Jock. Everything stayed in his-her repertoire, so Jock was still saying "Vote for Grayson" when Ramsey MacDonald became prime minister more than ten years later, and "Down with Asquith!" which delighted Shamus.

Shamus got a job in a lunatic asylum as a shorthand typist, which paid one pound more each week than he'd earned before—four pounds altogether. I thought we could buy anything when I first heard the good news, but Biddy soon set us right about that. Shamus celebrated with half a boiled pig's head and I got a penny extra for cleaning the kitchen tap. Shamus was full of stories about the tricks that the asylum staff played on the lunatics, like nailing a scrub brush to the floor when the patient who was a cleaner was in the w.c. We laughed ourselves silly although we were all very kind people really.

If Biddy looked for loopholes in the law, Shamus looked for them in the Bible. He'd often sit by the kitchen stove reading plainly illogical passages aloud and laughing his head off. In our house we always spelled *God* with a small *g*. A group of atheist friends published leaflets quoting Bible tales that could not possibly be factual, and I even distributed a few of these outside the Sunday School at the end of Leathwaite Road. Then I began to think that if these people were so certain there was no God, it was just as silly as someone who is certain there is a God. Even a child likes to have proof. I was almost relieved to find the word *agnostic* in the dictionary. That's what I was and it was nice to know. Thank goodness religion was not a subject at Mr. Kettle's. You did and thought what you liked.

Mr. Kettle was a London County Council examiner, so at the end of the L.C.C. school term, two great square baskets full of examination papers would be delivered to the big house in front of the school. The boys and I helped correct some of these papers. Of course, we all had the answers but it gave us confidence in ourselves. I know I felt positively powerful. We did not have exams ourselves—we at Mr. Kettle's were not encouraged to compete. We did play cricket, football, and rounders. Mr. Kettle sometimes joined in, especially when we went out onto the Common to play. He kept up with us in his own wild way and he looked very like Mark Twain. I don't even remember winning or losing.

Maybe because it was a boys' school and most boys relish cruelty (they seem to go to war like ducks to water), or maybe they sort of showed off in front of Miss Kettle, or even me, but they played some cruel games and I joined in. One term we had a black boy in school. He was about twelve, the son of an African studying law at Oxford. The boy was rather fat and was dressed in suits that were much too tight. He did not like rounders or cricket. One day to avoid playing, he managed to climb up the fig tree in the playground. We started to throw things at him—the ball, a stone or two, bits of wood—and we shouted, "Come down!" As he had no choice, he finally started to climb down. Unfortunately he had a bottle of perfume in his pocket, which broke and ran down his legs. The smell was ghastly and his shame was pitiful. All my life this scene will stay with me along with the secret regret that I just watched without any compassion. Mr. Kettle gave us a severe lecture. The boy didn't stay long after that.

Another nasty thing we did was to shut up a boy named Ernest Hunter in the laboratory. We put burning sulfur in saucers on the tops of the high chemistry cupboards and locked him in. Then we rammed the door with some poles that were lying around and shouted, "A la Bastille!" The boy was blond and harmless, but he wore thick eyeglasses and had a weak chin, so we always had and always did call him "Stinkpot." Mr. Kettle again talked seriously to us, but a fat lot of good that did. Madge Kettle was adored by many of the boys and she was a wicked flirt, so I suppose she lit this flame of cruelty. For my part, I shyly played my cards with her, occasionally bringing her a flower and one Christmas a growing red tulip in a small blue-and-white china bowl with handles. It was a Delft sugar bowl, and I didn't like giving it away, but after all I wanted her to like me, too.

I began to make friends on Leathwaite Road, starting off with children of fellow socialists. Mrs. Mary Gray, who had backed Biddy during the stormy days before I was born when the Lanchester-Sullivan Case was raging, had a granddaughter, Olive Moody, and she was my best friend. We started the Classical Dance Club and had blue buttons with the letters *CDC* chain-stitched in yellow. We circulated the one copy of our magazine, *La Dance,* among the ten or twelve members. I wrote everything in the magazine, painted the pictures, and also taught the classes (in our front room). It is obvious why Olive and I soon quarreled. She started her own club, the Roller Skating Club. The *RSC* buttons were white and mauve. Olive Moody couldn't dance and looked awful, anyway, with her mouse-colored hair and skin. Her personality was olive and moody, and her *RSC* buttons got dirty very quickly. Our falling out notwithstanding, Mrs. Mary Gray and Biddy and Shamus went on being very close comrades.

Waldo and I argued a lot. I said that my handwriting was better than his. Then he shoved a plate of butter toward me one day and broke a piece off one of my teeth. We also were quite bitter about sharing our gramophone. I used it for the dancing classes and I liked to play "Because" and "Home to Our Mountains," while Waldo liked to mess around with the sapphire needle and the inner workings. But Waldo and I got on very well together when I helped him with the dynamo that we made to give electric-shock parties. I spent hours winding green, silk-covered wire onto a coil. For the electric shocks, we and the neighbor children would sit in a semicircle with our bare feet in basins of water; the person at each end would hold the connected brass handles. When Waldo decided to give us the electric shock the suspense was thrilling and the screams divine. Soon afterward my brother was apprenticed to a scientific instrument maker.

Across the top of Leathwaite Road ran a wide avenue with big square houses built on large square gardens, with large old trees shading everything. Only the old white- or mauve-painted houses ever saw the sunlight. It was an eerie and lovely place to walk, very dark, cool green light and shade. At night, lovers stood like darker patches against the fences. Waldo and I often went up there with our street friends. The sidewalks were gravel, and there were always a lot of young green frogs around. We all liked to catch a few and take them home to put them in a water tank with rocks. Once a tiny frog escaped in our front room. It disappeared completely. In the morning Waldo and I moved every single bit of furniture to try to rescue the frog, if it was still alive. When we moved the huge box where we kept the coal, there it was, the frog. It was squashed quite flat and was as dry and thin as a piece of paper. For some reason, perhaps to give it a decent funeral, we put it in a sink full of water. Within an hour the frog had swelled back to normal and was hopping about the kitchen. We put it back in the tank and we named it Lazarus.

In the front room, along with a bed, we also had a loom. We wove a lot of our own clothes and even spun enough wool for a few blankets and a coat for me—very itchy. To lay the warp we had to stretch the full length of wool out the door and down the hallway. There was also an upright piano (Keith-Prowse) that Biddy's older sister, my Aunt Mary, had and didn't want. I was supposed to learn to play but the lessons didn't take. Nor did my violin lessons. On the front panel of the piano Aunt Mary had painted a rustic scene with satyrs and virgins —at least they were females and seemed to be running away. And besides the big loom, the piano, and the bed, we had two little hand looms, a spinning wheel, the Pathe gramophone (with the sapphire), and a lot of bookshelves—with Shakespeare, Dickens, the Bible, the *Children's Encyclopaedia* (a monthly magazine), dictionaries, and a vast selection of classics. (*Madame Bovary* had a powerful influence on me.) I would guess the room to have been no more than fourteen by eighteen feet, with a small suburban bay window and a small black iron fireplace. The room was full up, but as I'd not yet learned that space was a pleasure I didn't mind the lack of it.

The Kitchen really was a better place for Shamus to sit, though he liked to build the fire in the front room. He was very skilled at laying a fire. It always burned beautifully and quickly, although he put coal at the bottom, with the firewood next and then the paper on the top. His method remained a mystery to everyone, but it always worked.

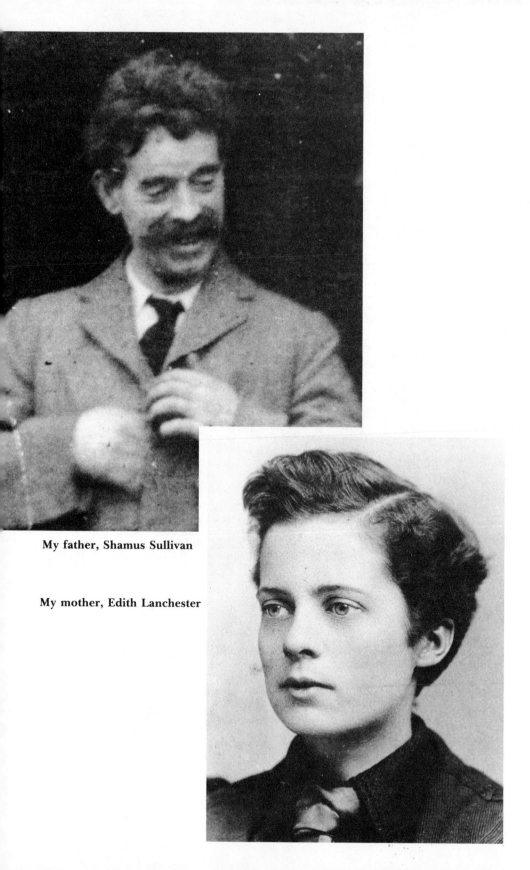

My father, Shamus Sullivan

My mother, Edith Lanchester

With my teddy bear, at age four and a half;
painting by my aunt, Mary Lanchester

Waldo and Elsa Sullivan Lanchester

My Oriental dances:
very, very graceful
and madly artistic

As a young dancer

n The Cave of Harmony: one of my
irst numbers, wearing a paper skirt

Dressed as Winnie Mable (age 12)
in *Payment Deferred*

Our engagement makes the newspaper

ROMANCE OF THE NEW MR. PICKWICK

Charles Laughton as Mr.
Proback in Arnold Bennett's
play of that name—

—as Mr. Pickwick, the part
he is now playing at the
Haymarket Theatre—

Elsa Lanchester, the actress, whose engagement is
announced to Charles Laughton, the brilliant young
character actor who in three years has risen from
obscurity to the pinnacle of fame.

—in the title part in " The
Man with Red Hair," and—

—as himself.

"Stapledown," our tree house in Surrey

At Sadler's Wells, in *Danse Arabe* (1934); costume is by Oliver Messel

Charles as Prospero, me as Ariel in *The Tempest*

Another scene from *The Tempest*

Ariel again

Charles played Canon Chasuble
and I played Miss Prim
in *The Importance of Being Earnest*

Charles and I in
The Cherry Orchard

We arrive in Hollywood in 1932

As a Florentine page
(singing "Take, O Take Those Lips Away")
in *Measure for Measure*

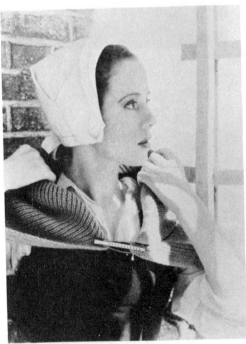

As Hendrickje Stoffels

Charles as Rembrandt van Rijn

As I looked in 1935

Charles and I
in *The Beachcomber*

In *The Beachcomber*

As Mary Shelley in the often-cut opening scene of *The Bride of Frankenstein* (Universal Pictures)

Making up for *The Bride* (Universal Pictures)

The Bride again (Universal Pictures)

The Bride of Frankenstein
(Universal Pictures)

**With Colin Clive
(Universal Pictures)**

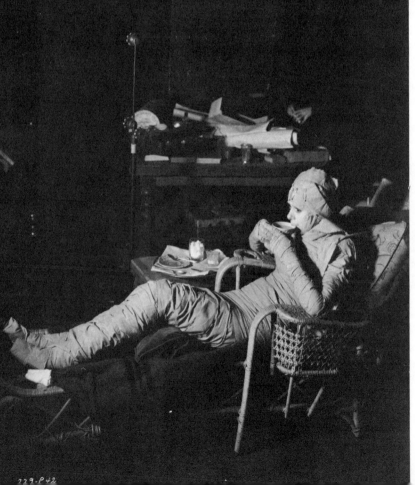

**Teatime on
the set of**
*The Bride of
Frankenstein*
(Universal Pictures)

729.P42

When I was about eleven, Raymond Duncan told Biddy that his sister, Isadora Duncan, was opening a school for talented children in Paris—"To Teach the World to Dance." All expenses would be paid. I was a chosen child, one of about twenty in the world—Isadora's world. So I was enrolled in the school at Bellevue on the outskirts of Paris. Biddy rather pushily came, too, and got a part-time job at the school so she could hover over me.

One wet day, after I'd been at Isadora's for about a week, Biddy took me round Paris to get a few things for school. Under an umbrella at a tram stop she tried very hard to tell me what happened to girls every month. "*It* starts," she said, "sometimes when girls are only ten and sometimes at fifteen or sixteen." I was embarrassed and frightened, but I soon forgot about *it,* though I always carried several hankerchiefs with me, just in case. Finally *it* started when I was about fourteen, on a Saturday morning at art school. Appropriately, at the time I was drawing an egg with charcoal. All artists should be able to draw a perfect egg. It's like the theory of music to a musician and a vocabulary to a writer.

The school building at Bellevue had been given to Isadora Duncan by a very wealthy gentleman called Paris Singer, of the Singer Sewing Machine family.

Bellevue had been a large hotel with 150 bedrooms. It was still furnished in the manner of the nineteenth century, with brass bedsteads glittering with knobs that we would all screw on and off during idle hours and on wet days. We each had our individual grand suite with vast black-and-white tiled bathrooms with bidets. After getting over the shock of what a bidet was for, we children had a lot of fun with our miniature Versailles.

When I joined the school, Isadora was pregnant and, I believe, having one of her lawsuits with the dancer Loie Fuller. Swathed in draperies, she did most of her teaching lying on a chaise lounge, only occasionally getting up to move about. Isadora was usually covered from head to foot, even her face, with the finest veiling of the palest cream color. Through this cocoon you could catch a glimpse of her hennaed hair (in those days hair dyed red had brassy purple highlights in it) and a glimpse of her plump white arms and hands with red-painted fingernails. I had good reason to notice those nails because each morning we had to line up to kiss her hand and say, "Good morning, Miss Duncan." I just pretended to kiss it because the gesture was too much like bowing before royalty—a practice not favored in Biddy's and Shamus's world.

Although it was a great honor to be recruited as a talented child, I soon learned that all Isadora could do was teach us to run away from or toward an enemy or to become an autumn leaf . . . or something. As a matter of fact, she had no technique of her own that she could pass on to others—she could not teach any of her pupils to be the beautiful, sexy girl she had been. So we just walked and ran and jumped, each in his or her own way. Or we'd listen to something like Schumann's "Traumerei," and when the notes of the melody went up, our arms went up. This was known to us as Interpreting the Music.

Sometimes Isadora would rise from her divan and herd us over to one of the great long windows overlooking the Seine. She would point to some climbing pink roses growing wildly over an old trellis pergola, and, as a few of the petals fell, she would say, "They dance, now *you* dance!" Then, with a Christlike gesture—both hands outturned—she would bid us scatter. And we did.

We did a few limbering-up exercises under the leadership of some teen-age students who had been "borrowed" from her sister Elizabeth's school in Darmstadt. These nice young German girls remained borrowed and never went home. After all, the Isadora emporium off-ered superb food, good clothes, trips in Rolls-Royces to the Louvre and Versailles. We were all beautifully dressed, and each of us had a warm coat of a different color. We must have looked like a living rainbow, and we all loved the attention we got! My coat was a clay-colored brown, which made me very envious of the others who mostly had brightly colored ones. We were shepherded about Paris like valu-able Pekinese.

At Bellevue in the blue salon we children wore blue chiffon, and for the white salon we wore white chiffon. We danced for three hours every morning, then we had lunch. Our food was the most superb French cuisine imaginable. There was often a stream of famous visitors to watch us dance and eat. They were the cream of French and Italian society and would pat us on the head as if our youth and talent might rub off on their gloved hands. The names did not mean anything to me at the time, but I have since read that Rodin was among them. Many of his famous watercolor sketches are supposed to have been done in our salon. Often we would have to sit for two or three hours just listening to music, the classics played by Paderewski and other great pianists of the day. Once I overheard an old lady called the Queen of Naples say in a low voice to Isadora, "If some of the children sit very, very still it shows they are musical." I can tell you I often got pins and needles from sitting still.

Three children were brought over from Russia soon after I arrived at Bellevue. Two of the older Darmstadt pupil-teachers had been sent to St. Petersburg to search and hold auditions. The three Russian girls who came back were Valla, age eleven, Valla, age ten, and Alla, age three. They were all willingly thrust out of Russia by their ambitious parents. The older Valla had not been chosen by the Darmstadt teachers at first, but she came to the station in St. Petersburg anyway and was dragged along by the moving train for a few feet before she finally was pulled into the carriage. How could they refuse her? Such desire for this other life, the dancing life, showed such a passion for the touch of Isadora—the teachers felt this must make a great dancer! The disillusionment on both sides was immediate. The three Russian children were no Pavlovas. They were hopeless and untalented and had stolid peasant figures. Their first day was pretty frightening, I must say. A good hairdresser cut off all their long hair because they had nits. This was done, as it happened, during a great thunderstorm that broke from a night-black sky at four o'clock on their first afternoon. Valla, Valla, and Alla had their luggage removed and their little possessions thrown out—icons and perfumed pink soap. I can still hear their screams. God knows what happened to them, the two Vallas and the plump little Alla. Alla was only three and cross-eyed, and could keep time to music . . . I hope Paderewski was impressed.

We seemed to spend a great deal of time playing croquet in the rose garden and riding on a dilapidated funicular railway that went down to the Seine. Somehow, amid all this activity, we also managed a few desultory school lessons. Fraulein Winter, our teacher-governess, was hired to instruct us in the three Rs, but we spoiled, naughty children soon put a stop to that. The dark-haired, darker-eyed Fraulein sat more or less alone in her schoolroom, giving guttural orders that we all found very funny. After all, we were geniuses and more powerful than Miss Winter.

There were other childish hijinks. One night a French boy named

Jean started playing a game with some of the others that seemed very popular. They all knelt on a big double bed and started to fart, or tried to. Jean roughly pulled me over to the group shouting, "Tu fait un canon! Attendez, je fait un grand canon!" He certainly was very good at it, but I was horrified. Though children do not smell as bad as older people.

Another what you might call musical experience came from this same boy Jean. He knew a lot of songs. I thought one especially was nice and wicked. It was about cabbages and was called "Un Bon Mouvement." You see, in England babies are supposed to come from under gooseberry bushes. In America the stork is supposed to bring them. But in France they are supposed to come from cabbages. Well, this song told about the thirty-two ways of planting cabbages.

Isadora Duncan's admirers have said, as she herself said in her autobiography, that she "adored children," and I'm sure she did. She certainly did adore her image as a great earth mother. The loss of her own two children, who were drowned in the Seine, must have affected her behavior and approach to life. The accident happened in less than a minute. The car they were riding in had stalled on a bridge. The chauffeur got out to investigate, then the car started suddenly, knocked down the chauffeur, and rolled down a ramp into the Seine.

There were two others besides me who were from England. However, they were not with us to learn to dance. Isadora had been shown a photograph of the children, who were about seven or eight years old, and she had been struck by their resemblance to her own lost children. She had begged their parents to let them join her school, saying she would make them great dancers. Biddy was told that Isadora had actually gone down on her knees, weeping, as she begged to be allowed to teach these children. The duplicates were nice enough kids, plump and pretty, and had been given pageboy haircuts to enhance their resemblance to Isadora's children. They stood or knelt one on each side of Miss Duncan on all possible occasions but were rather lumpy in class.

With war in the air, most of us who had homes were sent back. The remaining children and student-teachers drifted to Russia with Isadora and so melted away into history. If I had stayed longer at Isadora's school, I would probably have become a classical dancer in the worst sense of the term, backed by no knowledge of life and with no sense of responsibility. I was fortunate not to have been caught up in that particular art eddy. After all, bare feet are no longer naughty and nobody can make a living today by imitating rose petals.

Some years later Biddy and I went to see Isadora dancing in London. She was, I remember, quite pale and rather flabby. To quote

John Dos Passos in *U.S.A.*, "She took to drinking too much and stepping to the footlights and bawling out the boxholders." Isadora was still imitating autumn leaves and running to and from some enemy. In her interpretation of Chopin's "Funeral March" she was hidden beneath a big piece of purple velvet that blanketed her completely. Then she let one arm come up into view, and in her exposed hand was a lily, which she slowly placed on the velvet. Biddy whispered to me, "Anybody can do that."

Dos Passos had gone on to say, "She couldn't keep her hands off good-looking young men, couldn't bother to keep her figure in shape, never could keep track of her money . . . if she got any cash she threw a party or gave it away." Isadora was tolerated with amusement and even affection as a young girl in the 1890s. She was the sex symbol-artist-plaything of the intellectuals of her day, attracting painters and literary giants and wealthy patrons, and she thrived on all that attention. But later on Isadora also attracted mockery and unkind notoriety. Getting older was the most ungraceful thing she ever did. And that came after too many other ungraceful happenings.

It could be, with the trend for courtesans and beauties becoming famous actresses today, and vice versa, that Isadora might have achieved more in her rather loose art and left behind her more than a wisp of chiffon and a tragic life story. Today she is still remembered and respected in spite of the mockery. In her own time, she presented herself with true showmanship, instinctively cashing in on the then-current trend toward female emancipation. She inspired followers to loosen their corsets as the Women's Suffrage Movement and the Fabian Society were flourishing.

Biddy's mother, Octavia Lanchester, had tried to be a little friendly over the years—to forgive and forget—sending us a crate of food at Christmas, oranges, and a Christmas pudding (we gave away the mince pie because it had suet in it), and sometimes a dress for me. Henry Lanchester, Biddy's father, didn't seem to exist. I think he must have had a stroke and was kept upstairs in bed at their home in Linfield, Hayward's Heath. We visited the house two or three times a year from 1908 on, and by then I think my grandfather was dead. Anyway, I never saw him. Biddy always called her parents Mater and Pater. Biddy's elder sister, my Aunt Mary, lived with Octavia, and Octavia also had a companion, Miss Pierce. I always saw my grandmother in a bath chair. She was a birdlike little old lady who wore purple or gray silk, a lot of jet, and a cream lace cap. She sat up at the head of the dining table in the dining room. This room was very dim and the mahogany furniture and the fine linen and silver made me so frightened that I cannot recall eating anything. But my Aunt Mary, although not a very attractive spinster, was full of interesting talents. She was an exquisite painter of flowers and the English countryside, and was well-known being the president of the English Tempera Society. She had the whole top floor of the house at Linfield, where she painted in bad weather and made and carved her own frames, gilding them with real gold leaf. She also made her own tempera there—a sort of mixture of eggs and clay—and I loved helping in that studio. Down below in the garden, Waldo and I and Miss Pierce played croquet and took a lot of photos with a Brownie camera, developing them under blankets at night with a red glass oil lamp. Aunt Mary gave me a nice little conifer in a tub for my roof garden. She also made me a shantung dress with every animal in the zoo that you could think of embroidered round the neck in white silk.

I roamed far into Sussex and Kent with Aunt Mary, by bicycle, and occasionally we stayed at small farms. I always carried her easel and stool into the fields or rolling hills, where she would settle down for the day and paint a patch of wild flowers and grasses with unbelievable perfection. On our trips Aunt Mary always carried a small bag of poppy seeds—the common scarlet poppies that grow in cornfields all over England. The farmers try to get rid of them to keep them out of the final threshed corn, but Aunt Mary had other ideas. We both scattered the seeds far and wide. The yellow cornfields in summer with their splashes of scarlet inspired some of her loveliest paintings.

Aunt Mary also had a kitchen garden at the end of the lawn and annual beds at the Linfield house and grew all possible fresh vegetables. She was a vegetarian like us, and so was considered by the family to be eccentric, too. My grandfather (not that I ever used the despised word) is supposed to have said, "Why are my five sons all so brilliant and my three daughters so unbalanced?"

Another aunt, Aunt Carrie, was six feet tall. She was the one who married her first cousin, John (or Jack) Ward, who was younger than she, and shorter. Aunt Carrie was over forty when her daughter Blanche was born, who was also said to be "unusual." Biddy said she hoped Blanche would be "all right."

I met my cousin Blanche just once when she was a child. I think I was about nine and Blanche was about three or four, certainly a lively little girl. Too lively. She made me quite nervous—if at nine one can be called nervous. The Wards lived somewhere on the outskirts of London, and their little house was a very long walk from the bus. The long road was lined with trees and bushes, and the walk back seemed to go on forever. It had been raining, and in the endless English dusk the gray drip-drip went down our backs and into our shoes. Blanche kept kicking up the wet gravel at us and wouldn't stop, though Aunt Carrie tried to stop her. You could see it was hopeless trying to make Blanche obedient. Freedom is one thing, but just being cussed is quite different. Waldo, Biddy, and I were all glad to get back on the bus and head home.

Biddy's brothers were fairly brilliant. Fred had invented the Lanchester car and first fluid flywheel. Harry was a British government architect and town planner for New Delhi, India. But then, they had helped kidnap Biddy, so to us this bigoted bunch were the unbalanced ones. We despised showing gratitude for any miserable effort any one of them might make, and at home we laughed at them in a mocking kind of way. One younger brother, Frank, sent boxes of his old clothes for Shamus, which were useful when altered a little. Frank was a businessman, so Shamus was a very well-dressed clerk. The first thing that we did when the clothes arrived was to turn out the pockets, but all we ever found was a "French letter." We didn't know what it was so we put it on the mantelpiece in the Kitchen. There it stayed for two or three weeks, looking like a big rubber thimble, until at last a comrade explained its use to Shamus or Biddy. After great pressure from me, Biddy finally told us about it, passing it off with a slight joke: "Isn't it funny that the English call them 'French letters' and the French call them 'Capot Anglais'?"

I learned the word *cock*, as well as other four-letter words, from neighbor children but never from the boys at school. That word seemed particularly horrid because the family across the road from us were called Cocks. It was a nasty name for anyone, but this family had eleven children and they weren't even Catholics, so it must have been the name that did it. That the wisdom of Malthus should be unknown to them seemed disgusting—we were very snobbish about people who had big families. Dr. Malthus preached at the end of the eighteenth century that the population tends to increase faster than food supplies. He believed that war or disease would kill us all if people didn't stop having children.

Gracie Cocks was the eldest daughter and she was getting married. On the big day everyone on Leathwaite Road looked out their window or stood by their gates. As the Cocks children were got ready, they started to seep out onto the street: three boys and seven girls, leaning against the iron railings gingerly. The boys wore little black suits with long trousers and celluloid collars, and the girls wore white broidery Anglaise dresses with blue satin sashes and big bows on their low behinds (only rich people seemed to have long legs), plus white stockings and black shoes. Their hair had been transformed into thick sausages held back by blue bows over each temple. All the Cockses had dull-colored hair, not really mouse-colored but rat-colored. They were a plain family except for one boy, about four years old, who looked like an angel from a religious painting. I'd noticed other big families that had just one lovely child. Sometimes that one was epileptic.

As the five horse carriages drove off to church down Leathwaite Road, I rushed out with a dustpan and hoe to scrape up the horse dung. This was the neighborhood routine after any horse traffic. The important thing was to be first on the scene. We put the dung on our bit of front garden, under the privet bushes, and mixed it with some soil to use on the roof garden. We were getting ambitious and tried to grow some beans, not very successfully, but the radishes were huge and the privet was unnaturally healthy.

I began to be very pleased with the name Lanchester. How sad to be called Cocks or Bottoms! About three weeks after Gracie Cocks' wedding I saw a tinted photograph of the bride and groom and won-

dered what it was like to lie in the same bed together every night forever.

Biddy and her advanced methods and efforts to tell me all the facts
about our bodies was agony to her and left me with a disgust about how
I must have been created. No children like the idea applied to their
own mother and father and Biddy did not improve matters by her
prophylactic plumbing approach.

After Isadora and before the war—around 1913—Aunt Mary got a
commission to write and illustrate a book called *The River Severn from
Source to Mouth.* She planned to travel by bicycle, with sketchbook, pen,
ink, paint and pencil, camping equipment—and me. With great excitement, I packed my water colors and chalks, and we started off at the
beginning of July.

First we took the train to Llandudno, in the heart of Wales, and
stayed overnight at the local commercial hotel. The hotel was one of
those ugly wedge-shaped buildings built in the Victorian era, and it
faced the cattle market. As Aunt Mary and I ate poached eggs on toast
for breakfast in our triangular room, the noise of a cattle sale was
deafening. I looked out the window, feeling my first pang of homesick-
ness, and saw a bull servicing a cow. I didn't say a word, of course. Aunt
Mary wouldn't know about those things, and, anyway, she was busy
spreading marmalade on her toast.

We took several days to reach the source of the Severn. Buying
food, setting up our tent at sunset, washing in streams, and repacking
every morning, we worked very hard. The Severn rises on Plinlimmon,
a mountain that is green and hilly all the way up, with small sheep
farms here and there and waterfalls getting smaller at every turn of the
hills. The farmhouses on Plinlimmon are connected by yellow-sand
cart roads divided by gates. Of course, the lovely stream-threaded hills
got steeper and greener all the time on the way to the top. But I didn't
have much time to really enjoy the scenery. Aunt Mary made me cycle
ahead to open the gates while she sailed through. Then I had to shut
the gate and overtake her and open the next gate. I suppose we passed
through at least fifty gates. Maybe she was old and I was young, but
I hadn't come along on this adventure to just be a *tweeny.* Finally, we
left our bikes at the last farmhouse, Blaen Hafren, and walked the final
two miles to the source. At the top, which was really a moist field, there
were about five damp, boggy springs that collected into a little rivulet
. . . drip . . . drip . . . drip . . . and on to the sea two hundred miles
away.

Coming back downhill, I thought it would be easier to open the
gates, but Aunt Mary went faster than ever, although she did stop to

sketch all the time. Even then I had tasks—to cut bracken for our pillows and string up the tent and peg it out, sometimes to cut two larch saplings and strip them to hold the tent up. I was delighted when, one morning at six o'clock, a gamekeeper caught my aunt in the nude having a really good wash in a trout stream. She had soap and flannel and everything. The keeper just shouted, "Off my property!" Of course, I don't know how long he'd been looking—probably not long, because Aunt Mary was nothing to write home about. Nobody likes looking at old people with nothing on. It's funny that even the most broad-minded people never mention it.

After nine days' traveling down Plinlimmon, I got tired of my aunt and very homesick. One night we stayed in a small hotel at Shrewsbury, and as I heard the trains shunting and clanging, I made up my mind. In the morning, I quite simply said to Aunt Mary, "I'm going home." I had to transfer my train ticket, check in my bike at the luggage office, and wait for a train. Biddy and Shamus seemed surprised to see me and yet seemed to half expect me, too.

5

On Sunday, June 28, 1914, Archduke Francis Ferdinand was assassinated in Austria-Hungary. Just another headline to me. It first appeared in the *Stop Press News*, soon grew into anti-German propaganda, and then flared into anti–Kaiser Wilhelm propaganda, with songs and jokes for the children.

> Belgium put the kibosh on the Kaiser,
> Gave him a kick and made him sore . . .

Biddy and Shamus were violently antiwar, of course, and pacifism roared through the Kitchen. Contrary as usual, I had secret jingoistic thoughts. Waldo learned to drive a truck—in case. A sort of fear was everywhere—*sort of,* because it almost became routine. Our roof was a splendid place to observe the war sights. We saw the daylight air raids and watched the German zeppelin come down in flames at Cuffley, blazing in the sky. One gentle, sunny day we saw the first German planes, like mosquitos high in the sky.

Mr. Kettle's school closed soon after the war started. There were only six boys and me left. I think Mr. Kettle wanted to retire and Miss Kettle got married. For me, it was about time the school closed. I was developing quite a bustline, and when the boys dragged me around the playground with their hands under my arms, clenched across my chest, it did hurt a lot.

But I was only twelve, and fourteen was the legal minimum age to leave school and go to work. So I was sent to a coeducational boarding school for rather prosperous children at Kings Langley, Berkshire. I was to teach dancing classes two or three times each week in exchange for my education and food. One wet autumn evening, I arrived at the Kings Langley station with a feeling of hopeless despair. I had to walk two miles from the station on a country road, carrying my wicker clothesbox tied with a leather strap. I knew I was quite unfit to learn or teach. The sky and the trees were dripping after a storm, and it was nearly dark when I reached the school. The children were having dinner as Miss Coombs, the headmistress, took me around for introductions. I sat with the students at one of the long oak tables—about thirty boys and girls. Miss Coombs had a rather cruel face and looked like a currant bun: two currants for eyes, two for nostrils, and three for a pinched little mouth all pushed deep into the bun. Her skin was pale and puffy—yes, an uncooked yet severe currant bun.

All the children were gaily discussing whether their quarantine was over: "I won't be out for two days . . ." "I'm lucky I haven't got it yet." The disease turned out to be chicken pox, which luckily I had had, but I was shocked. Miss Coombs couldn't fix up a bed for me that night in a room or dormitory, so I slept on a straw-stuffed mattress on a stone balcony under a metal roof, with another girl who was older than I. She was out there by choice—toughening herself for life, I think. The school was run on ascetic lines. You could call it an "advanced" school—expensive to go to and cheap to run—but the result was very uncomfortable. The food was awful, but then the blockade of England had started and no one had made much progress with austerity. I'd always had to eat a lot of porridge, and now I ate more than ever. After pommes soufflé in Paris, I was not gracious at Kings Langley.

The girl on the other mattress, on my first night, was named Barbara Burnham. We talked all night or at least till it began to get light. There wasn't enough straw in my mattress and the cold stone floor struck right through to my bones, but our conversation seemed wonderful and profound. My first experience, I suppose, with the pleasures of logic and mental honesty from a bright young thing. Straw and damp morning air can smell very haunting.

My education at Mr. Kettle's made me a misfit among the other pupils. I didn't know what grammar was or verbs or nouns—I'd never learned history but loved mathematics and drawing. When I taught my dancing classes, I had no authority over the rather sophisticated bunch of young people, nearly all claiming to have chicken pox, who lounged around the huge fireplace in the "great barn" playroom. I was quite an expert at Raymond Duncan's Greek Rhythmic Gymnastics, and one or two children took an interest. I got on very well with a Scottish boy named Rory Stewart Richardson. His mother, Lady Constance Stewart Richardson, was a dancer, so I probably didn't seem so strange to him.

But things went from bad to worse. Sleeping six to a dormitory, I lay awake among the chattering poxy monkeys. I was unable to eat the food, and Miss Coombs lashed out at me because I didn't fit any pattern. The school prided itself on developing individuality in the young, so those in authority had to work by rigid rule of thumb methods. From that experience and from Biddy and Mr. Kettle I learned the trick of being a free individual behind a rather conventional facade. Nothing like it!

After ten days I gave notice, and taking my wicker basket, I walked to Kings Langley station to wait for a train to London. I reached Leathwaite Road very late at night. As before, when I came back alone from Wales, Biddy and Shamus took it as a matter of course. "Oh," said Biddy, "you didn't like it there?" I felt pleased and vindicated when Lady Constance invited me to go camping in the Sherwood Forest with her and Rory and his brothers. I dreamed of what to wear and what to pack, and even bought a set of hairbrushes with silver backs—or rather *Silware* backs, as the patent called it. Biddy called them a "ghastly purchase," and she was right—ghastly for camping out in the forest. But we never did hear any more from Lady Constance Stewart Richardson or Rory, and the Silware brush set tarnished in no time.

Uncle Harry was the oldest of the Lanchester children and the least aggressive of the trio that kidnapped Biddy—though he had been violent toward Mrs. Gray. Rather late in life—he must have been around fifty—he married Ann Gilchrist, a musical comedy actress, whom we called Aunt Nancy. Biddy, Shamus, Waldo, and I were soon invited to their house at Weybridge. The big, gently terraced garden went down to the river and they had two rowing boats and a punt in the boathouse. There was a tennis court, a pine wood, and in the vegetable garden there were plenty of raspberry canes. Aunt Nancy was very, very Scottish. When she sang "The Songs of the Hebrides" and Hungarian folk songs, I was swept off my feet. She became my first idol. She sensed this and used to say, "Kiss Auntie," when we met or parted, which caused me agonies of embarrassment. Biddy grew to dislike Aunt Nancy and would often say mockingly, "Kiss Auntie." Biddy could sneer in a most unpleasant way.

Although I did not see my aunt and uncle very often over the years, I always liked staying at Weybridge—that is, without Biddy. I spent lovely days there wandering around the garden and sitting in a boat tied up under willow trees. Sometimes I wheeled Harry's and Nancy's first child, Robbie, in his pram up and down the terraces. I often whispered to him how he was born, with a few medical details thrown in. He was only one year old so it did no harm. My bedroom at Weybridge was at the top of the house, but it was fit for a dairymaid, with white dimity curtains over the two dormer windows and wallpaper with tiny blue flowers all over it. It was my first experience with daintiness and spotlessness.

Being an authority on Raymond Duncan's Greek Rhythmic Gymnastics and with the added glamour of my life with Isadora, at age thirteen I was a full-fledged assistant, ready and willing to work. My first assignment after Kings Langley came from Miss Rose Benton, one of Raymond Duncan's adult pupils, who took me on a lecture tour. She was a dark, quite muscular spinster with a beak of a nose—a strict, dehydrated, noncompanionable lady like many of Raymond Duncan's followers (who, by the way, lived on a diet of rice and spinach). She lectured about *things* Grecian and the Duncan System, describing the movements and talking about their creation from Greek vase decorations, dressed in a hand-woven Greek gown like The Master. Wearing a linen and silk Greek dress that I'd woven myself, I demonstrated most gracefully as she talked or while she got her breath back. The audience, I felt, loved me but I was uncertain why.

In each town we visited, we stayed with sponsors in their private houses. In Edinburgh, in rather an elegant house, I had to share a big bed with a girl of about seventeen, who had long black hair down to her knees. I didn't like the arrangement at all. She insisted on washing my hair that night, saying that I would love the smell of the orrisroot shampoo. In bed, she kept inching over to my side bit by bit. I lay rigid as a punt pole, edging farther away, until I very nearly fell out of bed. Thank God she gave up. At breakfast the girl's mother and Miss Benton thought I smelled funny—the smell of the orrisroot hung on and on. I looked it up in the dictionary and found out that it was used for making sachets and powder. It certainly spoiled my excellent bacon and eggs. Finally the tour fizzled out. I only got paid a few shillings for each performance. I earned much more—one shilling per hour—sitting for artists.

Miss Benton later was enamored of a group of Hindus, their way of life and their philosophy. I went to a few meetings with her but really didn't absorb anything much. A jolly, short, fat Hindu offered to give me some lessons in Indian dancing so I started on that and proved almost to be born for it. His name was Ali Khan but they all seemed to be called that. They (the Hindu group) took over a large, double-fronted late Georgian house on Holland Road, Bayswater, and furnished it as only self-denialists can, with Oriental rugs and only one or two wooden chairs. When I went for my lessons on summer afternoons, the sun came in through the unwashed windows in opaque shafts. Maybe the other parts of the house were quite different, but that's how the big front drawing room was where he and I worked. Ali Khan, who had a very fat stomach, taught me to bend over backward and touch the floor with my head, as he held my waist from the front so I wouldn't fall. I didn't like it, and I didn't think I could do it, but he said, "Yes, you can." I could and I was very surprised. I learned how to move my head sideways like a snake, and my hips, too, keeping my torso between quite still. I don't know whether a snake dancer is supposed to be imitating a snake or mesmerizing a snake, but I was very snaky and supple and I suppose Eastern. I found that I had what some people call double-joints, and learned what some people call bumps and grinds and others call belly dancing.

I didn't have many lessons, but enough. Holland Road was a long way from Clapham Common, and I only wanted to learn a smattering of other dance systems. I realized a smattering was enough to be an authority, which was all I wanted to be.

The next smattering I got was of was Dalcroze Eurhythmics. Basically Dalcroze was musical training. You learned to conduct or beat time with your hands and feet, which grew really difficult in the later phases. For example, you had to beat four-time with one hand, three-time with the other hand, and two-time with your feet. You also learned to conduct groups of students into a planned but loose formation, then move them around the studio to a classical composition played by the teacher. I learned a lot about phrasing and musical structure from Dalcroze, as well as the fun of being a kind of King Canute pushing the waters back. Even now I can't really sit through a concert because I start to conduct or rather create an imaginary ballet.

So, by the time I started to teach, I had a lot to pass on. I never gave it a moment's constructive thought, but I certainly could have called it "my system."

The war was under way when I started to go to Margaret Morris' school in Chelsea. Besides dancing it offered art classes, a little acting, and lessons in singing and speech by a Mrs. Glover. Margaret Morris gave a few shows to display herself and her star pupils, and also sent out assistants to teach on the outskirts of London. She was a lithe woman, like a Modigliani model, a remarkable personality and dancer —someone I could envy, admire, and not dislike too much. She lived with a man called Mr. Ferguson, who looked like a bull. I found him scary.

Two girls at the school became my best friends—Angela Baddeley and her sister Hermione (then called Toti). I stayed with them for a few weeks in their flat somewhere in the suburbs, while their mother was away, looking after their pregnant sister, Muriel. We three had quite a time tending their monkey, Mona, and cleaning up her cage. We also went to the public swimming pool, and although public pools were really filthy, we survived. We heard that a drowned child had been lying at the deep end for three days but couldn't be seen owing to the murk. You couldn't see your feet below you, anyway. We three agreed we hadn't been swimming since the child had been missing, and we never went back again. Angela was a star pupil at Margaret Morris's mainly because she was so very charming and such a good dancer. We both decided never to grow old. We just would not let it creep up on us—ever, ever.

I was an assistant teacher at the school, assigned to help a teacher called Una Minchin. Every Saturday, we went out by bus to Golders Green and taught at the house of a Mrs. Garrett. The class was organized to glorify Mrs. Garrett's little girl Joan-Mary, truly a beautiful child with gold-colored hair. I painted a semireligious picture of her with a golden halo and blue background, which the Garretts framed. It became a kind of iconlike centerpiece on their living room wall. They asked me to one or two evenings at their house, where I danced more or less naked for their guests after dinner. I wore a string Maori skirt that Shamus had brought home from the office years before. His boss then, Mr. Oxley, must have been an importer because Shamus was always bringing home odd things that came from foreign parts—Jock the parrot had come from that office.

The trip from the Margaret Morris School took about forty-five minutes, by bus and tram and walking. The German planes came over every few nights, more often on moonlit nights because then the Germans could catch the reflection of the river Thames. That would indicate the Houses of Parliament and other locations. A few times I got caught by the air-raid warnings on my way home. I never thought I would be killed by the planes, but I was really terrified of knocking at unknown doors and talking to absolute strangers until the all clear. And I felt very alone, thinking that Biddy and Shamus and Waldo could be wiped out and that they would be feeling the same about me. A lot of people who have not been through war feel that it brings families closer together, but that doesn't always seem to be so. Likes and dislikes, loves and hates, stay the same.

At home we all went down to the coal cellar during the raids. Once a bit of shrapnel whizzed through the roof, passed my bed, and went on through the floor into the kitchen. All of us were in the cellar except Shamus, who sat in the dark upstairs. "He only does it to annoy," complained Biddy. The piece of shrapnel became a showpiece on the mantelpiece.

Once a house up Leathwaite Road got a direct hit. Down in the coal cellar, I was lifted right off the ground. A bomb blast turns you into a feather, and as I floated back to the floor I clearly remember deciding that having children was not a good idea. I was sure that

Biddy and Shamus had not had war in mind for Waldo and me. No one should have children and that was that—how right Dr. Malthus had been. As for God, the war seemed the best proof yet that there was no one up there and that believers in a Creator were weak in the head. I thought that the story of the devil was more likely, especially since my book *Chips from the Earth's Crust* described the core of the earth as still being hot. Just because there was evil didn't prove that there *had* to be good. In the morning we all went to see the bombed house. It was a clean-cut space between two other houses. "If there's a God, he's certainly a good dentist," said Shamus.

That year, Margaret Morris opened a summer school in the Isle of Wight, taught by Miss Minchin and me. Besides dancing, for some reason I was to teach abstract art. The Isle of Wight was very lovely, hilly, and green, and the area where we lived, called Seaview, was on the beach. We went north to Ryde and faced the Solent, where yachts still race. Across the water we could see the white and olive camouflage round the Portsmouth shipping activity.

Promotion for the school started with a show and a party. Angela Baddeley and one or two others were on hand to perform, along with Margaret Morris, of course. She found families to lodge Miss Minchin and me for the month. At first, Angela and I stayed in a little room in an old stone cottage. We rehearsed our show, and Margaret Morris generously allowed me to perform a composition of my own, "Maori Dance," set to music by Coleridge-Taylor, inspired by the string skirt that Shamus had given me. (The string skirt, like Jock, had come from Mr. Oxley's office.) I was told that I must use depilatory to remove the hair under my arms. Angela seemed to know a little about it because she had older sisters—what a relief! We bought the stuff and followed the instructions. It was a powder that became active when mixed with water. When I put it under my arms it itched, and its sulfurous stink was overpowering. Then we didn't know how to get it off. Finally Angela scraped it with a teaspoon, and we threw the mess into some stinging nettles outside the window. We thought it was the funniest thing that had ever happened to us, funnier than Mona the monkey.

The "Maori Dance" was the most successful number on the program, and I had several curtain calls. Definitely surprised, Margaret Morris didn't praise me at all. I got more applause than she did for her numbers but she had to answer questions graciously about that "remarkable red-headed girl." Miss Minchin was rather sour about my success because of her loyalty to Miss Morris, whom she worshiped. She was a Christian Scientist so it wasn't difficult for her to seem neutral. Angela was simply delighted for me. She was incapable of an ill thought.

After the show came the party. My first real party, with food, music, dancing, talking, and laughing. Some bright lights and some soft, pretty lights in the garden. Young couples waltzing and doing some tangolike steps. Miss Morris danced with everyone, including me. She was wearing a magenta sheath dress, and her shining straight black hair hung in a low, loose knot. She probably wore some exotic jewelry, bracelets . . . I don't know. I think she wore bright green shoes. She led me up and down the room in an exhibitionistic tango of her own invention, which frightened me out of my wits. Her body thrust forward at the hips, and with her thighs gripping me I felt trapped by a sort of steel animal. Of course, I exaggerate, but I was so embarrassed that I made some excuse and ran. I didn't know I was a shy person until then—I mean not a daring person. I didn't know what I felt.

My classes were pleasant and calm, and I loved my title of Art Teacher. I liked being with Miss Minchin, who had great reserve and a talent for quietude. We hired bicycles and made many trips together round the island. I even copied her way of writing a Greek capital *E*. Then the gossip began about Margaret Morris. Two or three mothers got together to talk and then blamed each other for possibly libelous remarks. In the end they decided that a red-headed girl had not only started the rumors but must now be saved. One night after dinner I was called into a conference and they gave me the third degree. I was mystified by what they were talking about, completely. Finally, I said that I didn't like dancing with Margaret Morris. Yes, I thought it was disgusting. Apparently she had danced with them all—like *that*. I was sent outside to walk on the beach. I was full of hatred and felt wronged from an unknown direction. I will never know what really happened, but it seems now that I had become a scapegoat for idle gossips.

That night I was moved to another room in another house. My new hostess, who wanted to "help" me, was a Mrs. Gawthorne, and there and then I realized that in the future I would never trust anyone, no matter who. I was being wronged by these adult fiends, without any redress . . . I was sent back to London the next day. When I got home to Leathwaite Road, I was greeted with the usual "Oh, you're back" from Biddy. I never saw Miss Morris or Miss Minchin again.

But I did see Mrs. Gawthorne, my accuser-defender on the Isle of Wight. The Gawthornes had three beautiful little blond daughters, and they asked me to give them private dancing lessons twice a week at their elegant house on Sloane Street, Knightsbridge. I taught the children for several months and always had a delicious tea with the family afterward—thin cucumber sandwiches, cakes, and sweet biscuits of every kind. But then Mr. Gawthorne started kissing me earnestly as he gallantly saw me to the front door. He held my nose to make me open my mouth. One day I got a sweet letter written on thick, deep blue paper saying the children would not be taking lessons anymore. I was not displeased.

What with removing the hair under my arms, being slandered, and kissing and everything, I was more or less grown-up.

My earliest effort to get a job in the theatre might well have put me off the business forever. Some friends of Biddy's and Shamus's, a Mr. and Mrs. Priest, brought round a copy of *The Era*. It was the organ of showpeople, a weekly paper crammed with news of music hall acts, stage companies, and touring companies. There were advertisements for "artistes" and for "digs" (rooms) where "theatricals" were welcome. In *The Era*'s ads I found the call: "Wanted, snake dancer. Young, attractive, for 'A Night in Egypt.' Apply Ida Barr, Edmondton Royal Theatre, £2 per week."

Miss Barr was an enormous woman with paper-white puffy flesh, a hoarse voice, and hennaed hair. One twist of my sinuous arms and I was engaged. I started in two days, with no rehearsal. As the act began Ida Barr, wearing a glittering cloak and tights, stood in front of the red velvet curtains making a stream of jokes: "A man said to me at the stage door, 'What's your name?' and I said, 'Ida Barr,' and he said, 'Ida Barr? Why, you're big enough to 'ide a pub!' " Then came "A Night in Egypt." The curtain rose on a desert scene, a cracked backdrop, with stars twinkling through. Ida Barr came onstage without cloak but wearing a peacock blue chiffon overgown. On a silver clarinet she played "The William Tell Overture" in deafening fashion, her little white, fat fingers flashing on the stops. Then I made my entrance. I wore a short little brown crepe nothing of a dress, in bare feet, and insinuated myself snakelike through a side wing to squirm my way into the hearts of the audience, while Ida Barr played sinuous Eastern music on her instrument. My encore was "Ballet Egyptian."

At the time it was not funny to me—only sordid. We did three shows a day at the Royal Edmondton, and I got back to Leathwaite road by late bus. Ida Barr thought I was lovely—"like a little fawn," she said—and wanted me to go on tour with her, but Biddy and I agreed that it was no life for me and I left at the end of the week. Truly, I left mostly because I couldn't stand dressing in the same room with this corseted white barrel, who had no modesty. She was very annoyed with me for leaving, but still quite kind. "You're really too good for this, you know, and you'll be a big success someday—you'll see," she said.

During the early war years, Biddy had a growing interest in the Quakers—not because of their lack of dogma but because of their pacifist beliefs. The Society of Friends opposed war in any form and preached nonviolence between countries. Most Quakers refused to fight but the decision was personal. The sect and its history strongly appealed to me, too, but Shamus thought it was a lot of rot and Waldo thought it was all right—that is, if he had an opinion then.

Biddy learned of a proposed Quaker community, a village in the Cotswold Hills, to be called "Jordans." It would be designed and built by the Quakers and their sympathizers. With the war under way and the bombs falling, Jordans seemed, from the literature, to be a dream of perfect peace for the future. Sensitive and knowledgeable about current events, Biddy must have longed to have some money to invest in Jordans.

When Waldo was about eighteen, his apprenticeship to the scientific instrument-maker came to an end. The time had come for him to be conscripted into the army. He had silently waited, no doubt dreading what would happen to him. I took it as a matter of course that Waldo would go into the army and felt an obscure depression on his account and a sense of foggy-ended destiny for all young men.

Then the name Clifford Allen sprang up in our Kitchen. He was the first to articulate the point of view of the noncombatant in wartime. All over England tribunals were set up, consisting of a judge and a group of gentlemen past military age, to screen applicants for noncombatant status. Each "objector" had a chance to state his reasons for not fighting and to appeal his conscription. Through the leadership and example of Clifford Allen, along with several members of Parliament, the conscientious objector—the C.O., the "Conchy"—was born.

Of course, Waldo would try to become a conscientious objector. Biddy, Waldo, and I attended a meeting where Clifford Allen spoke to learn what Waldo would be up against when he was cross-examined by a tribunal. We began to collect information and newspaper cuttings, which we pinned up in the Kitchen on a cupboard door by Jock's cage.

Some judges, it seemed, were gentler than others, but all were unrelenting. Our district, Battersea, which happened to be the same as Clifford Allen's, had a Tribunal that was particularly harsh. It dispensed longer sentences to prison and more hard labor if the answers from the objector were not servile. Biddy thought that moving to another district was the solution. So she and I went house-hunting in the Wandsworth area. We found nothing at the low rent of Leathwaite Road. It seemed hopeless.

Then we read in *The London Times* of Wednesday, March 15, 1916:

> Mr. Clifford Allen, chairman of the No-Conscription Fellowship, applied at the Battersea Tribunal last night for absolute exemption on conscientious grounds. The application was refused.

And a month later:

SERVICE TRIBUNALS

THE "NO CONSCRIPTION" FELLOWSHIP

> At the London Appeal Tribunal (City section) yesterday, Reginald Clifford Allen, chairman of the "No-Conscription" Fellowship, appealed against the decision of the Battersea Local Tribunal ordering him to undertake noncombatant service. He claimed absolute exemption on the grounds of conscience.
>
> The appellant said that, as a Socialist, he considered his life and personality sacred. He refused to take any part whatever in war. He considered that he could render the best service by advocating the cause of peace.
>
> Major Lionel de Rothschild, M.P., the military representative, submitted that the appellant had no religious conscientious objection, and only those were recognized by the Act.
>
> George Lansbury, who was present, exclaimed: "Shame on you, Rothschild. Herbert Samuel said that a moral objection is as good as a religious objection. You ought to be ashamed of yourself."

Eventually *the* day came for Waldo. I can remember lying awake the night before, and then the color of the day—the dim, pale, dusty sun coming through the courtroom windows. It must have been winter because I was wearing mittens. It wasn't exactly a courtroom—more like a large committee room with dusty kitchen chairs and benches for people to sit on. There were about thirty tense, almost weeping watchers. Mostly mothers, I think. Waldo was battered by a battery of the same questions. My poor brother.

"If you were attacked by a German, would you fight back?"

"If a German attacked your mother, what would you do?"

"What would you feel if the Kaiser ruled England?"

"What would you do if a Prussian soldier raped your sister?"

"Would you take on noncombatant work?"

"Can you drive a truck?"

Waldo said nothing or "No" or "I don't know." The judge was a happy beast enjoying his work. I like to remember him as frothing at the mouth. He sent Waldo to Wormwood Scrubbs Prison for one year.

We all visited Waldo in prison, not often but when it was allowed. Then I became a little "jingo" for a few months and missed one visit. I was eaten up by the thought that Waldo *had* learned to drive a truck, in case. I was sure that Waldo's being a C.O. was due to Biddy's influence. I was too young and too confused to know what to think. Before the end of the war Waldo was recommitted to prison several more times.

Of course, there were many funny stories about "Conchies," but they didn't surface for us at the time. In Douglas Goldring's book, *The Nineteen Twenties*, published in 1945, he described them as

certainly the oddest lot of people ever temporarily united under one banner. Some of them carried their dislike of killing so far that they existed only on vegetables. Others would not even hurt the feelings of a vegetable by cooking it, and lived on unfired food. Perhaps the strangest figure who ever appeared before a Tribunal was the late Lytton Strachey. The dignified bearded historian, on arriving in Court, calmly inflated an air cushion before seating himself to discuss with the tribunes, in his high-pitched voice, what he would do if he came upon a Hun in the act of molesting one of his female relatives. Another Conchy was a musician who had the honesty to admit his physical disability. "Quite apart from my hatred of war," he explained to a friend, "I am entirely devoid of all the more obvious forms of physical courage. I can not bear explosions or thunderstorms, always avoid fields containing cattle, cannot use my fists . . . and always feel faint at the sight of blood. It is the way I am made—just as some men are born deaf or short-sighted." The tribunes were, of course, unanimous in refusing him any kind of exemption. Fortunately a sympathetic doctor fitted him out with a pair of flat feet, so he was able to go on playing his piano undisturbed.

Occasionally we would read a fading snatch or two about Clifford Allen. Nothing stays on a front page for long, and he was soon relegated to the chit-chat columns.

The London Times, May 14, 1917:

NEWS IN BRIEF

Colonel Rudge, 79, formerly in command of the Lincolnshire Regimental District, was choked while dining. It was found that a piece of chicken had blocked the opening of the windpipe.

Clifford Allen, chairman of the No-Conscription Fellowship, having finished his second term of 112 days' imprisonment with hard labour for refusal to obey military orders, was released on Saturday from Maidstone Gaol and handed over to a military escort to be returned to his unit at Andover. He will be Court-martialled for a third time in a few days.

While gathering seagulls' eggs on Little Ormes Head, Llandudno, on Wednesday night, Albert Brown, age 14, fell about 150 feet on to the rocks below and was killed.

Biddy's mother, Octavia, died in 1916 at the age of eighty-two, leaving Biddy four hundred pounds. Biddy invested all the money in Jordans, but the Quaker community project never came to anything. We couldn't even get a reply from them, just more brochures—no dividends or an option on a place to live. Once we made a trip to see the place. It was just a few muddy yellow-clay roads and piles of brick. We weren't even absolutely sure it was the right place. It didn't say Jordans anywhere.

After the war Waldo was released from prison and came home to Leathwaite Road. There was a big demand for hand looms, and Waldo started to manufacture them for Biddy's many connections. He also started to make puppets and gradually built up a performing group. He got a few commercial jobs, including one with the gas company. Later Biddy acquired a studio in the Richmond area where she and Waldo could both function, making puppets, teaching weaving, giving shows and lessons. They developed quite a coterie of friends and helpers, who were just names to me. By then I was off on my own, collecting a group of friends who were in turn strangers to Biddy.

One was Lady Firenza Montagu, an energetic society woman whose pet charity was "The Happy Evenings Association." It was an effort to create active evenings for children and young people, "to keep them off the streets." Lady Montagu had the use of a school in Soho, and I was put in charge of about thirty young people for two evenings each week. I taught them everything I'd learned about movement and dancing. They were nearly all attractive and clever—mostly Jews, the children of first- and second-generation immigrants from all over Europe, and from poverty-stricken homes. And for them I was a lively, forthright, and graceful young leader.

I had begun to feel some creeping authority in myself with everyone I met. I'd always had opinions but now they were framed, as it were, and my new confidence must have made me a rather brassy young teenager.

In the summer Lady Montagu went away on a long holiday with her husband and two children, so it was back to the street for my charges just when they most needed an occupation. During the second summer that I worked for Lady Montagu I rented by the hour a small hall in Soho at 110 Charlotte Street, and gathered all the children together again. I always had an itch to organize everybody round me, and as I loved dancing itself, I wanted to continue teaching. Harold Scott, the pianist from The Happy Evenings Association, joined me, with a few friends. We called this new enterprise the Children's Theatre.

By now I was living on my own, quite happy to get by on next to nothing. I used to eat in a cheap Italian restaurant in Charlotte Street. The place was always full of taxi drivers. I had a bowl of minestrone with bread and a big handful of green olives, all for nine pence. I taught a large dancing class once a week at Bedales, a big coeducational school near Petersfield. My salary of £2 a week paid the rent and gas for the room that I had taken off Baker Street. Biddy had always encouraged me to be independent but when the time came she was nevertheless shaken.

For many months I had also been giving private dance lessons to the two Montagu children, traveling by train to Farnham, Surrey once a week and staying overnight. I began to reject my hand-woven arty garb and found it very disturbing not to have the right clothes for such high society. I did have a nice blue Liberty dress, but I longed to have something different to wear for breakfast. Breakfast there meant a sideboard loaded with everything I'd ever read about in books—York ham, kedgeree, any kind of eggs, kidneys, mushrooms and kippers and bacon. Through the windows, you could see dewy lawns and flowerbeds, and then pine woods beyond. It was a beautiful, romantic old country house, where James Barrie had written *Peter Pan*. When I started the Children's Theatre, that ended my trips to the Montagus. I missed the loaded breakfast sideboard that had become my ideal in the food department.

My Children's Theatre absorbed most of Lady Montagu's group —sadly for her, the most attractive and talented children—because it was more fun and we took no holidays. Our classes were free, of course, so we put together shows to pay the rent. Lessons came to be called rehearsals. Harold Scott organized a folk-singing group, and someone else helped the children make costumes. They made most of them out of cheap stuff—casement cloth at sixpence halfpenny a yard and printer's muslin, the cotton run through the press to clean the type, which we got free from the dustbins of Fleet Street. By then the stuff had black-and-blue stripes and blurs across it—a ghostly version of a daily paper.

From the start the Children's Theatre attracted a great deal of publicity. The children and I developed a taste for hard work. Our shows were models of orderliness and consisted of songs, dances, and short and long plays. We did adaptations from Hans Christian Andersen's "The Nightingale" and "The Emperor's New Clothes," and a very early piece of work by Jane Austen.

Our most elaborate production was *Tom Thumb* (or *The Tragedy of Tragedies*) by Henry Fielding. I made my first linocut for the bill we sent out for our first performance. The robust verse of this lovely and brilliant little drama was full of charm and wisecracks that were not above the heads of the children. Most of them were from the heart of London and had a bit of the alert gutter rat in them, as I did. From their sprightly delivery (especially from the little girl who played Tom Thumb, Leah Birnberg), I learned a lot myself about acting. The children did the play with superb gusto and heartfelt sincerity. The ending of the little tragedy was not unlike *Hamlet*'s, with stabbings all around. Tom Thumb had been swallowed by a cow just before this bloodbath:

LORD GRIZZLE.   Thanks, O ye Stars, my Vengeance
                                 is restor'd,
                    Nor shalt thou fly me—for I'll
                                    kill the Ghost.
                                 (Kills the Ghost
                                 of Tom Thumb.)

HUNCAMUNCA.　O barbarous Deed—I will revenge him so.
                    (Kills Griz.)

MR. DOODLE.　Ha! Grizzle kill'd—then Murtheress beware.
                    (Kills Hunc.)

QUEEN.　O wretch—have at thee.
                    (Kills Dood.)

MR. NOODLE.　And have at thee too.
                    (Kills the Queen.)

CLEORA.　Thou'st killed the Queen.
                    (Kills Nood.)

MUSTACHA.　And thou hast kill'd my Lover.
                    (Kills Cleo.)

KING.　Ha! Murtheress vile, take that.
                    (Kills Must.)
And take thou this.
                    (Kills himself.)

This finished off the entire cast, except for a crowd of followers and courtiers who fell down anyway in horror and dismay.

Most of the children in the theatre were very good at *something*. If a child could walk on her toes without shoes, we dressed her as a violet and she did a violet dance. If a child was double-jointed, he or she played a circus contortionist or mimed walking on a wire. They all did what they could do well and the audience was very impressed, so I got the reputation for being a brilliant teacher. But with more well-off pupils, the more money I was offered for teaching, the less talent the child seemed to have. Several of these students were little horrors. The besotted mothers often came to me and said right in front of their tots, "My little girl I *know* will be another Pavlova! *You'll* see. You simply *must* take her as a pupil. And I want her to have *private lessons.*" I took them, poor little things. I had to earn a living.

I adapted our Jane Austen piece from a book of her letters and early works called *Love and Freindship* (the misspelling was hers). It made a very delicious half-hour satire, poking fun at the idle rich. It was good exercise for the children to learn the stance and behavior of another period. To complete the evening's program, we added solo and group dances and songs. The shows became nearly self-supporting. This fact, combined with our production of *Love and Freindship*, was our downfall. The London County Council stepped in with its red tape and rules. I was called before a board of ancient gentlemen who said that I was exploiting children and quoted the Child Slave Act to me. On top of that they said, "And how dare you presume to teach children when you yourself cannot even spell 'friendship'?" It was a pleasure to put the gentlemen right. Although they turned rather red, they forbade us to give the final performance of *Love and Freindship*. But, shades of Biddy, I told them that for all I cared they could arrest me.

We held the last show on a Sunday afternoon in our own practice hall on Charlotte Street. The house was full (150 in attendance) and the performance went without a hitch. Several L.C.C. gentlemen turned up but they disappeared quickly. They could do nothing because we had previously given several shows in aid of the Save the Children Fund, and that society had kindly allowed me to put slips to that effect in the program. Biddy wasn't the only one who could crow over the London County Council. She admired me for tricking her old enemy the Law.

7

This hurdle was crossed, but the children were growing a little older, a little less pretty, and perhaps a shade boy-and-girl conscious. New students came in but the fire of the Children's Theatre was fading out. I don't know when it actually ended and our new project began.

It was a nightclub Harold Scott and I started to put on one-act plays at midnight. We called the club the Cave of Harmony. With the help of a few friends, we began to rehearse several plays that were little classics in the hall at 107 Charlotte Street. We couldn't get a liquor license, so I must admit that we left the tops off bottles of cider, which in two weeks would become a little alcoholic. Our meager profits we shared among the partners: a young newspaper critic, Matthew Norgate; a songwriter-actor, Philip Godfrey; Harold; me; and a rather large lady named Helen Egli who, wearing sequins, feathers, and a fringe, could really put across a song. Harold was the emcee and also sang at the piano. I suppose I was the dancing soubrette, as well as the head cook and bottle washer. Besides addressing envelopes, making linocuts, and painting scenery I began singing out-of-print songs Harold and I collected. We had spent hours researching in the British Museum to find songs such as "Please Sell No More Drink to My Father," written as a serious Temperance song, and "The Ratcatcher's Daughter." We re-created the Victorian era in a weekly act under the title of "The Old Mahogany Bar." The "All-British Russian Choir" was another popular standby. This loony act was just a catchall for the four of us—Helen, Harold, Philip, and me—to do anything we wanted, using old wigs, boots, and furs.

It wasn't very practical to rent a hall by the hour, so we eventually moved to a perfect little place with an entrance in a cobblestone mews. We painted the walls pink, the woodwork yellow, and put up red velvet curtains. It was a lovely firetrap, illuminated only by candlelight. Sometimes we did a midnight one-act play and sometimes we put together a cabaret show. We had a little trio of violin, piano, and drums, and when the dancing stopped, people sat on the floor to watch the show.

The Journal of Arnold Bennett described us in those days:

Tuesday, June 17th, 1924:

Elsa Lanchester and Harold Scott came to lunch yesterday. She had a most charming dress, homemade. She said she had made it out of dusters, and I believe she had. Very young. A lovely complexion, wonderful shock of copper hair; a rather queerly blunted nose. Harold staggered her and D. [Dorothy Cheston, actress friend of Bennett] by arriving in a hat. He never wears hats, but had apparently decided to learn to dress. Both deeply interested in their cabaret schemes. Discussing it among themselves and with Dorothy. Largely ignoring me, though with no conscious rudeness. Youthful severity on older people. I offered to pay for some chairs and tables for their cabaret, but they were not at all keen on them, apparently preferring the audience to sit on the floor. However, they took them. I should say that these people are bound to do something good. They are full of *original* inventiveness and of distinction.

During this time I often slept at the Cave of Harmony, in a kind of balcony-loft that I had built at one end. To get to it I climbed up a ladder and through a trapdoor. In this comfortable den I felt independent and secure. I could see down onto the dance floor through a small square window and could retire if I wanted to and just listen to the music and general babble.

Because our performances took place after theatre time, we were able to get distinguished actors and actresses to appear for us. We staged the one-act plays of famous writers such as Pirandello and Chekhov—plays that most people never saw performed—and actors were anxious to appear in them. I also worked up an act with Angela Baddeley. We invented two charwomen, Mrs. Bricketts and Mrs. Du Bellamy. We always opened with our feet in basins of hot water and a clothesline of laundry strung across the front of the stage, and we could chat, completely impromptu, about anything that was in the daily headlines. This "turn" was very popular, and the great point of the act was to surprise each other and break each other up.

Harold Scott was a superb accompanist and a good composer and arranger and he was a perfect young man friend to me. Blond, with a rather overpink face, he was thirteen years older than I. He had been married to a singer of French folk songs called Raymonde Collingnon, a miniature blonde like one from a painting by Fra Filippo Lippi, who had a tiny singing voice that was so clear you could swear she was a little bird. Harold knew the countryside around London and he also knew a lot about wildflowers. We spent a lot of time walking in the same woodland area in Surrey where I had camped out years ago with Biddy.

Biddy didn't like Harold Scott. She said, "He's not the type that I'd have hoped for you at all." I was annoyed because I should have thought he *was* the type. Apart from his talent, he was erudite and certainly continued my general education where Mr. Kettle's school left off. I was annoyed, too, with Biddy when she read one of the letters Harold wrote me when I was staying again for a few days at Leathwaite Road. Biddy, Biddy, Biddy. It's not a thing girls forgive their mothers for.

I did lots of things to earn a living in those days—sat for painters and photographers and sculptors. The photographers were "art" photographers. *Art* was a word that cloaked oceans of naughtiness, and I mostly posed in the nude. I often dropped by the elegant art store under the portico of the Ritz Hotel to look at my photos in the window. Once or twice I brought along some dear old admirer who had given me lunch to see them. The pictures were almost indecently respectable. Biddy told me she often dropped by to see them, too, when she was in the area. It was probably the only way she could see how I was developing physically.

A lot of rather famous people started dropping in at the Cave of Harmony—writers, poets and painters, musicians. H. G. Wells, Aldous Huxley, Evelyn Waugh, and James Whale. Sometimes someone would write a song for me, like Herbert Farjeon:

> I may be fast, I may be loose,
> I may be easy to seduce.
> I may not be particular
> To keep the perpendicular.
> But all my horizontal friends
> Are Princes, Peers and Reverends.
> When Tom or Dick or Bertie call,
> You'll find me strictly vertical!

Evelyn Waugh came to the Cave of Harmony quite often. Usually he seemed to have been somewhere else before and my place was part of the night out. He and his friends were usually half drunk and I expect that they brought a bottle with them. Evelyn Waugh was not at all attractive looking. Not very tall, he had a pink face. That is, not all over pink, pink in patches as if he had a bad cold. Therefore the features were not well-defined and the bitter-witty-cruel mind shone through the pinkness. Evelyn Waugh and his companions at this time decided to make a film for fun—*The Scarlet Woman.* I don't know why the film was called *The Scarlet Woman.* I don't know who owned the camera or who held it. It was a Papish plot with the Pope trying to force the return of England to the Church of Rome. This was to be achieved by the Prince of Wales being seduced, forced, and persuaded. Three enforcers were used and I was the woman. It was all much more complicated than that—the big cast raced around Hampstead Heath and Kensington Gardens. There was lots of drinking in the bedroom scenes—bottles of liquor at every turn. I know the Scarlet Woman had plenty of bottles under her bed. The Pope and the Prince of Wales were also surrounded by liquor. The film was awful though we laughed hysterically.

Waugh was the same age as I—to the day (he said to the hour). Also he came to the club especially to hear me sing "My Yiddisher Boy (With His Yoy, Yoy, Yoy)."

John Armstrong joined our group when he was an unknown painter. He not only helped design the scenery and costumes (as well as addressing envelopes) but he also wrote plays and brilliant limericks. He created a coffee stall decorated elaborately with a cornucopia and made wonderful sandwiches that he sold for sixpence each. His specialty was mushroom and paté. A poem John wrote one night while counting out the night's take in his niche in the wall showed the jolly mood that we were usually in:

> Remember the wages of sin is death,
> So when on your deathbed you draw your last breath
> Say to yourself, as your relatives pray,
> "Hurrah, hurrah, it's pay-day today!"

Those were wonderful days and nights of staying up and having eggs and bacon at Lyon's Corner House at four in the morning. Then on to Covent Garden to see the flowers and vegetables come in, the greengrocers, the florists, and restaurant owners choosing the very best. How beautiful and fresh everything was. Then, as it got light, home to bed. What a sleep that was.

We also went to shows, movies, circuses, and music halls. Once at the Olympia, a huge stadium, we all saw the Barnum and Bailey Circus. Having gone on all the big amusement rides, we decided to try the sordid side shows. There were always some very small tents on the outer edges, housing fortune-tellers and the like. One that looked particularly seedy was called "A Night in Paris," and it was only tuppence to go in. So we trooped in through the entrance, an opening in an old sheet, and between two dusty black velvet curtains. Newspaper cuttings and a few torn photos were pinned up. Suddenly there was a yell of glee. Among the nudes was one of the old art photos of me! A spider's web had been drawn in behind me, and the title said, "Caught in the Web."

They were four wonderful years—the shows, the friends, my private loft, the audiences, the early morning meals and talks. During these years Biddy never visited the Cave of Harmony except in the cold light of day. She grizzled because it was not the Children's Theatre anymore.

I was always in need of money to pay for food and rent but one way or another I managed to pick up enough to keep an account going at the National Provincial Bank. I was so precise and honest about money that they always let me overdraw up to two pounds. Among other odd jobs, I occasionally did some housecleaning. Washing the white molding round windows is not easy work, but I did it very well. A Mr. and Mrs. Kapp kindly let me clean their London flat. They both played recorders and entertained at the Cave several times. Kapp was a famous caricaturist and she was a magazine writer. They had a little daughter. They were both good friends of mine, but they *both* made passes at me. I was very shocked, especially by hers. I was curious enough try anything once—but not *that*. The cleaning-the-flat job ended, but I always wondered if they talked about me with each other. Had it been a plan between them? We stayed good friends for many years, but I never felt flattered.

A better paying job was being corespondent to couples who wouldn't get an "honest" divorce. This situation arose from the very Old World notion that an unfaithful wife had to be protected from being branded a scarlet woman. To be a "gentleman," the husband took the blame. So, when a man's wife had a lover, he wouldn't sink to spending the night with a whore, he would hire me. For £100 or more, we would spend one pure night in a hotel, be "discovered" together, and the divorce would go through.

The government office, the King's Proctor, frowned on such collusions. I only engaged in these transactions a few times, as they were no doubt punishable offenses, although I only did them through a lawyer. For my part, I thought these cooked-up divorces terribly funny. I was never bored with my part in the little drama. After all, it was acting—being entertaining, making jokes and playing cards all night

—a kind of show. In the morning we both got into our pajama tops in the bathroom (one at a time, of course), then sat up in bed to be seen by the maid. Duty done, cash paid, bill paid at the hotel desk. It was just thank you and good-bye.

The maid who served breakfast in the hotel had to appear in court as a witness when the case was heard and testify that it was not the gentleman's wife who was with him in the bedroom. As the maid stated in court in my first case: "I knew they weren't married because he asked her if she took sugar." Then the wife would dab her eyes with a handkerchief, probably provided by the lawyer. The unknown woman (me!) of course did not have to appear. If the *wife* was found by the King's Proctor in *flagrante delicto,* the whole case would be rescinded and the husband and wife would have to wait a whole year and start again. Once more Biddy rather admired me for tricking the old enemy the Law.

I sang this song at the Cave of Harmony. It was written by Herbert Farjeon.

> I've got those King's Proctor Blues.
> Oh, doctor,
> Say, have you heard the news!
> Pamela's hopes have all gone spinning,
> She's got to start from the very beginning,
> She's more rescinded against than sinning—
> She's got those King's Proctor Blues.
>
> You never know where he is for certain.
> Under the bed or behind the curtain,
> Ready to spring if he finds you're flirtin'—
> I've got those King's Proctor Blues.

Shamus wore his mother's guard ring until sometime around 1918, when he gave it to me. I was, of course, getting jewelry-conscious and had often tried on curtain rings for size when I was a child. I found the guard ring quite useful when I started going around with young men and later when I got those corespondent jobs. I never knew why Shamus wore the guard ring. Perhaps he remembered his mother fondly, or in a tiny gesture of defiance he wanted to telegraph to Biddy that it made him feel a little bit properly married. Or maybe he wanted to cover up a blue ring he had tattooed on that fatal finger. He had several other small tattoos, and all I ever knew was that they were done in his youth. It didn't occur to me to ask why. Now I do wonder about that prophetic tattoo on his wedding ring finger covered by the guard ring. To Biddy the ring must have symbolized the failure of her powers of persuasion. She had conspicuously never worn any ring at all, and so she strongly objected to my wearing one. She often asked me, "Why wear a guard ring—what's it supposed to guard?"

For somewhere to go in the daytime I now belonged to a club— the 1917 Club. Harold, who had been a conscientious objector, introduced me to it, and Biddy was proud that I was its youngest member. I'm sure I was accepted more as a mascot than anything. Some of the members were very famous—E. M. Forster, H. G. Wells, Sir Osbert Sitwell, Aldous Huxley. Ramsey MacDonald was the president. Biddy said that I had sat on his knee at a socialist meeting in Caxton Hall when I was two years old.

As Douglas Goldring described the club in *The Nineteen Twenties:*

> The premises . . . at 4 Gerrard Street, Soho, had all the squalor and dinginess associated in the popular imagination with a conspiratorial den of Bolsheviks and thieves. . Cranks of all varieties—vegetarians . . . mystics, progressives of all sorts and descriptions, Quakers, poets and a queer crowd of *avant-gardists* of every creed, colour and social and ethical background . . .

The club had political overtones—1917 being the year of the Russian Revolution—although under that roof the members were fairly conservative socialists, according to the Biddy doctrine. Biddy had rather rapidly turned into a communist and referred to socialists as being "practically Tories," having "no guts," who had "let the workers down." The Communist Party was taking on some of the early fire of the Labour Party, and the 1917 Club was a representative meeting ground for this exchange of ideas.

The club seemed to have a very resigned and gentle atmosphere under the benign eye of the secretary, Miss Sprott, who sat at the door. After lunch the place was fairly empty, and if stragglers felt like talking they just got into conversations. Quite often Chaim Weizmann and I sat and talked there of an afternoon. Sunk in a deep, ancient armchair I'm sure I looked very intelligent. I always had a talent for becoming a chameleon if I wanted to. Some call it acting.

He was a great chemist and the great Zionist leader, and he told me very quietly and gently about world affairs. He probably felt he was informing a child, that his time was not wasted in helping to mold the future. I liked to hear him talk but didn't really try to understand what he said about Theodor Herzl, the first Zionist, or the hopes for Jews in Palestine. It was all too far away from any basic knowledge I had.

Once I went to dinner at Weizmann's house. It was just the two of us—I think that he had a wife or maybe a sister somewhere upstairs, but she was never well, I believe. It was a hot summer evening, and his house was somewhere in the grayer reaches of Kensington. I went by taxi. He lived in one of those triangular buildings that looked like a large piece of cheese, and the rooms inside were more or less triangular, too. There was a heavy dimness inside, the sort of curtains that light never really comes through. Maybe the house was only rented or belonged to a relative, I don't know. The dinner was served by a very silent servant in a white apron, and I do not remember what we ate at all. I instinctively looked serious and intent and eager to learn—and I was, but I couldn't. I just studied him and breathed in the atmosphere of the scene. I gave him respectful and adoring looks, and I'm sure I managed to ask bright questions for my age. He just brushed his stubby beard against my face, and we shook hands firmly when I left. Maybe he thought that I would be a young disciple of Zionism, and we did go on talking at the 1917 Club until he stopped appearing.

I was beginning to feel my lack of formal education—the art of learning how to learn, to apply yourself to a subject. Intense curiosity is not quite the same thing. I felt that in my conversations with Weizmann I was only smart at seeming to be smart, like the good old gutter rat of years ago.

An evening that I'd forgotten but Douglas Goldring remembered in his book:

I was sent tickets for the premiere of *Hassan* at His Majesty's, and took with me Elsa Lanchester, who was then scarcely out of her teens. Her flaming red-gold hair, exotic costume and *gamine* appearance had—much to my amusement—a startling effect on all the stuffed shirts who beheld her. "Who's that girl?" I heard people murmuring in the entr'acte.

Elsa became one of the shining lights of the 1917 Club and soon acquired numerous admirers in the world of art and literature. Among them was a young artist [John Armstrong], now one of our most gifted painters, whose fidelity made him occasionally visit Gerrard Street in search of her. He was not apparently favourably impressed by her surroundings . . as [his] following ribald and wholly libellous poem . . indicates:

In nineteen seventeen they founded a Club,
Partly as brothel and partly as pub.
The members were all of them horrible bores,
Except for the Girl in Giotto-pink drawers.

Not quite correct. The exact words of John Armstrong's poem were:

> In nineteen one seven they founded a Club
> Partly as brothel & partly as pub,
> With a membership mainly of literary bores
> Redeemed by a girl in Giotto-pink drawers.

Douglas Goldring concluded with:

> I hasten to add that the colour of Elsa's alleged "drawers" was
> an innocent club joke, the point of which I have forgotten.

And I have forgotten, too. I don't recall having any pink drawers, being more partial to white. But the principal in a "legend" is the last person to know its causes.

JA

Geoffrey Dunlop, also a 1917 member, added to the rumours with this rather bitter poem—but then Geoffrey was bitter about everything (mostly himself):

> Pink drawers alas—why should her drawers be pink
> Their colour gives me furiously to think—
> Pink drawers—and do they never turn to red
> Flushed at their mistress' sin while she's in bed.
> No they are pink, as peonies their faint hue
> Their innocence remains forever new.

62

In London I walked everywhere with daring and confidence, alone and with friends—I was becoming very conspicuous. Passersby always stared at me, and no wonder—I had a mass of curly auburn hair and usually wore a homemade cloak. I did not know for one moment that I had some sort of compulsion to be different. Even at parties I nearly always wore a severe suit, with a gardenia, when others wore evening dress, or vice versa. I was funny and loud when things were quiet and silent and wide-eyed when gatherings were noisy. I know that if I'd had enough money I would have conformed, as I did later. But in those days I had to be advised like a child about what to wear. What to wear will always be a mystery to me—a decision that sometimes made me withdraw from events.

Biddy grew concerned when I turned up less and less at Leathwaite Road. I didn't feel I had to account for myself in any way. After all, independence was one of Biddy's causes, and she was very proud of the freedom that she practiced. I suppose she was as surprised as I was to find that she was hanging on to me, clinging to every move of my private life. Maybe Biddy was not aware of her changing patterns, or mine. Maybe she thought I was too young to be gallivanting about. She was changing very slowly, and the more curious she became about my life the more withdrawn I became from her. I just thought she was nosey. Her daughter was not the homing pigeon she had expected, but a strange and hurtful boomerang. I suppose it was natural enough for a mother to say, "Don't leave home, not yet," but the innocent and slow change in Biddy's own emotions seemed out of character to me. Since my whole upbringing had conditioned me toward self-sufficiency, Biddy did not have any valid argument, so she was tentative in her criticism of me—whimpering and, of course, quietly sarcastic. It crossed my mind even then that Biddy may have been thinking back on the sorrow she caused her own mother and father. I remembered my grandmother then with a little warmth. As for Shamus, he was much too embarrassed to say anything but "Hello, girlie" when I saw him.

Unexpectedly, Biddy was quite proud of some of my habits. I didn't wear a hat, and she liked to hear people say that I belonged to the "hatless brigade." But she was very annoyed when people in the street called out, "Ginger, you're balmy, get your hair cut!"

8

It must have been spring. Anyway, on a fine day walking in the country with a friend, what do you expect? It was under a may tree near Warlingham in Surrey, quite near the copse where the caterpillars fell on me when I was a child, in a little area with the unfortunate name of Titsey Wood. Many of my friends who might have been thought to be lovers were just friends, and here and there a friend was a lover. Distance had to be planted at the very beginning, I found. Bohemian life being what it was at the time, relationships, unless openly passionate, were often kept under a cover of almost Victorian reserve. My own reputation was rather pure, for I was only close to people I liked, and after an affair I usually went into a virginal shell of my own invention. I think I preferred the role of the Untouchable Young Woman to a close relationship. At no time did I want to make a little home. I didn't mind saying good-bye to men, but I hated saying good-bye to household possessions—saucepans and so on. I found a sort of power in periodically living serenely alone because I despised women who had to have a sex life. I thought, "I'll show them." There was no element of keeping pure for anyone—just for myself.

Ties were something that I was always running away from. I'm sure that couples do get bored with each other owing to the bed being the same old bed in the same old place. I would say that I needed a change of place rather than a change of person. Yes, I was a topographical lover. Different places—woodlands, friendly farmhouses, village pubs that let rooms, the English countryside. I remember lying in a bluebell wood in Surrey—blue as far as the eye could see through the trees—then having a picnic of hard-boiled eggs, bread, and cheese. But I cannot remember who I was lying with. I don't mean that there were so many men to choose from—there were not. But the face faded completely out of the picture like the Cheshire Cat in *Alice in Wonderland*.

One summer a friend and I walked all the way from London to Brighton with packs on our backs, stopping at a cottage or farmhouse each night. In an old orchard, very overgrown and decayed, we sat with our bread and cheese and apples and watched a sunset. Herbs had crept through the fence into the long grass—thyme, marjoram, mint. The pungent smell of the herbs we crushed has stayed in my memory forever. When I made a stew in later years it would all come back to me—the thyme, the marjoram—not too flattering to the young man to be remembered by a stew.

One of the times when I was tired of attachments—I think it was after Harold Scott—I moved to 43 Belsize Park Gardens. Harold had taken up with a girl called Dulcie who was not very strong and died in a sad manner at Fontainebleau, a farm for intellectual people who couldn't face life. Once I opened a letter from Dulcie to Harold in the 1917 Club washroom. The envelope filled up with hot tap water, and I handed Harold a very waterlogged letter.

So I moved to 43 Belsize Park Gardens. I had a very large room with a piano, a camp bed, and quite bohemian kitchen privileges in a large mid-Victorian stucco house owned by the writer Mary Butts. She was a rather handsome, angular lady, breathing erudition, with a gentle family background. She had thin carrot-colored hair that was almost pink, and pale, pale skin. Both she and the house were something of a legend. Virgil Thomson says in a book about his own life that "Mary Butts was English, an adept at magic, a smoker of opium, a poet, an author of novels and stories."

Mary Butts was a writer of distinction and certainly part of the intellectual wave that thrived between the turn of the century and the second World War, reaching its peak in the twenties. Artistically she never reached the crystalline heights of Katherine Mansfield, Virginia Woolf, or Gertrude Stein, but she was of that school of writers who observed life in all its autumnal introversion. So many creative artists around the twenties—painters as well as writers—seem to have expressed a prophetic doom that certainly came to pass. At that time I had absorbed de Maupassant, Flaubert, Gogol, and Chekhov, and Mary introduced me to Krafft-Ebing for laughs—I felt ready for anything. This literature exactly suited the teenager I was, who needed an endless supply of agonizing sorrow to wallow in—the sob sister and the soap opera came later.

At that time Mary was living with a man called Cecil Maitland, who was thickset with a rather red skin and black hair. He was either drunk or seemed to be most of the time, but maybe he was sniffing something. I didn't like Maitland at all. He frightened me. Once, in a playful manner, I suppose, he pulled me onto their studio bed by the hair. I gave him the knee in the groin and he laughed it off. We were all having tea at the time in Mary's study. Tea was quite often a meeting time for droppers-in. Mary had some fine china and used it. Knowing the riotous life that sometimes went on, I was amazed that the tea set was not all smashed up.

Mary had a small daughter by her marriage to a poet, John Rodker. Camilla was under three years old and she came to No. 43 only to visit. I saw her occasionally at the house where she lived, just up the road, which was peopled with flotsam and jetsam. Most of its inhabitants were followers of Diaghilev's Russian Ballet—the most conspicuous among them being "Poppy." Poppy had colorless hair that I think had never been washed or combed or cut. Perhaps it just broke off. Every night she could be seen in the front row of the gallery with her bare feet hanging over the rail. Anton Dolin was a friend of hers and used to sit around her house, often in the nude. Once when Camilla was crawling along the floor she made her way under Dolin's chair and sighting something unusual clutched hold of his testicles and said in lisping innocence, "One-two." It was funny, but Mary thought it was magnificent—obviously foreseeing that her daughter promised to be a brilliant mathematician.

At No. 43 there were both permanent and temporary lodgers. Upstairs lived two lovely serene sisters, a sculptress and a painter. The novelist Douglas Goldring, who was a tenant for a short time, was almost stupefied with love for the eldest, Gladys Hines. I was always a willing listener for anyone who wanted to talk. The more outlandish the problem the better. The Goldring-Hines "case" was, of course, uncomplicated but very enjoyable. Douglas Goldring and I were always good friends. In fact, I played his corespondent when he wanted a divorce. How we laughed.

For a short time there was a tenant called "The Lady in Red." She was the companion of Aleister Crowley, a Black Magician, who had his headquarters or "temple" in Cefalù in Sicily. Mary Butts said the temple was eight-sided with a sort of sacrificial altar where they occasionally killed a cat. The ritual sounded ghastly to me. I suppose that's where the opium (or cocaine) came from. Once I saw Aleister Crowley when he came to the house at Belsize Park. He had a bicycle and his head was shaved. He was wearing a yellow kilt. Apparently he was always an odd dresser, as *The Journal of Arnold Bennett* relates:

1904. Tuesday, April 26th.
    I went to lunch with Aleister Crowley and his wife . . . today at Paillard's. He had been made a "Khan" in the East, and was

wearing a heavily jewelled red waistcoat and the largest ring I ever saw on a human hand. I rather liked him . . .

1905. Thursday, March 9th.
    I dined at the Chat Blanc. Aleister Crowley was there with dirty hands, immense rings, presumably dyed hair, a fancy waistcoat, a fur coat, and tennis shoes . . .

I helped him find The Lady in Red. She was down in the kitchen, stirring a large pot on the stove. It could have been stew or dirty washing.

Mary and her lover Cecil were sometimes very odd, and I went in to visit them at teatime less and less often. Once Mary invited me to come to tea to meet a famous attorney and writer, E. S. P. Haynes, who she said, admired me. So I decided to go. The lecherous old attorney, this E. S. P. Haynes, the author of *The Decline of Liberty in England, The Case for Liberty,* and so on, was large and fat. He wore a shiny steel plate to support his stomach, which he insisted on demonstrating to me, though I did not want to see it. I think the others had seen the show before. He then said he would like to see me in the nude, so I stripped immediately, sat down again, and went on sipping my tea from one of Mary Butts' dainty china cups. Everybody in the room enjoyed the gesture, which oddly enough was quite decent. E. S. P. Haynes looked like a stuck pig.

Behind these mid-Victorian houses were long gardens with some nice trees and bushes, but behind No. 43 the garden was unkempt and usually rather muddy, with some rank grass. Even in summer the bushes looked the same as in winter, yet not exactly dead. Someone gave Mary Butts a white chicken, which was named Charlotte the Harlot, and this garden was her home. Charlotte laid about one egg a day for a time and then stopped, so we called up *The London Times* —it had a general information department. They said the chicken must be "egg-bound," and the cure was a "soot pill made of some common soot from the chimney mixed with butter." As Mary held Charlotte, I opened the beak and pushed in the pill. After a few treatments the chicken was cured. She produced a chain of gradated eggs joined together like a row of sloppy pearls and then went back to normal.

Whirling down Shaftesbury Avenue one day, I passed a wild-looking man with thin, untidy hair, loose clothes, and a free-flowing tie. I turned around to look at him, and he turned around to look at me. He walked back to me and said, "I am Jacob Epstein." Introductions over, he asked me if I would sit for him. I started the next week and was honored by sitting for, even then, a famous sculptor. But all the same it was a strain, never easy. We did not communicate.

Jacob Epstein had a scandalous reputation and was credited with having wild times with his models—many great but interesting beauties—and riotous evenings at the Cafe Royale, a large restaurant in Regent street. The Cafe Royale was always packed with celebrities, artists, and wealthy dilettantes—and even poor dilettants. Mahogany walls and baroque gold-framed mirrors, always smoke-filled and probably gaslit before my time.

No doubt to make me less nervous, Epstein explained to me why his reputation as a bohemian was so unjust. He said, "As I work at home, it is unfair to say I go out to lead an immoral life away from my family. What is a home for—a place to go back to—so how can I come back home if I don't go out?" He also told me that he would like me to pose as Peter Pan for him. That is, when the official request came through for the full-size figure for Kensington Gardens.

Epstein worked in the first-floor front room in a house on Guildford Street in Bloomsbury. It was exciting to see his "heads," finished and unfinished, all around. There were many heads of his famous model, Oriel, as well as those of his daughter Peggy—the now famous heads of Peggy as a baby, executed with the love and softness of Renoir's paintings of his son.

Sittings started about nine-thirty or ten and went on till lunch, which was served in the front room on the ground floor. His wife, a nice plump lady, cooked economically and was not attractive enough to protest about or even feel hurt about his other life. I'm sure she was just proud to be Mrs. Jacob Epstein, and to be the mother of his daughter, Peggy. Peggy was now about seven years old and spent most of the lunchtime under the table, being disobedient. She obviously didn't like me—or anyone from upstairs, I suspect. One lunchtime, toward the end of my sittings, she totally disappeared. When I prepared to leave that afternoon I couldn't find my hat. I had spent a lot on that hat and was on the verge of being a more fashionable woman —a big step. Well, that horrid child Peggy had forced my hat down the w.c. and blocked up the plumbing. Father was slightly angry, mother felt too unworthy to complain, and I decided not to sit for Peter Pan with this hated little Peggy in power.

Biddy and I didn't have much in common. By this time she was a communist and very pro-Russian, and very involved with weaving, hating meat, and complaining about Shamus' lethargy. When I talked to Biddy she might well have thought that I was taking after Shamus because I seemed lethargic, too, when I was with her. When I saw her now it was usually for lunch or a very early dinner on the long summer evenings—nothing expensive because neither of us had money to spare. We would go to Shearns, the vegetarian restaurant in Tottenham Court Road. It also had a very large and good fruit and vegetable shop, and like Little Red Riding Hood, Biddy usually took a basket of goods home with her. Although Biddy seemed to think it was quite a treat, I could not stand the food at Shearns: nut cutlets, fruit-nut wafers (mostly figs), and of course, fresh fruit. With Postum. We also went to Eustace-Miles off Charing Cross Road, but that was much more expensive and not good. The menu mostly offered imitations of something you wouldn't know what the original was anyway.

I felt very far away from Biddy, and she gazed at me as if I were going to bite her head off. Fortunately she had lots of friends, many younger than she and some contemporary. They all had one thing in common—they admired her for her early stand against marriage and her fight against her beastly father when she was abducted and falsely committed.

We would talk about the old Children's Theatre, all my ex-pupils, and the Cave of Harmony, or my classes at Bedales, the large coeducational school near Petersfield an association that pleased Biddy. Like any Victorian middle-class mother, she wanted security for me. She took pot shots at my insecurity: "How is Harold Scott?" (long after his day). "Where are you living now?" "What do you eat?" and "How's the bank account?" From freedom to hypocrisy is a giant jump, and I couldn't get on with any human being who thought he or she had rights. I can only wish now that I could have dissembled a bit then, but that art is acquired later in life.

When Biddy's kidnapping case occurred in the 1890s, her mother and father must have been in their vulnerable middle years. In the 1920s, when I was living through my own eccentric times, Biddy and Shamus were suffering through *their* vulnerable middle years. I doubt that they ever thought that love conquered all, but Biddy and Shamus, like all human beings, probably felt that their dream would be fulfilled. Instead, the usual disillusionment crept up on them from day to day. Freedom, it turned out, was not really freedom. So their children's own freedoms took its place. Biddy was drifting into a vicarious existence through me in the twilight of her relationship with Shamus. It was felicitous to be born in 1902. Anyone born around that time hit a jackpot era—that is, if they lived through the two wars. Science, medicine, and the arts in this century tumbled over each other at such speed that our human span of three score years and ten seems more like living two hundred years.

Biddy reminded me that once I pulled a kaleidoscope apart because I wanted to write my name on a piece of the colored glass—green. I did, and my brother Waldo had to put it together again. I felt that I was preordained to be better than other people, and Biddy seemed to think so as well—almost too heartily. She even went as far as to have my horoscope made when I was about eight years old—quite an elaborate one, too. I shall never forget it. Biddy often read it to friends and neighbors. "Ideas will fly from her like sparks from an anvil." I lived with that in mind, with the added spur of my kaleidoscope and piece of ever-changing green glass. So through the Children's Theatre days, the 1917 Club days, the Cave of Harmony and Belsize Park days, my confidence in myself was helped by a bit of superstition.

At 43 Belsize Park Gardens I really needed self-confidence. Mary Butts was strong meat for anyone, and I was only about nineteen. Over time I seemed to survive the power of her talent-personality. She remained a friend, though rather an out-of-focus friend due to her drug habits, I'm sure. She often came to my very large room, with the piano, to watch me practice dancing and create numbers for the Cave of Harmony shows. I often noticed her sniffing the back of her hand. She was a vague but fascinating person, with or without cocaine.

A pianist friend, Alfred T. Chenhalls, played for me and composed music for my ideas, which were original, to say the least. One dance was based on Krafft-Ebing, Case No. 74B of Zurich. A nun called Blankebin spent her time looking for the foreskin that was cut from Christ when he was circumcised. She pursued this batty occupation all over the church and occasionally thought that she had found it. Oh, joy.

Like so many brilliant musicians, Alfred Chenhalls was also a brilliant mathematician. When he was in his very early twenties he worked for a large firm of accountants, and he bought out his bosses within two years. Chennie, as we called him, introduced me to Schoenberg's music. I pretended to understand it, but I never did really, though I composed some outlandishly abstract, expressionist, and revolutionary dance movements to his pieces. The audiences at the Cave thought I was very clever. That's how vogues often start.

Chennie proposed to almost every woman he met, carrying an engagement ring in his waistcoat pocket at all times. I am sure he often found it a shortcut to the bed—but not for me. He was quite nice, but his pin-striped business suit and pink, round face only made me laugh. He looked very, very much like Winston Churchill.

Another true friend through all the years was John Armstrong. He came to the Cave of Harmony very early and grew with it. At the time he shared a studio with another painter, Harry Jonas. Harry was Jewish, sardonic, and attractive. At the Cave he danced the gliding type of dance or tango in a way very "fascinating to women." John Armstrong danced like a bunch of thin slats hung on a wire and jerked gaily unaware round the dance floor. During the war he had been an officer in the Royal Field Artillery. A photograph of him in uniform on a horse made him look very distinguished, like a soldier in a painting by Sargent.

I sat for both John and Harry in their big studio on Warwick Road. They did portraits, very pre-Raphaelite, and nudes. Sometimes I slept at the studio. John used to give up his narrow bed to me and he slept on the floor. John seemed to enjoy the sacrifice, and I noticed a benign smile on his face at all times when I stayed there. He made incredibly delicious breakfasts and woke me up with a kiss on the hand and a cup of tea, and sometimes a poem. John had various crushes and relationships, as I did, and we also had in common food, flowers, and London walks. Sometimes we would talk nearly all night—till four or five in the morning—then he would walk me home to Belsize Park from the studio, a good eight miles.

The crosscurrents of friendships in your life can build a structure that makes a well-rounded existence. Starting in a small way in my teens, that structure made me into a presentable person for any company. Of course you cannot organize your own crosscurrents, but for me there were some pretty fortunate connections—from Aunt Mary to John Armstrong; from Biddy the nonconformist to Mary Butts' form of freedom; from socialist theories in the Clapham Common Kitchen to the 1917 Club, with its writers and intellectuals; from Isadora to Margaret Morris. And a hundred other crosscurrents forced me to leap mentally from crag to crag—very good exercise. And a perfectly good replacement for what is called "an education."

Querschnitt (*Crosscurrents*), published in Berlin, was the first magazine I ever bought and went on buying. It was almost entirely made up of pairs of photographs of related things or people, such as two chickens beak-to-beak having a squabble, and opposite, two women cackling across a fence. In these comparisons in *Querschnitt* I learned a lot about behavior and so a lot about acting.

Most of my friends from the 1917 Club and the Cave knew each other a little but never well. I would say they drifted by each other. I think that was my unknowing method: Keep each person separate in your heart. Don't have two sex patterns going at the same time. And don't ever join a conversation about something you know nothing about.

9

After a year or two I was on the move from my Belsize Park room. As Mary Butts and Cecil Maitland went abroad more and more, the big house seemed to have a lot of empty rooms and it echoed coldly. For about a year I lived in the balcony-loft of the Cave of Harmony, then I moved to Doughty Street, Bloomsbury. I shared the rent of this ground-floor flat with a writer. He had the front room and I had the back room. Quite separate. Then he left and I rented the room to John Collier as an office. Collier was a very close friend of Philip Godfrey of our Cave of Harmony group. Many a fine time we all had at Doughty Street singing through the night hours with Philip playing the guitar. Both Collier and Godfrey were incurably fascinated by oily cockneys and unctuous characters. In fact, everyone I knew liked to undermine hypocrisy. It was the mood of the day.

Collier needed the office because he was working for a friend who had a "method" and gambled on the stock market. This man, Geoffrey Pike, was mysterious and wealthy and used his money to run an exceedingly modern school for boys of all ages. The financial chart on the office wall was about eight feet long, and John Collier delighted in marking down the "hot" news every morning, along with instructions from Geoffrey Pike. Then Collier would be on the phone for hours, juggling with buyers and sellers. Every morning he shone with fun and joy as he performed the role of financial wizard. For these transactions with the stock exchange, he liked to borrow my silk top hat, which I used at the Cave of Harmony in a couple of songs—"The Boatman's Dance" and "Buffalo Gals." Once when he made a very big coup, he dragged me off to the Waldorf Hotel in Aldwych, very grand and stuffy, and he ordered a feast of raspberries and cream. The eerie winds of his macabre point of view started to fan that sort of humor in me.

Doughty Street had a sort of after-show atmosphere, and Collier was the leader of some of the childlike wickedness. He was very attached to Helen Kapp, sister of caricaturist Peter Kapp, and once, out of sheer excess energy, he tied her up in a bedsheet and bumped her on the floor, not much, but enough, while he laughed his antic heart out. At the London Zoo, one of Collier's favorite stomping grounds, he invented wonderful conversations between the chimps—talks about big business and high finance or the country life of English gentlemen: "Hunting and shooting . . . what." These chimps had long, pensive pauses as they found momentary sex pastimes or chased an autumn leaf. "Excuse me a moment, sir, just a little business." A fine preview of *His Monkey Wife*.

Doughty Street ran only one long block, but it was full of interest —very wide, with perfect, untouched, good, solid nineteenth-century houses, each with a basement and three floors. One morning when I lived there I was awakened by a sanctimonious voice announcing from an open charabanc, "We will now take a ramble down Doughty Street!" There were many blue plaques on the houses marking the famous who had lived there, but the present residents were noteworthy too: James Agate, the dean of theatre critics; Paul Robeson; and from my own past, Harold Scott, who was now married to Audrey Lucas, the daughter of E. V. Lucas. And just around the corner on Guildford Street was Jacob Epstein; and in the Bloomsbury squares were the Meynells of Nonesuch Press fame; John Maynard Keynes and his young Lopokova from the Russian ballet; and Miles Malleson, the actor, at whose flat in earlier years I nearly lost my virginity when he and Harold Scott combed my hair until I nearly swooned.

Bloomsbury was a name that conjured up an era of painters, poets, musicians, and writers. It was a little decayed in the 1920s, for some of the wide streets and large green squares, with their beautiful nineteenth-century architecture, were turning into flats and boarding-houses. Still the very air of Bloomsbury was so thick with the past, present, and future that I almost choked with excitement half the time.

James Agate, with his manservant and two large white boxer dogs, lived across the street from me. Through him I met an oddball-caller, Jock Dent. Jock was a very poor but strong and ambitious young man, who actually walked from his home in Scotland to Agate's door and knocked. He wanted to learn about the theatre and become a critic, too. At first, Jock ran errands for Agate—Jock would do anything for him—but he gradually impressed Jimmy.

Jock dropped over to visit me quite often, just for a chat and a cup of tea. He may have got fed up with Jimmy's obedient manservant and the two white boxers—boxers, if trained, are known to go for the throat, for their owner's protection. These two dogs certainly scared me, although they were always kept on leashes.

One foggy day when Jock came over to visit, I opened the door and said, "Oh, it's foggy!" From then on, *he* got to be called "Foggy." His mother sent me delicious shortbread from Scotland. Foggy (in his strong Scottish accent) told me that Jimmy's sister, before she came into the room to meet visitors, always had to wash her knees. I found him rather weirdly interesting.

Now Foggy is a most distinguished drama critic in London, under the name of Alan Dent. Jimmy Agate had a heart attack; and a frightening rumor had it that he lay dead and his ferocious dogs stood over him for some days until he was found.

Among this galaxy of friends was a woman whom I would know most of my life—or, rather, I should say, all of her life—Iris Barry. She was known and admired over the years by countless segments of artists. I met her at a rather voguish party, and by chance, she lived a half a block from me. So we dropped in on each other frequently, for drinks or tea or a little attention during colds or influenza.

This amazing woman sprang from a pure gypsy background. Her mother had actually told fortunes, so I think. Iris was self-educated to a much greater degree than I was. She lived with her heart and her heart was often broken; she wouldn't like me to say that. But her heartbreaks made her a very touching person to all people. She had lived with Wyndham Lewis and had two children by him, both put out for adoption. In spite of other affairs and marriages she could never forget him.

Iris was an up-and-coming film critic on *The Daily Mail* and, of course, had the entree to English film studios. She introduced me to her friend Sidney Bernstein, whose father had invented the movie house tip-up seat. Thus born with money, Sidney grew to become the head of I.T.V. (the pay television network in England) and is now Lord Sidney Bernstein. Iris engaged his help in organizing the London Film Society. Iris provided her vast film knowledge, inspiration, and drive to bring it to life.

Iris, Sidney Bernstein, and I sometimes went out to dinner because Sidney preferred to go out with two women rather than one, being afraid of becoming involved. Iris and I were pretty relieved to get a free dinner at the time, but when he took us back in a taxi, he always fumbled in his pockets for change. He never had any. So Iris and I always had to pay out more than the price of a cheap meal. How we laughed at him.

The 1917 Club carried on but was getting rather tatty. In *The Nineteen Twenties*, Douglas Goldring told how it declined:

The 1917 Club, which had decayed into a cheap lunching place for civil servants and minor Labour Party officials, was dreary beyond belief, and obviously on its last legs. All the excitement, all the hope, all the seething life and vitality of the early 'twenties seemed to have been smothered under a concrete layer of frustration.

I didn't go there very often anymore but enough to start a rather uncomfortable relationship with a White Russian. It was uncomfortable because I didn't have cerebral control, which had been my great protection. I had picked up the word *cerebral* when I was about fifteen and it had a great influence on me, like a magic power word. Other words that helped me live were *resilience* and *survival.*

This Russian could have been a spy, for all I knew, but I found him rather attractive—enough to make my singing and dancing and acting more vivid. He gave me that extra excitement that a creative person needs to excite others. I tried to observe this effect for later use.

Nigel Playfair was another follower of life at the Cave. He had even taken part in a few of our one-act plays. He was a highly successful London producer and director, and he cast me in his productions, beginning with *The Insect Play.* John Gielgud was in it, too, along with Angela Baddeley and Claude Rains. It was Gielgud's first professional job, I was told, since his Royal Academy of Dramatic Art days. He played a butterfly. Angela Baddeley was a female beetle. I played The Larva, a tiny but pivotal part, and I was staggered when I walked off with rave reviews. It was all new to me. I knew it was the part itself and not really me. I didn't understand the power of the printed word or why the reviews would cause the slightly cold shoulder from some of my fellow actors—or, at least, some glassy looks. I felt almost guilty and didn't enjoy my first success. It was very confusing. Even Biddy said I was "terrific" in the part, but I knew I had done nothing much and was suspicious of all compliments, and suspected Biddy's general wisdom again. The mystery of what personality *is* is still unsolved. It has a new name—*charisma*—but that does not help at all. Personality has always been an elusive commodity, whatever its name.

The next production I was in was *The Way of the World,* which featured Edith Evans as Millamant. I played a sluttish maid and later in the same show also did a dance based on Hogarth's "Shrimp Girl," to music by Purcell played on a harpsichord. Next, I appeared in Sheridan's *Duenna,* in which Angela Baddeley and I were twin pages who did just about everything. We were acolytes and carried torches, and we danced a number with Nigel Playfair himself. He really only pointed his toes to the music, while Angela and I dashed around him.

We were all three dressed in mauve—even shoes and stockings and buttons and bows. In *The Merry Wives of Windsor* (another Playfair production) I understudied the part of Anne Page. I didn't attend to the idea of what an understudy was, so I didn't learn the words. Luckily, it was for a short run and the girl I understudied was never off, though she was very late once. Had she not shown up, I cannot imagine what I would have done!

Finally Nigel Playfair put me in his revue, *Riverside Nights,* performed at the Lyric Theatre, Hammersmith, newly made popular by his sensational revival of *The Beggar's Opera.* I sang four or five songs in the show—a group with Harold Scott—and danced some character into all of them. No member of the cast was really the "lead," but when *Riverside Nights* was published, I was rather surprised to find myself on the cover.

As it happened, my young man friend from Russia lived on a long, gray suburban street about a mile away from the Lyric, so I had somewhere to go between matinee and evening shows. Otherwise I had to take the Underground and a bus back to Doughty Street. The Russian, whom I will call Stanis, had a furnished room that was sordid because it was so very adequate—wallpaper, linoleum, and wooden chairs all clean but dingy, and the bed was not comfortable. But Stanis had an endless supply of caviar. I suppose he got it at cost from the Argus Club. He served it very correctly with finely chopped onion, chopped white of egg, grated yolk, a wedge of lemon, and very thin toast. In the otherwise cold room there was a nice bright flickering coalfire in the Victorian grate. Unfortunately, at this time I had to have an abortion, but I did not miss a performance of the now long-running *Riverside Nights.* Stanis asked me to marry him, but by then I was in one of my virtuous virginal periods and Stanis looked like a piece of ectoplasm.

During the run of *Riverside Nights* I also started working in *The Midnight Follies* at the Metropole Hotel. I rode in a hired limousine from one show to the other. One night the car was stopped by a policeman who wondered what was going on behind the temporarily covered windows. It was me changing costumes from my "Please Sell No More Drink to My Father" black cotton stockings and Victorian middy blouse to become Nell Gwynne with her busty bodice. In *The Midnight Follies* I did a number called "Spare a Copper for the Lucky Baby," written by A. P. Herbert, the great English wit and poet, and beloved contributor to *Punch* and author of *Riverside Nights.* Anyway, in that number I was a very glamorous gypsy on Derby Day wearing a rather grand satin patchwork shawl and holding a baby in my arms.

> Spare a copper for the lucky baby
> And a blessing shall be your reward.

She's a regular fairy,
Brought luck to Queen Mary,
Health and wealth to the motherless lord!

Who sent the kind stork
To the Duchess of York
And cured our dear Prince of his pain?
Well, you ask the Prince
If he's had the croup since—
He was good to Elizabeth Jane!

The Prince referred to was the then Prince of Wales, later the King, and *later* the Duke of Windsor. He was offended by the reference to his family and walked out of the theatre, saying as he left, "This is very unusual." The manager of the Metropole said, "We can't afford to offend a good customer." So I got the sack.

Another after-show job I had was at the Cavour in Leicester Square. I sang three songs after supper. There were two others on the bill—a French singer called Helene Shappi, and a man, Harry something. We all three opened in a "Hello" sort of number, and finished the show with "Bye, Bye Blackbird," a handwritten copy of which we found in a stack of original compositions in a big music store, Francis, Day and Hunter, in Charing Cross Road.

The very, *very* French performers always tickled me pink, and I had many laughs back at the Cave doing imitations or, rather, mockeries of their style. Helene Shappi had sung:

Vy vaste your luff, ven you can giff it to me,
Vy break your aching heart, ven you can giff it to me—
I vant it!

After the show at the Cavour, we could go and sit with friends in the audience. Occasionally I did. One night my savior in the near past, Tallulah Bankhead, who had introduced me to an abortionist, was there with her latest boy, Lord Ivor Churchill. Tallulah was rather drunk—and this was the outcome:

TALLULAH: "Waiter, waiter!"

WAITER: "Yes, Miss Bankhead?"

TALLULAH: "Those two people at the next table are horribly ugly. Would you ask them to leave?"

WAITER: "I'm afraid I cannot, Miss Bankhead."

Tallulah then put her hand around a champagne glass and broke it. The waiter cleared the glass away. In about ten or fifteen minutes she repeated the scene again exactly. A little later, she turned to me and said, "Don't flirt with Ivor." And she ground her heel into my instep under the table. I did see Ivor Churchill once after that for a drink somewhere, but I found him tedious. I'm sure my forthright manner scared the ass off him.

I believe that A. P. Herbert, author of *Riverside Nights,* started out as a lawyer. He became a Member of Parliament and really stirred up the old unfair divorce laws in England. To know him and his wife and family was a benison. They lived in a house upriver, above Hammersmith. I often went there and so did John Armstrong, who found Gwen Herbert and the Herbert daughters enchanting. John had done the costumes for *Riverside Nights.* Gwen Herbert, who was a painter herself, also bought some of John Armstrong's work. It was all very close.

The cast often went to the Herbert house after the show. It always seemed like party time then, although there were very few organized gatherings. To feed twelve or more people leftovers or cheese from the family larder seemed no effort to Gwen. Even when she wasn't there, we found something or other to eat and trooped down to the semibasement dining area. Beyond the wall of their long thin garden, through a gate, and down the steps was the Thames—and the large Herbert rowing boat. They also had a barge with a motor. Sometimes after the show at night we all got into the rowing boat, and silently taking off our clothes in midriver, we slipped into the Thames. We would swim across and then back alongside the boat. We all hid, hanging on to one side, if and when a police patrol boat chugged by. Exciting silence and fiendish grins.

Nigel Playfair, who was quite short and round—he looked just like Mr. Pickwick—one day said to me surreptitiously, "I say, is it true that you all go swimming with nothing on?" "Yes," I replied, and he said —looking as sweet as a young puppy—"Do you think I could join you?" So he did. But that night when we all stepped through the garden gate, Nigel Playfair was quite nude in all his white roundness, and we all had on bathing suits. We were too modest to undress in front of our producer. Nevertheless, seeing his awful predicament, we all stripped immediately and he smiled like the Mona Lisa. That is, if Mr. Pickwick could smile like La Gioconda. Nigel Playfair was a lovable father image to me. I think I loved him. Everybody did. And it was good for me to know that type of affection at last.

The critics began to mean more to me. Some were really constructive, over and above their line of duty. James Agate, critic for *The London*

Times, once wrote that although I was "brilliant" satirizing "Please Sell No More Drink to My Father," I should "take warning" that it would never be an important art to mock a piece of material that was never good in the first place, anyway. Then, again, on my own I learned that the most satisfactory reward for my work was to make another person wax poetic about it. Not a big audience applauding or hands reaching up from the crowd—just one person's mind rising to lyric heights, ideally a brilliant mind. I can't resist quoting Herbert Farjeon (from *Vogue* magazine): "Her hair is in the chestnut trees of London and her feet are in the mud of the Thames."

Biddy collected press cuttings about me, and all her friends kept a sharp lookout for her. Even the Lanchester family came to ask "the latest" about me now and then, and although Biddy dropped this news to me overcasually, she was very pleased. The printed word helped hammer the nail home further. My sitting for Epstein, among other jobs, was very distinguished. Biddy's eyes lit up like beacons at the prospect of my having some sort of career in the theatre. After all, the Lanchesters would see that I had turned out better than the other nieces and nephews. She would to some extent justify her own battle with her family through me, by having a bright child to prove her early actions were right. She'd show them—and in a way I wanted to show them, too.

I hardly ever saw Shamus, but according to Biddy he pepped up for days after seeing me. With him and Biddy I visited his sister, Aunt Nell, once or twice at their place near Euston Station and had tea with her and her daughter and usually another of Shamus's sisters, Mary. I once took them all out to dinner at the Paddington Hotel, which was not very far away and quite incidentally had a very fine dining room. It catered to businessmen from the North, no doubt. Anyway, Aunt Nell, looking at me with beseeching eyes, asked if she could order turbot, which was a little bit more expensive than the other things on the menu. So the dinner became quite an event. To order what you really wanted caused great gaiety, and I wish all life could be as care-free as moments like this. Just because of a piece of turbot. Of course, Biddy had vegetables and the waiter was concerned: "Not a little sole, Madam, or a little chicken breast, perhaps?" "Urg," said Biddy. Shamus enjoyed his pork.

Then it was back to Aunt Nell's flat and more tea. Shamus standing with his back to the little fire, hands clutching his lapels just like a politician, full of confidence, stroking his mustache now and then with a twirl and upward, as he gazed benignly over the scene. I could not enjoy the excitement that I seemed to produce by being there. I only enjoyed seeing Shamus looking proud—well, just plain cocky. I really did want to justify Shamus's shining moment, so I behaved very well—never showing that I wanted to get away, hating the strong tea (mostly tannin) and the prospect of going down the narrow stairs with brown embossed wallpaper and out into the street near smelly Euston.

At the end of the 1920s, Biddy and Shamus were still living in Leathwaite Road, but Biddy had a weaving and puppet studio somewhere else. She talked about Waldo and his work and shows, and also about a place that he had in Malvern where he spent most of his time. He didn't come to London often. Then he met a lady potter called Muriel and they got married.

I also got married. Biddy and Shamus were glittering with delight at my wedding—one of the many paradoxical twists to their life. In 1895 the phrase What will people think? was dismissed by Biddy, but now it must have seemed very sweet. I'm sure that this irony didn't cross Biddy's or Shamus's mind, nor did I think of it at the time. Their bright expressions shone with illogical satisfaction.

Our marriage was announced on the front page of *The Tatler* in 1929. In the *Tatler* photograph, taken especially by a fashionable photographer, we looked like a pair of rather stodgy society people. A slap in the eye for the wicked uncles. The early years of my freedom were gone and I would guess that Biddy and Shamus were just plain relieved. Their daughter was safe—at last.

I met Charles Laughton in 1927 at the first rehearsal of the play *Mr. Prohack* by Arnold Bennett. I had arrived early and was talking to Arthur Macrae, who was the assistant stage manager. Arthur and I remained friends over the years. It was a laughing relationship built around jokes that were personal to us.

For rehearsal the stage was, as usual, lit by a couple of bare "working lights" on iron standards or hanging from above on a long wire. I remember Charles wandering in. He looked quite without color —pale plump face, mouse-colored hair—wearing wrinkled clothes, arms hanging rather listlessly at his sides with the backs of his hands facing forward. Nevertheless, the actor-personality was strong. My first impression was that he looked like a baker's assistant who'd just left a bakery and was dusty with flour.

The company knew that Charles had been referred to as a genius by a few critics, including James Agate, and that made everyone rather shy. But Charles seemed to try to hide from himself and become an obscure bundle. He was playing Mr. Prohack, and I was his secretary, Mimi Winstock.

The actors sat on wooden chairs in a circle, and Theodore Komis-sarjevsky, the director, was on stage in front of the footlights—probably pacing. Nobody could possibly look his or her best, and it seemed almost the professional thing not even to try.

ELSA (to Charles): "James Agate talks about you a lot. He said that you were the only actor who should play the part with me in *The Pool.*"

CHARLES: "So we nearly met before this play."

ELSA: "Yes, I suppose so. Tony Bertram is a friend of Jimmy Agate. He wrote *The Pool.* It wasn't a very good play. I don't think I was very good, anyway."

CHARLES: "I suppose I was doing *The Happy Husband.*"

ELSA: "Anyway, it's a good thing you weren't in it, *The Pool.*"

CHARLES: Yes, I suppose so. Anyway, here we are."

ELSA: "Yeah. He, Jimmy Agate, lives opposite to me, on Doughty Street. That's in Bloomsbury, sort of."

We began the "cold" (first) reading. Charles, who had been trained at Royal Academy of Dramatic Art, was stumbling but good. I was awkward and probably appalling—never could read well. Both Charles and I were persecuted by our two forms of imaginary incompetence. Lydia Sherwood, the young leading lady, who also went to R.A.D.A, said that all the students envied actors like myself who were successful without the benefit of instruction. She said that we were their inspiration. Lydia had a crush on "Komis," the director, and later married him. One of his many marriages.

Since everybody was dismissed for lunch at the same time, there was a general hubbub:

"Does anyone know a restaurant?"

"There's a cheap one across Sloane Square."

"There's the pub—if you want cold beef and pickles."

"There's a better one—French—but it's probably full."

In two minutes everyone had gone off.

Charles, Arthur, Lydia, and I went to the cheaper place a few times. Then groups of varying number tried the other places. Charles and I did not attempt to be alone—it did not occur to us. Once after a hard day's rehearsal, near production time, Charles and I did go to the French restaurant for dinner. We talked mostly about food and his family's hotels in Scarborough. Charles ordered Sole Veronique for me. Lydia and a painter friend, Mark Gertler, joined us in the middle of the meal, and at the end, Charles paid for my dinner. I probably would not have let him do that as I was so voraciously independent, but since he had a hotel behind him it seemed okay. I was in the habit of worrying about money. It was a built-in problem that I had grown up with. Being scrupulously honest and prompt, I could always depend on a small bank overdraft until the next job. All the same, the meetings with Charles did have overtones of financial worry.

82

After a time, Charles admitted that he had seen me twice in *Riverside Nights* and dreamed that he would meet me. No wonder he was so doubly shy at that first rehearsal. We found in each other a friendship that we both needed badly—Charles because he felt lonely and was called ugly, and I because I was too "bohemian," with too many odd friends who stayed up half the night. I was probably drinking sherry or maybe port, and dancing the Charleston, and soon progressing to dry martinis and body-close dancing. This was beginning to add up to despair within myself.

From talking about his family's hotels, it was natural for Charles to move on to his mother and his brothers and his beloved Aunt Mary. Aunt Mary approved of his going on the stage, and above all she loved flowers. She had a green thumb and her garden was small and beautiful. She had a great knowledge of ceramics and Charles learned about beautiful china from her. They went to antique shops and took walks on the Yorkshire moors together. From Charles' Aunt Mary we naturally got to talking about my own Aunt Mary and how I got my knowledge about flowers—and my mother.

We planned to take walks in the country. Actually, I think our first one started off from the Waterloo Railway Station during the run of *Mr. Prohack,* on a Sunday morning, and we came back that Sunday night. We did not yet talk about the possibility of staying overnight. We would not have risked staying away when the play was running.

On that first walk we visited a house where I'd been before, one built by Clifford Allen, the first conscientious objector, and his wife. Red brick, modern for its time, two stories high, it sat in the middle of the country on a small hill above a stream. Allen was highly literate and educated. Charles found him an over-ascetic stuffed shirt and a prig. The house had many visitors. There was a lot of reading aloud from Heroditus, *The Decline and Fall of the Roman Empire,* and Petronius and having violent political arguments.

I think I was welcome there because of my notorious Lanchester background and my involvement with 1917 Club, the Cave of Harmony, and so on.

Charles did not enjoy it at all—it was too far from his hotel background. But the six- or seven-mile walk to and from the railway station was after his own heart. We wandered along the streambed and across the fields, picking bunches of king cups and forget-me-nots and daisies. We were very, very silent then, and even on later walks hardly talked at all.

There was no element of frankness or honesty at all in our conversations. Nor was there any element of calculation or thoughts of the future. For two people who were twenty-five and twenty-eight years old, who had both had various previous associations, our lack of curiosity about each other was, I would think, a sort of subconscious cleansing process. A making of a space between the past and the present. Later, the past boomeranged back.

When I first met Charles, H. G. Wells was a friend of mine, and he wrote three silent short films for me. I was supposed to do six a year. Just for fun, Charles played a little part in each one. He was paid six pounds and six shillings for his work in the films—in those days there were no union problems or anything. The filming began on August 20 and took about three weeks to complete. We went on location near Rye for some ocean shots, and the whole company stayed in various small hotels in the area. They were good days. I guess we were all in our twenties, including the cameraman, who was Fred Young. Young is a famous top-flight cameraman now.

One weekend, while we we making the films, I think Charles went with me down to Wells' place. We were invited to a Lady Warwick's for a dinner so elaborate that it was indigestion-making. During those days, Charles was more or less subservient to people like Wells and his friends. He was impressed and quiet, absorbing and drawing from their words of wisdom, which he later was not above using himself. Wells, stuttering but effective, had the great art of simplicity that always seemed to elude Charles when he later became an imposing figure himself with listeners at his feet. Among other basic simplicities, Wells said that weekend that having a child was really like boiling an egg. Charles and I didn't even spend the night at the Wells domain but drove down in the morning and back the same night to London.

When we had finished three films for Wells, the "talkies" were just beginning. At the time, I remember, Wells said, "I am not going to write any more stories for you. No future in talkies, no future in talkies at all!"

After the show one night, toward the end of the run of *Mr. Prohack*, I took Charles along to a party given by Gerald Barry and his wife. Later Sir Gerald Barry—he was the editor of *New Statesman*—and his guests were the usual collection of Bloomsbury intellectuals. *Probably*, Maynard Keynes, Lytton Strachey, Francis and Vera Meynell, and a few Russian ballet people were there. I enjoyed introducing Charles to James Agate. I danced with a lot of people and maybe alone. Anyway, it was "show off" time for me.

Charles sat looking his usual pale self at the side of a buffet table. I kept coming over to him, then dashing off again. I was wearing an evening dress with a silver lamé tight-fitting bodice and a skirt with mauve taffeta ruffles, short in front and long at the back, and an amethyst necklace!

84

Around three o'clock in the morning, when half the party had broken up and the buffet table was just a white cloth with empty dishes and crumbs, Charles and I decided to order a taxi. He would drop me at my flat only two blocks away and then he would go on to his place. When it came to say good night, we awkwardly and embarrassingly kissed in rather a conventional way. Then, staring at each other in utter surprise, we clung together. Charles came into my flat and we sat around for an hour or so. It was a bohemian sort of place—wicker armchair, box spring, gas fire with a shilling meter, hand-woven rug from my past, and two wooden wheel-back chairs that I'd painted green; a collage on the wall by the door, a few pictures, and costume designs by my old friend John Armstrong. That night, for the first time, we realized that we wanted to be together.

My flat was always filled with friends, dropping by out of habit— John Collier, Tony Bertram, James Agate, John Armstrong, Jock Dent, and friends of theirs. I never had any privacy. Charles boarded in the apartment of a Mrs. Forster, who was very attached to her "lodger," so it was impossible for us to meet *there*. We both decided to move— Charles into the Garlands Hotel and I to a room in an apartment house in another square in Bloomsbury. It was sordid and strict and respect-able—*no* gentlemen allowed, two pence for a hot bath.

At the time we were not even thinking of marriage—just a general getting-together. But this first move from our two original bases had some advantages. For one thing, the Garlands Hotel had a good dining room. The Laughton hoteliers would call it a "good kitchen." Charles had a bedroom and sitting room, and we had our dinners sent up.

Occasionally Charles' mother came down from Scarborough on shopping trips. This time she came to dinner—so we met. At Charles' suggestion I wore a conservative little black dress with a green sash and the green amber beads that had been his first gift to me. She came to dinner in the small, austere dining room of the Garlands Hotel. We sat nervously making conversation in the mahogany-paneled, white dam-ask atmosphere.

After dinner, we went upstairs to Charles' sitting room. Mrs. Laughton showed no sign of what she probably felt. We just made small talk, sitting around a small coal fire. She laughed when I told her that, since my eyes rather popped out, I had to poke a hole in the pillow at night to be comfortable. I did not attempt to shock her. Afterward, Charles told me that I spoke beautiful English when I was with her and that it pleased him very much.

She was a tiny but dominating woman, a Catholic and a strict one. The former Eliza Conlin, she had been a barmaid in a Scarborough hotel and had married Charles' father who then, I think, was a butler or held some position similar to hers. They saved and saved and eventually, I suppose, got a bank loan and bought a hotel of their own. In time they were able to buy the Pavillion Hotel in Scarborough. The trade there is seasonal, so they did a very profitable thing—that is, take advantage of every conceivable holiday. They always had festivities of some sort: celebrations for Christmas, Easter, Whitsun, bank holidays (every four months), Guy Fawkes Day ("Remember, Remember the fifth of November; Gunpowder, treason and plot!"); New Year's, Twelfth Night (January 6); and all kinds of summer dances and spring banquets. I drew many program covers for these events, and so did John Armstrong.

Charles' mother was determined that her three boys should not be "trade." England has "upper classes" and "trade" and "lower classes."

Eliza Conlin Laughton was a ruthless hotelkeeper. She wasn't above booking a couple that she knew wasn't married, but it was never spoken about—or even *three* people in a room in a pinch. She saved and saved for her three sons and insisted on sending them to Stonyhurst, the great Jesuit college in the north of England. I don't think any of them were very happy there. Charles liked flowers and walking in the woods and things, when the other students were at sports. So they decided to haze him, painting his behind with eucalyptus and hitting him, wrapping him in a sheet, and pushing him around. They called him fat and names that were degrading.

Charles was the oldest, then came Tom, who was a businessman, and then Frank, who was considered not very strong. They were all brought up as strict Catholics. Then they became not very good Catholics, and finally not Catholics at all.

Charles began to question his faith when he was in his late teens. Once, during confession, the Jesuit priest wormed out of Charles an admission of performing that "wicked habit." The priest said to him, "For that, you will be punished in hell, my boy, through all eternity. First your little finger will be worn away and then another finger." Then he said, "Do you know, my boy, what all eternity is? Imagine that the world is a steel globe, and that a bird passes that steel globe every thousand years and its wing touches that steel globe; and when the earth is worn away by the touch of that bird's wing, that will be all eternity!" Well, Charles said to the priest, "But, Father, what about this all-forgiving God? If one has done wrong, why does God punish us by sending us to hell?" And the priest answered, "My son, we are told there is a hell, but are we told that there is anybody in it?" And this is when Charles began to have doubts.

Charles' mother was a very well-dressed woman, and Charles was very proud of her. He loved to hear people say around his home town of Scarborough, in Yorkshire, "Oh, yes, Charles Laughton's mother is a very 'smart' woman." Charles was rather puzzled as to how she acquired her taste, but since she bought safe, expensive clothes, it was not really a great mystery. She seemed to have cupboards full of the best suits from the best tailors and the finest blouses. She also had quite a lot of antique jewelry and plenty of furs. When I first went up to Scarborough, Charles was very nervous about my appearance. He was very nervous, period. His mother had once said to him, "Charles, never marry an actress or a red-headed woman," and I was both.

I was not as eccentric as I had been in my teens, and I certainly wanted to dress well, but then I had very little money. So I made a lot of my own clothes and they looked it. Charles insisted on taking me to a dressmaker, a Madame Helene Galin, to buy some better clothes. For some reason I always felt I should pay my own way in everything. But I couldn't afford Madame Galin. Charles and I just didn't talk about money. Charles had always had just enough from his family allowance and I'd lived between jobs as well as I could. There is a difference between knowing where your next penny will come from and not knowing.

Charles finally had to pay and resented my resentment about it. We never did quite recover from this financial tennis match about my wardrobe, nor have I yet recovered from his pressure that I follow his taste. I didn't ever have a chance to learn from my own mistakes. His ideas and taste were very good, nevertheless, and no one could resist his enormous enjoyment of a few hours at the dressmaker's.

Some of the clothes we saw at Madame Galin's flat were imported from houses in Paris, but they were too expensive for Charles and me. Yet we never forgot them. We talked about them for years, and later, long after they had gone out of fashion (when we could have afforded them), we redescribed them to each other and regretted not having owned such and such a masterpiece.

Eventually Charles' mother got to like me in my little suits and cocky felt hats, and black or white net or chiffon dresses for evenings. Charles also took me to Hermine in Bond Street to have some underwear and some pajamas made. This was a shop where his mother went for most of her blouses; all the work was done by nuns, and very fine it was. Some of the flowered chiffon underwear that Charles ordered specially for me must have given the nuns quite a turn. Nevertheless, the stitches were uniformly tiny and the lace sewn on most exquisitely. I wonder if an awful lot of atonement is made through tiny stitches.

During these days, I was out of work and Charles was rehearsing and then playing in *The Man with Red Hair*. He spent a lot of time under the arches of Charing Cross, learning to use a bullwhip for the play. I felt slightly nauseated by the whole thing, but Charles took it as a matter of course in his preparation. He did the same thorough work and research for every part.

The Man with Red Hair—a very special opening night. I had made myself an evening dress from a pale blue Indian sari of the finest, almost transparent wool I have ever seen. As I stood in the middle of the first nighters in the foyer of the Little Theatre, I heard a few people say, "That's Charles Laughton's girl, you know." I must admit, it made me feel extraordinarily proud—and virginal, with my halo of auburn hair adding to the effect, I'm sure.

Charles attacked the part with a fury of precision. As usual with Charles the actor, he made audiences understand the man but made them recoil too from the horrifying character. In every part he played Charles created understanding and respect and therefore forced tolerance on the audience. Charles' powerful interpretation of the role overwhelmed everyone, including the author Hugh Walpole and the cast: actors James Whale (the stage manager, actor, and scene designer in *Riverside Nights*), Gillian Lind (later in Charles' *On The Spot*), and J. H. Roberts (later in Charles' *Alibi*). He equally overwhelmed the press. In its November 30, 1928 issue, *The Tatler* paid tribute to Charles in poetry:

> Hail to thee, LAUGHTON, idol of the hour!
> Hail, newly-risen star of the West End!
> Whose rugged *genius* and explosive pow'r
> Critics and even *connoisseurs* commend!
> First in the shilling shocker WALPOLE penned,
> Red-haired, fat-fingered, and with greedy glance . . .

And so on, for three stanzas.

Charles and I started going to The Dog and Duck, a small pub-hotel in Sussex, for weekends. We had an old car, and Charles' dresser at the theatre would serve as chauffeur. He would drive us down to The Dog and Duck, then take us around the countryside during the day. At night I would hear Charles' words, sitting around a small coalfire, and then we would go to bed on a feather mattress, once considered a luxury, but it was lumpy. We had many pleasant nights in the hotel, except for the inconvenience of the bathroom, which was down a narrow hallway, up a few steps, and down a few more. The water was cold and the door wouldn't lock.

Charles always wanted to talk until he fell asleep—about plays, about furnishing a flat to live in, and once he talked about having children and dramatized an imaginary hospital scene. He thought it would be beautiful, but I didn't. I said nothing. We never said anything about children again. (Occasionally, after a dry martini or two, when he was in his frustrated fifties, he would get quite belligerent about not having children.)

One night we discussed getting married, obviously because the public was crowding in and gossip was bothering us. Career-wise, and morally, I did not care at all about marriage, but Charles did. We always registered as Mr. and Mrs. Laughton at the hotel. The proprietors were very kind and considerate and seemed to think we were two well-known people who must have been secretly married. Later Charles and I felt rather guilty when we did marry and the event was on the front page of all the newspapers. After all, the hotelkeepers and their small staff felt as if they had been the proud owners of a secret, but the Laughtons had let them down. We never went back to the hotel as man and wife.

Around this time I got pregnant—I blamed the cold water at The Dog and Duck—and had to find a doctor who would give me what was politely called a "curette." It was a trying time. Neither of us even considered having the baby, and yet we at the same time were talking about getting married. Public opinion led us to the brink of respectability—a respectability we weren't living.

After the abortion, we decided to get our own flat, a beautifully furnished one in Dean Street in Soho. It was a top floor *pied-à-terre* of the Clifford Allens. There I began to cook a little and we entertained our friends and Charles' brothers. The house had belonged to Karl Marx, and it had a blue plaque on the front of the building to mark the fact. Kenneth (*The Wind in the Willows*) Grahame lived right behind us. We used to wave to each other and met and talked a few times.

By this time, Charles must have been in the play *Alibi,* by Agatha Christie. I was doing nothing, having by then given up the Cave of Harmony, and I began to learn about buying, cooking, caring for food from Charles' brother Frank. Thoroughly informed about food, he was known as a dictator to be feared in the Laughtons' hotel kitchens. We had several *haute cuisine* cooking sessions together in Dean Street. Charles generally disapproved of the way his brother behaved in restaurants. Frank was highly critical—too much salt, too much pepper, soup thickened with flour, not enough gravy, too much gravy, too hot, too cold. Charles didn't like attracting attention—at least, unless he was the one attracting it.

Eventually Clifford Allen needed the Dean Street place again, so Charles and I began looking for a flat of our own.

Finally, we found a very small, top-floor flat in Percy Street, off

Tottenham Court Road. It had been, presumably, servants' quarters in a modest old house built around 1850. It was the equivalent of a small New York City brownstone. Two rooms had been made into one, and there was a tiny extra room, plus a slip of a kitchen and a bathroom—that was it. Then we began looking for furniture—a new experience for me. Charles had had practical training in the Laughton Hotels, along with a good taste that was born in him, developed, and raced in all directions.

Every few weeks Charles and I visited Scarborough together and stayed at the Laughtons' Pavillion Hotel, in separate rooms, of course. We walked on the moors in the heather. We scoured antique shops full of dirt-cheap beautiful objects. We bought furniture that stayed with us and was eventually sent to America. Charles loved antiques then, but later his taste forged ahead to more modern styles, especially in painting. He loved the Impressionists and the Post-Impressionists, as well as primitive, abstract, and Oriental art.

That first year that Charles and I lived together on Percy street was rather like being married.

Charles used to think I looked like the Nubian boy Titania and Oberon fight over in *A Midsummer Night's Dream*. He got to calling me Nubian, and then shortened it to Nub, and I started calling him Nubitz or Nubbins. I looked Nubbin up in the dictionary and found it is a rotten or a dwarfed ear of corn—something very unflattering. So I later tried to cut it out.

One night we came home from the theatre—Charles was in a play—to find bedbugs. It was absolutely horrifying to see these on the clean white sheets. And they got worse and worse. They'd walk across the ceiling and when they got over the bed, or over the warmth of a human being—they'd drop! Only a few intimate friends, such as John Armstrong, knew about the bugs. John and I would play chess together, and we'd keep looking up at the ceiling. The trouble with bedbugs is that they can live in the wall. If you seal up the wall, bedbugs can live for four years without water. They're very difficult to get rid of, so we had to move to a hotel while we got the place fumigated.

We kept talking vaguely about marriage.

Charles and I were too shy to remain unmarried, if that can explain it. To go on living together was just too embarrassing for us to cope with. Certainly, it would have acted as a brake to Charles' growing career and also hurt his northern hotelier family and his Catholic mother. These people would have been made ill rather than shocked. I felt rather blank about the whole thing, having had no moral pressures in my life. One day I asked Arthur Macrae, a friend from *Mr. Prohack* days, who later became a writer of musical revues, "Should I marry Charles?" All Arthur said was, "If you can stay with him, why not?"

Finally Charles and I decided to get married, but we kept the news very quiet. We were both pretty well known, running neck and neck at that time, and the press was after us. To avoid publicity, we planned to get married on a Sunday. We paid the Registry Office at Henrietta Street extra money to come in on a Sunday and do the deed.

But on that Sunday our street was thick with journalists. We couldn't get out to get married. I thought it was all pretty silly, but Charles was quite scared, I think. First, Charles called a taxi and raced out separately, and the journalists followed him. Then I left the flat, as Charles came back. There were still one or two journalists hovering about. Then *I* returned to the flat, and then we *both* went to the Registry Office in separate taxis. It was like a French farce, with all these exits and entrances. We got all the reporters very confused.

Charles thought I should wear a hat and suit, so we bought a gray felt hat with red and white feathers, turned up on one side. I also wore a buttonhole of grape hyacinths. I think I must have looked like a French Legionnaire. When we got to the Registry Office it was pouring rain. John Armstrong and Iris Barry were waiting there; Biddy and Shamus met us back at the Percy Street flat later.

We went to Switzerland on our honeymoon—a rather comical word when a couple has been living together before a wedding ceremony. We brought Charles' mother because he wanted to show her Switzerland, and his brother Frank came, too. All my friends found it hilarious.

I got on very well with Charles' mother in Switzerland, but it made me feel I had to be a good bride. It made me conscious of my nails if they weren't groomed. It made me very constipated. Charles' mother was at dinner every night. After two weeks, we left her and went on alone to Italy.

First we stayed a few days in Naples to see Pompeii and Paestum and go up Vesuvius. In Naples the bedroom was salmon pink, much, much too pink—sofa, chairs, big bed, ceiling, and walls. It was not pleasurable at all. I looked quite gray in the nude, and I guess Charles did, too. We were used to uncomfortable beds (from The Dog and Duck, etc.), but now our aesthetic senses were assaulted, which was worse in a way than a lumpy mattress supported by years of dead, squeaky springs. It was more like the color when a person first gets a black eye. To us, who had so recently been collecting some sweet Meissen pieces and endearing Staffordshire pieces of china, the room was awful.

Naples snapped at us; Pompeii, though, was lovely with sun and rain and wear and tear. We made a trip to Paestum to see the temples. We traveled in an open hotel car through a dusty thirty miles. We set out fresh and early and came back in the evening totally covered in dust—looking like the same honeymoon couple eighty years later. The big wash in the pink bath took hours.

The next day we went up Vesuvius on Cook's Railway. I was fantastically excited, as I am by all elemental phenomena, and went right to the very edge of the open crater—as far as the rope, that is. Charles backed away from the edge, with his hair standing on end with fear. My own was standing on end from excitement. From then on Charles called me a harpie, but that day served me very well when I came to play Ariel in *The Tempest* at the Old Vic.

Then we went on to Ravello, where we stayed at the Hotel Caruso, run by the Caruso family, who also owned vineyards and a winery. They exported an excellent white wine and a rosé that we could usually get at Italian shops. Charles and I drank a lot of it.

In the small town of Amalfi that lies on the coast road below Ravello, we found friends from England, Osbert Sitwell and William Walton, who often came up for lunch and a glass of rosé. Sir Osbert Sitwell writes in his autobiography, The *Scarlet Tree:*

> He [Charles] and his wife—whose character and wit matched his own—used to stay at Ravello every winter, for several years running, while I was a mile or so away, downhill, at Amalfi. Certainly Charles Laughton, like myself, found here some attraction that he could not define or resist. If the landscape had a fault, it was that the ruins of its ancient towers and castles and Saracenic palaces rendered it a little dead, a little morbid; but the spectacle of Charles and Elsa, with her flaming red hair, and their friend John Armstrong, the painter, who often accompanied them, climbing up the rocks and among the crenelated gray walls like goats and, however tired, triumphing with a worthy ardor over every obstacle, added as much to the liveliness of it as did their talk of an evening.

The sheer clifflike drop below Ravello had been given to a certain Padre Pantalione to create a church and sanctuary for the poor and some lepers. The donor of this vertical cliff owned the Villa Cimbrone on the top. How noble, how kind, how bountiful to give this vertical cliff to the Padre Pantalione. The Villa Cimbrone, incidentally, at this time had been loaned to Greta Garbo, who was closeted there with Leopold Stokowski. Whether it was true or not, rumor had it that she only carried a small suitcase with a nightshirt, a toothbrush, and a jar of honey.

Padre Pantalione was, I think, close to eighty years old, but a mountain goat crossed with a bank robber couldn't have been more agile and ingenious. Cutting steps out of the cliff itself from bottom to oh-so-near the top to gouge out a sizable church, he discovered cave after cave filled with hanging stalactites and sharp stalagmites. The padre developed little belvederes around these areas where he grew horse beans and raised little black pigs that often followed him around.

Once, Padre Pantalione drew Charles and me up the cement steps after him, saying, "Come . . . bella vista, bella vista!" Then, right at the top, "Aspete . . . wait, wait." Flying down the steps, he returned in no time at all carrying a long, luscious apple flan. He cut off a piece for each of us, and I took a great bite—but there were no apples inside. They were whole cloves of garlic. I swallowed it somehow but was not at all well for twenty-four hours.

The old padre came up to the Hotel Caruso quite often to talk to us and have a drink. He did not drink the local rosé wine. He liked green chartreuse. Once, as we three sat together in the hotel room, I raised my thimble-size liqueur glass and said, "Well, here's to God." Charles covered his face and cried, "Oh, no. Oh, no!" But the Padre Pantalione threw himself back on the bed, kicking his legs in the air, and laughed like the Fiend himself.

When we got back to England we seriously started to search for a place in the country. Our friendship, our growing intimacy, and our marriage had grown and basically flourished in the countryside of England. Our love of the outdoors proved to be the foremost ruling theme in our life together. Acting, food, art collecting were each powerful in their turn, but the pleasure of each other's company was felt most strongly among trees and flowers.

During these months, Charles was having a terrible time with his voice. It is hard to believe that Charles' speaking voice was once raspy and weak. He was always having bad throats and tracheal coughs, and the apartment was covered with throat sprays and other medication for his condition. His voice grew steadily worse and Charles became worried about his career. Critics remarked on the difficulty of hearing him on stage and began speculating as to how long his voice would last. Charles started dreading having to appear. Eventually a doctor pressed Charles to have his tonsils out. The prospect of the operation, the terror and the pain nearly turned Charles into a madman. But finally (especially after a critic said that he had "little hope for a brilliant future") Charles developed a little faith in a throat specialist, and out came his tonsils. And good heavens, it worked! Charles' voice got better, and he never looked back—vocally.

To recover, Charles and I went off to Ravello again, taking John Armstrong, on what a few of our more gaga friends called a second honeymoon. Charles brought along a play by Edgar Wallace, *On the Spot.* The character he was to play, Tony Perelli, was an Italian-American gangster, so Charles talked with all sorts of Italians, studying their mannerisms. He also read everything he could about Al Capone, on whom the character was based. With all the lurid stories we read about the gangsters in newspapers, we were later apprehensive about our first trip to America. When we got back from Italy, Charles went to a voice teacher, Ernesto Boraldi, to learn how to place his voice and how to protect it. By the time Charles went into rehearsals for *On the Spot*, he had relearned to use his voice.

On the Spot was a colossal success. But every night before his performance, Charles would have to lie on his back, remaining perfectly quiet and breathing deeply for over an hour. The doctor told Charles to spend as much time in the country as possible in order to keep his health. So we spent most of our weekends away from London —walking about and looking for a place at the same time.

As Charles was working every night in *On the Spot*, I spent a lot of time alone. One night I went to a dinner party at the house of Clough Williams-Ellis, the architect and the creator of the famous village of Portmeirion in Wales, and his wife Amabel. I told Clough of our hunt for a country house. Next thing, he had a large map out on the table, covering London and all the surrounding areas. I stared at it rather blankly. I shall never forget how Clough looked over at his wife and said, "Do you think they'll do?" Do? And Amabel answered, "Yes, I think they'll do." They were talking about their *own* cottage in Surrey, which Clough had built himself! They were planning to spend more of their time in Wales, so the Surrey place was for sale—but only to someone who was right for it. Charles and I.

When Clough started to describe the cottage I began to shake like a leaf, and I flew to the telephone. The curtain had just come down on Charles' play, and I remember I talked to him as if I were sending an economical telegram: "Come at once Clough's party thatched wooden cabin twenty-eight miles London 625 feet up heart of wild woods bracken up to front door two miles nearest village no water no lights pine trees bluebells."

The next day Charles and I were walking through lanes and copses toward the wood—there were no roads—without a single doubt in our minds that we had found our country place. We knew for certain it was where we were going to live, although we had never even seen it. It was a bright, warm spring day and we sat down among the wild anemones and had a picnic lunch. Then we started walking again—and there it was. With four pine trees actually growing right through it! A wonderful thatched wooden structure surrounded by thirty-two acres of woodland, and the miles of surrounding country were untouched by civilization. We closed the deal at once. Though Clough called it a cottage, it was more like a hut supported by the trunks of pine trees, one foot from the ground. It was called Stapledown. Journalists, when they wrote about it, called it "the Laughton house in the tree-tops." Another journalist simply said that we were "living up a tree."

We had paths cut in the wood. Then Charles and I furnished the place cheaply and quickly—in two weeks exactly. We moved in, in time for the bluebells, and had friends staying with us almost at once. Our guests had to work for their supper—chopping logs, fetching drinking water from a half mile away, and finding ways to kill ants.

At that time we knew Constant Lambert and Paul Draper, the dancer. I wanted to buy a piano, and Lambert went with me to select it. After several trips he spotted a Bluthner medium grand, which I still have today. We had wonderful sessions at Percy Street, with Constant playing the piano and Paul dancing. Charles was working every night in *On the Spot,* so he wasn't always there, which was fortunate, for he disliked Paul Draper very much. The son of Muriel Draper, Paul was a brash American, rambunctious, cocky, and flip. Charles didn't like people like that. Besides, at the time, Paul was having an affair with my close friend, Iris Barry, whom Charles adored. He was sorry to see Paul breaking Iris' heart, although I thought Iris could look after herself. Iris, in love, ashamed that she was older than Paul, was now not being witty at all because Paul was no better than a blind puppy as a listener. Paul and Iris often came to visit us at Stapledown, but Charles never really joined in the frivolity. He was like an older gentleman, although he wasn't thirty yet. He watched us enjoy ourselves.

The walls and floor at Stapledown were made only of great wooden planks. One quiet night I was awakened by a regular pumping sound that went on and on. "How thoughtless of Paul and Iris to make such a noise," I thought. And I listened and listened. It seemed endless. It was my own heart beating.

Then came *Payment Deferred,* a play Jeffrey Dell adapted from the book by C. S. Forester. The powerful part of Willie Marble was perfect for Charles. There was a good part for me, too—Winnie Marble, his daughter.

In spring 1930, before rehearsals began on *Payment Deferred,* Charles and I went down to Jeffrey Dell's home in Brighton to discuss the play and polish the dialogue. Jeffrey, who was also a lawyer, lived in what was a rather ordinary, dismally furnished ground-floor flat with his girlfriend Eileen. He probably had very little money then, as he'd left a wife and maybe a child to start this new household. The four of us had many wonderful lighthearted days, talking, laughing, going out to restaurants, and walking on the beach. Jeffrey and Eileen came to the hut at Stapledown very often for weekends.

Payment Deferred went into rehearsal for the usual three-week period. At least we were prepared. But Charles almost immediately began to suffer the agonies that the character Willie Marble went through. Unhappy, complaining, Charles blamed the director, H. K.

Ayliffe, for being destructive and stuffy. Charles deeply searched the character of the murderer he played to find the essence of what made him tick, so that he might make the audience understand what it felt like to be driven to murder. I would say that this is what made the play have a comparatively short run. The audience also felt guilty.

Charles also took a violent interest in how I should be dressed in my part as his daughter, Winnie, age twelve. Charles was a great believer in getting the very top craftsmen to carry out his vision of each character, down to creating his own stage (and later, film) clothes and everybody else's in any production. Part of Charles' secret as an actor was that he looked for the tramp in a king and the king in a tramp, and only the finest craftsmen could make costumes for any rags or riches role that he did.

By the time we were getting ready for *Payment Deferred*, Charles and I had been married about two years. One night, Charles went out with Jeffrey Dell and when they got back to our flat, the police stopped Charles at the door. The police held a boy who they said presumably wanted to get money from Charles.

I was in bed when Charles came upstairs with Jeffrey. "Something awful has happened," he said to me. "I have something to confess." He asked Jeffrey Dell to go into the kitchen while he told me what had happened. He said that he had picked up the boy, and it wasn't the first time he had done it; that he was homosexual partly, and he cried. I said, "It's perfectly all right, it doesn't matter. I understand it. Don't worry about it."

That's why he cried. When I told him it didn't matter. Then Jeffrey came in and we sat and drank, and Charles was tear-stained and felt very bad. It was a shock to both of us. Jeffrey, who was still going with Eileen, suggested that we should all go off to Salzburg on a two-week holiday before rehearsals started. I said I didn't want to go. It was too awful—four of us to go away. I just didn't want to go, to somehow pretend it was a second honeymoon. I couldn't go along with it. The hypocrisy of that I couldn't face. So they went off without me.

When the case came up in court, Charles had to appear as a witness. He must have given the boy five shillings, or something, which the judge called "misguided generosity." There was a little paragraph about two or three inches from the bottom of the page in a newspaper that said: "Actor warned about misguided generosity." It gave only the boy's name.

The only obvious effect the incident had on me was that during the run of *Payment Deferred*, I became deaf for about a week. I suppose I shut my ears off, probably as a reaction to the news I hadn't wanted to hear. Later on, I would ask Charles what really happened, and once he told me that he had had a fellow on our sofa. The only thing I said was, "Fine, okay, but get rid of the sofa." We did. We sold it.

Reviewing Charles' performance in *Payment Deferred*, A. E. Wilson wrote in *The Star:*

> The acting of Charles Laughton was astonishing. At times I found it almost unendurable to contemplate the agonies and fears of the murderer. There was a moment when, thinking his wife had discovered his secret, he collapses into hysteria. Here was an utter abandonment to funk and terror; no detail was spared. The sight of the quivering, blubbering wretch aroused mingled feelings of disgust and pity.

Jeffrey and I used to talk in the dressing room when Charles was on stage during *Payment Deferred.* And we even had calls on the phone to Brighton and back. Although I had said to Charles that "it" was perfectly all right, underneath I had to empty my feelings out to somebody. I turned to friends and I turned to Jeffrey. He sensed I needed affection and help. We had actually a sort of quietly passionate time —not actually an affair. It was partly because there was no opportunity. He lived in Brighton, and we lived in London. If it had been convenient, there might have been.

It was only *afterward*, in later years, that the boy episode proved to grow into a great wall—never mentioned, but distinctly *there*. I can think of no indication whatsoever that Charles liked young men prior to that time. Obviously, he needed secret and degrading episodes. I would say that he only began to "love" young men when he reached the age of about forty. It was his change of life. Then I was relieved. It was so safe.

Perhaps my overtolerance in the beginning did Charles—and me —more harm than good. If I had known all this before we were married it might have been very different, one way or another. But the deception is what hurt so deeply.

I don't know whether Charles' jealousy played a part in his effort to break out in a little freedom—that could be. After we were married, I was working in a film and had to be taken to an outlying studio about six in the morning. The assistant would pick me up in a car. Charles always would stand at the door on Percy Street to say good-bye, looking angry. The assistant thought I was married to a grouse and was very sympathetic.

Later, when I played in *The Outskirts*, I had endless passionate scenes with an actor called Derrick de Marney. Between matinees and evening shows, I used to sleep in my dressing room. Soon after we opened, Charles unexpectedly and loudly burst into my room and actually blurted out, "I thought Derrick was in here . . . he's not in his room!" This dramatic, suspicious entrance was more like cheap melodrama than flattering. Actually I thought Derrick de Marney was rather awful—all tongue and little acting technique on the stage. At the end of the play he had to strangle me—and nearly did—every night.

I didn't say anything to Charles about his dashing in like that, but I felt his jealousy unpromising for our future. But it never showed itself again.

Charles was not able to unfold his problems to me or anybody else, including the brilliant and famous analyst Ernest Jones. Rather, Charles felt that he knew himself, and that he alone was the expert on himself. His seeing Dr. Jones was the only time that Charles made a voluntary plea for help from another human being, and he was driven to that by sheer terror at my discovery of his sofa episode. Even so, Charles almost immediately stopped keeping his appointments. The nurse called three times to ask, "Where is he?" or "Is he just late?" Charles would tell me, "Jones agrees with me that I know more about myself than he can ever know or find out." Many a one of Charles' friends felt that he alone was the only one to whom Charles had opened his very guts, but it always turned out that Charles had revealed only a facet or two of the complicated turmoil within him. Everyone shows different facets of himself to different people. The more you search and delve into a person, the more you find. But people who make a big splash in life seem to be more interesting, to have more information within them to grip and amuse others.

I remember that it rained nearly every day during *Payment Deferred*, which only added to all the dreariness. When the curtain fell every night, we would all have a whiskey to pick us up. It was a fine play but it hit bottom. Charles was trying to make the audience feel that any one of them might, under similar circumstances, perform a criminal act himself, so the audience would feel, if only temporarily, some tolerance and compassion for the weaknesses and aberrations of others. Charles wrote to a close personal friend during the play's run:

> Poor, rigid, hide-bound Mr. Marble, the laugh is with him and on the audience. They crucified him, and by the end of the play they know they did it in secret fear of their own hidden loves under a mask of virtue. By that time they naturally want to crucify me for telling them so.

I suppose too many members of the audience may have felt the very truth that Charles expressed in his letter, because, though highly praised, *Payment Deferred* never had a wide appeal and it ran for only three months.

Therefore, it came as an exciting surprise when a successful New York producer, Gilbert Miller, saw the play and decided to import it to New York, along with most of the cast. We were to open in September of 1931. We had a pretty ugly picture of the United States—a lot of people in England thought that everyone in America wore feathers and made war whoops—but nevertheless we prepared to go. We spoke to Clough Williams-Ellis about enlarging our country hut while we were out of the country, And we gave up our flat in Percy Street. A good thing we did, too, because an Indian restaurant had opened up underneath us, and the smell of garlic and curry was everywhere in our apartment.

Charles and I came over to the United States on the S. S. *Olympic*. The easy life from soup to dessert, with no decisions to make, was a luxury unknown to us. Gilbert Miller was footing the first-class bill, and we didn't have to study lines—we knew the parts. Charles was a bit seasick for two rough days, but we got out for walks. And we ordered delicious little cantaloupe melons at practically every meal.

During this first trip across the Atlantic, Charles and I brought a pornographic book to read for fun. We were getting on fine in those days, despite the sofa incident. The book's cover said *The War of 1872 in Armenia*, or a title something like that, but inside I think it was called *Cherry Blossoms in Beachtime*—one of those titles. It had been printed in France. It was the usual thing about a young girl and a great buck running down the beach, how her backside shook, and a rape in a cave and all that. Anyway, as we got nearer and nearer to New York, Charles and I started to get scared that the customs people might find the book. So we ripped it apart and threw it out the porthole. But we'd thrown the pages upwind, and the waves had caught them, so when we docked the entire side of the boat was spattered with the pages of the dirty book.

In 1931, seeing New York City for the first time from an ocean liner was an event. Of course, plenty of passengers were old hands at crossing the Atlantic and were getting drunk in the bar, or were asleep in their bunks, or doing the cocoon bit in blankets on deck. For others (some who had never surfaced during the trip, even for shuffleboard), it was an emotional moment.

I suppose it was about three or four o'clock on an early autumn afternoon that a small crowd collected on the prow, walking around and keeping warm. We had left the muggy Gulf Stream, the ocean was a misty gray-blue, and so was the sky. There was no horizon to be seen. First we imagined we could see New York—but where to look? Up, down, straight, right, or left? Anyway, after a long, long time there seemed to be an opal forming, a marquise-shaped opal. Then an isosceles triangle. Then one and yet another glitter flash (probably the Chrysler Building). And then the little putt-putt barges and the immigration officers came to help the *Olympic* and us in.

Then the press and the cameramen were let aboard, and Charles and I had that dear, sweet, Old World experience of being cross-examined by these verbal sob-sisters and their brother snipers. And just as I'd been told they would, the photographers said to me, "Sit on this rail, cross your legs, skirt above your knees please—no, not that far—and smile, and say *cheese.*"

Dear Iris Barry (at this time, Mrs. Alan Porter) was there too, dissolved in tears, mixed with some sort of gin. After going through customs with some fear, for I'd heard of Ellis Island, we took off in a taxi for the Chatham Hotel.

In our hotel room, Iris sat on the bed and said to me, "Now you're in America, Towser, don't trust anyone—even your own mother. And don't forget, the only thing that counts is the dollar." Then she fell back, much to Charles' sorrow, and half seemed to fall asleep—after asking for another drink.

It was near the end of Prohibition. Iris used to get so drunk on bathtub gin that she'd fall across the bed and you couldn't move her. She smelled like a polecat. The gin was coming out of her skin. Porter, her husband, was an English teacher at Vassar. He had been a sort of makeshift at some point and she drifted along with him to America. He was very deaf and not a proper husband for Iris.

In New York, *Payment Deferred* did not run long, although the reviews for Charles were very fine. The play again made the audiences feel guilty and once more gave them the fearsome feeling "It might be me." Charles yet again, as he would many times later, had demonstrated his special talent in finding the lowest common denominator in us all. People who saw the play said, as they had in England, "I thought it was great but I wouldn't want my sister or mother to see it." This does not help to make for a word-of-mouth audience.

Payment Deferred went on to Chicago for a limited run, and Charles was hailed once again. The press said that he was even greater than "the great Ivan Pavlenko from Russia," who had just been in town. But since Charles and I had never heard of Pavlenko, it didn't feel much like a compliment.

We loved Chicago. We lived high up in a great apartment (with kitchen!) overlooking Lake Michigan. The weather was wild and icy, and you had to hold on to a rope to walk on Michigan Avenue.

Back in New York Charles and I went to see *The Churchmouse* with Ruth Gordon. We were so overwhelmed by Ruth Gordon that we had nerve enough to go backstage, hoping that she knew about Charles and *Payment Deferred*. We got to know her very well and very quickly. After her show and our show, at night we very often went to her house—or was it Jed Harris' house?—a small, elegant brownstone. There would be light food and drinks and theatre talk. Thornton Wilder would be there, reading from his plays. Charles would read and expound. Jed Harris, producer and director, would dominate and sparkle. And somewhere upstairs there was a baby and a nurse.

As a result of those evenings, Jed greedily gobbled up Charles to present him in his London success, *Alibi*, retitled *The Fatal Alibi* in New York. In his further efforts to Americanize Agatha Christie's masterly play, Harris hung himself with the green rope of envy. Up until rehearsals began, Jed was very friendly to us. Afterward Jed claimed that he hated the play and said that he only produced it in New York to show off Charles. I'm sure he also thought it would make money. After all, the play had been a huge hit in England.

It was during the run of *The Fatal Alibi* in New York that our friendship with Joe Losey grew. He had come to England during the run of *Payment Deferred* in 1931, and at that time I wasn't sure what his connection to the play was—but he was there studying it. Then, when Gilbert Miller took *Payment Deferred* to New York, Losey was stage manager.

Whenever Charles was deeply unhappy in a play or a film, he often started to bully me. Joe Losey increasingly took my side after these bitter arguments and privately sympathized with me. Although I became close him, I never told him about Charles. I never told him about my problem marriage. For that matter, I never told anyone. Toward the end of the run of *Fatal Alibi*, Joe got the mumps—but we went on talking on the phone and then wrote each other letters for months— until we bored each other to tears. If Joe hadn't gotten the mumps, we might have become involved—two lost, angry people floating around, overshadowed by Charles.

Joe Losey was a great friend of John Hammond, and the two of them took me to Harlem and introduced me to some of the greatest jazz musicians in some of the smallest, murkiest cellars—the mind boggles when trying to describe them. Very stuffy, dark basements, smoky and eerie and very sickly sweet. We also went to the Cotton Club, where I first saw girls waiting in line behind a rope for dancing partners. It was called Lovers' Lane. Charles came with us once, but Harlem frightened him. Also, he never had my insatiable curiosity.

One fine Sunday Joe and John took me to a wealthy home in Mount Kisco for cocktails. There were many idle-rich types there. Apparently, it was very smart then to go to Russia and study the workers, after cocktails and speakeasies had lost their charm. Several of the guests had just returned from Russia with photos. They had intended to stay and "study" Russia for five weeks but left in three days owing to acute indigestion. They ate too much caviar and rich food, administered, I imagine, by a clever Soviet government. Their snobbish prejudices certainly made me feel very pro-Russian.

When I returned to America later, I saw Joe in New York one last time. We met for an early dinner at his sister's flat. Joe cooked oysters, a quite elaborate dish served in shells on rock salt. I disliked oysters very much—years before in England a distinguished old barrister had patted my knee and said, "If oysters are really fresh they should twitch in your mouth." So my meeting with Joe, and his oysters, in every way fell flat. A great relief!

During *Payment Deferred* telegrams had started coming from Hollywood. When we got back to England, the telegrams became more
urgent—especially the ones from an old friend and playwright, Benn
Levy, who was writing screenplays for Paramount Studios. Charles
cabled Benn: SHALL I TAKE THIS OFFER FOR "THE DEVIL AND THE DEEP"?
He cabled back: YES. COULDN'T FAIL IF I PLAYED THE PART MYSELF. So,
turning right around, Charles and I sailed back to America, and on to
Hollywood.

Before Charles left for England he signed for *The Devil and the Deep*
at Paramount, with Tallulah Bankhead, Gary Cooper, and Cary Grant
(in a small part), but the script was not ready yet, so he was loaned to
Universal Studios for *The Old Dark House*, directed by James Whale.
Paramount pushed Charles into the arrangement on the condition that
The Devil and the Deep would be released first. Charles was very irritated.
It took a little while to get used to the ways of Hollywood.

There was no smog in Southern California in 1932, and after
London with its pea-soup fog, we could not believe colors we saw
around us. The sky in Los Angeles seemed almost navy blue, and so
were the shadows on the ground. In England, the yellow tinge of the
very air, by comparison, I found saddening. Apart from the lovely
brightness in Hollywood, though, I found "the big pink pup" and
"giant frog" sort of restaurants horrifying. You walked into the giant
mouth of a frog to get a meal! Also, the workmanship on little summer
dresses that Charles bought for me there was pathetic. The first time
I wore one, the hem fell down in a few minutes. In a taxi, Charles and
I stuck it up with postage stamps.

James Whale had first come to Hollywood to film *Journey's End,*
which he'd directed as a play in London and New York, and this picture

was followed soon after by his famous *Frankenstein*. Of course, we were very happy to see him again, although Charles wasn't particularly close to him. He found James Whale a little showy—Charles himself veering away from that sort of thing.

On our first night in Hollywood, we three went to the Brown Derby Restaurant for dinner. (Not a frog or a pink pup, but a bowler hat!) Jimmy Whale said, "You will love it here in Hollywood, Charles. I'm pouring the gold through my hair and enjoying every minute of it!" Charles was horrified by that. But Jimmy did love money. He came from a poverty-stricken English family, and I had heard him describe the tiny little fire in the tiny little grate in the rooms where he was brought up. While we were at dinner, Tallulah Bankhead came over to our table and said, "Charlie, I hear you're going to be in *my* new picture!" It certainly was also Charles' picture, and of course Gary Cooper's, too.

Charles and I rented a house in Hollywood. It was the last one on La Brea Avenue—La Brea Terrace—like a finger going up into the hills.

I often climbed the hill behind the house, through mariposa tulips and yuccas, and so on, up to where the huge sign said OUTPOST, wearing shorts and shirt and bare legs. How I avoided getting bitten by rattlers and tarantulas I don't know. Never heard of them, I suppose. I always got rather bloody from scratches. Once I persuaded Charles to battle his way to the top, and he was enchanted to find the sandy mesa place alive with butterflies—black and yellow—thousands of them.

Charles at this time was working, of course; I was not. I found myself cut off from the world for months, which became a sort of illness, mentally. I was so unhappy, so lonely. A new country. An isolated house. So I was pleased to have people to dinner sometimes.

There were many English people connected with *The Old Dark House*—among them, James Whale, Lillian Bond, and Ernest Thesiger. A man called Rogers was our cook, houseman, and chauffeur, who took Charles to the studio every morning and picked him up at night. We would invite these people—Whale and Lillian and her mother, and Thesiger—over to the house, and Rogers would quite routinely cook dinner for six.

To me, American cooking was so odd. You know, mayonnaise on peaches, the odd combinations of foods. I remember Rogers bringing in some stewed apples to go with the lamb—which was fine—but the apples were bright green! Nobody wanted to eat them. When he saw them, Ernest Thesiger (who would later play the mad scientist in Whale's *The Bride of Frankenstein*)—said, "Oh, arsenic apples!" I remember Thesiger coming up to see us one day, bringing two full-length yuccas wrapped in a piece of newspaper. You know, one was (and is) forbidden to pick yuccas from the hills. They are treated like English swans. Or sacred cows in India. Well, when I saw the yuccas in his arms, I said, "What have you done? *You* picked them?" Thesiger said with a grin, "I walked along Hollywood Boulevard and nobody took any notice at all."

In *The Devil and the Deep*, Charles was a tyrannical, jealous sea captain. Everyone on the set was driven throbbing-head mad by Tallulah, who played the same phonograph record over and over again. The song was certainly about love, but whether it was frustrated or fulfilled, I forget. I think the title was "Falling in Love Again," or something like that. And nothing would stop her—not even her current crush on Gary Cooper, a fact she would rasp out proudly to anyone who would listen. I kept away from the set. Charles preferred it.

But one night, I was on the set, with Scotch and blankets, when Charles did his big sinking ship and drowning scene. The ship's captain's cabin was specially built in the studio tank so its ceiling was level with the studio floor. They could fill it up with water as the ship supposedly sank. Charles was to sit in his chair at a desk and willfully let himself drown. He was very nervous, of course, having to hold his breath until the water rose authentically high above him. But, oh hell, the water had barely covered his forehead when his officer's hat floated away. Stagehands plunged in to pull out Charles. It took a full hour to dry off the cabin, and many hot whiskeys to help Charles through the night. When they got the shot right it was 4:30 A.M. And, oh yes, they stuck Charles' hat on with tape and spirit gum to be certain it wouldn't float off again. Thank goodness, Tallulah was not in the scene, with her awful sex-song box.

I shouldn't really dislike Tallulah after what she did for me in London in the 1920s—generously risking her reputation by sending me to an abortion doctor. But she was always so coarsely rude to Charles. Once at a very large New York party, she stood at the bar and kept repeating, "Look how ugly he is! Charles Laughton . . . look how ugly he is!" Even after Charles had died, she said she would not talk about him. "He had such dirty nails," was her last witless remark.

Charles' next film was *The Sign of the Cross*, and as usual, he was at his wit's end on what to make of his character, Nero. Cecil B. De Mille, the director, wanted a portrait of the real man. But what, one wonders, was that? A very noisy beast? An English feudal lord? Or a flaming fairy?

Finally Charles came up with his divine ace card—the grape sucking, wild Wilde Nero. De Mille didn't expect the audiences to scream with laughter. All De Mille had seen during the shooting was "the real man." De Mille saw the evil, and there was evil in this Nero; but Charles made you laugh at it. Cecil B. De Mille never knew quite what hit him. And I'm sure that role did Charles more good than going to a psychiatrist.

Iris Barry came out to stay with us in Hollywood—or, more than that, to be with us. She settled into a studio connecting to our house. Charles had brought home a black kitten from Paramount, so we naturally called it "Nero." Things were looking up, emotionally. We all went to see the wild flowers in the desert, with Rogers driving.

During *The Sign of the Cross*, Metro-Goldwyn-Mayer planned to film *Payment Deferred* and offered Charles the Willie Marble part. Since the studio was only photographing a play, they thought it would be quick and cheap. Charles was so unquestionably brilliant in the part, it seemed a sure-fire idea. But for the female part they wanted another big name to bolster the box office. I was shocked when Maureen O'Sullivan was cast in my original role of the daughter, and Charles joined me in my despair. I was said to be so extraordinarily good in the part—why? how could this happen? Iris said, "That's life, Towser." I nearly became blind with crying and wanting to scream for England and our bluebell woods. I soon left Hollywood and went home. The train trip alone, and then the boat trip, helped me to forget the pain.

When I was traveling alone on the ship, I was very afraid at first of leaving my cabin. But tradition demanded that twelve miles outside the limit everyone dash to the bar and have a champagne cocktail—a lump of sugar with three drops of Angostura bitters, a dash of brandy, a twist of orange peel, then the rest champagne. Afterward everyone straightaway proceeded to his cabin—home base. Whenever I left the cabin, from fear of talking to strangers I would walk fiercely round the deck with my head down—long strides, heels first.

On one of my trips round the deck, a lady got out of her deck chair and stopped me. "I say," she said, "do please sit down with us for a minute. You look as if you're stalking a bug." So I sat down with her and her friends. She said, "I am Lady Moray. And this is Mrs. Otto Kahn," and so on and so forth. So I amused the rich with funny remarks about New York for a while. I told them about a little shop I'd seen in Times Square—this was still during Prohibition—just a hole in a wall with room for a narrow door. It sold only one thing—apparently reddish-purplish house bricks. Actually, they were dried pressed grapes, and round each brick was a label that read:

Do NOT put this in three quarts of water at a temperature of 76 degrees and leave uncovered for three weeks, then strain and cover and leave for six more weeks, as it will become alcoholic, and *this is against the law!*

And I added that I thought New Yorkers all had furry tongues and bad breath from drinking bathtub gin, which made plain water taste horrible. I was sure there was nothing wrong with the hotel tap water. "Oh," squeaked Mrs. Otto Kahn, "tap water, tap water, what does it taste like?"

After the trip I exchanged a couple of letters with Lady Moray and wish I had kept up with her. We really got on very well. She lived in Scotland in some castle or other—Moray Castle, I imagine. And soon she became the Countess of Moray. I was curious about the life-style in the Scottish highlands, and what must have been glorious surrounding country. But I have always been as scared as a wild rabbit of such social situations—about what to wear and when, what knife, what fork at table. And heavens, all those miles of spoons and crystal glass. So I stopped writing and the connection fizzled out. I could never ride and gain confidence on my so-called talent or name. Just let me get home and peel a potato.

My escape from what I thought was cruel Hollywood soon grew into my first experience of life away from Charles. I had a slight feeling of cowardice and the quite strong feeling that I had duties. Duty? That was a new word that soon was a ruling element in my life. Over the following years of our marriage Charles and I were both bound by that unexpectedly protective word. Freedoms can be taken and meted out by a person under the immunity that strict duty provides. Immunity from guilts. Duty is a good roof for anyone who needs shelter, and at the time I did.

Back in London, I stayed over The Etoile, a small restaurant in Charlotte Street, Soho. The owners, the Rossis, two or three generations of them, lived in the same building above. The restaurant is now a four-star landmark for gourmets. In the twenties the food was wonderful and inexpensive, thanks to the artists. Italian wine and lots of mirrors. You could see yourself a hundred times over as you leaned on the cool, marble-topped tables. In time there were white cloths and little bunches of fresh flowers. A few special people were welcome to stay in the two or three rooms that were for rent. The bathroom was up or down the stairs on a landing.

I had a very small room with a small window overlooking Charlotte Street. On the Italianate ceiling were painted nude cherubs, blue skies, fluffy clouds, and wreaths of pink roses. There was really hardly room for my cabin trunk, but I lived out of it like a closet and chest, and lay and gazed at the ceiling a lot thinking about my life and duty.

The bluebells at Stapledown were nearly gone and the bracken was leaping up, fingering its way to the sky, covering up what I suppose nature thinks is leftover untidiness—crab apple trees and blasts of foxgloves. What a place and what a cure for hurt pride. My friends were a consolation, too. John Armstrong was his brilliant, adoring, tall, wispy self, painting well and having fun with models that he pursued like a lepidopterist. For me this lifelong friend wrote letters, poems, and limericks of such scholarly quality that I have never come across any since with quite that touch of wit. Many are quite unprintable. I still have them.

I saw quite a lot of Biddy and Shamus, but I was rather nervous because Biddy got in a few neighbors and I hadn't learned at that time to be nice. Right or wrong, the neighbors praised my hair and skin and even my beauty—to please Biddy. After Maureen O'Sullivan had gotten my part in Hollywood, I couldn't take it. It made me feel a fraud. To them I was a big success, but to myself I felt a kind of disgrace.

I took Biddy to some of the old haunts and vegetarian restaurants and even made a trip to Brighton where Biddy was born and where we had spent some summer holidays when Waldo and I were children. On the way to Brighton we stopped by Aunt Mary's shack in Forest Row in Sussex. Aunt Mary was still painting away and making her own tempera from the clay in her acre field. She had built a most ungainly structure of red brick, two stories high, a studio on top of a studio. The upper one with a north light always leaked in the wet weather, and the floor was covered with cups and saucers from my grandparents' golden wedding set. But from gaining the amused respect of a few wealthy families in the area—who helped occasionally over tea and crumpets by buying a picture—to finding water wherever she dug at the bottom of her field, Aunt Mary flourished. She dug four or five square holes in the clay about two feet by two feet, and three or four feet deep. Water was in all of them and she bailed it out with a small bucket, one well at a time. The water made good tea, and of course she could wash in it. Probably very good for the skin. Aunt Mary made her "field shoes" from old car tires. What a sight she looked. But she could put on a tweed suit and Liberty blouse to go up to London as president of the Tempera Society and look quite respectable.

Biddy began to talk more and more about the Lanchester family. She somehow had become rather proud of them—those who had distinguished themselves. She had actually done some research on the Lanchesters. I also had a kind of pride-hatred feeling about the Lanchester family, their prestige versus their part in the kidnapping.

I even remember being quite proud seeing the chimney of the Lanchester car factory on the way into Birmingham, with the name LANCHESTER printed in vast letters down the side. Although it was Fred Lanchester who was the least kind of the brothers at the kidnapping, Biddy nevertheless found it impossible to contain her pride about his inventing the fluid flywheel in the Lanchester car. But she also delighted in undermining the wicked brother, and told us with ironical glee about a 1919 model of his car, an ornate four-seater "saloon" with inlaid marquetry roof, which King George V remarked was "more suited to a prostitute than a prince."

Once, over tea, with a little audience of old socialists, Biddy told about our blue-blooded background, as she recalled a piece of gossip about the Earl of Onslow. It seems that my great-great-grandfather, the Reverend Lanchester, was the presiding chaplain on the Onslow Estate in Surrey. The Earl of Onslow had got a chambermaid into trouble and he married the poor girl off to the Reverend Lanchester. Bar sinister number one. So Waldo and I could be said to have inherited a second bar sinister.

Biddy did all the talking. Shamus just sat by himself, sometimes listening, mostly dozing.

Letters to and from Charles in Hollywood went painfully on. We missed each other, but there was nothing to be done about it. It was at about this time that Charles slipped into a jewel of a performance in a film for Paramount Studios. But more important, it was a film segment directed by Ernst Lubitsch. The film was *If I Had a Million.* If only Charles had had more associations with great directors—or even the great in any field—his whole life story would have been elevated to a much more interesting level.

If I Had a Million was released at some point around the time Charles and I appeared at the Old Vic. Lubitsch and Charles really adored each other, and even in passing in the commissary or at casual parties, the warmth between them was contagious.

If I Had a Million was a film of many episodes. Charles played a bank clerk—one of a sea of two or three hundred bank clerks. The premise of each episode in the film was: What would your reaction be if you inherited a million dollars? An office boy approaches Charles with a telegram. Charles opens the telegram and without pause, gets up, passes dozens of desks, goes through swinging doors, up one, then two flights of stairs, then three, getting grander and more deeply carpeted, then he goes through more swinging doors and finally knocks gently at a vast, heavy, carved wooden door. A voice says, "Come in!" Charles goes in meekly and blows the largest raspberry that the world has probably ever heard; and, at the same time—the finger. In England during that era, the raspberry was not allowed by the film censors, so another take was made of the scene for the British. Charles gave a shrill whistle and a two-finger "up yours" gesture.

The coda of this story comes much later, in America, when a grip was talking to Charles on a film set. Charles said, "I wonder why one finger is allowed in America but not in England. There, two is okay. Just like hailing a taxi." "Oh," said the grip, "I guess, Mr. Laughton, the English have bigger assholes."

Out of the blue, Alexander Korda contacted me in London and I went to see him at his Grosvenor Street office. In those days Korda had already made the film *Service for Ladies* with Leslie Howard, as well as *Private Life of Helen of Troy.* He was becoming increasingly famous, and I had high hopes of getting a job. Well, in his witty, delightful, persuasive Hungarian way he led the subject around to Charles. Korda immediately suggested a delicious script called *A Gust of Wind,* in which he wanted Charles to play the leading role.

I wrote to Charles. He did not then believe in English films. He wanted to come back to London and work on the stage. He looked upon London as a place in which to work in the theatre, and Hollywood as the place to make films. Before the week was out, Korda had me up to his office again and he talked about another idea for Charles —and me, this time—*Henry the Eighth's Fifth Wife.* That is, Anne of Cleves.

My first impression of Alexander Korda had been that he resembled two directors Charles had worked with and liked: Komissarjevsky, of *Mr. Prohack* days, and E. A. Dupont, who had directed Charles in a tiny cameo in his first film, *Piccadilly.* Both these men had theatrical minds and ingratiating charm. So I wrote back to Charles that Korda was someone I thought he would like working with. Charles didn't reply. But he was coming back soon.

A few days later Korda called me again, with an even greater idea —he'd do all the wives of Henry the Eighth, and I would be one of them. All the time this schmaltz oozed out of Korda like toothpaste. I should have suspected his motives, of course. After all, Korda knew I was married to Charles. Oh, well, Anne of Cleves was a part for me —better than nothing.

In the meantime I found a great flat for Charles and me in Gordon Square, Bloomsbury—the top three floors of a five-story Georgian house. There were business offices below. The famous Bloomsbury houses are mostly built around lovely green squares and all have beautifully proportioned large rooms. At this time my friend John Armstrong was seeing a bright, handsome young woman called Benita

Jaeger, so we all three had conferences about the Gordon Square flat. Everything was in hand for Charles' return, awaiting his orders: the Gordon Square flat, Alexander Korda's film, and of course, lovely Stapledown.

The moment Charles came back to England, about six weeks after my first letter, his agent took him to see Korda. The two would meet frequently thereafter to discuss ideas for films, but Charles was still hoping to find a good play. Finally Korda changed Charles' program. Their meeting led to *The Private Life of Henry VIII*.

It began in a healthy fury—with Chinese firecrackers and squibs* going off all the time. Those were the days when one did the best one could with a piece of string and a drawing pin. *Henry VIII* was produced for about fifty thousand pounds, which even then was very little for a comparatively big picture. Charles took a great deal of trouble to probe the period and character of Henry the Eighth before he started work on the film. And he nagged at anyone connected with the film to research thoroughly. He dragged Korda down from his desk to Hampton Court, to see the architecture and gardens, and Korda's reaction was immediate and enthusiastic. As far as I know, Korda had never been there before. Zoltan Korda, Alex's brother, did the sets and, with Charles, dogged Henry the Eighth's footsteps. I also scraped the bottom of the barrel for all known facts about Anne of Cleves. She knew well the art of retiring from life without losing her head—or any other heads.

Korda's picture really had very little to do with history. Most of the audience would picture Henry the Eighth (if at all) as he appeared in the famous painting by Holbein, so Charles used that image as his basic model. From it he created a character of almost Rabelaisian mirth, with giant strokes and a broadness that would jolt the audiences out of their seats.

In my own way I was soaking up Anne of Cleves. Benita Jaeger by then had married John Armstrong, who designed the costumes for the picture, and she helped me with my German accent. I also studied the accent of the German actress Elizabeth Bergner, who was in England at the time.

There were so many alterations in the script and holdups during the filming that, in the end, Charles was called back to Hollywood before *Henry VIII* was finished. So they shot Charles in all his scenes, and the rest of us finished the film after he had left. Before his depar-

---

Squib: a firework, consisting of a tube filled with powder, which burns with a hissing noise, ending usually in a slight explosion.

ture he arranged to act with the Old Vic's company in the autumn season on his return. I would join the company, too, and play any parts that came my way.

Charles had been making films solidly for months, and he felt that he'd been away from the stage too long. But his movies were now being released all over the world. When he arrived in New York City, on his way back to Hollywood, he was stunned and even frightened by the crowd that stood outside his taxi, calling "Hey, Charlie!" It was at this moment, I think, that he realized fully the power of talking pictures. Obviously, films offered greater opportunities than the theatre to an actor whose first interest was to make a character understandable to the public. Not to please one man or woman, one intellectual or one critic, but all people.

On that trip, Charles made the film *White Woman*, with Carole Lombard. Though it was not an awfully good film, Charles was very funny in it—giving one of those lewd performances with that dirty red look in his eye. When he was in mid-Atlantic on his way back to England, a radiogram to the *Ile de France* told him to keep right on going from Plymouth to Cherbourg. I would meet him to travel to Paris for the world premiere of *The Private Life of Henry VIII*.

Alexander Korda (now London Film Productions) made all the arrangements. From Cherbourg, Charles and I rushed to Paris, arriving about seven o'clock. After checking into the Hotel Prince de Gaulle, having a bath, dressing, and grabbing a sandwich, we arrived at the theatre by eight o'clock. This was my first premiere of one of my own films, and I remember how every little cough or seat movement sawed through me like a rasp that night. I think my own heart beating made more noise than anything else. Charles and I were sitting next to an English princess, and they talked away before the film began. As the lights went down, Charles said to her, "By the way, I'm afraid I don't know how I ought to be addressing you." She whispered back, "Don't say I said so, but you ought to be calling me Ma'am." Afterward, she seemed genuinely delighted when Charles introduced her to Maurice Chevalier.

The French press raved about the film. Everybody said it was marvelous, and Charles and I joined Korda and his entourage for supper. We all wanted to go to a different restaurant—Korda to a Hungarian one, Charles and Georges Périnal, the cameraman, to a French one, me to a fish one, and so forth. Then Korda said, "The stomach is always a *patriot!*"—so everybody went to a Hungarian restaurant to celebrate with him. Charles and I got to bed very late, still hoping our success was all true. But however important it was, this premiere in Paris didn't give a hint of the furor that *Henry VIII* would create. It became the first great English film distributed in the United States.

After just a few hours of sleep, Charles and I rammed our evening clothes into our luggage and caught an early morning plane at Le Bourget, and in the afternoon we were both rehearsing for *The Cherry Orchard* at the Old Vic.

The London premiere of *The Private Life of Henry VIII* took place within a few days. Charles was to sit in the front row of the dress circle at the Leicester Square Theatre, with all of Henry's wives around him. I don't think this polygamous evening was very pleasant for Charles, and I certainly didn't care for an enforced night in a harem any more than Henry's other wives did. All of us took a call on the stage when the film was finished, looking very gay and smiling. But we were shocked the next morning to see pictures in the newspapers of Charles and his wives watching the movie. It was one of the first times infra-red lights had been used by press cameras, and everyone had been caught in unflattering and rather embarrassing shots.

13

For his performance as Henry the Eighth, Charles won the 1933 Academy Award. As for me, although *The Private Life of Henry VIII* brought me much praise, it brought few film offers. As Anne of Cleves I had done my best to look like hell in order to keep the character of Henry the Eighth at arm's length. I made myself look as ugly as possible and, in addition, the cameraman lit my nose so that it would look like a potato—knobbier than usual at the tip. And I spoke with an accent of the most guttural kind and wore a straight blond wig.

I eventually was to sign a contract with MGM, but they never knew quite what to do with the red-headed Londoner who turned up in Hollywood, instead of the blond German gawk they had expected.

I also received kind notices for *The Cherry Orchard*, in which I played the eccentric governess. Tyrone Guthrie said my performance gave "a haunting impression of loveliness." Charles did not fare so well. He had wanted to polish his acting craft quietly at the Old Vic, but it was too late for him to hide. His success had been too rapid and too great. He came back to London as a sitting pigeon for the press. He never had time or room in life to become the technician he should have been. Or perhaps he didn't want to be.

In his autobiography, *A Life in the Theatre*, Tyrone Guthrie writes about a meeting with Lilian Baylis, the matriarch of the Old Vic. The conversation, according to Guthrie, in part went like this:

MISS BAYLIS: "I saw Charles Laughton in that film. And in that play about a gangster in Chicago. Very clever, dear, of course. But I don't think my people would like him at the Vic."

GUTHRIE: "Why not, Miss Baylis?"

MISS BAYLIS: "I just don't think so, that's why."

(A pause. Then:)

"He's never played in Shakespeare, has he, dear? Why should I pay twenty pounds a week to a man who's never acted in Shakespeare?"

(Another pause.)

"Does he go to church, dear?"

Charles and Guthrie, then a young, up-and-coming director, had descended on Lilian Baylis with several new ideas for a season at the Old Vic. Miss Baylis listened, then said something to the effect that God had sent Charles to her, which at first took the wind out of Charles' sails, but he eventually got used to the idea. That season was to prove the first to make money, but Miss Baylis gave nobody credit for the profits. By the end of the season she had completely forgotten her gratitude to the Deity for sending Charles to her, referring to Charles only as "that rich film star."

In his autobiography Guthrie goes on to say that Miss Baylis felt Charles "could only be 'using' the Vic as a steppingstone to his own career. She treated him with an icy, rather naïve hauteur. To this, naturally, he reacted by imagining her to be a scheming, small-minded, mean-spirited old shrew."

When the Old Vic chose to do Shakespeare's *Henry the Eighth* in their seven-play season, they thought that they would cash in on the colossal success of the current film. Charles had Henry so in his bones that it was a foregone conclusion that he would give a great performance at the Old Vic. He did, but he suffered agonies in readjusting the celluloid character that he had already established. I think the result was disappointing to the public and the press. "It was a mistake," Harcourt Williams wrote in his *Old Vic Saga.* * "Perhaps the shadow of the over-flamboyant film fell too heavily across it." After seeing a closeup of a character on film, with more intimacy than the stage can ever show, a stage version is like seeing a person you know through the wrong end of a telescope. That is the danger of going from the films back to the stage. Once the public has tasted film blood, as it were —seen the very irises dilate in the hero's eyes—it has trouble accepting a distant figure beyond a proscenium arch, whose acting must be so broad that the back of the pit and gallery can both see and hear. In days

---

*Williams was a director for the Old Vic from 1929 through 1933.

before microphones, this could create what would now be called a "ham."

Charles wore the same hat and some of the same clothes for the stage Henry. Lilian Baylis appreciated the economy. She reigned over us all like a good or bad fairy according to the box office receipts.

You could admire her power to organize the great Old Vic and Sadler's Wells, but nobody liked her cruel undermining of top actors as well as underlings. I remember one night when a poor little understudy went on for somebody. She had learned the lines and was pretty poor, as understudies can be—especially in a company where half of them are American students paying fees to function in any capacity and learn from association. Anyway, the poor girl managed to get through the performance at short notice. When finally she staggered off the stage at the end of the play, the cast was applauding her because she had been so brave, and success apparently loomed ahead of her. The public had been served and she had kept up the Old Vic curtain. But Miss Baylis, standing there in the wings with her tight, crooked mouth and her strong glasses, said to the girl, "Well, dear, you've had your chance and lost it." That's not a nice person. Lilian Baylis also had a tiresome habit of making us go in groups on Sundays to a leper colony and perform for the lepers.

It took the whole of the nine months of the Old Vic season to get our permanent flat in Gordon Square prepared, because we enlarged the back windows and knocked two rooms into one on two floors. We completely gutted what had been a very Victorian overstuffed, dim flat, to let the sunlight in. So all through the Old Vic season Charles and I had no proper home in London—our trips back and forth to Hollywood had not allowed us to settle down yet. We lived in a service flat in Jermyn Street, which was convenient for the Old Vic. Although it was a poky sort of existence, working and living in a couple of rooms, we had a marvelous time.

Charles and I were fairly closely associated as actors during the Old Vic season—as we all were, in fact. We would often eat with some of the cast after performances. We nearly always went back to Jermyn Street. We'd all troop up, about eight, nine, or ten of us: Roger Livesy, Athene Seyler, Ursula Jeans, James Mason, Flora Robson, and Marius Goring. We'd sit shoulder-to-shoulder, drinking beer and eating cold tongue and potato salad, talking sometimes till two in the morning.

We had brought Rogers with us from Hollywood to be our general houseman and driver. Charles never did drive. Rogers was rather a motherly sort of man—I mean, he liked to look after people. He cooked exceedingly well, in spite of the arsenic apples, and made absolutely miraculous coffee in a kettle. He would throw a raw egg with shell into the kettle, mash it up with coffee, and it was the best coffee I've had in my life. Finally, when we went back to Hollywood, Rogers left us. I wasn't there when he left. There was some sort of scandal, but not between Charles and him. Next thing we knew, Rogers had hung out his shingle saying that he had been Charles' drama coach!

Among the Old Vic crowd, Roger Livesy was a practical joker. Charles and I couldn't stand practical jokers in the theatre, but jokes often start getting played on the stage during a long run and in repertory seasons. Anyway, as Miss Prism in *The Importance of Being Earnest*, I had to pick up and open a big black bag. The whole last act of that play centers around that bag. Roger had to carry it onstage and give it to me. One night, he put in two stage weights—at least thirty-five pounds each—but being a strong fellow, he brought the bag on like a feather. Of course, when the time came, I couldn't lift the bag from the floor! We had to finish the play from a kneeling position. For some days after that I feared that every prop I touched would jump into my face or be glued fast to the stage. I have always had a horror of unrehearsed effects. The audiences may laugh with the actor in a friendly way, and admire how he overcomes the practical joke, but still it is not what they came to see and pay for. Nevertheless, I was very happy when Ursula Jeans sawed Roger Livesy's stage walking stick nearly in half, and when he came on as Ernest and stamped his stick, it snapped with a bang at a critical moment. Ursula later married Roger Livesy.

The Importance of Being Earnest was one of the Old Vic's successes of that season, in spite of me as Miss Prism. Nothing is quite so lowering as being a miscast character actress. Charles fared little better as Canon Chasuble. Tyrone Guthrie, its director, wrote that *Earnest* was "was not a wise choice. Nobody was really well suited . . . The revival must be unique in that Canon Chasuble—Charles Laughton in a devastating, brilliant, and outrageous lampoon—appeared to be the leading part."

The Tempest was my star turn in the season. I played Ariel and Charles played Prospero. I think it was my most serious and most interesting acting relationship with Charles. We shared *Mr. Prohack, Payment Deferred, Henry VIII, The Beachcomber, Rembrandt, Peter Pan, Witness for the Prosecution.* But in *The Tempest* our performances were almost entirely interdependent.

Many people who acted with Charles have said that he was difficult to work with. But I found that there was no one easier. In *The Tempest* I began to learn to act rather than perform. I began to realize that I had started on a career in which the more I learned, the less I knew.

Dennis Arundell, who had also acted in Old Vic productions, composed the original music for *The Tempest* and worked with me on the songs. I did all the songs in that season that required a choirboy voice—for a young boy or a girl—a register I could produce. For example, in *Measure for Measure,* I was a Florentine boy standing on a bridge wearing white and green, singing a very beautiful song called "Take, O Take Those Lips Away." Also, as a sewing maid in *Henry the Eighth* I sang "Orpheus with His Lute," and modest though the contribution was, it was for me one of my high spots. "Orpheus" is one of the most lovely songs I know. If it hadn't been for my choirboy voice, I suppose I never would have been cast as Ariel. I also had a lot of fun choreographing when needed. A ballet for eight sailors was a good one in *Love for Love.*

Tyrone Guthrie directed *The Tempest,* and I found him rather petty. He made people do little military tricks on the stage. Describing Guthrie to a friend once, I called him "the butterfly that stamped," after the story by Rudyard Kipling. Guthrie was a tall man, but he was a great big butterfly.

Truthfully, I did not understand Prospero in *The Tempest,* although I read the part in an effort to help Charles. During rehearsals, Charles struggled desperately with Prospero, but Guthrie couldn't possibly clarify the part for him. Nor could Guthrie help me with Ariel. I sat with him for hours, trying to interpret one great long speech that was very confusing. It was a little like learning ten alphabets in Greek backward. Guthrie simply said that he didn't know what it meant either. I've read and reread that speech, and to this day I still cannot understand most of it. Some people say that Shakespeare couldn't possibly have written it, with all those commas and colons and parentheses—it's like a jigsaw puzzle. You need an expert director–Shakespearean scholar to help you in a case like that.

In his autobiography, Tyrone Guthrie described the play:

> Our season came to an end with what I think must be the worst production of *The Tempest* ever achieved . . . my direction was at once feeble and confused. The only good thing was Elsa Lanchester's Ariel, weird and lyrical in a balletic style which was at odds with everything else in the production and which better direction would never have permitted.

Harcourt Williams thought that I "gave a highly stylized interpretation of Ariel. The pitfall awaiting those who indulge in that particular form of art is that the spectator too often is set thinking about the style instead of about the character and its relation to the play."

A pleasanter and more comforting reaction came from the critic James Agate, who had once been so constructive during my old *Riverside Nights* days. He waxed poetic in his review:

ARIEL AT LAST
Thunder Over Islington

May I be forgiven for saying that until Miss Elsa Lanchester, the part of Ariel has never been acted? . . . Miss Lanchester has added lightness, or better, taken away weight . . . [She] has a radiance that cannot be explained, and by an ingenious, unwearying, yet unwearisome movement of the arms suggests kinship with that insect creation which, quivering in the sun, puts to shame the helicopter of human invention. Ariel speaks in a voice that is both shrill and soft, and in my view sings as well as Ariel should, since there is no excuse for a coloratura soprano with full bosom and empty head. In short, it is a lovely performance of exquisite invention.

And about Charles' Prospero, he wrote:

Alas, he made the old boy perform his hocus-pocus with a naughty little twinkle in his eye, and never for one moment suggested 'the potent wizard brooding in gloomy abstraction over the secrets of his art'!

In discussions of *The Tempest* years later, Charles talked about Ariel but avoided mentioning Prospero. But Ariel really is a projection of Prospero, in a way, and so I was a part of Prospero and part of Charles. I was *Charles'* Ariel.

Later, when Charles died, Prospero magically became crystal clear to me and of enduring solace.

The Sadler's Wells Ballet, inspired by Ninette de Valois, was also born and growing up in these years. As a result of my Ariel, I was loaned out to dance "Danse Arabe" in *The Nutcracker Suite*. Costumes by Oliver Messel and the orchestra conducted by Constant Lambert—need I say how happy this made me? Hearing my music cue with a full orchestra after only rehearsing with a cheap piano was nerve-racking. I had to be given a small push on the right beat. But Alicia Markova herself had to have a countdown and a push, also. She was the prima ballerina and needed a little shove for her Sugar Plum Fairy entrance.

The Old Vic season progressed. Charles loved doing *Measure for*

Measure. I think his performance as Angelo remains the best interpretation of a classic part that Charles has ever done. The costumes were designed by John Armstrong and were very sweeping and shadow-making—one cloak made Charles look almost like a bat at times. Two years before, John had suggested that Charles do *Measure for Measure* sometime, and between them they had gradually made the necessary cuts for an imaginary production. The result of these two years' soaking in the play inevitably showed in a production that had a kind of maturity not often seen in the theatre.

Harcourt Williams, in his *Old Vic Saga,* concurred:

> By the time *Measure for Measure* was reached, the company had learned to work together and a very fine performance was the result which drew the town—to the amazement of the management who had always listed this play with the unpopular ones . . . Charles Laughton's Angelo was, I think, the finest thing he did in that season. His scenes with Flora Robson as Isabella were admirably composed and carried out. The sinister streak often noticeable in his acting could not have been used to better advantage.

In moiling and toiling over the conflicting forces in the character of Angelo, Charles also seemed to clear up a kind of morose hangover that he had within himself. He needed a triumph, perhaps. He needed adulation, and *Measure for Measure* served that need.

That season James Mason was a member of the company—not one of the stars. He was in my bracket, on the second payroll. In *Measure for Measure* he had his first large part, Flora Robson's brother, Claudio. Mason was very beautiful, of course, and we all liked him very much. But he was terribly inexperienced then. It's hard to believe that he became such a fine actor when at the Old Vic he could not walk across the stage. He walked like a camel. I think Charles was too involved with himself and his roles to help anybody else at that time.

On to another production—*Love for Love.* I played Miss Prue and Charles was Mr. Tattle, a typical Restoration fop, who among other things seduces Prue, a country gossage, age fifteen, in one of the bawdiest scenes ever. The powers-that-be at the Old Vic were not happy with the licentiousness of that particular scene. The sections of the play where these two appear together have usually been cut to ribbons by producers or the police or the censors, but because in this case the parts were played by a married couple, everything seemed permissible and above-board. We could have got away with murder. Our private relationship brought a sort of decency to those parts of the play where none was intended. The scene was shown by the BBC, and relayed to the United States. "Shocking" was the verdict.

TATTLE: And won't you show me, pretty miss, where your bed-chamber is?

MISS PRUE: No, indeed, won't I; but I'll run there and hide myself from you behind the curtains.

TATTLE: I'll follow you.

MISS PRUE: Ah, but I'll hold the door with both hands, and be angry;—and you shall push me down before you come in.

TATTLE: No, I'll come in first, and push you down afterwards.

That is what people love—the Lunt and Fontanne thing. Not that Charles and I were known completely as an acting couple, but we were sufficiently a couple. Lunt and Fontanne set a superb example of what married people can do. They could do everything but take their pants off—and I think Alfred Lunt even did that in a play—because they were married in private life, and the audiences accepted and loved it.

Our final production was *Macbeth.* I think that Charles had some great moments, which came out of his ability to find structure and form in any play or film. Suddenly, from those bricks that were building the house that was *Macbeth,* the form was there; so that unexpectedly, in a high spot, Charles could make your blood run cold. But the actual execution of the role was unsatisfactory. He did not take flight, as it were. And it was not in him to make a real soldier.

I don't know whose fault it was—Tyrone Guthrie's or Charles'—but they both had big reputations beyond their experience. They both went to the Old Vic to hide and practice their art, and they were open to view like meat hanging in a butcher shop.

In his autobiography, Guthrie wrote:

Macbeth was to have been the high peak of the season. Laughton was longing to play it and full of interesting ideas. At the dress rehearsal his performance was electrifying . . . His acting that night bore the unmistakable stamp of genius. Alas, he never again, except momentarily, fitfully, recovered this greatness.

Charles was very dejected after the opening night of *Macbeth.* He knew the evening had not been a success and painfully aware that he did not meet his promise of the dress rehearsal. Tyrone Guthrie describes that evening:

At the end of the first performance, round to the dressing rooms comes Miss Baylis, aware of a need to administer cheerful but honest consolation to My Boys and Girls . . . If ever a human creature is vulnerable it is a leading man at the end of a long exhausting performance which he knows has been a disappointment.

Charles is at his dressing table, still made up as Macbeth. To him comes Miss Baylis in the full academic robes to which as an Honorary M.A. of Oxford she was entitled, and which she very sensibly put on for first nights: beaming benignly through her glasses upon the dejected actor, she gave what I knew was a laugh of embarrassment . . . Charles declares it was a hyena's yell of triumph. She then caught him a smart crack across the shoulder blades.

"Never mind, dear," she said, "I'm sure you did your best! . . ."

When the Old Vic season finished, we rushed back to Hollywood. Irving Thalberg had sent for Charles to play Father Barrett in *The Barretts of Wimpole Street*. The studio (Metro-Goldwyn-Mayer) had begun filming around Charles, shooting Norma Shearer in some of her scenes. Whenever we have gone to Hollywood it seems it has always been urgent, and then we wait once we arrive. Packing in a hurry means packing dirty as well as clean clothes. Dirty dresses at the end of a journey are expected, but it's a sordid way to start out.

We took the fastest boat possible to New York and stayed there overnight. Then the next morning we took a plane for Hollywood. The year before Charles had an ecstatic flight from Hollywood to New York —startling scenery and gorgeous skies. He sold me on the idea of a plane trip. Like praising a restaurant to a friend just before being served dreadful food, we started up on a lovely sunny morning, but it became one of the worst trips in that airline's experience. Bumps all the way. Even though the cardboard coffee cups were only half filled, it was impossible even to get them to our mouths without hitting our front teeth or spilling coffee all over our clothes.

At that time, the New York to Los Angeles plane trips were considered very fast, but in the course of that twenty-three-hour trip we changed planes about six times. On the last lap, which took place at night, we flew in a Boeing plane with blue flames from the exhaust streaming right past the window. Terrifying. The stewards offered me earplugs and aspirins and gently unstrapped us when we landed.

During one of the changeovers, at Chicago, in the midst of a dust storm, Thornton Wilder met us at the airport. At that time he was a professor at the University of Chicago. During the one-hour wait, he talked with great enthusiasm about us and our work. He always became very animated when talking of actors. He loved them.

Finally we got to California. Nearing Los Angeles, we could not see the ground at all through the thick fog below. We plunged down into nothingness, missed an airport tower, and tried again—four times in all. Charles and I did not speak. We held hands and looked at each other as if for the last time. Each time we dived through the fog, we would suddenly see below us motorcars, or laundry hanging on lines in backyards—then up we went again. It may have only taken a few more minutes before the safe landing, but it seemed to me to be at least an hour. So much for Charles' ecstasy the year before.

My first job in Hollywood was the small part of Clickett in Charles Dickens' *David Copperfield.* George Cukor directed, and Hugh Walpole, author of *The Man with Red Hair,* wrote the screenplay. Both Walpole and Cukor had decided that Charles would be perfect in the part of Mr. Macawber. Cukor had liked Charles in the silent rushes, but later Charles decided that he was unable to do the part. He seemed always to feel uncertain about the parts he played, but this time was different. Charles lost his confidence completely. The more he tried, the worse he felt he was. Eventually he convinced the powers-that-were that he could not play an actor acting. He considered Macawber a ham actor who was always "on." It's very difficult to explain why Charles feared playing this particular part. I suppose if Charles was to play a ham actor, he would have to make his own comment on the character. Dickens had made the comments about Macawber, and Charles felt he couldn't add to them. So W. C. Fields took over the role and was excellent.

I think if Charles had had his way, he never would have acted at all, because in every part he ever played—every single one—after the first two or three days' work he tried to get out of the picture. He'd say, "I can't do it. I am not suited to it!" and he gave valid, excellent reasons, and the directors and producers often started to agree with him. Luckily, they would still say, "But let's go on, Charles. If you cannot, in a week from now, we will have to agree with you." And so they would go on and the rushes would always get better. Charles would then say, "I will go on, on one condition; and that is, when we get to the end of the film, we reshoot the first three days' work." But by the end of the shooting, when the company would see the rough cut and Charles would be ready to pounce on the first three days' work to get it reshot, he could never spot the first three days. Nor could anybody else. The first few days had become a part of the whole film, the story, the whole performance.

As I worked on *David Copperfield,* Charles was finishing up Thalberg's *The Barretts of Wimpole Street.* Thalberg was Louis B. Mayer's fair-haired boy and the husband of Norma Shearer. Charles was happy with both of them. Unlike many Hollywood producers, Thalberg was respected, admired, and liked. He was straightforward in his dealings and his advice could be trusted. I used to go to see him in his office sometimes to discuss my contract with the studio. You see, when we got to Hollywood this time, I was given a courtesy contract by MGM —$150 a week—running concurrently with Charles' contract.

Thalberg advised me on *David Copperfield* and the do's and don't's of taking a screen test. He knew that Charles and I wanted to be together, as much as possible, in America, and so by helping me with my career he was also helping Charles. Often I used to walk into Thalberg's office after being out on the beach, with my hair all cockled up from the ocean, wearing ragamuffin-length coveralls. Once, when I had an interview with another producer, Thalberg said to me, "I must tell you, Elsa, that you cannot go and see other producers like this. Do something with your hair, and wear a skirt." So I smoothed down my hair and wore a suit, realizing that Thalberg had given me some very good practical advice. Hollywood was at a loss as to what to do with me in the first place, without my confusing them all the more. When you are at the top of the bill, you can take to your ragamuffin slacks again.

One of Thalberg's producer-friends was Hunt Stromberg. I quite liked him, and I guess he quite liked me. He had the habit of putting his arms around my waist—a little too far and a little too high. I got a very good part in his production of *Naughty Marietta.*

W. S. (Woody) Van Dyke was the director, and working with him was about the best experience I could have had then. Van Dyke was very famous, not so much for directing great movies, but for directing big movies in record time. He never went over budget—a kind of sainthood to Louis B. Mayer—because he insisted on printing the first and only take of a scene. It seemed to work because the first take did have a freshness no other take ever achieved. At least, it seemed to work for Van Dyke. And it helped me to think fast on my feet and get it right the first time.

Perhaps part of Woody Van Dyke's success can be credited to Christian Science. For example, when Charles was making *Mutiny on the Bounty* on Catalina Island, they were paralyzed for three days by fog. Van Dyke was shooting another picture on Catalina at the same time, and he said, "Oh, we'll soon get rid of this. I'll call my mother"—a Christian Science practitioner—"She'll disperse the fog." She did.

I did not meet Norma Shearer for some time, but Charles would bring home stories of how nice she was—and how she loved to eat. She had a colossal appetite, and there were continuous rounds of food consumed during *The Barretts of Wimpole Street*. Canadian bacon and marmalade on fried bread started the morning on the set. Soup at eleven. And so on. When I finally did meet Miss Shearer, I found her as charming as Charles had.

The parties at the Thalberg house were the only ones where Charles and I felt comfortable. Theirs was an easy household to move about in. Very well organized. The Thalbergs had a little boy. And when Miss Shearer was pregnant again, I knew they would have a girl. After all, they already had a boy, and her life was too well organized to have anything but a girl. And so they did.

That house was on the beach at Santa Monica. On one night of the year, during the full moon, I think, hundreds of little fish called grunion come up on the beach to breed. They balance on their tails and twiddle about, then go back to the deep water. It was a lovely sight to see them.

One night when Charles and I were at the Thalbergs', I saw Jean Harlow with a little fish wiggling in her hand. She put it in a bowl of flowers. I'd learned a little about grunion, and I figured that's what Miss Harlow had found and that the great grunion run was on. I knew her fish would die in the fresh water of the flower vase. So I stuck in my hand, took hold of the fish, and rushed outside, across a beach garden, and down onto the beach, to put it back home in the ocean. The shore was covered with grunion, and there were people every-where catching them in their hands and putting them in buckets. I kicked off my shoes and pulled my evening dress up round my knees and walked among the grunion in the moonlight. Thinking Charles might be interested, I ran back into the house again, shouting, "The grunion are running, the grunion are running!" I wonder what they thought of me. Most of the guests ignored me, except for Charles and Jeanette MacDonald. The three of us ran out onto the beach again, kicked off our shoes, and paddled about in the water. The ocean had so many grunion it felt as if our legs were being massaged. We didn't want to catch any, so we just splashed about and watched the grunion flip onto the beach and slip back into the ocean again. No breach of promise cases, no divorces—just twiddling around.

Jeanette MacDonald was the star of *Naughty Marietta*. I liked her from the beginning. She was an unaffected, gay, and natural person, who seemed to enjoy being successful and famous. Charles had met her before I did, during the filming of *The Barretts*. And it was from her that I acquired Louis, our second Hollywood cat, who had been left on her doorstep by a fan.

Nelson Eddy was, of course, Miss MacDonald's costar in *Naughty Marietta*. In this musical film their famous team was born. When the picture was finished, Van Dyke gave a large party for everyone from the studio. The house was packed. It was Christmas Eve and I became acquainted with a popular American drink called an Old Fashioned. I had a very good time at this party. I relaxed. I was even beginning not to mind Hollywood so much. It was becoming less of a foreign place.

I am aware that I have an unusual face, one that perhaps a painter or sculptor would want to record, but in Hollywood—where there are so many famous beauties—I wasn't sure that my face was an asset. But at this Christmas Eve party I became very gay, and a homesick expression that was always stuck on my face was wiped off. People looked *at* me, instead of past me. Having a good part in a big picture made this turning point for me that night, and I stopped being so snooty about Hollywood and the people who work there. When you've been in a strange town for many months, only working occasionally, and you feel lonely and miserable, and then people, strangers, look at you as if you were somebody, the ego is calmed and you feel a whole lot better. Anyway, I started to feel more sure of myself. I thought, "Well, I may not be a beautiful Hollywood blonde, but I am *something*. I am *somebody*." Not very profound, but I'm sure it made me better company for Charles.

All this time we had been living at the Garden of Allah Hotel, the old Nazimova home. It and its pool were peopled with the famous and hangers-on, the hopeful and a few forlorn lotus eaters. It was comparatively quiet. In Hollywood, Charles was being pulled this way and that by Paramount. He still owed them one picture, having fulfilled his other contractual commitments.

It was Charles who chose *Ruggles of Red Gap*. It was not a Paramount property. The studio bought it because Charles wanted to play the English butler who becomes an American, and Charles asked if he could have Leo McCarey to direct. Leo McCarey had done great films back in the Hal Roach days, the days of Laurel and Hardy, and Charles felt that *Ruggles of Red Gap* needed this exquisite humor and timing. And, sure enough, it was a great picture and Leo McCarey came back with a bang. When anybody did ask the silly question, "What is your favorite picture, Mr. Laughton?" Charles, floundering around and not knowing really what to say, finally had to admit, "I guess *Ruggles of Red Gap*," or maybe, "The picture I'm doing now."

Before *Ruggles* began shooting, Charles worked with McCarey and a writer or two on the script, but the necessary Englishness of Ruggles himself eluded them all. So, needing an ally to reinforce that side of the story, Charles asked for our old friend, Arthur Macrae—now a successful revue writer and playwright in England—to come and help. Arthur was delighted. He looked rather like Noel Coward and had a talent in that school—funny and frivolous. He came to Hollywood and stayed with us at the Garden of Allah. Arthur worked over the dialogue and the script and wrote some of the funniest lines in the film. But, alas, Charles became ill at this time and had to go to the hospital for an operation—a rectal fistula.

Charles had always refused to go out to be amused by Hollywood's various sideshows—among them, Aimee Semple McPherson, and her spinoff of lesser leaders, and dozens of related groups who offered faith and hope in various odd forms. Although for a while he had thought that Aimee Semple McPherson was an entertaining phenomenon on the radio, Charles found this whole business of exploiting religion shocking. (Even so, he very often said to me that if he hadn't been an actor, he would have been a damn good four-square gospel preacher.) In a town where most waitresses and garage attendants were frustrated actors, some of the wilder personalities got employment in the God business. Hollywood, I understand, has the largest number of cult groups in any city.

And there were the wrestling matches—rehearsed fights in the ring with artificial blood. After all, it's only acting in another form— and Arthur and I thought it was hilarious. Charles had gone to one wrestling match and did find the fledgling bouts before the main event quite funny. Little old ladies shouting, "Gouge his eyes out!" Young boys battling the air with gloves nearly as big as themselves. Skinny kids with combat in their tiny squinched-up eyes, and fat boys with faces like angry hamburger buns. You would never see a good-looking boy with large, luminous eyes—he'd have a film career in mind.

So, while Charles was in the hospital, Arthur Macrae became my escort to these events that I so much wanted to see. We had the time of our lives. Ocean Park pier and its entertainments from roller coasters to fortune tellers. We always went back to see poor Charles in bed. He was mostly in great pain, but we tried to cheer him up—we tried. We told him about our evening at the Angelus Temple and how Aimee Semple McPherson had been dressed as a picturesque flower seller, carrying two big baskets full of bunches of violets. She carried on in an almost sensual manner about her "Buddy," God, and what He could do for you. Her appeal as His Messenger was definitely sexy. She finally threw the violets to the audience (she had quite a strong pitching arm), and longing hands reached out to catch the talismans. After that, we had to hold hands with the strangers next to us. This was an order from On High—and Arthur and I had to do it so as not to offend anyone. We found it very embarrassing. (Except, I didn't mind holding Arthur's hand, as I was very fond of him.) Although we brought Charles all the color straight from the scene, in his hospital bed he only smiled weakly—all he really wanted was a shot of painkiller from his nurse. So Arthur and I sat with him until he drifted off to sleep. Charles always liked that.

It was during Charles' illness that I ran into W. C. Fields. One sunny afternoon after coming out of a dentist's office, I saw him standing on the corner of Vine Street and Yucca dressed fully as W. C. Fields in *My Little Chickadee*—with the great top hat and the cutaway coat and pin-striped trousers and the buttonhole. I told Fields about Charles' rectal abscess, and within a couple of hours a telegram arrived at the hospital addressed to CHARLES THESAURUS LAUGHTON. The telegram said: I HOPE THE HOLE THING IS BETTER, signed W. C. FIELDS.

In *Ruggles of Red Gap,* Charles read the Gettysburg Address. That was certainly one of the seeds that later sprouted into whole evenings of readings. People in this country just didn't seem to know it, or if they did, they knew it like the Lord's Prayer or the alphabet. They hadn't really listened to the words. Charles made every word ring true and go right home to every American who saw *Ruggles.* At the time he didn't know what he had done with that particular piece, but everyone on the set knew it was a great scene. I remember going to the sneak preview, feeling unsure about Americans' reactions to an Englishman telling them about being American. It turned the other way around: The audience just loved it, just loved learning something they should have known. In some rare, wonderful way, a great number of the Laurel and Hardy touches crept into the picture. If you look at *Ruggles* now, you will recognize Leo McCarey's hand, and Charles' admiration of and ease with McCarey's humor. He and Charles talked about doing another film together, but it never materialized.

Leo McCarey was very much in demand after *Ruggles of Red Gap.* He even appeared in person on the *Kraft Cheese Radio Show* to plug the film. He was to just say hello and a few words about the picture. Charles and I had been on the *Kraft Show* and were delighted to get the big basket of mixed cheeses that they gave all guests. Well, Leo was an extremely shy man but full of charm, with an apologetic smile that would melt an agent's gut. But he was terrified into absolute silence when he got to the Kraft microphone. He tried to talk and stuttered, then very rapidly blurted out on the air, "For Christ's sake, give me my cheese and let me go home!"

McCarey also had a weakness for pretty women and always fell in love with them. He told Charles he deeply regretted this, as he had a wife and daughter and didn't want to hurt them. "But," as he said to Charles, "here I am sitting opposite a girl in the commissary and I find myself saying to her, 'You eat your lettuce so pretty.' I'm in love and I can't help it."

After Charles finished *Ruggles of Red Gap,* he was loaned out to Twentieth Century-Fox for the part of police inspector Javert in *Les Miserables.* Victor Hugo's overpowering social conscience created a man, Javert, with letter-of-the-law mania, whose entire world is the pursuing of evil and the elimination of the guilty, embodied in the ex-prisoner Jean Valjean. But Javert in the end develops doubts and sees himself as guilty for trying to destroy Valjean. He kills himself because he cannot live with his own sin.

I give this preamble to hint at the parallel suffering that Charles went through as Inspector Javert. As an actor he probed his personal, innermost pain to bring Javert to the screen. At least Charles felt he'd achieved Victor Hugo's intent and, I would add, he gave one of those cleansing performances that brought him a little peace. In later years he was to do Victor Hugo's *The Hunchback of Notre Dame,* in which he took physical torture over and above what was needed—a sort of purging of his human weakness and general guilt. Not guilt for any piddling little act. Just guilt for an overall insufficiency of perfection in life and work.

Charles was busy working and I sailed back to England alone. I felt very much at home when I crossed the Atlantic on the *Champlain,* although the trip was the roughest I'd ever known. And it was a small ship. Not one passenger was to be seen and everything was strapped down. I ate with the French sailors and we managed somehow to understand each other. They called me their fiancée, pointing to the face of *Liberty* on a French postage stamp.

The seven-day trip took twelve days, and a few passengers were taken off the boat with broken ankles and so on. But during the trip I loved swinging round the ship and up and down staircases like a chimp. And being strapped in my bunk with an extra pillow on each side. You have hardly lived if you haven't seen waves so fierce and vast that the sky disappears until the ship rises again from the trough, and then down you go again. Thank goodness Charles was not on the *Champlain.* Later, during the war, it was destroyed by a German submarine. I felt it a personal loss.

I remember another solo trip, on the *Berengaria,* sailing from New York to Southampton. It was during Prohibition, and two acquaintances were aboard, fellows who were connected with a museum. I had brought a bottle of Scotch with me, and I used it to tempt them to talk. Like a sort of truth serum. Well, one of these fellows confided in me that he liked to wear a tiger-skin belt next to his skin—inside out, with the fur next to him. Facts like that make one feel blue-eyed and normal. I recalled the weirdness of Jimmy Agate's sister washing her knees before mixing socially with others.

On the *Berengaria,* Lady Castlerosse met Kitty Miller (Gilbert Miller's wife) head-on in the dining room of the ship, both wearing the same evening dress—a glittering, shimmering, swaying waterfall of silver diamante fringe. They stopped short and let out a sort of rattle, and with helms high they each steered a slightly different course. I think you could call this encounter a little disaster at sea.

Once more alone in London, I felt the restless annoyance of responsibility—Stapledown and Gordon Square had to be kept up diligently. I missed Charles very much because, having no one to consult, I felt like a lone watchdog, supervising incessant cleaning, plumbing, carpentering on the property, and keeping the people who looked after us feeling that they were appreciated. Charles, having been bred in the hotel business, was a tough taskmaster, though he never picked on me as the responsible person—but I was.

So when James Whale offered me a part in a film, I was glad to leave London for Hollywood. It was *The Bride of Frankenstein.* I only knew that the picture would be based on the book by Mary Wollstonecraft Shelley. Earlier, James Whale had made the first and very successful Frankenstein film, which made a star of Boris Karloff. And I was happy to be working with James, of course. I thought back on the Cave of Harmony days, when he was a wonderful tango dancer. And he always danced with Zinkheisen, a very beautiful and famous woman painter. James and she were engaged to be married, but at some point around the time when he was directing the play *Journey's End,* they parted. I don't think James Whale ever got over it. In Hollywood, James always had Zinkheisen's portrait at the end of his long dining room.

I suppose the quickest way you can shut me up nowadays is to ask me about *The Bride of Frankenstein.* To this day, nine out of ten photographs I get in the mail for autographing are of the Bride. I'm grateful for *The Bride of Frankenstein,* of course—it became a kind of trademark for me, in the same way that Captain Bligh and Henry the Eighth were for Charles. But such trademarks can cause typecasting and boomerang for some actors. Such actors work all the time, usually. Some like it. Some grumble.

There were *two* parts for me in *The Bride of Frankenstein.* In the opening scenes, I played Mary Wollstonecraft Shelley, dressed extremely elegantly, sweeter than sugar. I am delicately embroidering while sitting on a satin divan beside a crackling fire, as an electrical storm rages outside the window. My husband, Percy Bysshe Shelley, and his constant companion, Lord Byron, are arguing with me about the propriety of writing a gothic horror piece that is so sacrilegious—*Frankenstein.*

MARY SHELLEY (shuddering): "Lightning alarms me."

LORD BYRON (laughing): "Astonishing creature! You, my dear young lady, frightened of thunder?—when you have written a tale that froze my blood! How difficult to believe that that lovely brow conceived a monster created from the corpses of rifled graves!"

MARY SHELLEY: "And why shouldn't I write of monsters? My purpose was to write a moral lesson!"

In this prologue, Mary Shelley's dress was the most fairy-like creation that I have ever seen before or since in a film. It had a low neck, tiny puffed sleeves, and a bodice that continued in a long line to the floor and onto a train about seven feet long. The entire white net dress was embroidered with iridescent sequins—butterflies, stars, and moons. It took seventeen Mexican ladies twelve weeks to make it. The dress traveled around the country and appeared in the foyers of all the big openings of *The Bride of Frankenstein.*

It was James Whale's idea that, later in the film, Dr. Frankenstein's second creation, the strange and macabre female monster, should be played by the same actress. Quite a contrast to the sweet and dainty Mary Shelley. We shot the prologue first, and it took only two or three days. Then I worked another week or ten days as the Monster's Bride.

In March 1968, *Life* magazine published a essay on Mary Shelley and how she came to write *Frankenstein.* Samuel Rosenberg, its author, presented his thesis, thoroughly researched and sparked with his own wit. On the title page preceding Rosenberg's words, *Life* wrote:

THE HORRIBLE TRUTH ABOUT FRANKENSTEIN—What psychic forces drove Mary Shelley to write the most famous of all horror novels? What part did her husband play in the supernatural parlor games that produced *Frankenstein?* Did Mary have something in common with her creature?

I think James Whale felt that if this beautiful and innocent Mary Shelley could write such a horror story as *Frankenstein,* then somewhere she must have had a *fiend* within, dominating a part of her thoughts and her spirit—like ectoplasm flowing out of her to activate a monster. In this delicate little thing was an unexploded atom bomb. My playing both parts cemented that idea.

Charles had the definite theory that very, very sweet women were tough bitches underneath, and he'd often say in semifun, "Don't be frightened of Elsa if you find her too honest and she seems bitchy. She's really, you know, very nice inside."

Apart from the discomfort of the monster makeup and all the

hissing and screaming I had to do, I enjoyed working on the film. I admired Whale's directing and the waiting-for-something-to-happen atmosphere he was able to create around us. He and Jack Pierce, the makeup man, knew exactly what they wanted, so I didn't have to do many makeup tests. They had Queen Nefertiti in mind for the form and structure of the Bride's head.

I spent long hours in the makeup room. Jack Pierce, of course, was the creator of the first Frankenstein makeup, and so he was elevated even further in his own heaven when a Bride was to be born. He had his own *sanctum sanctorum,* and as you entered (you did not go in; you entered) *he* said good morning first. If I spoke first, he glared and slightly showed his upper teeth. He would be dressed in a full hospital doctor's operating outfit. At five in the morning, this made me dislike him intensely. Then, for three or four hours, the Lord would do his creative work, with never a word spoken as he built up the scars with spirit gum, pink putty, red paint, and so on. Nowadays, you can buy stick-on scars for a few cents at a joke shop. But Jack Pierce fancied himself The Maker of Monsters—meting out wrath and intolerance by the bucketful.

I've often been asked how my hair was made to stand on end. Well, from the top of my head they made four tiny, tight braids. On these was anchored a wired horsehair cage about five inches high. Then my own hair was brushed over this structure, and two white hair pieces—one from the right temple and the other from the left cheek-bone—were brushed onto the top.

I was bound in yards and yards of bandage most carefully wound by the studio nurse. I didn't particularly want to be seen by anyone. Nor did Boris Karloff. We weren't trying to be secretive. We just didn't want to be stared at. Poor Boris Karloff! When he ate in the studio commissary, he would cover up his head and shoulders with a piece of butter muslin, lifting it quickly like a curtain to pop some food into his mouth.

Sometimes members of the cast would have tea. After all, many English actors were in the cast. I may have been seen drinking tea, but I drank as little liquid as possible. It was too much of an ordeal to go to the bathroom—all those bandages—and having to be accompanied by my dresser!

A lot of opening shots were just of me lying on the table coming to life. The most magic moment was when one single bandaged finger . . . moved . . . very slightly. Another closeup that people seem to remember is the moment when some of my head bandages are peeled away and my eyes snap open. I am staring. And I had to just go right on staring. It had to be wide, unnatural, and with no blinks. They called

Cut! just before I blinked. My eyes were actually in pain, which must have only added to the look of horror I was supposed to show.

A word about the screams and that hissing sound I made to show my anger and terror when rebuffing my groom. Actually, I've always been fascinated by the sound that swans make. Regents Park in London has lots of them on the lake. Charles and I used to go and watch them very often. They're really very nasty creatures, always hissing at you. So I used the memory of that hiss. The sound men, in one or two cases, ran the hisses and screams backward to add to the strangeness. I spent so much time screaming that I lost my voice and I couldn't speak for days.

The publicity department at Universal had a field day selling *The Bride of Frankenstein.* Some of the shock lines used in the ads were:

> *Who will be the Bride of Frankenstein? Who will dare!*
>
> *Bolt your doors! Chain your windows! The monster is loose again and demands a bride!*
>
> *Torn between a desire to kill, maim, destroy—and mad with love for a creature like himself!*
>
> *Again he lives! And now he talks! He loves! He demands a mate! When he loved he was a fiend incarnate!*
>
> *A woman—could you call it that? . . .*

The review in *Variety* of *The Bride of Frankenstein* read:

> This tops all previous horror pictures in artistry and popular entertainment values . . The final action in the tower of doom is the most magnificent mechanical scene within recollection—awesome as a page from Genesis.

I got my own good notices, too. Carlos Clarens wrote in his *An Illustrated History of the Horror Film:*

> Elsa Lanchester in her white shroud and Nefertiti hairdo is a truly fantastic apparition . . . a delicate suggestion of both the wedding bed and the grave.

The Bride is one of the few films that has followed me all the time. It keeps popping up on television several times a year, especially at Halloween. Nowadays there seems to be a kind of underground cult around it—the face of the Bride is even featured in a New York disco.

I'm not unhappy that it happened. It's sometimes pleasant to have very young kids in markets or in the street recognize you as the Bride of Frankenstein. Because, changed as I have, obviously, I apparently haven't turned into a type that looks like everybody else. And I'm flattered that I'm recognizable in a part I played in the 1930s.

The poet Shelley had written that "poetry turns all things to loveliness; it exalts the beauty of that which is most beautiful, and it adds beauty to that which is most deformed." James Whale seemed to carry out this thought, giving his monsters spiritual beauty and pathos, over and above the horror. In discussing Whale in *An Illustrated History of the Horror Film,* author Carlos Clarens writes that Whale "met with some opposition from Universal when the Monster, trussed up and raised aloft on a cross by villagers, becomes a queer Christlike figure."

James Whale retired in 1941. Mostly he remained in his own private world, bitter yet dryly humorous, as always. As in his films, his choice of decor in his house was rather Italianate and a bit gothic.

In *Life* Magazine, Samuel Rosenberg observed that drownings ran throughout Mary Shelley's lifetime. Her husband's first wife, Harriet, having lost Percy to Mary, drowned herself in the Serpentine Lake in London's Hyde Park. Mary tried "to drown herself in a 'leap from the Putney Bridge into the Thames,' but the voluminous air-entrapping garments . . . kept her afloat . . ." Then "Shelley was drowned during a severe electrical storm while sailing in the Mediterranean." And then, in 1957, James Whale was found dead "under mysterious circumstances"—floating in his large pool at the foot of his hillside garden behind his Brentwood home.

During this visit to America, we were staying again at the Garden of Allah, this time in Nazimova's own original quarters—up one flight of tiled stairs and into the grandeur that was. A very large and high-ceiling living room and bedrooms with long crenelated windows remained here and there. And the bathroom—Charles and I thought it was a scream—large, with black tiles, even on the floor and ceiling. Hardly a home to go back to after days in a sewer for Charles, and being bandaged in a gothic structure during a thunderstorm for me. By almost freakish chance we both finished our films on the same day.

And all this time, from London Alexander Korda had been bombarding Charles with tempting telegrams and a positive kaleidoscope of ideas. One film Korda wanted to make was Rostand's *Cyrano de Bergerac,* and he had lined up the writer Leonard Woolf to do the screenplay. Charles was excited by the idea. Besides, we wanted to live in our flat in Gordon Square and our beautiful Stapledown. Bristling with plans, Korda got us onto the train to New York and ocean liner back to London. I still had not got my voice back from screaming and was taking codeine for the pain. Charles was sleeping all the time with an expression of virtuous relief—helped, I'm sure, by leaving Javert's heavy boots behind in Hollywood. Jobs well done.

We had a bit of an adventure on the Santa Fe train, just outside Raton, New Mexico. I was just leaving the dining car—Charles was still in the diner—when there was a terrific crash and a wrenching, and I slid on my feet all the way down the corridor and ruined a very good pair of shoes, stubbing the toes flat. Charles rushed out of the diner to see how I was, and I rushed back to the dining car to see how *he* was. We were both all right, but the engine driver was hurt. A few people got some bruises and strains, but it turned out to be a most miraculous day for us because, having got out of the train, we found that they couldn't send us on at once. The line was ripped up and another train couldn't be brought for six or seven hours.

It is a mountainous district, and they sent out a call for all foresters and miners to come down to put in a *shoofly line,* I think it's called. That's a line going around the wreck so they can bring in a new train. So we had hours in Raton and, naturally, Charles was recognized. We were taken into town, while all the other poor passengers were left standing in the cold or sitting upright in a carriage. Sometimes fame has benefits, however unfair to the nonfamous.

Raton is 6,000 feet up. In town we were taken to the newspaper office, where I was shown the print room and the typesetting. Then a little girl came in with daisies and a rose wrapped in green tissue paper to present to "Mrs. Laughton." We had arrived (or smashed) into Raton about two in the afternoon, and we got away about eleven that night. During that day, people showed us the Santa Fe Trail and told us about the views in the distance—those great caves where there are thousands of bats not thirty miles away in the hills, I forget what these caves are called. We just lived the life of a little town with crisp air and brilliant sunshine and such endearing little gifts and attentions. We really moved into that town, we were that town, we were Raton people for that day—not actors, not stage people.

When we got back to the train, the new train, the other end of the shoofly line was just being finished. It was night. All the men who had come down from the mountains had been working by torchlight. As we got aboard, they lined up on each side of the train with their torches and lanterns. Charles and I stood together on the platform between cars, looking down at them. It was so moving to pass through those lines of begrimed workmen sweating in the light of their torches, strong American mountainmen. As they waved back at us, we kept clapping and calling out, "Thank you, thank you very much!"

Before getting back on the train, I had picked up a piece of broken rail about nine inches long, which I put in my luggage. I could barely lift it, for even a small piece is pretty heavy. Charles was furious that I would carry this piece of rail with us, but I wanted that piece of the accident. The rail. To remember everything that happened that day. When we got to the Gotham Hotel in New York, the porter said that my luggage was very heavy.

I put the rail on the mantelpiece at the Gotham Hotel. Somebody came in and asked, "What the hell is that?" and I said, "That's a piece of the rail." He looked at it closely and then exclaimed, "Why, it's polarized!" *Polarized*—that means the metal has just given up. Oddly enough, in the typesetting room of the Raton paper, they had been changing some letters. When I asked why, the typesetter said, "Polarization. They might break at any time and clog the press." In other words, when metal sort of gives up the ghost, it magnetizes itself, or something like that. It made me wonder about airplanes, however—I mean, this polarization thing. Metal giving out when you're thirty thousand feet in the air is something else again.

Charles worried about the wreck getting into the newspapers, so the first thing that he did at Raton was cable his mother in England: BEEN IN A WRECK, BUT BOTH UNHURT, or words to that effect. Something reassuring. In fact, it turned out that the train wreck wasn't even reported in England, and Charles' mother didn't have any idea what the telegram was about.

Back home. Back home? I was beginning to wonder what that meant. We got back to London with all its hopes and pleasures: the Korda-Woolf *Cyrano* script; Gordon Square, now a gastronomic heaven with Nellie the cook; Stapledown, where some sloe gin that we had made was ready; and of course our friends, John Armstrong and Benita.

The *Cyrano* script was lagging pitifully with no immediate end in sight, and Irving Thalberg was calling to Charles to go back to Hollywood to make *Mutiny on the Bounty*. In the tug-of-war—with Korda at our end and Thalberg and MGM at the other end—MGM won out, and Charles once again left for Hollywood and *Mutiny*. Before he left London, when Charles knew that he was going to play Captain Bligh, he not only went to the Saville Row tailor who had the original measurements, bill, and receipt for Bligh's uniform but he also found the original hatmaker and saw to it that the naval tricorn hat was authentic also.

Before any production, Charles would play with his new props—putting on a hat and taking it off, hanging it up, putting it down, at home, in his dressing room, or in the producer's office. This was a time of fun for Charles and any audience around him. He could look at you from under a hat brim like nobody else could. He knew he could captivate and mesmerize.

His Henry the Eighth hat had been made for him by a Bond Street milliner called Miss Worth. It was a beautiful object, a copy from the Holbein painting. The hat that was made by a theatrical firm was cumbersome, with too many ostrich feathers, too many pearls that were too large—it weighed at least three times as much as Miss Worth's hat. Weight is one of the most important things to watch in making copies of costumes for theatrical use—the costumes must move well. The poor actors who lumber across a stage weighed down by about a ton of velvet and fur and lace and glass jewels have a tough time speaking trippingly on the tongue.

Edith Head, the famous Paramount costume designer, once said, "You always knew that when Charles Laughton had a fitting it would be at least a three-hour one. Put him in front of the three-way mirror and you were apt to get the whole play . . . Charles had the amazing ability to adjust his body to his clothes. You could put a suit on Charles and by his body control that suit could change amazingly before your eyes."

If Charles didn't like the suit and decided to change his shape when he was in it, woe be it to the fitter or the designer! I can do the same thing. Sometimes at Western Costume, when I was trying on an outfit, I would fold my arms, breathe deeply, and all the seams would split and I would say, "Oh, dear, I'm afraid this isn't going to be right at all."

So off Charles went, and I was left in London to pick up the hopes and pleasures on my own. It turned out well for me. *The Sunday Express* asked me if I would give our life story to the paper, a series to be called *Charles Laughton and I.* I was interviewed very skillfully for six days, and a court stenographer took it all down. I found I could certainly talk. The series ran for ten weeks at two thousand words an article. A big turning point, which led to the publication by Faber & Faber, in book form, of my life with Charles up to 1937.

Biddy and Shamus were still living at Leathwaite Road. The place still had a spinning wheel and a hand loom and all the same old friends, still cleaving together for better or worse. Biddy and Shamus had little security in their unplanned life. Not getting married was certainly a noble gesture, but they had no special freedom and no means of support, except for an allowance from Charles and me.

Charles needed his own kind of freedom and had a certain amount of it through the protection of our marriage. His security came through the plus that nature had given him—his art. Therefore, I enjoyed freedom, too. So in a way, we both had what we wanted.

In *Mutiny on the Bounty,* Charles had again taken on an unlovable character, while Clark Gable played the shining, handsome hero. Charles liked Gable very much. Gable once described a "siege of location blues" that Charles had. He discovered Charles out on a pier, sitting in the moonlight, just watching a fisherman in the bay. According to Gable, Charles muttered to himself, "I wish I were that man." The story is probably true, but I can't imagine Charles sitting and talking to himself. Charles mentioned to me once that, after some days of being tied up on Catalina, Gable took him to a brothel. I think that Charles was flattered. Still, *Mutiny on the Bounty* was a great strain on Charles. He had said to me, "When I have a part like Captain Bligh or Father Barrett, I hate the man's guts so much that I always have to stop myself overacting and be real. Parts like that make me physically sick!"

One day during the *Mutiny* filming, the phone rang in the London flat. It was *The Evening Standard*. They said, "The Bounty has sunk off Catalina, and they have no news as to the loss of life yet." Soon the rest of the press was on the phone. You can imagine the despair I felt while I waited for more news. Late that evening, *The Standard* called again and said that Charles was okay, the Bounty had not sunk. A raft had gone down and a member of the crew had drowned, but the paper didn't say who.

Nick Schenck, MGM's big boss in New York, ordered a private screening of *Mutiny*, to which he invited four hundred friends. Afterward, he gave his judgment: "Tell Thalberg it's the worst picture MGM ever made!" It won the Academy Award as the Best Picture of the year. In this 1935 Academy race, *three* of Charles' films—*Mutiny*, *Les Miserables*, and *Ruggles of Red Gap*—were nominated as Best Picture. Charles was nominated for Best Actor in *Mutiny* (along with Clark Gable and Franchot Tone), but Victor McLaglen won for his performance in *The Informer*. While Charles would never say so, he was very disappointed. But the New York Film Critics did choose Charles' Captain Bligh in *Mutiny on the Bounty* as the year's best performance by an actor.

Alexander Korda started to make a short film especially for me, *Miss Bracegirdle Does Her Duty*. He had a half-written script that promised to be a good adaptation of the original story by Stacy Aumonier. Korda actually started shooting a courtyard scene on a set already built for another film. The scene was the arrival of Miss Bracegirdle in France. Carpenters were busy building her hotel bedroom. But Charles was due back in a week, and I never had a studio call after that. The subject was never, never mentioned again. *Miss Bracegirdle Does Her Duty* could have been a brilliant comedy film—too bad, too bad. Korda was using this fake activity for me to ease Charles back to England. I was just a human shoehorn.

When Charles got back to London and Korda, the *Cyrano de Bergerac* script was still in sticky condition. Leonard Woolf had not nearly broken the back of his translation in verse or his adaptation for film. Charles found the verse impossible to speak, and Korda more or less agreed. So it became a long year of professional fury and frustration for Charles.

But our private life was good. We had a wonderful cook, Nellie Boxall, and her niece Grace, and a chauffeur. Boughs of trees from our Stapledown woodland were put in our great vases and pots at Gordon Square. We gave three rather good parties: one for Freddie and Florence March; one for Ruth Gordon and her opening at the Old Vic in *The Country Wife;* and a Christmas party, where we provided everyone with funny hats and wigs. It was Korda's fate that evening to be stuck with a blonde little Lord Fauntleroy wig that he wouldn't take off. And we replaced the mottos in the Christmas crackers, so he got the choicest of John Armstrong's bawdy lines:

> Christmas comes but once a year;
> Not like you and me I fear.

But the *Cyrano* script didn't come. Just Korda with his eternal charm, ideas, and promises.

During this endless wait, Charles and I went to Paris, where he made a most daring appearance at the Comédie Française as Sganarelle in Moliére's *Le Médecin Malgré Lui* ("The Doctor in Spite of Himself"). For total moral support and coaching, Charles took with him Madame Alice Gachet, who had been one of his teachers at the Royal Academy of Dramatic Art. Without her driving sponsorship, Charles always said that he would have had no career. Later, when she became very old, Charles helped support her.

I sat across from the Royal Box where I could see the Premier of France. The newspapers called Charles' appearance at the Comédie Française a spectacular success. The dramatic critic for *The Evening Standard* wrote:

> He has completely won the hearts of the company at the Comédie Française . . . by force of character and stern professional integrity.
>
> I talked with several members of Comédie Française last night. Never have I heard actors so generous. Every voice was lifted high in his praise . . .
>
> "Il est adorable" I heard on all sides . . . It is undoubtedly France's verdict on Charles Laughton, and he will bring pride to all men and women in England who still care for the delicate and imperishable art of the theatre.

The Evening News was even more enthusiastic. A banner headline read: BRILLIANT MR. CHARLES LAUGHTON MAKES A BIG HIT IN PARIS.

Gordon Square and Stapledown offered welcome serenity after our ecstatic Comédie Française experience. We had been very lucky to get Nellie Boxall, our cook, for on first sight she had been very uncertain that *she* would work for *us*. Former cook of Virginia Woolf, she had been sent to study cooking with the great Marcel Boulestin. Nellie had cooked for and knew the very heart of the Bloomsbury Group—writers, painters, poets. John Armstrong's wife, Benita, was closely involved with these groups, for she knew Clive Bell very well and was a superb comforter in times of complication—as when Vanessa Bell, Virginia Woolf's sister, left Clive Bell for painter Duncan Grant. The crisscrossing of lives seems endless. Anyway, Nellie, who was so loath to work for us, took one look at our wooden salt and pepper grinders, and in her raised cockney voice said, "Oww—just like the *click!*" She took the job.

Nellie's "click," which was the Bloomsbury Group, has since then come to define an important historical literary period. Without knowing it, I had moved on its outer edges, or perhaps I was part of the clique, through the 1917 Club, the Cave of Harmony, and now our location in Gordon Square. The air around the Bloomsbury Group was undoubtedly rarefied, and now, in retrospect, I visualize them as communicating with each other under a misty cloud that held them in a gentle embrace. God knows what games of musical chairs were played, and what fights raged in the nooks and crannies and bedrooms of these intellectual Beautiful People. Biographies and autobiographies have cemented the Bloomsbury Group into a unit, although those books always read like dream sequences to me. My name often comes up, and it seems a great thing to have been born when I was and to have tasted at this feast without knowing it. I wish now that I had tried harder. When I should have joined in conversations, I was . . . well . . . nervous. Once, I remember, Francis Meynell asked me out to dinner to the Cafe Royale, and I went almost trembling with anxiety. Meynell was very good-looking and I seemed like a ready and suitable companion. But we found nothing to talk about at all, and even an attempt to exchange flirtatious looks turned to pure stone. I think we both hoped for a good little friendship that could turn into a mild passion, but of course, in this case, that was putting the cart before the horse. Passion first and intellectual contact later was the required style. Perhaps seduction was in his mind, but who was to seduce whom I didn't know and never will.

Looking back on my first meeting with Alexander Korda I see now that I should have been a mind reader. I still had not learned the ways of the wicked world. No wonder the thirties were sometimes painful, for Charles and I wanted to be together and the only way seemed to be acting in the same picture. Korda fought quite hard *not* to help us and, indeed, the situation activated his fairly open criticism of me. So when Charles and Korda were together planning *Rembrandt,* I could only wonder what they said about me. Probably Korda said, Okay, she can play Hendrickje Stoffels—after all, she doesn't come on until the second half. And, also, Korda was tempting Charles because he wanted him for another picture, *I Claudius.* Yes, I felt a bit persecuted.

It was quite obvious that when I did a part in an Alexander Korda film, I had damn well better be good. The same applied later to Erich Pommer (of *The Beachcomber*) and a few other Laughton-grabbers. *Life* magazine went so far as to say, "Actor Laughton seems not to like American producers because . . . they want his wife, Elsa Lanchester, to play horror roles." Thus, "If Charles works, Elsa must be used, too," seemed to be more than a rumor, so that in a way, I was losing ground professionally. After my rather glamorous *Riverside Nights* years, I looked in the mirror a lot and felt time was passing me by.

Around this time Charles went to Paris with Korda to get away from everything and discuss *Rembrandt.* I suppose they had a good time because they had many a drink with Winston Churchill. Charles loathed Churchill as an overpowering vulgarian and an ass, but time heeled that a little. Alone in London, I planned a trip with John Armstrong and Benita to see Charles' mother and brothers in Scarborough. The journey was inspired by the fact that John was painting panels for the hotel dining room, and brother Tom wanted a conference. Tom admired John Armstrong and had bought many of his paintings.

We set out in our chauffeured car and were bowling along the highway—John was dozing as Benita and I played chess in the back of the car—when screaming wheels and a crash threw me from the backseat onto the steering wheel. Next thing, I was lying on a damp green grassy bank at the side of the road, and Benita was saying, "Oh, ducky, it would be the film star!"

A passing jalopy driven by a farmer took us into York and the hospital. I was bleeding like a pig from a deep cut through my left eyebrow. I would not let the York Hospital doctors sew me up. A few years before, a facial surgeon—who was a friend and had been knighted for his pioneering work rebuilding faces during the first World War—had said to me, "If you're ever in any accident, send for me. A wound should not be closed up immediately, so it can bleed itself clean. Don't let anyone else touch you."

So the York doctors just put a strap on the cut. They were furious. John located my doctor friend, who was playing golf on the Isle of Wight, and also informed Charles in France. Then John, Benita, and I caught a milk train from York to London. It was naturally a very slow train, and we sat swilling straight brandy. When we reached London it was just getting light. I had a crying bout from shock. Benita kept saying, "Oh, ducky, it would be the film star! Why not me?" Well, we all converged on the London Clinic—Charles, Korda, Benita and John, and my doctor friend.

So it became a long race between my scar and Hendrickje Stoffels. In the end, with a little extra help from makeup, I made it. To this day my left eyebrow is short of hair at one end, and when I wake up in the morning I stagger to the bathroom where an eyebrow pencil is at the ready and draw in the missing inch. Only an earthquake would change this habit—no, not even an earthquake.

Gertrude Lawrence played the second woman in Rembrandt's life, his housekeeper and presumed mistress Geertke Dirx. On the set she was very flip all the time, telling funny stories and keeping everyone entertained. Everyone? Charles didn't want to hear her stories during work. He was trying to do something great, like the Song of David speech ("The Lord is my Shepherd . . ."), which he made deeply moving, new, and fresh. He rehearsed the speech over and over again, with Gertrude Lawrence telling stories—making everyone, including Korda, shriek with laughter:

An English officer picked up a London tart. At her flat, he said, "I should know your name, young lady."

146

And she said, "I won't tell you!"
"Oh, come on, tell me."
"I'll give you three guesses."
He said, "Well, give me a hint."
"Well, it's a flower."
"Rose?"
"No."
"Daisy?"
"No."
"Iris?"
"No! I'll give you another hint: It's on a wall."
"Oh, shit!"
"No! *Ivy.*"

It was very painful for Charles. He had a screen put around the set to keep away the chattering and flittering of her voice. But Korda hadn't much respect for needed peace and quiet. He preferred to be on the other side of the screen with Gertrude Lawrence most of the time, except when the camera was rolling or near rolling.

In one of my first scenes with Charles, I had to sit for Rembrandt as the kitchenmaid Hendrickje Stoffels, the third woman in Rembrandt's life. We had the screen round us. I remember I heard someone giggling on the other side of the screen, and it disturbed me. Here I was doing this closeup in a scene where two people are about to fall in love, and I felt that I was being laughed at. My own insecurity.

Eventually I got to like the privacy very much. Unless you get a disciplined director, say, like Billy Wilder, it is rarely quiet on a set. A professional director is usually a splendid martinet. He insists on silence. And there is silence. Nobody talks or tells stories. It's like a royal condition.

Gertrude Lawrence despised films so much that she wouldn't even attempt to learn the words. Her costume had large white cuffs, so she'd write her part on these cuffs or on the back of a chair. If you went to a chair, you'd often find a bit of paper where she had written her lines, hanging down the back. But on the stage she was a lovely actress and a brilliant performer in musicals. She could kick high, and she didn't care if her voice was a little out of tune—she had a compelling charm.

Marlene Dietrich was filming at the Denham studio at the same time as we were making *Rembrandt.* Miss Dietrich once told a reporter that she would rather act in a love scene with Charles than with any other actor in the world. Her quote made small headlines in the evening papers. When Charles read the statement in print he was deeply flattered. He actually cheered and did a little jig. And I must say, it was a kind of indirect compliment for me. After meeting her in a Denham corridor one morning, Charles told me that in private life she had the art of casually putting on a very little makeup that looked slightly smeared, as if she had just got out of bed after a night of it. Obviously, these two should have got together somehow.

Korda and Charles thought about showing many of Rembrandt's masterpieces on the screen, but they realized that the dramatic interest of the story lay in the creative needs that drove Rembrandt to paint. The actual masterpieces, if shown, would only be a reminder to audiences that Charles was not really a painter. So the camera showed Charles painting at the easel, but never the actual brush on the canvas. The lighting by cameraman Georges Périnal was in itself inspiring. *The New Republic* praised Périnal for "finding beauty all along the way in a bridge, a kitchen corner, an angled roof, windows."

At one point in the story, a song was needed for Hendrickje to sing, a simple theme suggesting remembrance of flat land and windmills. No such folk song could be found, so I wrote one for myself. Charles suggested this not be made public. After all, I was playing the part of a simple country girl and seeming clever might detract from my performance. Though technically I scarcely know how to write music, I had a drink of gin and something, then sat down and wrote the words and music in less than an hour, picking out the tune with one finger on the piano:

> Green hills . . .
> Red clover . . .
> Distant sky . . .
> Far sea . . . far—sea.
>
> Yellow corn . . .
> Bright sand . . .
> Dark earth . . .
> Good land . . . good—land.

Korda liked it, and my melody was woven into the score. It became "Hendrickje's Theme," and I still draw a tiny royalty from it. I am grateful to Muir Matheson, who directed the full score, for letting my contribution be registered with ASCAP.

When Charles and I were working together, although we played other people, we had to be as natural and relaxed as ourselves. Quite ordinary, everyday things in our life became colored by the characters we were playing. I don't think that there is a single interviewer who has not asked, "And Mrs. Laughton, does Mr. Laughton bring his characters home with him at night?" Well, I suppose our personal relation-ship did change during some of Charles' more colorful parts. I remem-ber that when Charles was acting in *The Barretts of Wimpole Street*, several times he came home with that dominating father still in his system. Rather like a dog bringing a bone into the house. He was very jolly during *Ruggles of Red Gap*. The dog brought in cotton candy.

In *Rembrandt* our private relationship helped our acting relation-ship, and vice versa. But that sort of thing can become dangerous. It was a danger Charles and I had both felt before, never so strongly as during *Rembrandt*—but this time it worked to the good. Revealing myself as Hendrickje was not too great a problem for me, but Charles had a much more difficult job in showing what a creative genius is.

He had gone to Holland several times before *Rembrandt* started shooting. As usual, he haunted and hunted every museum where there were paintings by Rembrandt. He stayed at The Hague and visited many places where Rembrandt had been. And he always brought something back with him. The first time—it must have been spring—he brought back loads of tulips crisply fresh with brilliant enamellike colors. Some were just tulip heads that the Dutch growers cut off to make the bulbs flourish. Of course, we never see this enameled bril-liance in the tulips that we buy, even from Dutch bulbs. All over the world nature likes to stay home when it comes to color.

I went with Charles on one of these trips to the Hague, and we traveled on one of those lovely round, tubby overnight boats. At break-fast you got various kinds of bread and the usual things, but on the tray was a jigger of Hollands—that's their make of gin. (Among London's poorer people, hot Hollands is thought to ease cramps in women or even achieve an abortion.) On this trip my husband the pack rat bought a few Dutch plates and a birdcage Delft plaque. It's looking at me now this minute. We also got a couple of embroidered blouses, and then, back on the tubby overnight boat to England. A three-day holiday.

Rembrandt opened in Holland at the Hague City Theatre, and we were all there—more or less the same group as in Paris for the *Henry VIII* opening. The streets from our hotel to the theatre were lined with cheering people. A gentle snow was falling, the setting sun sent up a few Rembrandt-like beams. Charles was presented with a wreath so large he couldn't lift it. I received a huge bouquet of pink roses ad-dressed to "Gertrude Lawrence," and the Burgomaster, in his welcom-ing speech, addressed me as "Mrs. Korda."

One speech from *Rembrandt* has remained famous all these years. It is a speech that Rembrandt makes about women, a memory of his first wife, Saskia. There have been literally thousands of requests for a copy of this piece. Charles read it to wounded soldiers in hospitals, and later he included it in his reading tours. The demand for it seems to be insatiable. It goes like this:

> There was a man in the land of Ouse and the Lord gave him all that the human heart could desire—but beyond all this, this man was in love with his wife. He had a vision once.
>
> A creature—half child, half woman, half angel, half lover—crossed his path and of a sudden he knew that when one woman gives herself to you, you possess all women. Women of every age and race and kind. And more than that—the moon, the stars, all miracles and legends are yours. The brown-skinned girls who inflame your senses with their play. The cool yellow-haired women who entice and escape you. The gentle ones who serve you, the slender ones who torment you, the mothers who bore and suckled you.
>
> All women whom God created out of the teeming fullness of the earth are yours in the love of one woman. Throw a purple garment lightly over her shoulders and she becomes a Queen of Sheba. Lay your tousled head blindly upon her breast and she is a Delilah waiting to enthrall you. Take her garments from her, strip the last veil from her body, and she is a chaste Susannah covering her nakedness with fluttering hands. Gaze upon her as you would gaze upon a thousand strange women but never call her yours—for her secrets are inexhaustible. Call her by one name only—I call her Saskia.

Carl Zuckmayer wrote the speech, and he obviously warmed the hearts of a lot of married couples.

I wish that film acting didn't involve being exhibited to the public in person. I know it has to be done to promote the picture and many actors love it. I've said it before, and I say it again, though it may sound uncivil of me—I would rather be home peeling potatoes.

Peter Pan is a part that many actresses want to play. Over the years it has come to represent a stamp of success and approval, almost like being given a medal. Charles and I were first approached by the Daniel Mayer Company about playing Captain Hook and Peter in 1935. But Korda said no, we were soon starting a film. Then in 1936 we were asked again. But James Barrie always had the final word on casting, and he wrote to us saying we weren't suitable for the parts—he didn't want us to play them.

So off we went to Barrie's flat in Adelphi Terrace, and with fear and trembling climbed the stairs. We were shown into the great man's study. Barrie at once said, "I'm afraid you will terrify the children, Mr. Laughton, and Hook must never do that." I suppose that Sir James had visions of Charles as Captain Bligh and Nero. Charles said as gently as possible that he would not. Barrie had never seen me perform and he studied me carefully. Fortunately, a few minutes after we'd been there, the German actress, Elizabeth Bergner, rang up Barrie. He asked her what she thought, and she told Barrie that Charles and I would be wonderful in the parts and that it would be a great mistake not to let us do it. So Barrie gave us permission. At that time, Charles and I had never met Miss Bergner, but I've always been grateful to her.

I have never thought of *Peter Pan* as being a children's play. If you read the preface and full stage directions of the original play very carefully, you will suspect that Sir James Barrie had a twinkle in his eye as he was writing. I'm really not sure whether Sir James liked or disliked children. The more I rehearsed my part, the more I saw that Peter was like a little general—ordering the children about and being very officious. In other words, enjoying power. At one of the rehearsals James Barrie sat in front, and he insisted that I wear the conventional costume. I wanted to look more original, less elfin, but Barrie was adamant. No changes. And he was right. But he did say that he liked me in the part.

In our production of *Peter Pan* we added a few flights to the traditional stage business. The flying presented no problems. Having been a dancer, I introduced some movements in the air that suggested flight, which I had also used as Ariel in *The Tempest*—but without wires.

Charles always wanted to do Captain Hook again. He felt he had been too gentle as Hook—not fearful enough—in order to please Barrie. And I would have liked to play Peter again, but Hitler was on the rise and a little dictator (as I played him) was unwelcome. Tyrone Guthrie, in his *A Life in the Theatre,* wrote:

> An interesting revival of the piece was given in London in the thirties. Charles Laughton played Captain Hook; his wife, a glittering and satiric sprite called Elsa Lanchester, played Peter. Hook, a heavyweight Don Quixote, became the hero of the evening. It was when Peter Pan came on that little children hid their faces in their mothers' skirts and strong men shook with fear.

We also added the Lagoon Scene, its first performance in years. This made it a three-and-a-half-hour show. The Lagoon Scene has a famous line. When Peter appears doomed to drown, he says full out to the

audience of little children: "To die will be an awfully big adventure."
Brave little soldier. A few years ago, an article appeared in *The New York Times* written by Edmund Fuller, which said, "On a recent talk show, Elsa Lanchester tossed off to David Frost the comment that 'Peter Pan is a dominating little snit who orders people around.' Back in the era of Maude Adams that would have carried the shock of a desecration of the flag . . . But Miss Lanchester's casual quip has a shrewd truth to it. Also, it was Walter Kerr, we think, who succinctly said of *The Sound of Music* that it 'is for people who find James M. Barrie a little on the brutal side.' "

I think present-day interpretations of *Peter Pan* are really a long way from Barrie's conception. People seize on the sentiment and distort the play so that it comes out treacle—all those songs and what not. The original music was superb and haunting. And the actresses who play Peter nowadays don't really fly any more. They simply swing on the wire like dolls on a string.

Sir James Barrie died during the year following our Christmas production. I was, therefore, the last Peter Pan ever chosen by him. I always felt fortunate.

Every *Peter Pan* has to tour the English provinces and Scotland for three months after its Christmas month at the Palladium. A second company tours over the holidays at the same time. *That* company has another Peter Pan and Wendy, so when the London Peter joined the tour, I took over Peter Pan, while *that* tour's Peter became Wendy. Then the touring Wendy became one of the lost children—the confusion reminds me of one of James Barrie's more whimsical speeches from the play, when Wendy says, "The mauve fairies are boys and the white ones are girls, and there are some colors who don't know what they are."

Charles did not tour with *Peter Pan* because *I Claudius* was imminent.

In every town on the tour, Larry Adler, the harmonica virtuoso, was playing simultaneously at the vaudeville houses. We often met for food after the show, with others from our company—including our good stage manager who persuaded me to enjoy seeing football games. In spite of my getting two cracked ribs from an accidental jerk on my flying wire, I hardly noticed the pain, and time flew (ha ha) by.

Finishing in Liverpool at the same time, Larry and I traveled back to London on the same train first thing on Sunday morning. In the next carriage to us—the train was nearly empty—we had the pleasure of having Neville Chamberlain, the "peace in our time" boy, for our neighbor. Larry played appropriate and inappropriate tunes as loudly as possible during the whole trip. On the station platform, looking at

Chamberlain, we didn't seem to have made any impression on him. Charles met us on the platform, and we felt let down because we thought that Chamberlain might have said thank you for the music, but he just stalked away with his newspaper under his arm and his famous umbrella.

I had thought Charles and Larry would get on well together, but they were poles apart politically. At least, Charles just didn't have any political pole to be apart from, and he was very bored by being button-holed by opinionated people. Nevertheless, we often had dinner with Larry and his future wife, Eileen. The two of them came to Stapledown several times and, even to Charles, it was irresistible to walk through the woods with Larry playing his harmonica all the way.

I Claudius was looming nearer and nearer and Charles was beginning his usual preliminary birth pangs—not sleeping at night, expounding to Korda all day. Charles was always a controversial actor, and slowly, very slowly, it became clear that Korda would not face directing him. He began to suggest persuasively, "Maybe . . . someone else? Eh, Charles? . . . maybe Joe—good, dear, brilliant Joe? . . . Josef von Sternberg? . . . "

So Mr. Josef von Sternberg arrived, expecting a grand reception —which Korda gave him—and insisting all the time that it was *von* Sternberg and not Sternberg. Charles put up a good front and an even better front when von Sternberg got influenza and went to hospital. Charles took him grapes, and it's said that they spent a happy after-noon together vowing to make a great film, happily plotting to show the world the fall of the Roman Empire and point up the comparison with the current unsettled times. The Prince of Wales had abdicated, Chamberlain and his White Paper had turned out to be just that—a scrap of paper—and above all there was the growing power of Hitler.

Finally von Sternberg rose from his hospital bed like the phoenix. The wedding over between him and Charles, the hopeful honeymoon began. Soon, von Sternberg's light wit turned to humorlessness, and he arrived for the first day's work in riding boots and jacket and a sort of wide Eastern head binder. It became quite clear that von Sternberg the director did not like actors—as many directors do not, apparently —unless the actors were totally subservient to him. (For example, René Clair, if he wanted a taxi driver, would use a real one rather than an actor.) A famous "women's director" with Marlene Dietrich, now in his past, he must been feeling his hypnotic powers failing. But he was a vain man, and he still persisted with the tenets of his trade: "I am, therefore I am; you are under my direction, do what I tell you and it will be right."

At first, Charles came home every night not believing that this change was possible. Soon he grew full of venom, feeling that he was going to be destroyed. Sometimes he actually wept, tears trickling through his fingers as he covered his face. He was as innocent as a child with regard to his own achievement, never knowing what was great, always shuddering at how bad he could be, always setting off bravely for the impossible mountain as each new project came up—then backing away from it with fear once the climb began.

Korda had told von Sternberg from the outset that he could no longer handle Charles the actor, and as a producer Korda became helpless to pacify these two colorful antagonists. Charles felt more and more martyred and set out for the studio every day as if he had been called to the rack.

Merle Oberon was to play Messalina. She was patient and, I believe, held Charles' hand to comfort him. She was in a difficult position because Korda was in love with her, but his divorce had not yet gone through. (His wife, Maria, had made scenes in public and is said to have once stubbed out Korda's cigar on his face.) Korda and Merle saw *I Claudius* as a vehicle for her. Maybe it would have finished up as *I Messalina*. For charm, persuasiveness, and duplicity Korda was without peer.

Then the Great Producer in the sky put a finger in the pie. Going home in her chauffeured limousine, Merle woke up in hospital with a concussion and bad facial cuts. Lloyds of London, who insured the film, and the Bank of England, who put up the money, wanted to replace her, but Korda, being in love with her, refused point-blank to have anyone else in the part. I even heard that when one of the backers of the film said, "Well, why can't Elsa Lanchester play Messalina? It's a shame to scrap the film," Alexander Korda replied, "I would not have her play the part for the world. She looks like a horse." (Probably a reference to my role as Anne of Cleves, who was known as "The Mare of Flanders.")

The accident put an end to the agonizing project, which was a relief for everyone. After his many weeks of suffering, Charles came home that evening with no regrets and enjoyed the first passing flash of ecstasy for a time.

Charles and I sign autographs
in Raton, New Mexico

We inspect the train wreck
in Raton, New Mexico

Sketch of the two of us, 1937

The outdoor life:
Charles picking flowers;
I am climbing trees

Charles at Idyllwild

Bertold Brecht and Charles
in our garden at
Pacific Palisades,
late 1940s

I entertained some of
Charles' students at
Palos Verdes (Charles is
hosing in the
background.)

Charles as Galileo

**Rehearsing with
Ray Henderson**

**Costume sketch and photo
from "When a Lady Has a Piazza"**

Costume sketch for
Elsa Lanchester, Herself

Costume sketch and photo from "The Yasmak Song" (photo: Ernest A. Bachrach)

The Turnabout Theater cast (from top to bottom): Forman Brown, Elsa, Harry Burnett, Frances Osborne, Lotte Gosler, and Dorothy Neumann

Opposite page: "When A Lady Has A Piazza" (Forman Brown) was my trade mark if ever I had one. This is the dress. The lace was left to me in a will. Wear and tear was such that I had to have it copied three times, but the lace was much coarser in these others.

The "gown" was made of cream Taffeta. The lace was worked with small mauve ribbon baskets filled with midget pink roses (photo: John Alfred Piver).

Charles, Norman Corwin, and I appear on Norman's "The Pursuit of Happiness" radio show

Charles and I on "The Pursuit of Happiness" radio show, New York
(photo: Frank Bresee)

elsa **Lanchester**
HERSELF
WITH **RAY HENDERSON** AT THE PIANO

A caricature by Al Hirschfeld
for my show

Anne Baxter, Tyrone Power, and Raymond Massey rehearsing
John Brown's Body.

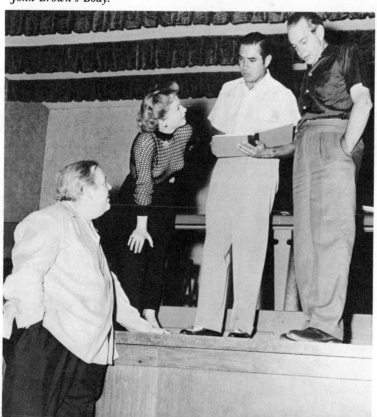

Scenes from three of my films
(top to bottom)
Ladies in Retirement,
Witness for the Prosecution,
and *Northwest Outpost*

WP-639

ith Charles in *The Party* (*The Sunday Times*, London)

Paths cross—I was touring, Adlai Stevenson was campaigning, 1951

LAUGHTONS BECOME CITIZENS

We celebrate becoming citizens, April 28, 1950
(*Los Angeles Daily News*)

In 1936 Erich Pommer came to England to get away from Nazi Germany. Although I do not know his actual reasons and emotions at that time, I am sure he never expected to go back, for he brought his son John and his wife Gertrude with him. They appeared to be prosperous. Pommer's original connection in England seems to have been with John Maxwell of ABP (Associated British Pictures). Pommer knew that Charles was about to be associated with Irving Thalberg at MGM and he, of course, knew of the tie-up with Korda and the current production, *I Claudius*. But when Thalberg died and then *Claudius* became a fiasco, Pommer became the link between Maxwell, the business promoter, and Charles the actor. Everything was ripe for the formation of the new trio. Their company was called The Mayflower Pictures Corporation.

Charles began going to the office every day. He had never felt he could or should try that uncomfortable seat on the other side of the desk. But now, off he went in suit and tie. Pommer had come from Germany as the head of UFA. He had vast credits to his name, among them *The Cabinet of Dr. Caligari*, *Metropolis* and, later, *The Blue Angel*, which had given birth to the careers of Emil Jannings and Dietrich—to list them all would be overrepeating known film history. Some reached splendor in Hollywood, some stayed behind when Pommer came to England to go on building his distinguished career.

The first film they were to make was *The Vessel of Wrath* by Somerset Maugham, adapted for the screen by Bartlett Cormack. It was a brilliant vehicle for Charles and me, showing two sides of two people. Charles played a drunken bum and I a frigid, narrow-minded spinster. Each tries to reform the other and they become deeply close. In the end, he confesses that his father was a clergyman and she confesses that her father was an alcoholic. All this in the middle of a savage South Sea island. The missionary and the bum. In America, the film was called *The Beachcomber.*

We started shooting in the south of France in September 1937, and the film opened in London March 4, 1938, at the Marble Arch Theatre. In the meantime, a new production, *St. Martin's Lane,* with a script by Clemence Dane, was being rushed ahead. It would star Charles and Vivien Leigh. My book, *Charles Laughton and I,* came out in 1937 and would be released in America in December 1938. Charles found time to promote *The Beachcomber* for about one week before filming began on *St. Martin's Lane.* So he and I took off from the south to the north of England, and on to Scotland.

It was fall. We made our first shy and nervous stage appearance at Brighton, on the stage of a large movie theatre. I say "shy," but perhaps that was an act. I can say that our approach was "tentative." After all, the film was Charles' own company's first effort. Let's say our manner was modest. We were presented by the mayor himself. He and some local town councillors met us backstage. There were a lot of hands to be shaken, of course, and the mayor said that mine was cold. I suppose it was fear that made me too flip. I made a few corny jokes about the big brass chain that the mayor wore round his neck—"I see you're weighed down by your office!" I don't remember whether he laughed or not. Charles called him "Your Honor," which at the time made me squirm. I just thought how pleased Charles' mother would be—and how my mother Biddy would not be.

The next day, we started off for Birmingham, Manchester, Liverpool, Glasgow, and Edinburgh. During this short personal appearance tour we planned to spend a day or two in the Lake District between York and Liverpool, and a day or two in Scotland round the lochs. We spent one day on Loch Katrine, chugging round on a lovely little tubby steamer. The day was very beautiful with very clear, ominous gray clouds, yet the sun shone through in beams and shafts—it seemed, on us—and in patches on the green land round the loch. A hundred tiny, tumbling rivulets emptied into the water, jumping through ferns and grasses. We were enchanted and happy.

As we went north by car and train, we wondered why so many soldiers were going south—very young boys, territorials, in badly fitting uniforms. Charles was almost oblivious to the political situation. Neville Chamberlain was Prime Minister at this time, and England constantly feared invasion by Hitler's Germany. War seemed inevitable. We picked up a newspaper—or perhaps we listened to the radio—in a little hotel, a country pub with rooms, about twenty miles outside Glasgow. The news was ominous.

Our sitting room was small and triangular. It had old peacock-blue paper on the walls and a chocolate-colored dado, with painfully uncomfortable Victorian furniture, a worn Axminster rug, and a table with a moss-green chenille cloth on it. We had a fairly good English pub dinner: boiled mutton, potatoes, and sprouts, reaching to the very edge of the plate. As we crouched near the gas fire, realizing that war was expected, we wondered if we should go back to London. However, we decided to stick to our schedule—there were only three more days to go—and finish with a fair in Edinburgh and one more lovely drive to Glamis Castle.

We arrived in great style at the fair. We wanted to make the most of the publicity, and what fair also doesn't want to make the most of anything. We were transferred into an open barouche—I suppose a Rolls-Royce convertible limousine, probably left over from some coronation or jubilee of some sort. In it we drove through cheering crowds that were standing, sitting, and perching in banks on our left and right. Since they strained to see us, we sat up on the back of the car with our feet resting on the rear seat. The autumn sun was low in the sky, but not setting yet. The Scottish mists were rising and the light was pinkish-yellow. I kept thinking to myself, "What am I doing here, anyway, sitting up here and waving to all these cheering people? Where did I come from?" I never did ask Charles what he thought of it all.

In the automobile on the drive to Glamis, we had the radio on again. The crisis. The King (George VI) was about to speak to the people of Great Britain. We should keep calm, obey instructions, learn to use gas masks, and with the help of God have courage to face the enemy and defend the country—and to win. This speech was to be made in Liverpool, I believe, but the King, who always had a weak chest, developed laryngitis, and became quite ill. So a last-minute emergency change was made, and Queen Elizabeth (Elizabeth the Second's mother) made the speech instead.

Queen Elizabeth was a cheerful but shy woman who had made many personal appearances for charities but had never touched politics or influenced people's opinions. Certainly she had never made a public speech of such gigantic import. The country was tremulous with hopes and wishes for her brave effort. Could she touch the people— as was necessary? She did. I have never heard a voice, let alone a royal voice, ring out in such a bell-like, truth-searching fashion. It was a moment to weep—for many reasons.

The Scottish countryside never looked lovelier. In its great forests and blue mists, everything looked so deep and so distant. A nostalgic and now sorrowful autumn. It was about four o'clock and we were going now to Glamis Castle for tea. Glamis Castle is where the Queen was born and where King George fell in love with her, and where her father, the Earl of Strathmore, was still living. We were going to have tea with Lady Rose, the Queen's sister.

Our chauffeur retired as we rang—or, rather, pulled at—the great front doorbell. Whoever answered the door dissolved into the rather high, dark hallway of the castle, and stepping into the light, Lady Rose came to meet us—quite surrounded by her teenage children and their friends, about five or six of them. They all wanted to meet Captain Bligh.

We said to Lady Rose that we'd been deeply moved by the Queen's speech. Lady Rose said, "Yes, she was quite splendid, wasn't she?" We asked if perhaps we should go—the impact of the speech and all, the pressures—but she waved it all aside. "No, no. We'll have tea," she said. And by then one of the boys was pulling Charles by the arm, saying, "You've got to see the place where Duncan was murdered! You can actually see the blood on the floor."

After going round the many halls and rooms of the castle with the children telling us blow-by-blow historical and bloodcurdling tales, we finished up in a large, cheerful drawing room. A huge blazing fire, an enormous round table set with a silver tea service, and beautiful china. There was a great feeling of comfortable, velvet warmth in the air. A smell of buttered crumpets, fruitcake, and cucumber sandwiches. Another table was set up for the noisy young people through an archway that led to a sort of anteroom. Equally warm and lively. After we'd started tea, the Earl of Strathmore came in. No affected apologies, he just came booming in, absolutely covered in sawdust. He sat down and began expounding on the importance of afforestation. He was a great tall tree of a man who seemed about eighty in his wisdom, and yet a boy in his excitement. Then he left quite abruptly—perhaps to saw off another branch before the sun left the forest. He left a trail of sawdust on the carpet.

That night we traveled to London by train and were lucky even to get seats. All classes of carriage were full of territorials. The train kept stopping and picking up more and more boys. When we got to our flat in London, it was just getting light, and we had breakfast. John and Benita were there to meet us with the latest news, and to hold a conclave to discuss the plans for all of us, together or apart.

First of all, we went to get our gas masks—everyone having been instructed to do this by newspaper and radio. We went to our local distribution center and waited in line for some hours to get them. Charles and John Armstrong, having been in the First World War, were the experts. They decided that Benita and I should go down to our place in Stapledown, twenty-eight miles away from London, and volunteer to learn about poison gases and firefighting. We were to join the local village war-instruction unit with the idea of passing on the knowledge to farming families in more outlying districts.

That evening we all took off from London by car, and the next night Benita and I walked two miles in the dark to our first lesson in civilian defense and gas warfare. Charles and John stayed back at the cottage and drank. This went on for some time. The lady-colonel-instructor said to the class, "First, we'll have a crowd of you, like tonight"—about thirty people—"then there will be twenty, then ten. Please determine now, each one of you, to continue this course." She was a squat, masculine lady, with a wart on her chin and some odd hairs whirling off her face; and her golden epaulets, with fringe, glittered in the miserable bare-bulb light of the school hall. For a while, Benita and I went our rounds, showing frightened country folk how to use a gas mask—and Charles and John didn't do anything much. Charles, of course, was in touch with Erich Pommer about their next movie, but no business was being done at that time.

Then Prime Minister Chamberlain went to Berlin and returned in triumph with his umbrella in one hand and the White Paper in the other. London went mad with relief, and everything started up again.

Some time later, at a party given by the publishers Faber & Faber (where, incidentally, I met John Heywood, a writer-invalid, and his dear companion, T. S. Eliot), I found myself talking to a handsome young woman. She was introduced as, I believe, Lady or the Honorable Miss Bowes-Lyon—the maiden name of the family that we had met at Glamis Castle. I realized that this was Lady Rose's daughter, one of the teenagers dashing round us on the tour of the castle. I recalled to her how her mother had behaved so incredibly well, and how beautifully poised she had been on the sad afternoon of the Queen's speech. I told her that I would have expected her to show some emotion, or at least to have appeared only at tea—we would have understood. The girl looked hard at me and said, "Mother had been crying, but she was all right for your visit, of course."

Christmas, 1938, I took off alone for New York and Canada to sell *The Beachcomber* and the American edition of my book, *Charles Laughton and I. The Beachcomber* opened at the old Rialto Theatre in Times Square on Christmas Eve and I was there to make a speech before the film—but some union ruling would not allow me to go on the stage. So I appeared *after* the film (much more effective) on the big oval balcony as the audience went out, and I shouted, "A Merry Christmas! ... I hope you liked the film," down to hundreds of people. Everybody shouted back, and the whole scene was very exciting. This was my first public speech really. I was wearing a voluminous black satin coat-dress, and a little wreath of tiny pink roses in my hair. I was flanked by Iris Barry and her then-husband John Abbott (treasurer of the Museum of Modern Art). I stayed with them in their brownstone in New York for my interviews and publicity for the following two weeks—fifty-three interviews!

The book, combined with *The Beachcomber*, made easy talk. I was assigned a publicity organizer by Paramount Studios—George Fraser —who finally took me to Canada (Toronto) to go on selling the book and the picture.

After my Rialto appearance in New York City, Iris and John Abbott took me straight on to Milford, Delaware, for a real Christmas day with his parents. We scampered on Rehoboth Beach, and I still have a big crab shell that I picked up.

I had done a good selling job and Erich Pommer came to the station in London to meet me, and gave me a good embrace of surprise and thanks. *St. Martin's Lane* (*Sidewalks of London* in America) rolled along, overlapping business talks about the next film, *Jamaica Inn*, directed by Alfred Hitchcock. I kept well out of the way.

Later, Alfred Hitchcock commented that no director could direct Charles, really.

> Charles was a very, very oblique early Method actor—not exactly Method. Let me put it this way: There are many, many artists in the world who are extremely talented and are geniuses, but they never become a pro. I think that was one of his problems— Charles never became a craft professional. He was always an artist and a genius, and he worked that way, so it became a disordered lack of control . . . Very often when we say a pro, it's in the pro the art is concealed.

One day I was asked to join Erich Pommer and Charles at our Gordon Square flat to meet their new discovery, Maureen O'Hara. She sat close to her mother, Mrs. Fitzsimmons, and Maureen certainly was a really beautiful young girl, with a healthy mop of dark chestnut hair. I suppose I represented the respectability that Maureen would be surrounded with. Anyway, I have never, never experienced the sight of such fresh, innocent youth.

Apparently she had first been spotted by Harry Richmond, an American talent scout, who went all over the world giving auditions to discover stars. He hired theatres and held talent contests. Maureen was discovered by him. Erich Pommer heard about Maureen somehow, and then Charles saw her. They were very proud of their find. And she turned out to be a remarkably good actress, too.

Maureen O'Hara never felt that Charles was the boss. She thought that Pommer was very severe, and if anything was going wrong, she could go to Charles—but not Pommer. Charles would tell Maureen that he'd always wanted to have children, particularly a daughter. At one point he asked her, "Do you think your mother and father would let me adopt you?"

Maureen's family were strict Catholics. So, of course, Maureen was a good girl. There's a short story by Saki called "The Story Teller," about a good little girl, which describes her well. (Look it up!) Maureen has always looked fresh and innocent, and that look gave me a tough time in 1939 when Charles left with her (and her mother) for America and *The Hunchback of Notre Dame.* Pommer and Charles easily persuaded R.K.O. Pictures to cast her as the gypsy girl Esmeralda.

Very early one morning, I saw Maureen, her mother, and Charles off at Victoria Station. On the platform I could tell that Maureen was feeling guilty about something. George Brown, a production assistant from *Jamaica Inn,* was there, too. She looked very pale and her hair was a bit untidy, as though it had been pulled through a bramble bush.

No sooner did the boat dock in America than rumors about Charles and his very young protégée sprang back at me. I didn't enjoy the printed words in the paper, something like "The Beauty and the Beast Arrive in America." The next thing, *The Evening Standard* called me and I was told that in New York Charles had put his arms around Maureen O'Hara. Of course, there were reporters on the dock taking pictures. And Charles was a star, so these pictures were in all the newspapers. *The Evening Standard* asked, "What about it? What is this, with your husband traveling abroad with a young girl?" With her mother as chaperone, of course.

I said, "Well, I don't know what Miss O'Hara or any others have been saying, but she's an actress who is going to appear with Charles in his next picture. He found her, discovered her, and so on—and there's just nothing to it." Then, a short transatlantic call from Charles made me laugh like a lunatic. It seems that on the boat trip across, Mrs. Fitzsimmons was going through her daughter's handbag and found a wedding ring in it. Her mother told Charles and the two of them confronted Maureen. Maureen admitted she had married George Brown. Too late, dammit! She'd been wedded and bedded already. Charles kept it very quiet because Esmeralda just had to be a virgin.

This time, alone in London, I was having a great time. There were parties and I felt popular then. It seemed as though Penguin might bring out *Charles Laughton and I* in paperback. Alan Lane of Penguin books took me out for a day or two on his little boat, *The Penguin*—with his brother!—and we sailed in the estuary north of the Isle of Wight. We slept on the boat, cooked breakfast, then landed at small towns with good pubs. When we three got back to Stapledown, there was a telegram waiting from Charles: LEAVE IMMEDIATELY FOR HOLLYWOOD. CANNOT CALL NOW. WILL EXPLAIN LATER.

So I packed and left on the first possible ocean liner. I didn't know what the urgency was about—I just went. I didn't know if it was a part in a film, or what. But I got on the boat, and I remember shedding a few tears as I looked out of the porthole and saw the cliffs and hills of England. I remember whispering to myself, over and over, "Poor little England, poor little England." I don't know why. Four weeks later, England declared war on Germany.

When I arrived in Los Angeles, the studio sent a limousine to bring me directly to meet Charles at a Hollywood party, and God knows how many other stars were there. I sat on the stairs and had a long conversation with Charles and Leo McCarey. McCarey asked me if I would ever settle down and like America. I said, "Maybe I could like America if I had an affair with an American man." He said, "Don't be so goddamned courteous." He was right, of course. Charles enjoyed a good belly laugh.

When I finally saw Maureen O'Hara again, I asked her, "What on earth was it you said when you arrived here? I had the backwash of that!" And she said, "They seemed to think that Charles and I were having an affair. I may have said something wrong." So I said, "If you'd gone to confession because you felt it was a sin, okay. But you might say now that you're sorry." Maureen was slightly arrogant, and I admit I wasn't very friendly to her—I was younger then. I shouldn't have taken any notice.

Some years later I ran into Maureen in the elevator at I. Magnin's. She was wearing a white dimity dress with a wide mauve satin sash and was still a fine broth of a woman, young and beautiful as ever. Her daughter, Bronwyn, who was then a chubby young teen-ager, stood there next to her, and there were lots of other people in the elevator, too. Maureen introduced her daughter to me. I said, "How nice to meet you, Bronwyn," or something like that. And Maureen said, "Oh, she's so horribly fat, isn't she a great fat thing?" This, in front of everyone in the elevator. I said, "I don't know. I was fat when I was her age" (which I wasn't, but I was trying to make the young girl feel better). The elevator unloaded its crowd of shopping ladies and everyone scattered—in discomfort, I'm sure.

Bronwyn's father, Will Price, had long ago been relegated to a back room where he had his meals until his divorce. At home, Maureen made an almost holy picture as she had done from her earliest days. Among other things, she would sit and sew with the tiniest, tiniest stitches. I have said that nuns are able either to atone for being alive or to feel themselves brides of Christ as they stitch, stitch, stitch. I find atoning for sin a fascinating subject in itself, but there is no way to account for some people's attraction to guilt. I am certain that Maureen O'Hara is a good woman and a nice woman, and certainly a sexy woman. It's just the little, tiny stitches that are difficult for me to understand.

19.

William Dieterle directed Charles and Maureen in *The Hunchback of Notre Dame.* Dieterle wrote that he "could not imagine any other actor in the title part but Charles Laughton. Charles started the part with a kind of theatrical idea, which he carried around inside him as a pregnant woman does her baby. He was not able to play his part until it was ripe within himself. As we were shooting the first scene in *The Hunchback of Notre Dame,* Laughton declared suddenly that he was unable to play his scene that day, not being ready for it yet. Since he had no dialogue at all (Quasimodo being deaf and dumb), his peculiarity was incomprehensible to me. I asked him, 'Please, Charles, the next time you are not yet ready, let me know it previously so I can plan accordingly.' Sweltering in his heavy rubber makeup, Charles muttered in a tormented voice, 'I am sorry, I am so sorry, but I thought I was ready, but it just did not come, but it will come and will be good.' Finally when Laughton acted the scene on the wheel, enduring the terrible torture, he was not the poor crippled creature expecting compassion from the mob, but rather oppressed and enslaved mankind, suffering the most awful injustice."

The Hunchback of Notre Dame was filmed during one of the hottest summers in Southern California. The temperature rose—107, 108, 109, 110 degrees—for about ten days. They kept saying that this brutal summer of 1939 was a record. The outdoor scenes were done in the San Fernando Valley on the old Universal lot, where there was a replica of Notre Dame, built for the first Lon Chaney *Hunchback* silent film.

Charles wore terribly heavy makeup. On his back he had about four or five inches of foam rubber for the hump, with a thin layer of rubber on top to make it resemble skin. This rubber skin went all the way down and over his shoulders and upper arms. We were staying at the Garden of Allah again and hotel living didn't make it any easier. He had to get up at 4:00 A.M. every morning for the makeup ordeal, and he never got much sleep. It was so hot that the only way we would get any sleep at all was to get in the bath with a sheet, nap for maybe ten or twenty minutes in the wet sheet, and then get up and wet it again!

Charles was on the revolving wheel and had to be lashed with a whip, his shirt ripped down to his waist. It was 110 in the shade—and this was in the sun. They actually had to lash him, to make it look real. You would think the lashing wouldn't hurt him, with all that foam rubber, but he would come home with welts on his arms or hips, groaning and weeping with pain. It was pitiful, but it went on for two or three days because they wanted to get the scene right. One day Charles was whipped for sixteen takes. His back was black and blue, in spite of the four-inch rubber hump. Then, after sixteen takes, Dieterle came up to Charles and—in the intimate tone directors use to confide their tricks, their genius, their wares, and ideas—he bent over Charles and whispered, "Now, Charles, listen to me. Let's do it one more time, but this time I want you . . . I want you to suffer." For this, Charles never forgave Dieterle, he always said to me he hated him. He thought that Dieterle was a mini-sadist. Somehow it was an added irritant to Charles that Dieterle always wore white gloves because he feared picking up germs.

When Charles finally saw the film at the Radio City Music Hall, he didn't recognize himself and hated what he saw. Again, the reviews of the picture were both negative and positive. From *The New York Times*, January 1, 1940:

> The Music Hall is the last place in the world where we should expect to find a freak show. It is to Mr. Laughton's credit that he is able to act at all under his make-up . . .

And from *Variety*, December 15, 1939:

> Great in his blending of the hideous and the spiritually beautiful is Charles Laughton's enactment of the deformed bell ringer of Notre Dame . . . the actor's revelation of the near imbecilic mind and tortured soul is magnificently impressive.

Around this time, my friend Arthur Macrae wrote to me from England. His letter began: *Dear Dame de Notre Hunchback* . . .

Charles was under contract to R.K.O. His next film was *They Knew What They Wanted*, produced by Erich Pommer and directed by Garson

Kanin, with Charles and Carole Lombard in the lead parts. Charles begged Pommer to replace Lombard—he felt he had suffered through *White Woman* with her—but Pommer and R.K.O. refused. Charles was miserable making the film, and the finished product showed it. Charles played an Italian immigrant farmer: Carol played a young waitress who marries him. I thought they were both miscast.

I went up to Napa Valley where they shot most of the picture, and Charles still wasn't getting on well with Miss Lombard. He didn't think she was a controlled actress. I don't know if I should feel that it was a bit of the pot calling the kettle black. So many people have said, more or less, that Charles was not a controlled actor, either. That was usually mid-high praise for his genius.

They Knew What They Wanted was not a success. Another sorrow for Erich Pommer.

He made one or two pictures for Paramount, but he didn't seem to have the heart to fight anymore. Charles was very busy and didn't see him. Mayflower Pictures had been dissolved, and Pommer went, he just disappeared, and I don't even know when or where. The other day on television I saw *Metropolis* (UFA, 1927) made by Pommer in his heyday in Germany. The score of this silent motion picture classic is in itself a torturous experience—little bird sounds, bird screeches, sirens, the hammering of metal on metal, clacks assault the ears in a dramatic accompaniment to this brutal film. Your guts seemed to take up low rumbling to fill the silences in this cacophony. I suppose that Fritz Lang created most of these effects—but with Erich Pommer. How sorrowful to think of Pommer's end so far from so high. He was so gentle, so sad-looking—but underneath, still more German than he seemed to be. What did he feel, I wonder, in this desert outpost, Hollywood?

I was getting rather worried about Biddy and Shamus in London. We could have got them out into the country, but a combination of fatalism, old age, and bravado made them, like so many others, absolutely immovable.

By now Charles and I had left the Garden of Allah for our first house —furnished!—on North Rockingham Avenue in Brentwood. Norman Corwin stayed there with us when he first arrived in California. And there Sheila Schwartz, brought over by us from England, began working for us.

We had first met Norman Corwin in New York City in the fall of 1939, when he was writing and producing a series, *The Pursuit of Happiness*, for CBS radio. Charles was influenced and intrigued by the possibilities of presenting literature in this form in front of a live audience.

The first program Charles and I appeared on was Stephen Vincent Benét's "John Brown's Body," using music, chorus, and sound effects. The other show we did with Norman was sections of Thomas Wolfe —"a melange of Wolfeiana," Corwin called it. Thomas Wolfe was so very American, and Charles during rehearsals would pace the stage trying to capture this giant of a writer and man. Eventually, he had a huge overstuffed armchair brought on stage. He sank into it and immediately became Thomas Wolfe. It turned out that that was how Thomas Wolfe lounged around while writing. Burgess Meredith hosted both productions.

Talking of those productions, Norman Corwin said:

> In those days, it was still possible for actors of the stature of the Laughtons to speak words written by writers of the stature of Thomas Wolfe and Stephen Vincent Benét on a commercial network . . . The experience was new for them, and they apparently enjoyed it . . . in a burst of cordiality, they invited me to be their guest if I should ever go to Hollywood. When soon afterward I signed up to write a movie, I notified the Laughtons . . . back came a telegram: DOG HOUSE IN GARDEN ALL READY FOR YOU WHAT TIME DO YOU ARRIVE BECAUSE WE WANT TO MEET YOU.

So we met Norman Corwin at the airport and parked him in the "dog house"—our guest house. We were quite a crowd: Charles and me, Sheila Schwartz, Corwin, a couple to look after us, our garden, our pool, an Irish setter (Sheila insisted on having a dog), five cats, and our paintings. The paintings were on loan to us from Albert Barnes of Philadelphia, who had generously let us have about fourteen pictures from his famous collection. He felt that Charles was his disciple and he was mentor. It was Barnes who "allowed" Charles to buy the very famous Renoir, *The Judgement of Paris,* which we fortunately were able to get to America in the mid-1940s.

We always had a cat, but we didn't ever go out and get a cat. Somehow the cats found us. When we moved to our house in Brentwood, one day we drove in and we heard a meeping and rustling in the driveway, and eventually we fished out five kittens from the ivy. In Hollywood, at least, if a poor family had a cat and it had kittens and they couldn't afford to have the mother cat "fixed," and they couldn't bring themselves to kill the kittens, they would put them in a basket and drop them in the gardens of the people who were better off. So we had cats. We kept them for a few weeks, all five, and we had five kittens chasing one another around the house—a great entertainment. It was much, much better than going to a ballet. Eventually we found homes for them all, except one—a ginger one—so this one was called "Mister Pinky" and he was considered Charles' cat. After that we always had ginger cats. For some reason, ginger cats always turned up.

Two doors away from the Brentwood house lived Henry Hathaway. He had an aunt and, I believe, a mother living there, two apparently rather deaf elderly ladies. One day their gardener told our gardener that "the Laughtons barbecue cats." We were infuriated. Tracing the atrocious statement to its source, we found that one old girl had said to the other, "You know, the Laughtons harbor cats," and the other deaf old girl heard "harbor" as "barbecue."

During his visit, Norman regaled us with two-line verses commenting on his stay with us:

In the most impeccable and proper House of Laughton
It is considered de rigeur to swim with not a jot on.

And if you have to go to pee
Be careful not to splash Dufy.

Or a four-liner:

In Brentwood's famous Laughton Hall
Which rents for many a shekel
Is written on a certain wall
SHEILA SHEILA TEKEL.

Charles and I had known Sheila Schwartz in England. She was an old friend of Charles'. She came from a fairly wealthy family and had a rather lantern-jawed Semitic-British face. Sheila was sort of in love with a divorced actor called Basil Gill, who became Charles' friend as well. He appeared with Charles in the films *St. Martin's Lane* and *Rembrandt*.

Basil Gill was a stage star in the grand manner, a matinee idol, and had been very, very good-looking. Sheila Schwartz had done a little acting by this time, and the two of them obviously needed to associate with a developing star, a person who was on the way up—Charles.

When I first knew Charles, he, Sheila, and Basil were very often together. Two or three times they had motored through France, with Basil driving, going to wonderful restaurants and places, driving through the wine districts, and talking about food. There must have been passions lurking in there somewhere. Certainly Sheila Schwartz must have been a bit put out when Charles married me. And later developments seemed to confirm this.

By the time Charles and I were married, I got on with Sheila very well. She would tell me all these little snippets about those days in France with Basil and Charles. Sometimes with little innuendos. She always made herself useful on her visits to Stapledown. Sheila could cook reasonably well, and she would wash up. After the war broke out, when Charles and I were in Hollywood working, the blitz was getting very bad and there was even a danger of the Germans invading England. We worried about Sheila, who was Jewish. As she was doing a few odd jobs for us in London, she would write reports to me . . .

Aug. 31, 1939

Darling,

I think the crisis is reaching its peak, the school children and Nellie and Gracie are being evacuated to-morrow, they have been angels and not a bit worried . . . Oh! Aggie dear I do wish that I was with you reading about all this from afar, or at any rate you were here . . . I do so hope that you and Charles are not worrying, not that you can stop, because honestly you have done everything that you possibly can, and anyhow there won't be a war!

A lot of love from,
"POOR LITTLE SHEILA"

Sheila

Eventually Charles said to me, "Can we have Sheila Schwartz out?" I said, "Of course. We must."

So we got Sheila Schwartz out of England. You had to put up five hundred dollars and say that you would be responsible for a person's keep. Sheila came out to us, to Hollywood; but for her own pride and Charles' convenience, she became his secretary. She didn't do shorthand, but she did speedwriting and typing. And she drove the car, so I didn't have to anymore. She would say, "Sheila will drive." She referred to herself in the third person. So Sheila drove. But she made it seem such a terrible chore. Charles would often ask her to back up somewhere to check on some wildflower, and Sheila would say, "Little Sheila can really drive."

The next addition to our Hollywood life was Albert Brush, a little autumn leaf of a man. The slightest breeze could have blown this dear ginger-headed fellow out of the room. He was very frail. It was I who introduced Albert Brush to Charles. Albert interviewed me on "The Beverly Hills Library Radio Show" to publicize the book *Charles Laugh-*

ton and I. So when Charles, much later, needed help in some research, I automatically thought of Albert. I just had the impression that he would be right for Charles and the job ahead. Albert Brush was like a piece of ectoplasm that knew everything. More than just knowledge-able, and I say *ectoplasm* because physically he was hardly there at all.

Charles liked Albert Brush immediately. Charles became the friend, the father, learner. He learned what Albert Brush had to give including Albert's knowledge of art, furniture, and oriental objects. He had such a delicacy of choice in all areas that I must use the word *taste*. I wish that word could be replaced by another, since there is no one definition for it. And Charles and he breathed the same language, which led to the basis of Charles' whole reading career.

Although Charles had a good education, Albert Brush helped him to fill in vacancies in his literary background. I think Charles felt the limitations we all feel. Some others who worked with Charles did not have the kind of intelligence to appreciate the gift that Albert had. With Albert Brush's help in collecting material, the project of putting together a reading program was not nearly as laborious as it might have been.

20

One day in 1941, I had lunch with Helen Deutsch, the screenwriter (*Lili, National Velvet, The Glass Slipper*), in a restaurant on Sunset strip in Hollywood. She said that there were three guys she knew (I think she said "crazy guys") opening a little theatre down on La Cienega Boulevard. They were known as the Yale Puppeteers, and their new theatre was to be called the Turnabout. They had designed and remodeled the theatre with two stages—one for puppets, one for actors —with old streetcar reversible seats for the audience in between. The plan called for an hour of puppets, then—turnabout!—an hour of live revue. Helen Deutsch thought it would be a good place for me to get up and try out my old collection of songs from the Cave of Harmony, my early research, and so on.

So after lunch we dropped in to see what the La Cienega place was like. The patio was a pile of rubble—things were in the usual pre-opening state of confusion—and the theatre smelled of new wood and not yet of paint. One of the partners, the actress Dorothy Neumann, was scrubbing away on the stage. The whole Turnabout idea had been thought up and carried out by Forman Brown (who wrote the material), Harry Burnett (who designed the puppets), and Roddy Brandon (the business manager)—The Three *B*'s, as they called themselves. It was the fulfillment of a wish to have their very own theatre after having toured America for years. And then I came into the picture, with all my old songs and new songs, pretty songs and wicked songs.

The four Turnabouters and I talked for a few minutes. They all seemed to like the idea of my appearing at the Turnabout. So I started to rehearse my numbers—of course, none of them written by Forman Brown at first.

I opened at Turnabout with three songs I knew very well. The first number was by A. P. Herbert, "He Didn't Oughter (Come to Bed in Boots)." The second song was "The Ratcatcher's Daughter," and the last one was "Somebody Broke Lola's Saucepan . . ."

> Just how she can't quite explain
> Somebody broke Lola's Saucepan,
> And she can't get it mended again . . .

For each song, I developed a characterization, each in a different costume. And this would remain the pattern I used at Turnabout.

Actually, I joined the company as a performer at the beginning of their *third* week, after making a lot of excuses about not wanting to interfere with their original plans. Part of the reason was Charles' idea that the Turnabouters should get one batch of publicity for their own publicized opening and then get another batch when I joined them several weeks later. But also I had wanted to do this kind of work again for a long time and had just not found the opportunity. When the chance did come, the truth was that I was just too scared to get up and do my songs in front of the Hollywood celebrities who would be coming on opening night. I was so nervous, in fact, that I wouldn't let Charles come to see me for weeks. When he did come, he brought Deanna Durbin, and I more or less lost my voice from sheer terror. In the beginning I was a wreck, and I recall reminding myself of Ruth Gordon's first-night experiences as an actress. Ruth loved first nights and told me she always stood in the wings of the stage and thought of herself as a dog on a leash—pulling to get on stage and start acting. So I pulled at my collar or dress at home and pretended to be Ruth. Also, I found it good advice to put my full weight on my heels.

The audiences liked me and understood me, too. Being from England, for me this American acceptance was of almost earth-shaking pleasure. After I was at the theatre for a short time, I rather tentatively asked what exactly their policy was. After all, I was being billed as a Guest Artist—and a self-invited one at that. I didn't really know if I was wanted, and they, on their part, were not so sure they should ask me to stay. So a roundabout series of conversations began about their "policy." I twisted myself into knots over it, and so did they. The truth was that the Yale Puppeteers didn't have a policy and, for that matter, never would. They all looked dreadfully worried at the prospect of acquiring one. It was agreed, however, that I should stay on. Well, I stayed . . . and stayed and stayed. For ten years.

The one "policy" at the Turnabout was that we would change the material as often as Forman Brown could produce it. And he produced a lot of material in those ten years. We arranged that I would receive no pay for my appearances, but all songs written for me would auto-matically become mine. The first year was, to a great extent, experi-mental. Finally, we had reduced all the best material to four complete and different shows. These were rotated and changed when Forman wrote new material, and audiences returned again and again to see their favorites.

Financially the venture was very successful, although the results might not have satisfied everybody. I suppose it depends on whether you want to earn a living or make lots of money. Although I continued to be called the Guest Artist, it was rather a joke after that first year. And since I didn't take a salary, it gave me the freedom to come and go if necessary—but I didn't.

None of us knew for sure why the Turnabout Theatre caught on and was such a success. We often used to sit around after the show and have coffee and cake and discuss the whole thing. Dorothy Neumann thought this and Forman thought that, and all of us dreamed about where it all might lead. Behind its popularity, I think, was the spirit that has started many famous companies on the road to success—we were a little group of people who were fascinated by making a commentary on our own time. A group of people who were able to entertain an audience with the same relish the talented amateur gets out of enter-taining his friends at a party. Not that the material was necessarily topical, but in it was an awareness of what makes people laugh and cry.

And as we were getting to know ourselves in relation to our audiences, Forman was getting to know us and what we did best. And this mutual sharpening of wits was, I believe, what sold out the theatre every night.

I knew that Forman had written all the puppet shows and all the songs for the other performers, and I had been waiting expectantly for *mine*. And I think the first song he wrote for me was "If You Can't Get in the Corners (You Might as Well Give Up)." It was about a cleaning lady. I did it with a duster in my hand. It brought back my *Riverside Nights* days.

Over all the years I was at Turnabout Theatre, Forman wrote fifty or sixty songs for me. My appearances in each of the revues consisted of three solo spots. As a performer known principally as a film person-ality, I hoped first of all to avoid the conventional movie image in my characterizations. I wanted to look unlike an actress trying to look more glamorous than she is. Therefore, in my first spot I became a kitchen slavey, a frowzy housewife, or a slum brat. A collection of distinctly unglamorous females. My second spot was usually a ballad. Since I was an actress, I tried to tell a story and create—in dance and song—a picturesque character. As these ballads were usually period pieces, they gave me a chance to move about the stage and dance in colorful costumes. And now, having shown myself looking my worst and best, for my last number I could be anything, however outrageous —a potentate's mistress, a lady of the night, and that sort of thing.

Whenever Forman came up with a new number, both of us immediately understood that it was destined for spot number one, spot number two, or spot number three. Charles once said that Forman and I made a true artistic marriage of talents—and a happy one. I believe he was right.

When Forman would play and sing a new number for me at the piano, I rarely reacted in any way. It must have been rather discouraging for him, as I think about it now—but what I was actually getting was my first vision of the person in the song, and I had learned that these first thoughts were never to be dismissed. If there is such a thing as inspiration, this first impression stayed uppermost with me. So I might add, discard, and change, but I rarely dismissed it.

Stuffing Forman's new song into my bag, I would rush to get home, get into my room, and read the words carefully, and then sleep on them. Then later I'd begin to appreciate the actual lines of the song and consider what I might do with them. I would roughly learn the tune on the piano with one finger. Then in the privacy of my room, usually late at night, I would move into the frame of an imaginary proscenium arch and start working out the movements for telling the song's story—pointing up jokes and double meanings with humble and naïve looks. Forman was a specialist in double entendres. But I sometimes topped him, for he would often say at an early rehearsal, "How *could* you think I meant *that?!*"

The art of selling the double entendre is making an audience feel almost guilty that such strange thoughts should pass through their minds. I have been told that my innocent expression prior to my understanding smile is my number one weapon. And I had plenty of time to polish and sharpen this weapon at Turnabout.

I began to visualize the costumes almost immediately when I was framing the movements, but in combing through the acres of clothes at Western Costume (an enormous warehouse catering to Hollywood studios), I often had to change the action of the song, sometimes for the better. Often, even, the costume came first. Once, for instance, I received an original Worth gown as a gift. It was too small for me, so I just left the lacing at the back undone. Charles thought of the title, "I'm Glad To See You're Back" (Your Back), and Forman wrote it.

In the 1930s, someone had left me a voluminous tea-colored petticoat covered with yards and yards of black lace, threaded with mauve ribbons. This was made into a grand first-night evening gown by Victor Stiebel in London. (He also dressed Princess Margaret.) Anyway, this dress served as the outfit for "When a Lady Has a Piazza." Over the years of wear and tear, I had to have it copied three times. So, the right dress for the right song.

Bertolt Brecht once made a comment about my work that I'd like to repeat here. I know it is rather vain to recall a compliment but, as I have said earlier, to be understood is the greatest pleasure that a performer can experience. Brecht said that I was the only person he had seen who filled in the frame of a proscenium arch the same way that the Japanese did in a print. I was enchanted with his observation, because I truly feel that a performer must be able to stand even in one corner of the stage and create rivers, houses, patios, laundromats, backyards, or whatever, for his audiences, without benefit of scenery or props.

Forman Brown and I were never at cross-purposes when it came to building a song. There was one general rule I did urge him to keep, a rule I only learned myself by trial and error. The songs should have upbeat endings. The ladies in our songs all had to like their lives in some way and be successful in the end. Forman, writer and poet, would occasionally indulge in creating sorrowful, picturesque scenes—for example, a woman sitting by candlelight and ruminating about days gone by. But I never wanted to leave an audience in a downbeat mood, and certainly not at the Turnabout. Audiences were there to be entertained, and Forman's upbeat endings were among his best inventions. Melinda Mame "rode in a barouche with four white horses," and Delphinia "was done up in pink and was having a drink with a couple of men at the Stork." Obviously, audiences were happy to hear it.

Nobody has a life plan that works exactly as expected. But I must say, looking back on the performing part of my life, that there is a distinct pattern. It seems quite clear to me that I had always been on the particular track that led me to the Turnabout Theatre in the 1940s. First there were the seaside shows when I was a child, then my early folk songs, and the days at the Cave of Harmony, the cabarets and nightspots, and the revue *Riverside Nights*.

Those years at the Turnabout, I can say, were truly growing years. And I literally *did* grow. I grew half an inch and my rib expansion gained two inches! I suppose the nightly workout, the singing and dancing, was as healthy as going to a gymnasium. Charles was happy that I had this second life, that I could find some professional satisfaction on a stage. I could still make films during the day, and any director would see that I was in time for the show at the famous Turnabout. I was able to pick from the hundreds of songs I had collected through all my years of research, plus the new ones Forman Brown had written for me. Pretty songs, funny songs, wicked songs . . .

> When a lady has a piazza, she has a prize indeed . . .
> She can look on her piazza as a friend in need,
> For a girl who has a piazza has a place on which to sit,
> And people know a piazza has a house attached to it.

And another song. "If You Peek in My Gazebo." You'll no longer be a free beau . . .

Charles loved the mountains, so between films, we would sometimes go out to the Hollywood Hills and drive around. He needed a weekend place, another Stapledown. I had been once or twice to a village called Idyllwild, above Palm Springs, so one day I had a look at a house for rent.

It was a perfect little wooden house with a great stone fireplace, three small bedrooms with double beds, and another one with fireplace and two bunks, a good kitchen, rocks, grass, and two or three acres of land. The rent was very reasonable, and the rural mountain agent didn't recognize me. So I said to him, "Well, the rent is rather high. If we take it for a year, it should be on account of purchase, don't you think? But maybe the people wouldn't want to sell it. Couldn't you make it a reasonable rent?"

The agent said, "I think you could buy it."

And I replied, "Well, I'd like to know how much."

"About two thousand," he said.

This fabulous place, with a full view of Lily Rock! "Well," I said, "that's rather a lot, but . . . I want to rent it and we do need it at once."

I knew we could drive down to Corona, where the bank was, so I told him, "I'll put a deposit down then."

When I got down to Corona, I said to the agent, "Well, I may as well pay for the whole thing." I gave him two thousand dollars, and the house was mine. Charles and I moved in two or three days later. But if the agent had known that I was married to Charles, the sale might have been a different story.

Charles went up to Idyllwild whenever he could, and I went up with the Turnabouters all the time. Clifford Odets came up to write— I don't know what Charles and he were working on, but I don't think it was a play. Once, Odets stayed there alone, but he was such a bad housekeeper that he nearly froze to death.

It was a wonderful place. During the war I sold it for five times the original price, only because we couldn't get gas to get up there to clear away the snow and the rats in the water tank and the mice in the quilts.

Through most of the Turnabout years, Charles and I lived in an elegant house on the Pacific Palisades, with an acre of garden running to the edge of the cliff overlooking the ocean. We furnished it with pieces designed by Paul Frankel, along with some things we were able to have sent from England—my Bluthner piano and some special chairs and chests from our early Yorkshire antique hunts.

Charles was still under contract to MGM and had started teaching a Shakespeare class. On Tuesdays, Thursdays, and Saturdays, ten to twenty youngish people trickled into the house just about the time I was driving to the theatre. But the queen of the class, Shelley Winters, said, "You must change it to Mondays, Wednesdays, and Fridays, because I have to fuck on Saturdays!" So the program was changed to suit her. Shelley also liked to park crosswise behind my car, and she was always late, so I would often have to rush into the classroom and say, "Hold it, please, I can't get my car out." I hated doing this because Charles resented interruptions and seemed to blame me, rather than Shelley. Charles adored Shelley and saw in her a delicate, sensitive female, a quality he brought out in the film he directed, *The Night of the Hunter*.

How Charles' opinion about Shakespeare had changed over the years! He was criticized at the Old Vic for denying the necessity of using the iambic pentameter. He said then that the story, the words to the story, the form, this came first, and any Shakespearean rule of verse after. He said that everyone in the cast was wrong, and the rhythm should fall where it may. During Charles' classes in Shakespeare at our house, Charles wouldn't budge from the iambic pentameter. His class was called the "Ti Tum, Ti Tum" class.

Because I was at the Turnabout Theatre every evening except Monday during all the years that Charles' class was in session, I really didn't have much of a chance to see him teaching. I do know that even as a teacher, Charles performed. By the time I came in at night—usually around eleven-thirty or midnight—he would be sitting in his big old armchair ordering everybody about: "*You*, get the vacuum cleaner! *You*, wash the glasses and coffee cups! Don't forget that ash on the floor! Open the windows!" It was all very well organized.

Charles didn't need me around as long as he had Kate Drain Lawson to supervise the cleaning up. She was a big lady who wore rather voluminous clothes, a kind of duenna or house mother or chaperone for the group. In fact, it was Kate Lawson who had first started an acting class, and Charles simply recruited her best students for his own—and finally the teacher herself.

Shelley Winters and Kate Lawson, Bill Phipps, Arthur O'Connell, and Denver Pyle were among Charles' students. But I don't think Charles really had any selection process going at all. His students were people whom he perhaps felt he liked or could communicate with, for after all, the teaching was also for his own benefit.

He admitted that he was learning while he taught. The classes also fulfilled an emotional need that Charles never spoke about—or, indeed, defined for himself. Like an alchemist, Charles had secrets that he wanted to pass on. But he needed to be the master.

Sometimes Charles would tell me about something one of his students had said or done, rather like the father bragging about his child's accomplishment. We would discuss material that the class might study. I remember once suggesting one of my favorite books of one-act plays, *Husbands and Lovers* by Molnar. The book is full of enormously funny and beautifully absurd dialogues. We had about a dozen moth-eaten copies of it lying around the schoolroom for a long time. The word *schoolroom* may sound silly but that is what Charles always wanted—a schoolroom where he could sit with his students all around him. So schoolroom it was.

Years earlier, the psychiatrist Ernest Jones had advised Charles to also try teaching. Sure enough, when he did, he became a happier, more contented man. He was less morose and actually seemed to enjoy his other activities more—his art collection, the garden, food, and his readings.

After Irving Thalberg's death, Charles was not happy at MGM. Thalberg was not only a friend but also an adviser and guide to Charles as an actor. Charles needed this Stradivarius of a businessman who made wise decisions and could carry through on productions with assurance and incredible taste and modesty. He felt lost without him. By comparison, Korda, although a great director, was a difficult and unreliable producer, always juggling art and money. Korda was with Charles when the news came of Thalberg's death. What a turmoil of mixed emotions must have swirled round them, Korda probably feeling about Charles, "Got him at last!"

Without the personal tie to Thalberg, Charles' MGM contract was artistically more or less a piece of paper. Thalberg had wanted Charles eventually to be a producer, and now no imaginative vehicles for Charles were likely to come from Louis B. Mayer. In the hangover years to come MGM would fulfill its contractual obligations by renting Charles out to other studios and casting him in a few stinkers of their own: *Stand by for Action, The Man from Down Under* and *The Bribe*—with the exception of *The Canterville Ghost*, which was rather good. Still, Charles loved some of the people he worked with—Margaret O'Brien, for instance. He swore that she must have been a changeling, somehow descended from royalty; perhaps, kidnapped from a Persian king.

When he was loaned out, at least, he was free to make a few good pictures at other studios: *It Started with Eve* with Deanna Durbin, whom Charles adored; *The Suspect; This Land Is Mine; The Big Clock*, with me; and *The Man on the Eiffel Tower*, which he unofficially codirected.

I think *The Suspect* was one of the best performances Charles ever gave, and to some extent I think he thought so, too. In the film, Charles murders his nagging wife and tries unsuccessfully to start a new life with young Ella Raines. It was played lightly. The murderer Charles played in *The Suspect* was similar to the one he played in *Payment Deferred*. But *Payment Deferred* was a photographed play, while *The Suspect* was a *film*. Robert Siodmak was a brilliant director and a dear, dryly humorous person. I liked him very much when he directed me in *The Spiral Staircase*. But he eventually left the country. He didn't feel comfortable with the way he was treated here in America, or he perhaps was simply here at the wrong time (the war years), when film moguls were nervous about certain directors. But he certainly should have worked with Charles again. And Charles wished that he had.

Most good actors' characterizations have something that everybody can identify with, and the more the people can recognize a character, the more the actor has succeeded. If I play an aunt, and somebody says to me, "I have an aunt just like that," I realize I have hit it. Watching Charles in old films on television, I see that time has shown him to be a much, much better actor than he ever thought himself. It is sad that he always denigrated himself. Apropos of these bad films where Charles was often extremely good, he and I often quoted an old English actor's description of working your ass off for nothing: "Grinding ice for father's piles."

The turning point of Charles' career came in these early 1940s. His Shakespeare class at the house became more and more the springboard for forming his own reading repertoire—with small captive audiences. Then he started reading to wounded soldiers in hospitals and on bond drives and war charities. His first stint was reading from the Bible for the soldiers at Birmingham Hospital in the San Fernando Valley, and this developed into another occupation. I cannot recall exactly how it came about, for I was so involved in working every night myself. Charles always credited me with saying, "Get off your ass and get active."

Sometimes Charles would come across a passage in a play or whatever, and he would read it aloud for me, trying it out. Charles had always liked to read aloud. I'm not sure that he wasn't developing the sound of his voice, like a singer. You hear about many actors of the last century with marvelous speaking voices—about how they rolled out words and about the depth and resonance of their voices. A beautiful voice, a rich voice alone was almost enough to fill a theatre—

something now completely outmoded, thanks to the microphone. I'm afraid if anybody tried to be as thunderous as the actors of the past, they'd be laughed off the stage.

To Charles the words were more important than the sound, although he became so famous for his speaking voice. On his reading tours, he would put his books on a couple of old soapboxes, or perhaps he had a stool from one of the college classrooms—whatever they had to offer. Usually they had nothing. They didn't have nice rostrums or anything like that. So Charles learned—he had to learn—that the less props you brought onstage, the better. He himself would sometimes carry on a soapbox or two, maybe a wooden 7-Up case. It made the audience relax.

As a reader, Charles has always created a large canvas and worked with a vast palette. He was no more natural than an artificial flower. It was a matter of deliberately setting the audience at its ease so *it* could feel natural. The first week at Birmingham Hospital, Charles got ten fellows in pajamas and wheelchairs to come and listen. Then it got to twenty the next week, and it got up to forty or fifty or sixty very quickly. The soldiers would ask Charles questions. It was like teaching —reading, explaining, expounding. Another classroom.

One place that made Charles very happy was a home for retarded and crippled children somewhere in Long Beach. I had also done a show for them. Charles went down there several times, and I still have an enchanting photograph of crippled children, clustered all around him as, book in hand, he read to them.

The readings became Charles' driving force and made the possible guilt of being in the Hollywood sunshine, overlooking the beautiful Pacific, at least tolerable—the guilt of not going back "to take the blitz" like others in England.

21

In England they were writing little stories about the "English Colony" in Hollywood, attacking Charles and me, among others, criticizing Charles for being in America and not back in England. This only added to Charles' doubts about himself. He often said to me, "I was in the First World War, in the trenches, bayoneting men, and getting gassed. I think once in a life is enough."

We had contributed several thousand dollars to *The Evening Standard* War Fund to aid the victims of the blitz, although we never publicized the fact. Once Nigel Bruce (Dr. Watson) actually stormed at us, banging at the front door, saying, "All the English contributed and you didn't!" When we showed him the telegram from *The Evening Standard* thanking us, he walked away down the garden path very cowed, very hangdog.

Of course, the war was always on our minds and with us. We carried out a host of the obligations that came with war. Nothing one should complain about or boast about. At this time, the early war years, the R.A.F. sent a batch of boys to America for desert training, and we gave them an enormous party. I think they were stationed out somewhere around Palm Springs. There were one hundred and fifty English boys stationed here. We got all one hundred fifty!

Well, we had to have starlets for them. So we called every studio, and each sent about ten starlets, with chaperones. The R.A.F. boys were bused in, and we had den mothers for them. Gladys Cooper was the chief den mother, and her name meant home to them all. She came and left with the boys. I suppose I was sort of one of the den mothers then, too. I was in between generations, you might say.

Charles had just made *It Started with Eve* with Deanna Durbin, so we asked her to sing at our party. They got along so well during the shooting of the film, she would have done anything for Charles. At the party, Deanna sat on the piano and sang like a bird—anything and everything they requested. Then she danced with as many of the English boys as she could. Afterward one of the boys said with sincere innocence, "It makes the war worthwhile."

As Charles had once been a hotelkeeper and I had run a nightclub, we were very good at organizing everything. The acre of land we had and the view from our cliff served beautifully that night. We had a huge cellophane tent over the whole lawn, with blazing braziers in the corners, for it was a lovely cold night. The R.A.F. boys could stand around warming themselves by the hot coals. A dance floor was constructed on the lawn. We provided all the foods they might have had back home in England—roast beef and Yorkshire pudding and trifle. It was one of the most successful parties I have ever attended, even if it was our own. It was just a magical night.

Sheila Schwartz was living with us all this time. She did our accounts for us as well as the interviews for changes in the staff—anything and everything. She was general factotum. The arrangement seemed fine. We would go to San Francisco or take long trips in the desert or country. Sheila drove. She was always with us.

It seemed that Sheila was always chattering about me to Charles and Bobby Benson, Charles' masseur. It was a sort of daisy chain of gossip. I never knew what she was actually saying, but she would feed Bobby Benson, and Bobby would feed it back to Charles, and Charles would then make a few odd remarks to me. Later I learned that Bobby spread rumors that Charles and I were separating—based on what Sheila had told him. Perhaps she fed him that kind of information all the time, and at the same time, she was feeding me stories about Charles having this liaison and that liaison, ad infinitum.

The most difficult thing to recall is a bad time in your life. This was a very evil time, and I was fairly innocent of it. Perhaps I was always much stronger, with a capacity to survive—a capacity that was greater than the whole lot of theirs put together. I would get down low, I'd have angry fits. I would cry—something I had always tried not to do. In a play, of course, I could force myself to cry. And, quite frankly, I suppose I used tears, as women do, if necessary. In those days, I felt as if I were living in the house with enemies, as if Bobby Benson and Sheila Schwartz and Charles were all together against me.

Bobby Benson was short, and one of his eyes had been punched a little crooked in a fight. He came to the house every day. He was a little fellow with blond, sort of greasy hair. He laughed a lot and made coarse jokes, and had a great German shepherd. We all used to meet

182

for coffee and breakfast, racing round the house in dressing gowns. Bobby Benson began to give me a massage every day or two, but he said to Charles that it was so exciting he had to go and dash cold water on himself. Maybe that was meant as a compliment, but it meant no more massages for me.

One day I was in our little office collecting bills for Mr. Williams, our income-tax business manager, and I came across a typed letter from Sheila to her sister in England. It could have been a copy of a letter that was mailed or just Sheila Shwartz's dream written down—I'll never know. It went something like this:

> That red-headed ——— is still here. I don't know if she'll ever go. The snub-nosed ——— seems to be a fixture."

Charles and I had a quick conference and that evening confronted her with the letter. Sheila did not crumple—she fell to the floor like a heavy plank. Without any words, she packed and went off in a taxi. I have not heard from her since. She went to work for a couple who shall be nameless. The couple separated after a year. Then she worked for a very well-known couple, who took Sheila to Europe as their secretary. They, too, separated within the year. All Charles ever said to me about Sheila was, "A true Iago by nature."

Norman Corwin—was he prophet or seer when he wrote that foreboding line, "Sheila Sheila Tekel," that paraphrase of the biblical handwriting on the wall.

It was the end of Charles' MGM era. They were giving him only bad pictures, and in those days Charles may have had a foreboding that his option would be dropped—as it eventually was. Another pressure was the discovery that the cliff below our house in Pacific Palisades was starting to slip: CHARLES LAUGHTON'S ESTATE ENDANGERED, a newspaper announced. Charles' state of mind was also slipping and he was also in despair.

Since Idyllwild had been sold, we had had no place to escape to when the pressures became too great. Charles and I bought fifteen acres of land on the Palos Verdes peninsula. It had been a millionaire's tropical orchard and aviary. We had a shack to sleep in that had been the bird hospital. We transformed this shack into a midget Mayo clinic —I mean, so white and clean. That was the good life then: cooking, walking, collecting shells in Abalone Cove; books, and friends.

The practical aspects of making a house functional were in the hands of a friend from Palos Verdes. He had been a submarine engineer and a captain on a liner for some years. By then he was piloting ships in and out of San Pedro harbor. The Captain told Charles and me not to come near him for one week. Then, there it was! How he did it was one of the mysteries of life. The nine-by-nine-foot kitchen had become a white and easy-to-run galley with space for six people to eat. Upstairs, against the hill, were two nine-by-nine-foot bedrooms —cubicles, really—and a nine-by-nine-foot bathroom. And surrounding us was a decayed tropical orchard, which we all tried to bring back to life. There were peacocks everywhere. Friends tried to describe the peacocks' screech. I thought that they cried "New York, New York!" Some said they sounded more like a lost person screaming "Hello, hello!"

Charles and I were very happy with this fifteen acres for more than fifteen years. "You'd think we were in France," Charles would say again and again to friends—as if in some way repaying France for the pleasant memories that that country had given him. He was particularly fond of a long grove of olive trees. We arranged for some Mexican families to pick the olives when they were ripe, but their children ate up all the guavas and figs, so we gave up that idea. Then Jean Renoir, who directed Charles and Maureen O'Hara in *This Land Is Mine*, became very enthusiastic about our olives. He and his wife, Dido, said, "We'll take the olives, we know what to do with them." So they packed them into boxes and sacks. The car was full of olives. I think it took two trips.

Jean and Dido put the olives in brine to "pickle" in a great barrel in the kitchen. The olives would soak in the brine for about six weeks, then the brine was supposed to be poured off and replaced with a fresh lot. One night Charles and I were going there for supper—late, because I was still performing at the Turnabout Theatre—and to help change the brine. As we began the process, suddenly the barrel creaked and a hoop slipped and the whole barrel gave up and burst, and the entire kitchen was about six inches deep in brine and olives. We spent the next two or three hours helping clean up, and Jean and Dido eventually gave up the whole project and threw all the olives away.

Of course, there were not enough trees to make picking the olives worthwhile to a manufacturer, so they fell to the ground or were eaten by the wild peacocks that roamed the Palos Verdes hills. You haven't lived until you've seen peacocks up olive trees in the sunset.

But the slipping cliff at the main house at Pacific Palisades was like the beginning of a series of illnesses for Charles. Perhaps it was. I often feel that too many deep sorrows can sow the seeds of illness. Compensating things like the Shakespeare class and the lovely surroundings of our homes healed many problems. These were also the exciting years at the Palisades house when Charles worked with Bertolt Brecht on *Galileo,* with Hanns Eisler often thumping away at the piano composing the music. My poor Bluthner piano! I suppose its German soul liked the beating.

Renoir's *This Land Is Mine* was produced by R.K.O. In it Charles played a cowardly French schoolteacher during the Nazi occupation who finds courage in the face of death. Charles would make impossible demands in order to bring the needed realism to the part, but, unlike many directors, Renoir was patient and understood. He called Charles one of the most brilliant actors he'd ever worked with.

> He was intelligent and wanted to know why he was being asked to do things. He had every right to know, and I appreciated the concern and concentration he showed all during the filming. You can divide actors into at least two major categories: those who are highly intelligent but not too gifted, and those who are highly gifted and not too intelligent. Charles was both intelligent and gifted, with an instinctive genius for acting.

Jean Renoir had been a Paramount director, and Charles and he had first met in the studio commissary. I don't think it was a big moment but, naturally, as Charles owned a painting by Jean Renoir's father, *The Judgement of Paris,* they talked about that. They became friends, and when Jean married Dido, his good companion and former girl friday, we held the ceremony at our house. It was during the war, so we put all our food stamps together to get a precious fillet of beef for their wedding. Sadly, the fillet got overcooked.

Charles and the Renoirs were very close for a long time, especially around and before and after *This Land Is Mine.* Jean was a man, just the way he lived, who could bring back the France that Charles loved —the France that he drove through with Basil Gill and Sheila Schwartz. The Renoirs' home was like a French farmhouse. There was a scrubbed table, a high fireplace with coals and grille, good sharp knives hanging on the wall, and over the square table a low-hanging lamp with a piece of paper wrapped around it to shadow the eyes restfully— better than candlelight. When you sat round the big square table at dinner, with that shaded light hanging from the ceiling, it was the Renoirs' own French world.

Without my drawing a diagram of this professional checkered life, I think it is fairly clear that Charles and I had to tighten our belts. No MGM income. The slipping cliff. Cook, maid, chauffeur, gardener to support. What we had saved was just eroding. We had to sell the Palisades house and find a cheaper way of life. But with the cliff slipping, house agents wouldn't touch the sale.

So the good Captain said, "Leave it to me!" Turning to his years of experience as an ocean liner captain, he simply said, "I'll know the right person when they come along, but you and Charles keep out of the way." So, cocking his naval cap at a certain angle, he began plotting his strategy.

Soon a rich fortyish lady with a twelve-year-old son and a devoted dark lover appeared in a limousine to answer the Captain's ad. Their enchantment was immediate. The bushy rim of our garden, newly planted with rhus integrifolia, made the Pacific Ocean beckon its arms toward the house on a sparkling day. Another attraction was the secret staircase between the downstairs bedroom and the upstairs bedroom.

Our client had to go to Carmel for a few days on business and a birthday party. How odd that the Captain had to be in nearby Monterey on business also. A full moon. A dinner. A Drambuie.

The Pacific Palisades house was sold at three times what we paid for it, and it went into immediate escrow—a down payment larger than usual. Only then did I meet the new owner for tea on the patio of the house. I had dashed in with a thick film script—Charles dashed in with an even thicker script and was moved gently out of the scene by the Captain. As I sipped my tea, I gave a sidelong glance or two toward the rhus integrifolia. Yes, *sidelong* is the word.

Looking for your next home should be a leisurely adventure, but this time around, it was like a shotgun wedding. I began the search with friends, or I looked alone or with the Captain. If I'd gone with Charles, it might have raised the price. The first thing is to feel like a jack rabbit and look for big, mature trees. Jump, as it were, like a jack rabbit—looking from left to right, spot the area where the wealthy live or have lived (and I don't mean in expensive Beverly Hills). Then drive around the area and find FOR SALE signs put out by the owner, not an agent. These signs are, or were, usually a bright, luminous, iridescent pink. The owner is probably frantic and the buyer cruelly calm. The Captain was very good at being that. And all the friends who came along were briefed: "Don't be enthusiastic!"

At the end of 1949 Charles and I moved from the Pacific Palisades slipping-cliff house to our new home in the heart of Hollywood, a short way up a hill. It was an old square house, but the designer-owner had dreams of medieval grandeur, and he built a kitty-cornered sunroom on the house with a turret on top. The house had an eighteen-by-thirty-foot living room, and by completely closing off a wall that had French doors, Charles got his schoolroom.

The garden: We put in a pool by Lloyd Wright, son of Frank Lloyd Wright. It took up the whole space at the side of the house. Charles was very proud of our pool. Lloyd Wright had made the outdoors look like the indoors, and vice versa—the best of two worlds. But with the discomforts of both worlds as well. If you sat on the benches, the cement grazed your shins, laddered your stockings, and induced the condition called nutmeg-grater-ass.

Before we came along the fine old house had fallen on hard times, and the owners had sold the frontage on our street. Charles and I could now be said to have a lot of backage, a tail of land that wound up into the hills. It used to be a woodland of pine trees, but they had been planted too close together and soon began to look like matchsticks. They would fall down occasionally in the wind, so gradually they all had to go. An old brick path wound to the top of our hill, lit by a string of electric lights dating from 1909 all the way up.

By this time, Charles and I had grown too far apart to be really honest with each other anymore. We were not often unhappy, but Charles showed a morose side to me, and I showed an increasingly flip side to him. We had been fed by too many professional "dividers": Alexander Korda, Erich Pommer, Sheila Schwartz, Bobby Benson, and there were more to come. Mostly, unattached people seem to take sides.

My success at the Turnabout Theatre was also a dividing element, as were my passing friendships that grew and fizzled out during all those years. Charles and I always seemed to have confidants who paralleled one another—the main evil being the confidant who listened and reported to both sides.

I can only compare Charles' and my tightly bound estrangement to the battle between Oberon and Titania in *A Midsummer Night's Dream* —although not in appearance, I fear. Nobody calculated intentionally to part us, nor did anybody try intentionally to get us together. We both needed some kind of help. We didn't get it.

But our house, our houses, survived, always. They endured, and somehow so did Charles and I. The physical structure was always secure.

Charles' classes—Shakespeare, rehearsals, sessions—came to rest at our house on Curson Avenue. Of course, as I was still involved at the Turnabout Theatre, we kept very different hours—hence the necessity of my having a separate kitchen, very tiny, in my bedroom, or we would have had to maintain a separate staff. I had an excellent routine going at the Turnabout, so I was always delighted that Charles had activities to occupy his evenings. The great thing about it was that Charles was admittedly learning as he taught and the students were learning something about behavior and life, too—if they were observant enough—though Charles didn't always have brilliant people around him. I think he just wanted people . . . followers.

The students discussed Stanislavski and the Comédie Français. In France and Russia, they took years to study one play. A play ripens. Charles and his students were patient, too, and proud of it. Infinite time was taken. They worked meticulously on *Twelfth Night* for well over a year and, unfortunately, never did it.

The large sofa in the schoolroom is now blue, but it was then white and always looked rather grubby. Since Charles always sank deeply into chairs, his students in emulation sank deep into the couch. Quite a lot of small change was retrieved from this generous sofa. And we had a pay telephone installed for all these "young" people, and I even think we made a profit out of it. When we went to empty out the money, there was often more than enough to pay the telephone bill.

The more important paintings we owned were hanging in this schoolroom: Renoir's *Judgement of Paris,* a Dufy, and a Utrillo. The large mantelpiece over the fireplace was loaded with thirty or forty pre-Columbian terra-cotta and stone figures. Some thirty more were placed around the room, and the rest in the house or in the garden by the pool. Paintings and drawings by Morris Graves were all over the place. Charles talked to his students with feeling and passion about being able to relate one art to another, and it was there for them to see.

Heidel came to us in 1947 or '48, after the Pacific Palisades house had slipped for the third time. She began as a maid, but she cooked so well that when we started to pull in the pursestrings and cut down on the staff, it was a great pleasure to keep her on as a housekeeper-cook. Our respect for her was a link, of sorts, for Charles and me. She survived the agony of the big move from the Palisades house to Curson Avenue.

Heidel was set in her religious faith, determined in her goodness, stubborn as a mule, and intelligent and well read. Perhaps she was a little inclined to proselytize, but the anti-Catholic (Charles) and the agnostic (me) knew how to steer clear of that. I think that occasionally I tried to probe the mystery of what "faith" really was, but I didn't get an answer from her or from anyone else. A gentle yet withering look was usually her response.

Just to please Heidel, Charles read two or three times on radio for *The Hour of St. Francis,* but he was horrified by the disproportionate amount of money that she gave to the church. He wished she would save more, partly because, being an actor, he knew his own future was uncertain, and wondered if Heidel thought we were the class of Europeans who looked after a "family retainer" in old age. Anyway, Heidel stayed with us right up until the 1959 production of *King Lear* in England, and is now happily employed with some wealthy people who, perhaps, not being in the creative field, are retainer-oriented. And are of the same faith.

Over the years, we changed Charles' "man" many times. You could call him Charles' houseman-valet-chauffeur-butler. Heidel wouldn't sit down and eat with any of these men. Whether this was personal with each one or a general fear of the male, or snobbishness,

I will never know. She just couldn't. Menservants often have preconceived dreams of sitting in the pantry cleaning silver (wearing a green baize apron) and performing other gentlemanly chores. But Charles and I had practically no silver. One cigarette box (a gift) and a set of German silver knives and forks were all.

It was always a problem to get a houseman since Charles was far from a conventional boss. I never enjoyed the chore of interviewing —listing duties, showing the house and rooms, and making the person feel that Charles and I were not monsters, yet talking with authority about an actor's life and hours. But when we moved into the new house, wonder of wonders, I hardly had a decision to make. I found Eddie Duncan, who had been batman to General Patton. It was immediately and mutually agreed. Eddie was a really good man's man for Charles, and he remained with us until after Charles died.

One reason that it was usually so difficult to find and keep a houseman was that Charles simply took no interest in his own appearance. He took the fullest advantage of all methods of dressing to achieve comfort. Everything he wore was too large for him, and he used the most peculiar things to hold up his trousers—old ties, pieces of rope or string, a leather luggage strap tied in a knot—usually tied rather tightly, well under the navel. He just seemed to have a thing against belts. But being a famous person did make it possible for him to be accepted, no matter what he wore. I thought Charles went a bit too far, privileged or not. He became "privileged" to such a degree that one time in New York his pants fell down in Times Square.

Also, it was horrendous for Charles to have to commit himself to when he would eat and where he would eat, and who else might be there. There was always a moment of passing fury if Charles was asked, and really he was right—how could he answer? In the mornings, Heidel would stand by my bed with a pencil and pad and ask me about dinner plans, and if I said I didn't know, Heidel occasionally told me that I ought to know! To her, unplanned food could not be as good as she would like it to be, and wasted food or spoiled food, of course, were beyond her compass of understanding—mine, too—and rather painful. I like a tight ship.

So round and round we went. Charles loved good food, but couldn't commit himself. He was no man to make a soufflé for. Eventually Heidel and I became experts at meals that didn't deteriorate if kept waiting for hours. We always had a high percentage of boiled dinners and stews when Charles was working. He was usually willing to wait the few minutes it took to cook green vegetables. Still, his habits were a strain on the staff. They were, after all, the first up in the morning to prepare for the day, and the last to get to bed after cleaning up.

190

Charles sometimes worried about this sort of problem when he saw how tired they looked.

In my early years of housekeeping with Charles, I sometimes said, "Oh, Charles, how I wish we could live in a hotel!" This proved to be one of the most hideous things that I could ever say to him. Having been born into the hotel business, Charles felt that owning and living in his own house was the answer to all his early frustrations and anxieties. He talked a lot about his "home," and he obviously enjoyed mouthing the word itself.

Nevertheless, he, as innocently as a child, continued to expect his home to be run like a hotel. A few superficial rules he made for himself seemed to prove to him that the great transition had been made. So he would not have bells in the house to call a servant. He preferred to say "Yoo-hoo!" though we did have a buzzer system on each telephone. Charles liked servants to go out on Christmas Day and other holidays, rather than have extra work. If Charles and I stayed in, we'd fix ourselves something simple—an almost defiant gesture against the elaborate family hotel celebrations he endured as a young man. Otherwise, Charles liked *ir*regularity. I shall remember Eddie for his capacity to cope with this.

I suppose we should have made more trips to the wildflowers, the mountains, deserts, and forests—but time was collapsing like a concertina. In the days when there was a little more time, a drive into the mountains or the deserts made Charles very happy. He loved to pick armfuls of flowers, to break off branches where it didn't hurt the tree and put them in the great vases and pots that we had collected over the years—pots by the Japanese artist Hamada, and by Hamada's contemporary English friend, Bernard Leach.

It was always interesting and satisfying, even exciting, to see Charles place a branch in a particular pot. He usually chose one that could sit in the pot in the precise position in which it had originally been growing. If it had been growing horizontally, Charles would counterbalance it with a rock, allowing the stalk to reach the water perhaps in a flat dish. I must admit I became rather expert, too—although different—at arranging oddly contrasting colors.

We used to enjoy all this without turning to the many Japanese books about flower arranging—some of which are appalling. In California the wildflowers gave Charles a new color experience, and I can only say that he felt free and ecstatic as he stood among them. For him those were rare times without anxiety. We would drive home exhausted, put the California poppies and lupins in our great pots or in aluminum saucepans in a casual mass, undisturbed, as we had picked them. The lupins, thrust in a kitchen bucket, would straighten up like ranks of soldiers in the sunlight the next morning.

But often when people came to the house, Charles would say to me, "If they say anything about the flowers, don't tell them I arranged them. Say you did it."

23

Several times I have been asked to remember my first meeting with Bertolt Brecht. It's not an occasion that I can recall; you only remember meeting people for the first time when they appeal to you. And Brecht didn't appeal to me particularly. He didn't have a very strong personality, as far as I could tell. He shambled along a little bit. I think there were many who didn't like him very much, but there were a great number of people who admired him tremendously, of course. Brecht had a lot of cronies.

I remember one of our lunches—fortunately, we often had them out of doors—when Brecht smelled so terribly of cigar smoke that I could hardly eat. He smoked awful cigars. Whether they were expensive ones or cheap ones, I don't know. Or perhaps the passing through Brecht made the smoke come out with the sourest, bitterest smell. He hadn't much money, so he wore overalls, all in one piece, washed-out blue. Not blue jeans—coveralls. Once there was a label hanging out the back of his neck. I pulled at the label and found that this outfit he was wearing was called a *Functional.* This really made him laugh. He hadn't many teeth and his mouth opened in a complete circle, so you'd see one or two little tombstones sticking out of this black hole. A very unpleasant sight.

Brecht had a coterie of mistresses, but I never saw him with a pretty woman. More your stolid spinsters. Women who fell in love with him fell in love with his intellect. To them Brecht was a giant. When he said something—whether it was a cliché or not—he said it with profound conviction.

He lived with his wife, Helene Weigel, and their two children in a small house in Santa Monica; the house was rather an untidy one, I must say. Brecht came to our house, but we'd occasionally go over there. I just remember a few things, like the toilet not working—and two or three weeks later it still wasn't working. And they had a wonderful apricot tree in the backyard, but I don't think they bothered about food very much. There were always a few very good chess sets around. Brecht obviously played a lot of chess with his European friends.

Helene Weigel was a wonderful actress and very loyal to her husband. She and Brecht understood each other. But at that time I had no opportunity to see her act because Brecht himself would not allow her to accept small character parts in Hollywood films. Of course, she had a German accent and it's highly improbable she ever would have got a lead. So she was rather an unhappy woman, I believe. I don't blame her, and I think that it might have changed her life and even the children's lives if she'd worked. She must have been absolutely boiling inside.

Charles and I didn't mix with the European side of Brecht's life at all—all his refugee friends from Hitler's regime.

It took Charles and Brecht two or three years to translate and rewrite *Galileo*. They worked together for several hours every day, and planned everything in the room we called the Library. Everything—the upholstery, the carpet, the curtains—had to be changed because you couldn't get the smell of Brecht's cigars out of them. Charles didn't speak a word of German and Brecht had a very small English vocabulary, and that with a very strong accent. Still, they managed to carve out the play. As Brecht described the process:

> The awkward circumstances that one translator knew no German and the other scarcely any English compelled us . . . from the outset to use acting as our means of translation . . .
>
> We had to decide the gist of each piece of dialogue by my acting it all in bad English or even in German, and his then acting it back in a variety of ways until I could say: that is it . . .
>
> We used to work in L.'s small library, in the mornings. But often L. would come and meet me in the garden, running barefoot in shirt and trousers over the damp grass . . . The gaiety and the beautiful proportions of this world of flowers overlapped in a most pleasant way into our work. For quite a while our work embraced everything we could lay our hands on.

Beyond acting, Charles' chief talent, I think, was construction. You might call it editing. He was never a creative playwright, but he was a master cutter. He would have liked to have been a writer, because in fact he really knew how to build a dramatic house, and Brecht spotted that. And Charles saw Brecht as one of the world's great playwrights.

Of course, Brecht was internationally known, but no one supposed then that he would end up the great figure he is today. But Charles had a sympathy with Brecht's brilliant mind. Perhaps, in a way, it's a pity they didn't make some kind of partnership of it and spend many more years together. But *Galileo* was their one and only collaboration. And it took such a long time because of the language barrier.

Hanns Eisler wrote the music for *Galileo*, so he often came to the house to help set the mood for Charles and Brecht. He was rather a short man, really rather like a sausage, and he stood at the piano—I think he got more force that way when he played. It sounded a bit like a Sousa band starting up. The clarion call rang out when Hanns Eisler started to extemporize for *Galileo*. Hanns was a jolly musician. He sort of stalked the instrument, and as he stood before it, his short fat fingers would come down on a chord that would shake the rafters. I believe the music he finally did for *Galileo* was very good, and the lyrics were adapted by Albert Brush.

When the play was completed, Charles and Brecht needed someone to oversee the production and keep it pulled together and well organized—in other words, a director. They approached Joe Losey, who was delighted. But he became, I am told, rather disenchanted during rehearsals.

Brecht was notorious for being a fiend incarnate in the theatre. Whenever anything of his was done in this country, he was an absolute devil at rehearsals. It was not personal malice. It was simply tremendous impatience when anything—the costumes, the scenery, the acting—was less than he wanted it to be. Charles generally agreed with his brilliant co-author.

On opening night, Norman Lloyd, who had founded the Coronet Theatre with John Houseman, visited Charles in his trailer dressing room. Charles was lying in the dark drinking soda water and, according to Lloyd, looking terrified. After all, it was Charles' first stage appearance since the Old Vic season years before. "Am I doing a terrible thing?" Charles asked him. "This could be a great setback in my career. But I have to do this, it is right. . . . This is a new play and it is of such stature! It is as important, if not even more important, than reviving the classics."

After the production Lloyd wrote:

> When it opened, it was a smash hit and . . . it probably could have run for a year, but it only ran two weeks because other productions had been scheduled. During the two weeks there was standing room only and people like Ingrid Bergman called and frantically begged to be given a seat.

But the reviews in New York were almost all unfavorable. The worst of them was by Brooks Atkinson in *The New York Times*. He found the play "loose and episodic," the performances "pretentious," especially Charles'. He "throws away his part, as though everyone were ashamed to be earnest about serious matters. . . . Although his Galileo is good Laughton, it is not Galileo. . . . He is casual and contemptuous; he is ponderous and condescending, and there is a great deal of old-fashioned fiddle-faddle. . . ."

Ironically, another play about Galileo, called *Lamp at Midnight*, opened off-Broadway around the same time, and it received better reviews than Brecht's. That nearly killed Charles. It was a terrible blow to him when the value of the play and the production were not recognized.

Many of Brecht's friends were thought to be Communists, but Charles, not politically minded at all, never gave that a thought. After all, Brecht was an artist, and so was Charles. Brecht himself did not have a Communist party card. He didn't belong to the Communist Party because, after all, if he *had*, he would have been anti-Communist. Brecht was anti-everything. The moment he became part of a country he was anti that country. He lived in America, but he was not a gracious guest—not here or anywhere. He wasn't a bitter man, I think. He was always funny about institutions and authority. He didn't want to be in power himself because he was anti-any power. And he wasn't destructive. He never tried to destroy a government with harsh words or anything like that. He was always humorous about the political news that came in.

Was it the ten or eleven unfriendly witnesses? Because I think that Brecht was the eleventh man and, as far as I know, he was the only one who really—what is the phrase?—"got away with it." He certainly wasn't given any particular reprimand or punishment by the House Un-American Activities Committee. Brecht was so honest, so innocent before the committee, and so funny—that was his saving grace. Plus, he had such a strong German accent that none of the committee members could understand a word he said. And of course when he spoke to them he saw to it that his English was even worse than usual.

"Mr. Brecht, since you have been in the United States, have you attended any Communist Party meetings?

"No, I don't think so."

"You don't think so?

"No."

196

"Well, aren't you certain?"

"No . . . I am certain. Yes."

Brecht also brought along an interpreter, who had an accent even worse than his own, so nobody could understand either of them. The smell of Brecht's awful cigars filled the large room. One of the men tried to make him stop smoking, but apparently Brecht couldn't function unless he was chewing on this wet, sour little cheroot, or whatever it was. The room stank, and people coughed, and they couldn't understand much of what he said—Brecht was just pixie enough in his nature to do all this on purpose, remember.

So they let Brecht go. They didn't even tell him to leave the country, but he was gone the very next day. Not only Brecht and his family, but Hanns Eisler, too—they all disappeared. Charles never saw any of them again.

Back in Europe, Brecht is supposed to have said: "The committee was very nice—they let me smoke. The Nazis would never have done that."

When Brecht died on August 14, 1956, someone sent a telegram asking Charles to prepare a message to be read at the funeral ceremony. But since the funeral would take place in East Germany, Charles didn't feel safe—that is, he didn't feel it would be the right thing to do —to send a message of good will or sympathy in response to the telegram, under the political circumstances. Our lawyer called up the FBI and informed them. The FBI said, "As you've told us of the whole thing, go ahead. You had the good sense to report it to us, so there will not be any repercussions." So Charles sent the telegram to Germany.

In 1954 a Kurt Singer, whom Charles and I had never met or spoken to, wrote the *unauthorized* biography of Charles, entitled *The Laughton Story, An Intimate Story of Charles Laughton.* And it was a story, filled with inaccuracies. Since the book was mostly endless flattery, our lawyers advised that little could be accomplished by a suit. We dropped the idea and dismissed Kurt Singer and his book from our minds. Charles would not autograph a copy for God or man.

Actually, the book is filled with so many inaccuracies that it becomes funny reading, sorting out the truth from fiction. In writing about Charles' *Galileo* experiences, Singer wrote:

The New York drama critics hailed Laughton's performance, and admired the skill with which he had adapted the original text, which was rather ponderous and wordy, into a fast-moving and stirring drama. However, the production soon ran into snags.

The trouble lay in the political affiliations of the playwright. Bertolt Brecht, for all his talent, was a dyed-in-the-wool Communist. . . . The musical score for the play on *Galileo* had been composed by Hanns Eisler, another convinced Communist who had composed many propaganda songs . . .

Laughton had gone into the project in complete innocence of the situation. He had, more or less, been "kidnapped" by the Communists, who were very happy to have a person of Laughton's stature to lend prestige to one of their propaganda fliers. . . . The tone of the production reeked of Communist influence. . . . the *Daily Worker* hailed it as the greatest thing on the American stage. . . . When the facts of the matter were put before Laughton by his manager, Charles saw that he was playing into Communist hands. He had fallen into bad company. There was nothing for him to do but to withdraw from the production of *Galileo*.

Singer's version was nonsense, of course. Charles went to New York with the production and stayed with it till the end. But twenty years later, the book surfaced again—and in a surprising way. Joe Losey, *Galileo's* director in name only, recalling the subpoena sent to him by the House Un-American Activities Committee, put down some "remembrances" with the help of writer Guy Flatley in an article that appeared in the drama section of the Sunday *Los Angeles Times*, March 9, 1975:

Who could have turned his name in to the committee?

"Charles Laughton turned my name in to the FBI. He went to them and denounced Brecht and me."

But why would Laughton do such a thing?

"Why did anybody talk to the FBI? To save their own necks. Laughton was a naturalized American, so maybe they threatened to have his citizenship revoked. . . . In his authorized biography, he claimed that he had been duped by Brecht and me. That wasn't true. He always knew where we stood. I was furious and horrified when I read that book."

Singers' statements are so full of inaccuracies and distortions, it is beyond me how Losey could ever have imagined such a book could be authorized by Charles. Had Joe Losey simply written to me or called me, he could have got the truth instantly. But some people are more comfortable feeling hurt and betrayed.

Anyway, I was also furious and horrified when I read Losey's quotes in that article. They smacked of paranoia and reckless misinformation. After speaking to my lawyer, we sent a letter off to *The Los Angeles Times*. My letter appeared in its drama section on the following March 30. In part it went:

> First of all, there has never been an "authorized biography" of Charles Laughton. There is no proof whatsoever for any of Losey's statements. Mr. Laughton . . . was just barely aware of the FBI. He was not motivated by fear of having his citizenship revoked, because Mr. Laughton did not become an American citizen until three years after the production of *Galileo,* and the termination of his association with Losey.
>
> The tactics Losey deplores, and which he says had caused him so much hardship, are the very ones he now finds the most useful in this article.

For the record, Brecht's own book, *Brecht on Theatre,* was published in 1964, seventeen years after his *Galileo* days. He devoted many pages to the time he spent with Charles, which express only admiration and appreciation. Brecht wrote:

> What attracted L. about *Galileo* was . . . he thought this might become what he called a *contribution.* And so great was his anxiety to show things as they really are that despite all his indifference (indeed timidity) in political matters he suggested and even demanded that not a few of the play's points should be made sharper. . . .

Charles, innocently enough, did not feel he ever really belonged in the human race, and no world tragedy made him at one with others, as is usually the case. Perhaps this is why Charles ignored most causes and was always unable to join. Another reason for not joining was our lawyer Loyd Wright. He protected us from groups of all sorts, as we planned to become American citizens. On Wright's advice, we did not apply for citizenship until after the war, for fear it would prejudice the sale of Charles' movies in England. So 1950 was the year we became United States citizens.

More and more, Charles and I were going to Palos Verdes separately. I often went there with my own friends, especially when Charles was away touring. Sometimes I went with a single friend, but more often with groups—musicians, the Turnabouters, and so on. Oddly enough,

I think Charles was more envious of my groups of friends than anything else. We'd have a barbecue or make a big pot of spaghetti, make silly movies, or take a lot of Polaroid pictures. We laughed a lot. But Charles, if he came along, just couldn't participate—he was a big child, as so many people have said, but he couldn't play.

Charles really didn't make friends very easily, but people soon focused on him. I would sometimes feel very annoyed at the way people would greet Charles enthusiastically and then, changing their focus, would add as an afterthought, "Oh, yes, and it's nice to meet you, too, Mrs. Laughton."

Eventually—and agonizingly—Charles told me that he only felt really comfortable with his "own kind." As the years went by, I suppose I just came to accept these friends as part of my life with Charles. I worried about him, and I was always glad if and when Charles met a man whom he was really fond of and who liked him. Charles would take him to Palos Verdes and stay there for a time. Perhaps it was unkind of me not to show disapproval. My acceptance may have been more cruel, in a way, and made Charles feel even more guilty about it all. He was a moral man—about everyone but himself. Himself he shocked; he horrified himself. And he suffered from the painful guilts of a highly moral man. It made me very sad that Charles should have to feel so guilty about it; that he seemed to need to be so secretive, all the while still wanting to be found out.

I remember resenting it very much when Charles said to me one day, "We've got to give up Palos Verdes, it's becoming a regular love nest and that's bad." Charles couldn't stand to think that our beautiful cottage was being contaminated, but I hated the way he said *we* and tried to make me feel immoral in order to ease his own conscience.

 24

With so few good film roles (*The Girl from Manhattan, The Strange Door, Abbott and Costello Meet Captain Kidd*), Charles was now reading publicly a lot—so much so that he was asked to read on the Sunday night *Ed Sullivan Show* in New York. It would excite interest, of course, because Charles was a film star. On that program he read *The Fiery Furnace* (Shadrach, Meshach, and Abed-Nego).

That Sunday evening Paul Gregory saw Charles on a television set in a New York bar. At the time he was working in the Concert Department of Music Corporation of America (M.C.A.), handling bookings for Spike Jones. Well, when Paul saw Charles on the screen, he flew out of the bar and round to the Broadway stage door of the Ed Sullivan theatre before Charles could have possibly left—even before the show was over. When Charles finally emerged, Gregory approached him, introduced himself, and said, "I have an idea for you!"

I don't know if Charles was alone when he first met Gregory or if he had somebody with him. You don't usually give a performance without someone around, probably an agent, or even go out and about alone at any time if you're well known. It's too hazardous and nerve-racking, as you never know what crowds of people might literally hang on to you for an autograph. Anyway, Paul and Charles met, and they went to a quiet bar to talk.

Paul Gregory, who had a mercurial mind, had had a brain wave. Since he was in the concert world, he suddenly had a vision of Henry the Eighth-Captain Bligh-Ruggles going round the country and reading, with all America sitting and listening. With his film career in the semidoldrums, Charles needed something to make him function again. Whatever else I might say about Paul Gregory, you cannot take that away from him—he came along when Charles needed him most.

Charles, enchanted with the idea, called me up at once. "There's an extraordinary young man I've run into," he said, very excited. "He'll be coming straight out to Hollywood. I'll be back in two days, and Paul will probably arrive two or three days after that." Then he added, "Don't be deceived by Paul's looks. He's overhandsome. He's right up in the Gregory Peck school of good looks." Charles guessed that I would be suspicious and assured me that Paul's brilliance overshadowed his appearance. I don't remember Charles saying that Paul was intelligent. He was *brilliant.* Maybe *intelligent* might have given the wrong impression.

From the time they met after the *Ed Sullivan Show,* the whole thing took form in seven or eight days. Soon Paul Gregory arrived in Hollywood with the M.C.A. concert booking files tucked underneath his arm. I remember the tall, dark figure I met at the front door. He hadn't even changed his M.C.A. charcoal suit to a "civilian" outfit. I figured that he must have just walked out on M.C.A. Rather proudly, in his own way (whether it was actually true or not), he said that he had stolen the card index of all the college auditoriums and women's clubs that M.C.A. had collected over many years. I supposed that he somehow already had a copy, because he felt he might one day be on his own and was just waiting for his chance. When it came, he would be ready to go—card index and all.

When I first saw Paul standing there in the doorway of our house, I quite agreed with Charles' report. He was handsome. And he was full of ideas. Later, I learned to be more suspicious. And afterward, I learned to be afraid of him.

The first thing Paul Gregory did was to order some note paper printed: PAUL GREGORY ASSOCIATES. He knew that print can be very impressive—*Incorporated* or *Associated.* Next, he found an office and a secretary. Then he and Charles went to our lawyer, Loyd Wright, and were advanced what was necessary to get started. Gregory started to book dates for Charles at impressive speed.

Charles' tours eventually influenced the whole world of performers going on one-man (or one-woman) lectures, shows—whatever category, whatever title. It is remarkable how many wonderful auditoriums across the country have superb lighting and sound equipment that is hardly used. Charles and Gregory pioneered the use of these semi-used theatres. Brochures, advance publicity, stage and lighting requirements, ticket sales—Gregory oversaw it all as he worked with clubs and organizations booking Charles. An "advance man" also was essential. Paul booked Charles for thirty-one appearances the first time, then forty the second time—all packed houses. And a new life for Charles—and Paul. They created their own red carpet.

As usual, at Christmastime Charles was back on radio and TV on the Edgar Bergen-Charlie McCarthy show. Charles would tell McCarthy the story of Christmas or would impersonate Santa Claus:

CHARLIE MCCARTHY: How'd you get in here, anyway? And don't give me that routine about the chimney!

LAUGHTON: Oh, so you don't believe I came down the chimney?

CHARLIE MCCARTHY: No, I don't. I look at you and I look at the fireplace—it can't be done!

LAUGHTON: Look at me! You've got me so excited my stomach is slipping its moorings.

CHARLIE MCCARTHY: Not only that, but your caboose is loose.

Paul and Charles knew it was great publicity for the tours. On this show and on other shows, Charles would sometimes try out material, so he could keep developing new segments—from Dickens to Kerouac and, more important, Thomas Wolfe.

Charles' reputation as a reader grew and grew. He read on the Dinah Shore and Jack Paar television programs, in the same way as other performers went on to sing or dance. He became Charles the Reader . . . and Teacher. Audiences wanted and waited for him to read and tell them stories about America.

Charles believed that in America people never stopped wanting to learn. That was one of the things that attracted Charles to reading in America in the first place—the eternal student point of view, the tendency of people of all ages to continue studying. Touring around the country, you might encounter a flighty, middle-aged bridge-playing lady with a purple orchid for the occasion, who insists on giving you a little supper after the show of maybe warm cranberry juice and cottage cheese with chives and Ritz crackers, and no liquor. But this woman also organized the program, sold the tickets, and so on, because she wanted to improve herself. Even if it only gave her a little power, a little identity in her community, she booked shows that she thought will bring culture to the town.

Charles' reading tours were for them like the *Reader's Digest,* which does pre-digest literature for people. He sorted out the literature and said, "I give you this piece of Shakespeare, this piece of the Bible, and just a little parsley on the side, with a slightly suggestive limerick," and then also fed them someone more difficult to understand, like Kerouac. Afterward, audiences possibly did tootle off to the library and take out books. Many of them might not even have remembered what

Charles read, but remembered the nice feeling when Charles read to them. They thought that they somehow grasped something that they didn't understand before, and I think they got the feeling that reading could actually be fun.

Charles' love and respect for America grew as he toured the little towns and cities across the country. Half his readings were at colleges and universities, and there—this is true—the sales of Thomas Wolfe actually rose. The college students were the most gratifying audiences to Charles. He talked to them afterward, and at colleges he always had supper with the dean, the teachers, and perhaps a student or two. Sometimes the dinners could be a chore, but usually, exhausted as Charles would be, he was renewed and exhilarated by them. To him the most important thing was simple, uncluttered contact existing between him and the audience; he felt that the actor-reader and his books should be the only things on the stage. Charles found the closeness in America, in small towns, in schools, in a way he never thought possible in England. So he learned to appreciate America through its authors: Mark Twain, Saroyan, Thurber.

Out of Charles' tours came all his appearances on television, and soon McGraw-Hill published his first book of readings, *Tell Me a Story.* Each story began with a personal piece or philosophical comment by Charles. He was really ahead of many educators in that his observations were quick and volatile—animal intuition and native intelligence. But Charles often doubted himself because he had not really gone straight to the sources of knowledge; he did it through research, through men like Albert Brush. He was served the choice morsels and he picked from these for the public. I'm sure these research people felt that he was fully equipped to turn these into theatrical gold.

Charles flourished in this world of knowledge. I, with my lack of formal education, became smart at dodging subjects I knew nothing about. I call it high education myself to know one's limitations—but Charles couldn't accept that. I think that, really, Charles had an inferiority complex about his trade background. We all do, when we see the size and quantity of literature in the world and we can't ever touch it, however long we live. "How little the wisest man knows . . ."

Through Albert Brush, Charles met the well-known art collector Walter Arensberg and his wife Lou. Generally speaking, Arensberg's tastes were different from Charles'. He said Charles had a "dancing" taste. Some things, even in a geometric line, can dance—as if the things that were made sprang from the passions of the artist. But the things that Walter Arensberg bought sprang from the intellect—cerebral, geometric, unpassionate. He was one of the first collectors of pre-Columbian figures, and his place was full of them, mainly stone figures, but also terra-cotta pieces, and every inch of the walls of his house in Hollywood was covered with pictures. He just had no more room, but he never sold any of them, and he kept acquiring more. They had great Persian carpets laid over other carpets—all beautiful.

I used to go to pick Charles up three, four, or even five nights a week at the Arensberg house. I was working at the Turnabout, and by the time I would arrive, the discussion among Charles and Walter and Lou Arensberg and Albert would be tapering off. It was then whiskey time—and sometimes they went right on talking. And, of course, there were the Monday nights when I wasn't working at the theatre, so I would sometimes spend a whole evening with Charles and Albert at the Arensbergs'.

The Stendahl Galleries in Los Angeles got a large shipment of objects from Mexico every few months, and the unpacking was very exciting. Arensberg had first choice, but Charles never once envied him—neither ever wanted anything the other did. I never bought anything, or certainly not anything of importance, and from experience I knew that whatever I did buy, Charles would not like it. In one unpacking ceremony, there was an object that Walter Arensberg didn't want. It was a warrior's head made of jadeite, a form of jade, and it was very heavy. It had full lips and there were remnants of gold in the eyesockets, where once there had been inlaid jewels. Warriors wore these masks on their chests to show their strength.

I fell in love with the mask. It was priced at $1,000, which was a lot of money for me then, but I wanted it, so I bought it anyway. The greenish head had an erotic expression so powerful that, I think, Charles was actually frightened of it. It was too masculine, too strong for him. But he said to me, "That's your taste. You like it, all right, that's fine. You should have something you like." Most people coming into our house liked it more than anything else we had. But when friends commented on the marvelous mask, Charles never explained to them that I had picked it out, that it was mine. Nothing was said.

Some years later, I went away on my first concert tour, which was directed and booked by Paul Gregory. When I returned home, my mask wasn't in the house anymore. Charles told me he had sold it to a dealer and got four terra-cotta figures in its place. Although I was hurt, I only said, "Oh, dear." Charles then apologized, "I know I shouldn't have done it." Nothing much more was said about it. But inside I really hated Charles for parting with it, and I would nurse that deep hatred through all the years.

One Christmas, when Charles was with the M.C.A. agency and sponsored by one of its executives, Taft Schreiber, there was a great exchange of presents. Taft Schreiber always gave very good and expensive gifts. Again, I was away during this time, and when I came back I saw the various Christmas gifts. One was a book displaying one of the most important pre-Columbian collections in the country—a great big art book, vast and expensive. Taft had given it to Charles. Charles had tried to keep the book from me, but after a few weeks I finally saw it—and the frontispiece was a color photograph of my green mask I had purchased and lost, which at that present date was worth twenty thousand dollars.

Charles came over to me and said, "I'm sorry." He was clutching the book and went absolutely rigid all over. He said, "I didn't want you to see it. I didn't want you to see it. Now that you have seen it, you might as well know that this is the most important piece in the entire collection."

I hadn't bought the mask as an investment, but the fact that it had become so vastly important in a matter of about four years just brought back all the pain, the deep fury I felt when Charles first sold it while I was away. I tried to put it out of my mind. I let it go, I just let it pass. Anger finally only ages a person. Charles knew he had made a terrible mistake, so what was the point of saying anything more?

Since that time, I have never bought anything like that of value— I dared not. Selling the mask was part of a killer thing in Charles, and it killed my taste and initiative. To this day I cannot bring myself to fall in love with objects or something I might want to possess. I suppose a psychiatrist could have a field day with that! But none of us copes too well with any loss. So I am simply protecting myself.

Between Charles and me, the incident finally got down to, well, not exactly a humorous level, but the issue lightened somewhat; because, over the years, if something cropped up—some disagreement or whatever—Charles would say, "I don't want to hear about the green mask." That meant, "Let's not talk about it!" Maybe the green mask represented a kind of threat to all his own fears and an undermining of his judgment in art.

Like a great number of people, Charles was always searching—not for a religion, not for truth—but for the connecting spark that made him the artist that he was. That compulsion is something I do not understand because I cannot identify with it. Charles always looked upon the painter Morris Graves, for example, as a mystic. It was this mystic quality that he first felt in Graves' paintings.

Charles and Morris Graves became very close as artists. Morris poured out letters to Charles, which I think he only half-answered, because he never really fully had a correspondence with anybody. It's a pity that Morris Graves' letters were never kept (Charles loved to fill a wastebasket—to file his conscience) for they were all expressions of mysticism. And as much as Graves enjoyed being a mystic to Charles, he was quite a tough businessman, too, and he had an eye to the future in relation to the sale of his paintings through Marion Willard and her gallery.

His art, of course, developed and changed while Charles was still alive. Marion Willard wanted Charles to have the best Graveses, so she would call him and say, "Come to the gallery. I have a new batch in." I personally felt a great empathy with Graves when he started to interpret his horror of noise in his paintings. I loved the noise paintings and wanted to buy a very black picture, with a tiny little bird fighting for its existence in a modern sort of dark, mechanized sky. Charles didn't like the painting and wouldn't have it in the house.

Marion Willard understood Charles well enough to show him the things that would act upon his emotions, because acquiring paintings was an emotional thing for Charles. They turned out always to be the food that sustained him in his acting. They excited him and inspired him. Charles could sit and handle a piece of sculpture—often pre-Columbian sculpture—or look at a painting literally for hours and hours.

A painting had to mean something to Charles. It had to fulfill a need or he would get rid of it. He never bought anything as an investment—which, of course, is what 80 percent of collectors do. It's not fashionable simply to say, "I am buying these things as an investment." So people buy paintings, they say, because they have a love for them —but Charles really lived on them. It was not just love, it was a necessity. It was like drinking water or breathing.

I remember, when I first knew Charles, how we went to antique shops and collected ceramics, furniture, and things that I still have around me in the house in Hollywood. The delicate little Meissen coffeepot we picked up in Yorkshire went next to a de Staël nude, each somehow bringing out the quality of the other. We always had modern furniture, and Charles always had great feeling for all things that had good lines, things made with passion and good craftsmanship.

Paul Gregory had a choral professor friend, Dr. Charles Hirt, at the University of Southern California. This friend would come to the house with teachers and students for Charles to read to for experimental practice with a small audience. At one of these sessions Paul introduced me to the musician Ray Henderson (who earlier had attended USC), who became my piano accompanist for singing engagements away from the Turnabout Theatre.

During some of the time that Charles was on tour, I performed at the Turnabout, but Ray Henderson and I also started to prepare a nightclub show. It was Paul who encouraged, even pressed, Ray and me to work up the nightclub act—Paul Gregory would promote it. Charles was very pleased with the idea that I, too, would get out and show myself in the big world. After all, I'd been at Turnabout for ten years. Paul was also tickled pink to separate me from "that little theatre."

So Ray and I began our rehearsals.

I had always been a research buff, and it comes naturally to me, for I rarely forget a song. I still remember those old socialist songs pleading for freedom and the earlier songs pleading for temperance that I uncovered in the Cave of Harmony days. And right up to Turnabout, of course.

Ray Henderson, on his side, never forgot a song once he heard it, so we had a high old time. Probably my biggest challenge was learning how to handle a microphone with ease. Charles insisted I should be a clotheshorse, so we invested in that as well. Paul booked us in Montreal in October 1950, then the Copley Plaza in Boston, and then the Persian Room in New York. As *The New Yorker* described my performance:

> There is a desperate quality about her art; in some curious way, she takes her listeners out of a close, tidy world and into a disquieting place filled with sharp winds and unsteady laughter.

We were good and bad to start with but got better and better, both in concerts and nightclubs, at charity dinners, and last but least, with some celebrating Shriners in the South. That's where I caught chiggers!

Charles and I were always considered very good material for interviewers. The two of us together—artistic and domestic—but better still as solo talkers. We always considered that a newspaper person had to earn his living, too, and personally I always tried never to repeat myself, especially if a bon mot or joke was involved. I also often made a remark or two of such a shocking or libelous nature that it couldn't possibly be printed. By doing that, I never had to fall back on the usual corny withdrawal remark, "Ooo-o, now don't you print that, will you," or, "Off the record, I'll tell really what happened." In the meantime, the journalist, with pencil poised, had a good time, and so did I.

Charles had a very funny time once with a bunch of photographers and writers who wanted to "do" our house for a big magazine. They had seen the art collection and were out by the pool. The press boys were all carrying Scotches by then, and Charles, waving his arms around, said, "Do you know how I got these paintings and this house and this swimming pool?"

"No, how?" they chorused.

"By reading the fucking Bible!" Charles answered.

25

Before Charles started a major new tour, Paul Gregory insisted that, since his film career was somewhat in the doldrums, he do a film, any film, to publicize his name as a reader. Motion pictures, of course, are a great outlet for reaching many millions of people. And the first offer that came along, Paul said to Charles, "If it's at all possible, you've got to do it!" Charles had been in the habit of getting $100,000 a picture then, and he had to go down to $25,000 because of his rating and comparative idleness in movies. Although Charles' readings were helping his rating to go up, they didn't easily penetrate the Hollywood moguls' notions of what was commercial. As Charles once said, "Contrary to what I'd been told in the entertainment industry, people everywhere have a common shy hunger for literature." The moguls didn't always agree with him.

Anyway, Charles did the film, a gothic melodrama costarring Boris Karloff, and I suppose it helped. Based on a story by Robert Louis Stevenson, it was called *The Strange Door*. As *Films in Review*, a bimonthly booklet devoted to motion pictures, described it: "Sadistic nobleman Laughton keeps his brother (Karloff) confined for twenty years and meets a watery death." I saw the film and enjoyed it very much. It was not a so-called big picture, but it was not a bad picture. Charles could not take the gothic tale seriously and made a delicious mockery of it—a horror put-on. He was so villainous and he shook his jowls with such relish and rolled his tongue around his mouth and spat out, and what with the rattling chains and creaking doors—well, it was exactly right for the story.

During the shooting, the director didn't know that Charles was being funny, and when the film was shown at a preview, the audience rocked with laughter at Charles' every movement and spit. Afterward, the director came and said, "Charles, they laughed at you! Isn't it terrible?" Shades of Cecil B. De Mille after Charles' Nero.

Charles secretly felt a personal triumph. He had been paid only $25,000 for the work, but it didn't seem to matter. I remember *Time* magazine giving Charles a marvelous review, saying the whole thing was very corny but it was a great evening to see Charles Laughton once more come back and ham it up and enjoy it so much, along with the audience. Charles was often criticized for being a ham, but his hamming in this case was an art and it was fun. More film offers started to come in after that. And the reading tours became a giant force, dominating our lives.

In these readings, Charles used to include pieces from Bernard Shaw's *Don Juan in Hell.* Just when and how the idea came about of other actors doing a whole piece like *Don Juan* I do not know firsthand. I do know that Charles had had it in mind ever since he first read pieces of it himself. I have also heard since that Gregory claims it was his idea. But Charles said in an article he wrote for *The New York Times,* March 23, 1952:

> Paul had the idea for a drama quartette in an automobile when we were on the way to Canada for some readings. He saw four stars standing up like musicians . . . and we thought of a lot of things to do but none of them would work until I remembered "Don Juan in Hell," which I read to him and he fell for it . . ."

In the spring of 1950 Charles first wrote to George Bernard Shaw asking permission to produce the *Don Juan in Hell* piece from *Man and Superman* for "a tour around the United States, which would largely consist of one-night stands at the universities and colleges . . ." Charles' letter went on:

> If you are sympathetic, I will immediately write you about the kind of grosses that are involved, which are considerable, and you can let me know your terms. The man who would be running this project would be one Paul Gregory . . . He is a vigorous young manager of imagination and integrity.

Shaw's answer to Charles included:

> The Hell Scene is such a queer business that I cannot honestly advise you to experiment with it; but I should certainly like you to try it. As you know, it is customarily omitted, and was never meant to be played . . .

Despite Shaw's lukewarm encouragement and his belief that audiences would "think it nothing but a pack of words," Charles and Gregory lost none of their enthusiasm for this play with "a cathedral of ideas," as Charles was quoted as saying.

Shaw's letter also contained some historical data about *Don Juan in Hell:*

> It was performed a few times . . . at the Court Theatre in London with Robert Loraine as Juan Tenorio . . . with splendid Spanish costumes blazing against a dead black background. . . . Lillah McCarthy as an Infanta was superbly gorgeous; and the Devil in a red costume covered with little hearts made a fine picture.
>
> No more was seen of it until years later, when Esmé Percy, then soldiering in France in the 1914–18 war, and getting up theatricals for the troops, was mad enough to treat them to the "entirety," Hell Scene and all. Later, when touring with the Macdona-Shaw company, he persuaded Mac to let him try the entirety for one evening in Glasgow. It lasted five hours and filled the house to capacity. . . . That is the ancient history of the scene.
>
> If you are willing to venture as you propose I shall not stand in your way.

Shaw concluded his letter with a personal word:

> I have a vivid recollection of chucking you in Gower Street because you played everyone bang off the stage. I spotted your future.

That last paragraph referred to the time, many years before, when Charles was attending the Royal Academy of Dramatic Art. He had won the academy's highest award, the Gold Medal, in his first year for his portrayal of Professor Higgins in Shaw's *Pygmalion,* and Shaw himself attended one of the rehearsals.

Charles' next letter to Shaw discussed further business details, then said:

> I remember very well indeed that day at the Academy of Dramatic Art. I was being very bad as Higgins, and you told me so, but told me I had a career in front of me. I boasted it constantly.

From the conception, I should think it took Charles and Paul at least six months to put *Don Juan in Hell* together: to edit it, cast it, and stage it. Charles started to cast fairly soon. I was very good at suggesting people in parts. I think I must have helped cast about 50 percent of the actors that were finally used in their productions. Paul Gregory never objected.

To get three really fine actors to tour with Charles, I think Gregory used the usual show-biz promotional method—that is, using one name to get another. Also, I think that he was clever in approaching actors who were no longer young and whose names were slightly on the wane —or perhaps I should say, actors who instinctively wanted to change their image in order to establish a longer career pattern. Charles was a prime example of this (when you consider a film like *Abbott and Costello Meet Captain Kidd*) and being a leader of the project, and a name, he had lessened the gamble a little. So Charles Boyer, Sir Cedric Hardwicke, and Agnes Moorehead joined *Don Juan in Hell*. Originally, Paul and Charles tried to get Madeleine Carroll for the part of Donna Ana, but she was unavailable, and Miss Moorehead was delighted when she was offered the role. (In a later production of the piece, they signed Boris Karloff for the part of the Devil, then changed their minds and Vincent Price played the part. Charles, however, often had other people do his dirty work—so the stage manager notified Karloff of the change.)

When Charles was functioning, he knew how to cut himself off from the whole world. Actors learn how to do that sort of thing. So I was cut off by Charles—actually, I too cut myself off from him. I cut off with pleasure. I didn't want to be asked questions. All I did was see that he got his eggs and bacon and lunch and dinner.

Though I tried to keep a distance, Charles and I had talked about what kind of setting should be used in *Don Juan*. He finally had the four actors sit on high stools, with lecterns in front of each one. No other scenery. In evening clothes (no Devil in a red costume covered with little hearts). Paul Gregory had wanted something like high ladders, with the Drama Quartette wearing very long cloaks with red lining. I had suggested to Charles several other ideas, including using simple screens, and I even made some rough drawings for him. But I was always aware that in having *any* ideas at all, my main contribution was giving Charles something to bat against. "No, no, no, *no!*" he would cry, and out of it usually came another and better idea.

Several nights before the first tryout was held in the small college town of Claremont, California, Charles went to a restaurant with the stage manager. After several martinis, Charles began to cry. He said, "I've destroyed these actors. I've fucked up their careers!" No argument could make him feel otherwise. At the performance there were not more than forty people in the audience. Charles Boyer and Cedric Hardwicke expected disaster. Instead, the response was tremendous.

After several more tryout performances, it was obvious that they had a huge hit on their hands.

The touring of *Don Juan in Hell* was triumphal, and as *Time* reported it:

> Audiences throughout the U.S. have been eating it up. Businessmen and bobbysoxers, college students and clubwomen have jammed theatres and auditoriums and high school gymnasiums to hear the Devil and Don Juan swap epigrams and arguments.

So much for Shaw's "pack of words" that no one would listen to.

Charles always complained bitterly about having to go on tour. On the phone he always told me how exhausted he was, but then when he came home he was glowing and full of excitement about his experiences and all the places he'd visited. I was quoted as having once said, after Charles returned from one of his grueling tours with *Don Juan,* "Charles, you look very tired . . . and fifteen years younger!" I suppose I did say something like that.

During the tour of *Don Juan in Hell,* Cedric Hardwicke, Charles Boyer, and Agnes Moorehead usually saw very little of Charles. As Hardwicke put it, Charles "would be off reciting the Gettysburg Address to any school or college within miles at the drop of a hat. 'Where's Charlie?' was the constant question at mealtimes. 'Off on his Four-Score-and-Ten' was the invariable reply." Hardwicke insisted they skip after-performance invitations if at all possible, for he was always very suspicious of faculty parties. They hardly ever served hard liquor. As a matter of fact, Cedric started calling the reading tour "the cranberry juice circuit." The name caught on with the rest of them.

On a train from Oregon—a late night train—some of the company went out onto the rear platform. Charles was also there, and he began to read aloud from Thomas Wolfe's *October,* a piece about trains. He read it to the rhythm of the clacking wheels. The others called it "a memorable moment."

Paul Gregory was later to say that he

> truly felt an evening with Charles Laughton was one of the most inspiring bits of exposure anyone could have . . . In fact, that's the only time Charles was ever a shining, glorious creature—when he was on that stage doing what he did better than anyone else. And before going on and immediately afterwards, he could vomit all over you; but while he was on, there was nothing that equaled him. I used to sit night after night and forget I even knew him. And when you can do that, it's something wonderful!

For Charles and Paul, *Don Juan in Hell* was more than a triumph—it was the culmination of a big gamble for them both. For Charles, it was a fulfillment of his earliest dream—to be a reader and a director. For Paul, it was the climax of his dream—to rise from poor boy to rich boy. Both their lives and careers had been at a low ebb, and this was their reward after many months of grinding work.

1951 was the year of the Festival of Britain. Charles and Paul decided they would take *Don Juan in Hell* to England for a run. But suddenly the United States government stepped in, blocking Cedric Hardwicke's departure from the country. He still owed taxes, it seemed —a large sum that he could not meet. As Hardwicke wrote in his autobiography, he was

> in the land of the lotus, suffering from the blight of soaring income tax, which makes it impossible for any seriously intentioned actor to hold on to enough money in Hollywood to justify his time there or to save him from burial in a pauper's grave.

By some mysterious maneuver, Paul Gregory found a way to satisfy the government (I think by simply paying up, and taking it out of Hardwicke's paychecks) and the Drama Quartette was off to England—only to be greeted with another disaster.

Lew Grade (now Lord) and his brother Leslie were in charge of British arrangements. But once the announcement was made that Charles Laughton was bringing *Don Juan* to London, the English producer John Clements decided he, too, would include *Don Juan in Hell* in his production of *Man and Superman* being done for the Festival. The British Council of Living Arts, headed by Laurence Olivier, gave Clements the go-ahead. At the time, Olivier was working up to his title and he was mixed up in diplomacy and the Home Office—who came into the country, who stayed out of the country. Olivier was a power behind the scenes. Clements' production meant that Charles' version could not be shown anywhere in London at the same time.

Charles and his *Don Juan in Hell* company arrived in England before they were told that all of their bookings would have to be outside London—in auditoriums in Manchester, Birmingham, Liverpool, and so on. Because the Festival of London would not support their visit, these auditoriums in the provinces were booked rather quickly through agents, and they often were too large for the kind of intimate presentation *Don Juan* demanded. The production should have first gone through the glamour stage of London, so it could be presented successfully elsewhere.

It was a very difficult tour for Charles and the others, and not much of a success. In his book, Cedric Hardwicke wrote about the English tour of *Don Juan in Hell:*

> I am not certain whether the two Grades (the producers) knew what our play was about, but the audiences most surely did not. They had expected to see . . . Hollywood stars glittering with wisecracks. They got the four of us . . . we played to half-empty theatres which normally resounded to the gurglings of rock-and-roll singers. . . . I was glad for only one thing—that the author was spared this sorry spectacle.

Shaw had died a year before.

Charles and I had become American citizens on April 29, 1950. On Loyd Wright's advice we waited until the war was over as Charles' films still had to be sold to the British market. But the British people seemed not to have forgiven us for being in the United States during the Battle of Britain. Feelings, apparently, ran high over it. And Charles had even more of it during the *Don Juan in Hell* tour.

Charles never quite forgave Laurence Olivier for what happened in England. Charles felt it was a personal insult—and just one more example of their attitude where Charles and I were concerned. As far as I know, Charles was never very fond of Olivier. It was an old jealousy thing. Laurence Olivier could play all the leading man roles that Charles physically was not able to play. And eventually he became *Sir* Laurence Olivier. Charles envied that, I think, American or not. In the unauthorized Singer book written about Charles in the fifties, he is quoted as saying, "Olivier . . . you are England!" I've always wondered where the writer got that. It doesn't sound a bit like Charles, and I do not remember him ever saying anything like it.

The English critic Kenneth Tynan interviewed Charles just before *Don Juan in Hell* opened in Birmingham. As Charles described him, Tynan was "sleek, slimy, eellike, oleaginous." Throughout the interview, Charles was very polite, despite his dislike. Tynan asked him about Olivier and he expressed his feelings about the whole *Don Juan* upset. After Tynan had left, Charles said, "That man is going to cut me apart. He'll tear me inside out, you watch." And when the article appeared the next day, that's exactly what Tynan did. "When I first encountered Mr. Laughton," he wrote, "he looked like a bank teller who had absconded with the funds." The article appeared in the Birmingham press and it hurt Charles tremendously, personally and at the box office.

Tynan blew up the Oliver conflict, so Charles later wrote to Olivier to explain about the interview. He answered him by letter, which said in part:

I didn't read it actually but was told about it, and I never for a moment thought blamefully of you, knowing so well how these things happen.

I was only distressed that you were bamboozled into giving the little fucker an interview.

Much later, long after Charles and Olivier worked together in Stanley Kubrick's *Spartacus,* Olivier recollected:

I have a slight tinge of memory that there was some friction between us, though what it was about I cannot now remember. It may *possibly* have been something to do with John Clements' production of *Man and Superman.* If it was to do with that, I would no doubt have been on John Clements' side as he was a closer friend of mine than Charles, and Charles seemed rather to be coming home a lot too late to make any claims upon the loyalties.

I had a lot of this snooty, superior attitude, too, when I took my nightclub show to London for four weeks at the Cafe de Paris. Ray Henderson accompanied me. Charles had had his rough time with *Don Juan in Hell* in England exactly six weeks before, now I had mine, but of course on a smaller scale. I was made very aware of the anti-Laughton feeling and was strongly criticized for having become an American. In a cab in London, the driver accused me of being some sort of traitor who sat out the war safely in America. He said, "We did a very good job of winning the war, didn't we? But you weren't here, were you? Pretty comfortable in Hollywood, was it?"

The English press said I had gone "Yankee," and asked where were my charming little English ditties that I used to sing years ago. I considered that I had made some changes and some progress after thirty years, but no, I had some bitter barbs from them, especially Tynan. Halfway through the job at the Cafe de Paris, the management asked me to take out "Somebody Broke Lola's Saucepan" (incidentally, written by British Philip Godfrey of the old Cave of Harmony days) because a certain Lord Portarlington had wandered out during the number, although he later came back. There seemed to be some doubt as to whether he objected to the song or merely went to the w.c. He was a rather doddering old gentleman who, I was told by a fellow in the band, often took such strolls during the show. Anyway, "Lola" was one of my best numbers and I just wouldn't take it out, so the management and I decided to part. Of course, they had to pay us.

So Ray Henderson and I had two weeks with loose money and expenses. I went to Brighton to see my mother and then on to Scarborough to see Charles' mother. On this trip Charles' brother Tom very kindly came by train to fetch me, and gently asked me about Charles' male companions—he was sympathetic, encouraging, and helpful. My talk with Tom seemed innocent enough. The third brother, Frank, shared a lovely house in the neighboring town of Scalby with a bright young man. During this time, Ray Henderson went to stay with his friend Benjamin Britten in Aldenburgh, Norfolk.

Then Ray and I met in London again and took off for Paris. We registered at the Prince de Galles Hotel. I asked for one room for Ray and two rooms for me, but they said, "Oh, no, Madame Laughton, the royal suite is quite free and you must have that!" So there Ray and I were, racing round and round thick pile carpets in high glee. We went to the Folies Bergère, the Lido, the Bal Tabarin, and took a limousine to see Chartres. The day was blackened by heavy clouds, and as we stepped into the cathedral the sky split open with thunder and lightning. The effect on the stained glass windows and the never-lit dark corners and the crash of the rain left an imprint on my mind that will never be wiped out. Yes, I am glad it was such a day as this.

Back at the Prince de Galles, Ray and I had some long, hot rum drinks and raced round our palace again—through sitting rooms and four bedrooms (with four bidets). Then, back to New York from Le Bourget Airport.

After the British Festival—if you can call it that—Charles and Paul went back to the American tour of *Don Juan in Hell,* working their way up to their climactic appearance at Carnegie Hall in New York. They decided to put on the dog and splurge on a suite at the Plaza Hotel to impress old friends and enemies and receive the clamoring press. And it was good business. I was on my way back from England with Ray, after the nightclub job and trip to Paris, for another job at The Blue Angel in New York. I stayed at the Algonquin Hotel. The next morning the telephone rang in my room. It was Valentina, the famous dressmaker.

"Elsa darling, can you tell me how I can possibly get tickets for tonight?"

"Tickets for what?"

"For Charles at Carnegie Hall!"

I asked, "Oh . . . what's he doing? Is he here?"

"At the Plaza, I think, but I can't get through."

So I called the Plaza and did get through. Charles was horrified that I was in New York and—what would people say?—we were at separate hotels!

"Look, Elsa, for God's sake, get in a cab and come here at once! I can't be at the Algonquin and there's no room here. This situation must not get out to the press. We'll have to go out and be seen everywhere together." We did. I sat in a box to see (and be seen at) *Don Juan in Hell* that night. And then, it was "21," Le Pavillon, Sardi's, and so on, places that were usually only on our agenda for business reasons—other than holding the marriage image together. So, the Laughtons were seen holding hands all over town.

Don Juan in Hell was an enormous success at Carnegie Hall. It topped anything that had gone before. When the advertisements in the newspapers announced the engagement, all seats for the first perform-ance were sold out in eight hours. The reviews were ecstatic.

Quite incidentally, only one year before, when I opened at the Persian Room at the Plaza Hotel, Charles had passed through New York for one night during a reading tour. Again the hotel was full. The desk clerk called up to me: "There's a man down here who says he's Charles Laughton. What shall I do?" Charles was very angry, naturally, but finally made his way up to my suite. The hotel moved a bed in for him.

Paul Gregory had had a good idea when he booked me at The Blue Angel in New York. That was an intimate room with an audience of people trained, as it were, to listen and laugh at more original or obscure material. Ray and I could work together in a more friendly fashion, with a few asides and impromptu remarks.

Then, back to Hollywood.

In October 1945, I received a telegram from Biddy telling of Shamus' death. Later Biddy's letter, dated October 24th, arrived, and this is the only reference she made to Shamus' death:

> It is difficult to say just what could have been done to help Shamus these last few years—That resentment against life seemed to grow on him and he was very stubborn in refusing any proffered kindness. It rather cut him off, as people feel a bit hurt if they don't understand—Still I feel it has happened for the best —I suppose because I am getting aged I look on death as just another incident. . . .

With the help of a secretary and friends, we had found a flat for Biddy in Brighton. Brighton is bright and brisk and known to be very healthy. Old people stroll on the Esplanade and live out their years there. Above all, Biddy was born there, and often returning to your place of birth can do wonders in old age. There seems to be more ozone in the air at Brighton, and the glittering electric lights all along the Front and the pier seem to reassure you that the past is still present. You don't have to say, "I remember when . . ."

While the flat was being got ready, Biddy stayed as a paying guest in a little house of a young married couple in Brighton. Biddy felt herself a most desirable personality to have around, having always had her entertaining past to attract attention. But this did not mean much to a new generation, and the host and hostess told me she must go soon. "Raising a very old lady out of the bath is not very pleasant," they said.

Biddy eventually was moved to her flat at Highcroft Villas. We fixed it up—including a hand rope for the bath. We set her up with proper heaters, which she fought against but soon couldn't live without. She was bitter that we paid a high rent, protesting in a querulous voice but only for a few days. She liked the year's lease with options. The place immediately looked the same as any other she'd lived in. You wouldn't think that such a mess could be duplicated.

Afterward, whenever I visited Biddy in England, it was always a hopeless task to try to get her to change to a life with a few more comforts. Any room that she lived in was without any order at all. Boxes full of letters and snapshots and old bills, scraps of cloth—all shoved under the bed or sofa—and something or other on every table and chair. Books, spools of wool, unfinished cups of tea. Somehow she and the room were very clean and it didn't smell. Her kitchen was the same, untidy with vegetarian oddments all over the place. A tomato here and an orange there and hard-boiled eggs galore, butter and brown bread and cheese in a crock. There were always dishes in the sink. When I saw Biddy I tried to wash up and put a few things away so that she could start fresh, but she always repeated, "Leave it, oh, *leave* it." We tried to get her to have a cleaning woman once a week, but she claimed she hated them all and would not have any part of any of them. But it was the cleaning women who wouldn't have any part of Biddy—"She's so rude if you move anything!"

Later, when Biddy was settled, we sent her on a trip round Europe. She had often regretted the fact that she'd never been anywhere and didn't expect to, so her lost "castle" suddenly came to life. She set off with no fellow travelers at all, sending us glowing descriptions on postcards from every hotel where she stayed, with her window marked by firm arrows or crosses.

There were still some shortages in England so there were more packages from us from California (mostly olive oil and tinned New Zealand butter) and, of course, flowers. With telephone calls and telegrams there was always communication, although when we made an overseas telephone call to Biddy, hearing a voice from so far scared her and she talked too fast because she thought it was so expensive.

26

I went back to the Turnabout Theatre for a limited period of time, and also took on a supper club job simultaneously! The club was The Bar of Music, also intimate. Ray again played there for me. Bobby Short was on the same bill, and we all three shared a dressing room. There was a dinner show—then a dash to Turnabout—then back to The Bar of Music for a supper show. I sang twenty-three songs in all each night during that time.

Paul Gregory seemed to be intrigued by my Turnabout songs and wanted to get a concert show together for a tour for me. He had a great itch to be creative and started to put *his* ideas into action—not with Charles and *not* the Turnabouters. It was to be called Elsa Lanchester's Private Music Hall. Since I am not first and foremost a singer, Paul insisted that I share the program with a quartet of men singers called the Mad Hatters (who had really good voices but didn't look too hot). They also backed me up vocally now and then. And last but not least was musician Ray Henderson, who held us together musically. He was by now musical director and arranger, and while I made my costume changes he played piano solos, including his own compositions.

Paul was very dominating and full of ideas, but mostly *not* listening to other ideas. When Charles was home from touring, Paul thought that he might interfere with rehearsals and give me complexes, so he would not ever let him come into the room for a moment while we worked. Charles hovered around a great deal, pressing his nose against the glass doors of the schoolroom like a child wanting to cry, but Paul wouldn't let him in. Now I realize that Paul's methods of getting me to perform—in rehearsal and on stage—were Simon Le-gree-ish and misguided. He certainly seemed to get a kind of enjoyment out of Charles and me not working together. Paul was singing one of the Greek choruses of my life: "Keep them separate, keep them separate."

We opened the Private Music Hall in Vancouver, and I must say that was a great success—in fact, an enormous success—but it was really only a medium good show. We did sixty performances round the country, driving 22,000 miles! (We never got one scratch or ticket.) We toured in two cars—the Mad Hatters and sound equipment in a station wagon, and Ray and I in a sedan with wardrobe. Paul Gregory's most insistent instruction was: "Never lose sight of each other on the road." We *never* saw each other on the road but all met punctually for every performance. Ray and I switched driving every two hours. The boys switched every hundred miles.

Paul had booked us for about sixty colleges and auditoriums, but the show did not quite live up to my first hopes. The auditoriums were always full and wild, but critics found too much similarity in the material, and so did I—chiefly because Paul used too many of my songs from the Turnabout. They were not spaced out with enough different material. Although I had a huge repertoire from England, Paul was insistent on this program. He had, of course, seen me perform at the Turnabout in Hollywood—and so that was what he envisioned. And Paul dominated rehearsals with dreams of being at the creative end of show business, and I was the guinea pig. I was happy enough until I learned better. And Charles, on the outer fringes, knew better all the time.

Twenty-two thousand miles, that's a lot of driving when the show "had to go on" every day except for a break or two with no bookings, or when the distance between two dates forced a driving-only-time— say, from Vancouver to Winnipeg, 1,640 miles, six days; Toronto to Jenkintown, Pennsylvania, 475 miles, two days; and many 300-mile stretches in one day. When you arrive, the first thing is to check the stage lighting, good or bad (a spotlight is specified on the contract with a No. 3 pink jell called tit-pink by stagehands), and during this, a wardrobe woman or a local lady presses the clothes; then to a hotel or motel, a bowl of pea soup for me and a short lie-down with luck (rather rare); then to the theatre, makeup, the show. One hour to clean up and that sort of thing. Swearing and cursing about the lights. Furious because the stage is dirty and balls of fluff sweep onto the costumes. No bathrooms some places. I don't know why one does it.

But when the music starts and I come floating out onto the stage, something happens. Something cleans me out. I feel alive. It's like a butterfly coming out of a dirty old chrysalis. I was aware that I was making my own memories.

And then afterward the big effort to get a decent meal—hotel

222

kitchens are closed, sponsors and college presidents offer Ritz crackers and lemonade. But through the rush, the strain, the nights with no sleep, I know that the unpleasant things will go—that later we will laugh about the hard times and cherish the good.

One trip on the Pennsylvania Turnpike was pretty bad. A snowstorm paralyzed all traffic and the long tunnels were filled with carbon monoxide. Cars crept out and parked and double-parked on the side of the road. As the sun was just about setting, Ray Henderson and I crept down on the shoulder of a tiny side road and at once found ourselves in the village of Dorset. We left the car at the one gas station, and they said they could put chains on the tires by morning.

We had to be at the Town Hall in Detroit for a show the next day. So Ray and I walked from pub to inn and house to house and eventually and grudgingly were allowed to stay in sort of a dressing room with a single bed. They did find us some soup and bread and cheese and took our shoes to dry. We had a little sleep—top to tail—and set off for Detroit, driving at about sixty miles an hour, with the chains, of course, ripping up the tires. Detroit—home of Cadillacs! We left the car for repairs and rented another, went to a hotel and got rooms to rest in and had breakfast, with hot black coffee and brandy.

The Mad Hatters, Ray Henderson, and I always tried to be on the same floor in a hotel so we could have coffee together before taking off for the day. The end of our tour was sometime toward the end of 1952, and one of our later dates was in Dallas. We got to Dallas in plenty of time for our show—that is, with several hours to look around. I think the Mad Hatters even went to a movie. Ray Henderson was arranging a long piece of religious music for organ and voices called "O Jesus Saviour Come to Me." As you may know, a full music manuscript is Scotch-taped together in one long piece and folded together like an accordion. Ray was doing his arranging in my sitting room because it was long enough so that he could lay the music out on the floor. I was writing letters and we were drinking milk.

The telephone rang and someone said, "Miss Lanchester?"

"Yes?"

"I want to talk to you about a private matter."

"Of course," I said. "Go ahead. What does it concern?"

"Well, it's about someone you are employing."

"Okay, come right up." I thought it must be some trouble back at the Hollywood house.

"We must see you alone," the voice said, "as it is about someone in your company."

So what could I do but ask Ray to go to his room across the

corridor. I was very curious but nervous, too, so we opened the transom over my door. So did Ray over his door.

The three gentlemen who came in were from the FBI and were looking for "a certain Ray Henderson. He's overdue for induction in the army," they said, "and we cannot catch up with him."

"Well," I said, "he's here and we've had a different address almost every day. He's received no papers and is certainly not running away from anything. I have a show on the road, you know." And I showed them a small poster.

But they said, "His first notice was two months ago."

"Yes, but we've been away for four months." I suppose they could have gone to Paul Gregory for our itinerary, but they hadn't used that approach.

They asked me endless questions as to whether Ray believed in God, whether I ever discussed with him any anti-American things, and whether he had any associates who might be Communists. I could only say we had never discussed anything like that. I said that the subjects would bore me. I also told them that his father was a Baptist minister and pointed out the endlessly long hymn stretching across the floor. I also gave the glasses of milk a desultory wave. I told them, too, when our last date would be and they seemed to think that Ray could finish the tour. The three gentlemen were most polite as time passed. I would like to have asked them if they could sing.

Ray went into the army on February 3, 1953, and went from playing the glockenspiel to conducting the band at Ford Ord in a short time. Right in the middle of Ray's basic training, I went up to Fort Ord and offered to do a show and met the head of Special Services. So we had to rehearse, naturally. I was escorted around the base in a grand car and was shown a display or two. If I had described all this to Biddy, my pacifist mother, I think she would have hissed herself to death.

While Ray was away, I returned to The Bar of Music, with another accompanist. One night I got a pain in my stomach—it was appendicitis, so I was off for several weeks. Paul Gregory sent a telegram to Ray Henderson at Fort Ord:

ELSA IN ST JOHN'S HOSPITAL SANTA MONICA CUTTING
OFF HER THING CALL HER COLLECT—PAUL

Since I had done this show at Ford Ord and promised another one, Ray's superior officer in Special Services sent him down to see me in St. John's Hospital the next day. We both felt rather important at such treatment. Ray got two days off!

As Charles was in New York, I went there to join him at the St.

Moritz Hotel and further recuperate. Charles was doing a reading at Town Hall. I believe he gave two performances there. I remember—as a complete side issue—that Charles was involved then with a young, ambitious fellow who was learning to act and thought that Charles would be able to teach him something. He became one of Charles' "road men." Every time Charles toured, he had to have a road man, under Gregory's supervision. One of his duties would be to pick up the check at the intermission. A performer would not go on with the second half of the program before picking up that check. You never knew when you would run into a sponsor who was underfunded!

Charles didn't want me to watch his performance at Town Hall. He very rarely liked me to see him in performance, and as I said, he had the road man. Charles had always needed looking after, and it was the road man's job to attend to all of Charles' needs. I quite liked this particular road man and he in turn did not feel uncomfortable with Mrs. Laughton, which was just fine. But later on I was to learn that this pleasant road man had said to someone about me, "She just won't let him go, will she?"

I truly didn't mind any association Charles had—I'd got quite used to them—just as long as these young men looked after Charles and didn't only use him. While Charles was performing at Town Hall, I went out and returned later to the hotel to wait for him. There were full ashtrays in the room and too many glasses from earlier in the day, so I started to clean up, putting them all on a tray. As I was doing this, Charles marched into the room with his road man. Charles was carrying a load of heavy books, and also his overcoat. The road man, arms empty, was munching on a snack.

I said to the young man, "Don't you ever carry the books when Charles is tired?" or words to that effect. He said No, quite simply. Charles hadn't heard what I'd said, but he started to help me pick up the rest of the glasses and ashtrays and get them out of the way. The young man just sat there, lit a cigarette, and watched us tidying up. Of course, I didn't mind the cleaning up but I resented this boy, on salary, letting Charles do this extra work after a hard performance.

I felt quite angry. I stood there with a tray in my hands and said to the young man, "You should be doing this." He looked up at me and answered, "I don't see why." So I threw the trayful of glasses and ashtrays right into his stomach. And I could see that Charles didn't mind my doing it at all. Charles knew that the young man should have been looking after him better. Why Charles put up with it, well, I never asked directly. But when the road man and I were alone, I said to him, "It's not really any of my business, but you really should think of Charles a little more. He is tired and he is fat and he is getting older,

and should be looked after. It's very ugly to see this kind of behavior."
I wanted people to be decent to Charles.

During one of Charles' cross-country reading tours, Paul Gregory
suddenly called me long-distance and told me that he had canceled
every date that he had booked for my second tour with Ray Henderson. I felt myself turn white during the phone call. I was surprised,
amazed, and staggered. I thought, he really is a man with an ax, like
Alexander Korda and Erich Pommer. They wanted to use Charles
alone, to make him shine for them—but not with his wife around.
When I recovered, I called the Gregory office in Hollywood and left
a message for Paul, asking why. Immediately I received this telegram
from him:

PLEASE DO NOT EVER LEAVE A MESSAGE WITH MY
EMPLOYEES INTENDED FOR ME LIKE THE ONE YOU LEFT
TODAY. AGAIN YOUR BAR OF MUSIC PROPOSITION CAME
UP WITHIN THE LAST THREE DAYS. MY FOX DEAL
PENDING PAST SIX MONTHS. WILL NOT TOLERATE YOUR
HYSTERICAL ABUSE. WHEN YOU DECIDE TO GO SANE
WILL BE GLAD TO TALK WITH YOU. PAUL.

The message that I left at Gregory's office was probably nothing more
than "Why am I canceled?"
    I'll never know exactly what he told the various sponsors of my
tour, but it must have been very damaging. I later heard that some
were told that my show was too risqué and would not be suitable for
colleges—which were always the greatest audiences we ever had. But
I'll never know the whole truth. And four months later, Paul released
me "from all contracts made with Gregory Associates, Inc." Then, to
drive the dividing knife home, Paul told Charles that I had told our
attorney Loyd Wright that Charles was homosexual.
    During Charles' English *Don Juan* tour, his brother Tom had ques-
tioned him about his relationships with young men. Tom asked me
about it when I was in England. Well, Charles was furious that I might
have talked to Tom about it. He was sure I was out to make mischief.
So, when Paul and Charles were coming back on the plane, Charles
said, "This time I'm going to do it, no two ways about it." He was
talking about divorce. Paul said to Charles, "Elsa doesn't have to tell
Loyd Wright about you, because he already knows." Charles said,
"How do you mean—he knows I'm homosexual?" And Paul told him
that he had had a conversation with Loyd Wright about another complicated thing involving *Confidential* Magazine—some article or other

226

that they proposed calling "The Unholy Four"—and said he bought them off for $1,000. Talking with Gregory, Loyd Wright said, "Well, of course, I know that Charles is homosexual. I know it just as Elsa knows it, too." But I had never talked to Wright about it.

Exactly why Paul canceled my second tour I cannot begin to guess, but I can only think it was either my conversation with Charles' brother Tom, who had asked me about "the dark man with Charles" (an actor-protégé who accompanied Charles to London) or the nonexistent, Paul-created Loyd Wright gossip. Paul and Charles obviously had worked themselves into a frenzy of anti-Elsa-ism, and thought of how to get rid of me. I was not only upset, I was frightened.

So when Charles got back to California the night before Thanksgiving and questioned me, I said, "This is Paul's invention. I have not talked to Loyd Wright at all or even seen him." But Charles believed Paul. He asked for a divorce. Serious as it all was at the time, it was a little comic, too. I was even obliged to threaten Charles with a conk on the head with a hairbrush. As a result, Charles promised to call Loyd Wright then and there, and he and Wright agreed to meet in the morning in Wright's law office. And Loyd Wright told Charles, "Elsa hasn't said any such thing to me, nor have I even seen her while you were away on tour. Paul, apparently, is feeling some kind of misguided jealousy." Then they called me on the phone and Charles said, without any apology, "No divorce."

Paul Gregory's most brilliant policy, which was his own sheer invention, was to book tours all over the country and be hailed in every town —and *then* go into New York. The critics were on the spot. The nationwide advance praise left them with no choice but adulation.

After the American success of *Don Juan in Hell*, Charles and Paul were searching around for another production. They realized there was a large audience for this kind of theatre. The piece they chose, Stephen Vincent Benét's *John Brown's Body*, dated back to the late 1930s, the days of radio and Norman Corwin's The Pursuit of Happiness programs. So when Charles went down to our house in Palos Verdes to edit and restructure the original Benét piece for a full evening's show, it caused somewhat of a breach with our old friend Norman Corwin. Corwin may have felt that Charles should have come to him and somehow involved him in the project. Gregory ended up giving Corwin $2,500 to forfeit all claims to Charles' version. But I don't really know the full story.

Paul Gregory remembers that when he sent Charles a copy of *John Brown's Body*, before Charles even read it he said, "Oh, it stinks, old boy, for chrissake, you don't want to do that goddamned thing!" Then suddenly, at four o'clock in the morning, Paul's phone rang and Charles was saying, "Paul, this is marvelous, it's marvelous, and I think your Tyrone Power idea is great!" So when Charles went round to Paul's, it was all *Charles'* idea—"which is how it should be, I suppose," Paul said.

Charles deeply admired Power. "He will someday be a great Hamlet," he said. But Tyrone Power always felt he had been held back by his good looks. His father had been a famous actor, too, so Tyrone had it in his blood all right.

Anyway, Charles and Paul went down to Mexico to see Tyrone Power about being in *John Brown's Body* and to make all the plans. Intrigued by the offer, Power was quoted as saying, "I was eager to get back on the stage. You go to the same studio every morning. You get the same kind of parts . . . When Charles Laughton asked me to do this, I'd have gone through almost anything to accept."

I knew Tyrone Power slightly from working with him in *Son of Fury* and also in Maugham's *The Razor's Edge*, which was made in 1945. Some time ago, I was interviewed for a book being written about him by Hector Arce. I said (and I must quote myself now): "Usually, I find good-looking people very boring. But Ty was very kind and helpful and a most gentle man. Yet . . . there was something . . . very feminine about his handshake. I know Charles adored Tyrone Power as a beauty. He was determined to make this straight actor with a beautiful face into a good actor . . . I know they had many long discussions about theatre." End of quote. I kept out of the way of all Charles' projects whenever I could. Ty Power *was* grateful to Charles, I know, and critics eventually discovered that Ty had the range, which came as a surprise to all.

Charles once said, "Ty Power is a storyteller, where Laurence Olivier, for instance, is not. Ty can say, 'Once there was a princess,' and you feel at home. You don't need the panoply of the theatre." He was right. And *John Brown's Body* was one of the best things Ty Power ever did.

Paul Gregory had this to say about it:

I think that Tyrone was so beautiful that Charles marveled at it . . . at any beautiful physical being. Charles wasn't intimidated by that sort of thing, however. But there were times when I felt terribly sorry for Charlie because he used to talk to me about his ugliness, and it was just tragic. I didn't really want to hear about it. As far as any advances to Tyrone Power, I wouldn't know. I know that Charles never did anything like that to me. Perhaps I wasn't attractive enough to him.

When Charles and Paul Gregory went to talk to Ty Power in Mexico, something happened that I could never understand. Paul Gregory, years later, told me his version of how it happened:

Tyrone Power was there in Mexico with his wife, Linda Christian. We gave him the script and Tyrone read it through; then he said, "You know, Paul, I don't know what the goddamned thing is about at all, but if you and Charles think it's gonna be something, I'll do it."

Charles was just obsessed and taken by Ty's house—even though it was unfinished; and so we were all sitting in this hall that still had a dirt floor, and Tyrone was saying, "This is going to be the living room here, and the fireplace there," and so on. Then Charles said, "And I have something to hang over your fireplace."

Tyrone said, "What?" and he was full of anticipation of what Charles was going to say. And when Charles said, "Siqueiros's Pancho Villa," Tyrone nearly fell over and he couldn't wait to get it.

Linda Christian hated the picture, and Tyrone loved it; but, of course, they never did a goddamned thing with that house in Mexico, and the Pancho Villa painting sat for years in the garage at the Powers' house in Hollywood after he died.

When Charles returned from Mexico, he said to me, "I've given the Pancho Villa away." And I said, "You must have done it over a dry martini." Charles said, "I don't want to hear any more about it." And he never did. But it was very cruel of Charles and, as a result, he was tortured by his own guilt for giving it away because he knew I liked that painting better than anything else in the house. The fact that I liked it so much almost seemed to be the cause of what he did. We had had two Siqueiros pictures, and the one he gave away was worth thousands of dollars. It was a pity, almost a tragedy to me, just as it was when Charles got rid of the green mask of mine. Once I saw the Siqueiros painting hanging at the Powers' house, over the fireplace.

Looking back, I can imagine other reasons that Charles gave the Siqueiros to Tyrone Power. I do know that Tyrone clung to Charles and learned a great deal about acting from him. After Tyrone Power's death, the Pancho Villa painting was on the market, and I went to the art dealer and said that I would like to buy it back, but it was too late. It had already been sold. The painting had increased in value and was worth far more than Charles paid for it.

It just happened like that—Charles giving things away, things that

I liked. It wasn't the money. It began to seem more and more that if I liked something, or bought something, or someone gave Charles something, then Charles would think it was a fake, of no value, and he wouldn't want it in the house. Six Rodin figure drawings disappeared. One of the boys had got them, apparently, and for a long time I didn't know for sure. When I mentioned them to Charles, he told me that they were fakes. Of course, they weren't—but Charles insisted.

Paul Gregory, years later, told me that he had seen three of the six drawings pinned up on a wall of the house of one of Charles' young friends. When Gregory asked him where he'd got the drawings, the young man said, "Charles gave them to me." Gregory then told the young man that he understood the drawings were stolen because Charles had mentioned that someone may have taken them. To me Charles just said, "I don't want to talk about it."

Later, another of Charles' friends came by one evening with a painting done by a friend of his. Not too bad—an abstract painting. Charles just looked at the young man and said, "You should not have done that, Peter." Afterward, Charles said to me, "Put it in the cupboard," and he never saw the young fellow again after that. He told me, "I do not like him. He shouldn't really bring me that painting!" You couldn't impose taste on Charles. There were a lot of things you couldn't impose on him, but above all, taste.

Once Tyrone Power was signed to do *John Brown's Body*, Paul went after Raymond Massey. Massey said of it: "I guess I had been kind of envious when I heard that Ty, a great, wonderful, beautiful, charming, naughty boy, had been signed for the production. So when Gregory offered me a part . . . I accepted immediately, even though I had no idea how they were going to do the famous poem that I and my wife loved so much."

Judith Anderson completed the trio of actors in *John Brown's Body*. Charles had talked to her when they worked together in *Salome* (he played Herod and Rita Hayworth, whom he adored, had the title role). According to a publicity story, Miss Anderson was supposed to have said, "I found myself wishing there was something in it for me; the next thing I knew, I was in it."

On November 1, 1952, the first real performance of *John Brown's Body* was given in Santa Barbara. The leading critic there, Ronald Scofield, headlined his review: A GREAT EVENT IN THEATRE, MAGNIFICENTLY PRESENTED. The show was a huge success across the country, and there was a large advance sale in New York. But eventually Judith Anderson was replaced by Anne Baxter, who had acted in several films with Ty Power.

According to Charles, Paul Gregory and Miss Anderson had had an unpleasant confrontation about billing or money or the comforts of travel or some such thing. She came down from Carpinteria, where she lived, to see him and talk about *John Brown's Body,* and he was very anxious to please her. But she came to stay at our house, and Charles did something I resented: He had me give up my room to her and go to the spare room. I had to take out boxes of odd things. Of course, the staff had to change their timing and look after her wants. I didn't like this arrangement, but it wasn't her fault. She was only in the house a couple of days, I believe, but it undermined my ability to run a house efficiently to have the staff see me put into another room—and not know why.

Charles was correct in wanting Judith Anderson. She was right for the play. Although Raymond Massey claimed innocence, he and Ty pushed the ultimatum that Gregory replace Miss Anderson. According to Paul:

> Judith Anderson had to be replaced, but Charles wouldn't talk to her at all when it happened. Judith Anderson came to my office, and Charlie was supposed to meet with her and me. After all, he was the director. It was unusual for the producer to have to fire someone, when it's a case of this kind. But Massey and Tyrone Power gave me an ultimatum that they would not play any longer with Judith. And so I had to get rid of Judith. Poor Judith was not well. . . . Opening night in New York the curtain didn't go up until 9:30. We were trying to get her out of the Maurice Hotel.

Later, Paul Gregory told me that he felt Charles had turned Power against him. Furthermore:

> No man had a right to have such a talent as Charles Laughton's. But Charlie also had to have utter chaos to make it go. If he didn't have fifty people absolutely miserable, he wasn't happy.

Charles was going to England to do the film *Hobson's Choice* for director
David Lean (in his early teens he had done the play at a community
playhouse). Before he left, he and Paul had a terrific fight in Jamaica
over a projected TV series. Charles was offered $25,000 a week, but
"our dear Charlie," as Paul said, wouldn't do it because he was afraid
of a series. As Paul recounted it:

> When I got into Miami I had a call from Jamaica. Charlie was
> there with this young fellow who was on the phone conveying
> messages to me from "Mr. Laughton." I was angry. I said to him,
> "Look, I don't want your messages from Charlie! If he wants to
> talk to me, he'll talk to me, and that's that!" Well, Charles called
> me back and he was wonderful and very persuasive. He said,
> "Paul, how can we just break off something that's been so won-
> derful as this?"
>   But I had gone through so much and I was so nervous, and
> I had these stomach pains. So I went to my doctor and he said,
> "All you have is Laughtonitis." Well, the outcome was, I flew on
> with Charlie to England and everything got all squared away. But
> we turned the series down.

While Charles was working on the movie, Paul returned to the States
to persuade Herman Wouk to write a play based on the court-martial
scene in his book, *The Caine Mutiny*. They would use no sets, just have
the judge's bench and the witness stand. Paul also signed Henry Fonda
to do the play before there was even a script. When Herman Wouk was
told that Fonda was signed, he agreed to go ahead with it. The first
time it was read by the cast it was four hours long. With Charles still

in England, Paul found it difficult to decide on anyone else to direct it. Dick Powell thought he'd "like to take a crack at it," and Paul, in this helpless moment, said, "Well, fine . . ."

In Paul's words:

> We'd been rehearsing about nine days when Charles arrived back. I thought the play was in serious trouble because Powell didn't know his ass from his elbow about directing on the stage. Charles said, "I'll be there, old boy, and I'll take a look at it."
>
> Charles came. He sat and watched it and it was endless. It had to be cut. The cast hoped Charles could do something, though no one had ever complained to me about it. Charles did do something—I don't know what the hell it was he did—and something wonderful came out of it. . . . The first thing he did was make Fonda and Dick Powell absolutely want to kill each other. But Laughton was going to be Jesus Christ and save everything. And he did. He saved the show.

Charles was growing into a great editor, as Herman Wouk would be the first to admit. He cut *Caine Mutiny* down to two hours and fifty-five minutes. And, as a matter of fact, Wouk dedicated the printed version of the play to him "in gratitude." Paul Gregory called the editing job "a goddamned bloody miracle, that's the genius this man had."

Herman Wouk worked with Charles at our house for ten days to two weeks. I remember I kept bacon, which I dearly love, out of the house because Wouk was very religious. I wondered if the dishes were washed properly and, of course, milk products and meat were never supposed to be in the same refrigerator. I didn't have much personal contact with Wouk. I only said hello to him every morning.

Charles was very excited and very happy. It was a businesslike carving job, and he and Wouk carved very well together. When it's a workable collaboration, it's wonderful, and you can never tell who did what where.

Before Charles stepped in, the play was not only too long, it was too funny. Dick Powell played too many of the characters for laughs. Charles, of course, redirected *The Caine Mutiny Court Martial.* Henry Fonda was unhappy when Charles started hacking hunks of the comedy out of the script, and Paul Gregory turned white, but Wouk and Charles kept rewriting and Charles kept editing at rehearsals. One member of the cast observed that Henry Fonda acted "as if he were Christ on the cross suffering" during these cutting sessions. Fonda also got very upset once when, during the tryout of the play, Charles sent him a telegram: LOVE YOU MADLY STOP ROSEBUD. It was, of course, meant humorously, but perhaps Fonda read it as some kind of insult. Fonda, then fifty, also objected to the fact that some of the silent jury were "handsome young guys" he would have to compete with onstage. James Bumgarten (later Garner) was one of them.

One funny thing happened during the performance of *The Caine Mutiny Court Martial*. As all of the play is about the court-martial, there had to be a jury of six men sitting on either side of the president of the court. The six men didn't have anything to say at all and just had to sit for two hours and listen. It isn't the easiest thing to be an entirely static actor. It's no problem in films, of course, where the camera can pick up the reactions of the jury in closeup. But to have to sit there on stage every night and listen and listen and listen. Well, anyway, the actors on the jury would sometimes fall asleep. So they painted *eyes* on their lids in case the lids started to droop! I don't think that Charles learned about the scheme until the play finished its run.

The tryout period of the play was full of problems. Henry Fonda was one of them, and he hurt Charles deeply. Paul Gregory wrote about it later:

Now, I will just say this about Henry Fonda: he is the most incomprehensible individual I have ever known. His treatment of Charles was absolutely the cruelest thing I've ever seen. Henry was furious because Charles cut scenes that he had. But if you're going to cut, you have to cut . . . So out of his fear, Fonda insisted on having a chance at a drunk scene on stage.

During one rehearsal, Henry Fonda behaved miserably and insulted Charles like I have never heard anyone insult him or anybody else in all my life—and in front of the whole company. Right from the stage, Fonda looked at Charles and said, "What do you know about men, you fat, ugly homosexual." And Fonda went into a thing, and Charles just sat there saying, "Oh, no . . . oh, no. . . . Take him out of here, take him out of here"; and Charles had ahold of Elliot Norton, the critic. Norton had already reviewed the play, but wanted to come and watch a rehearsal. Charles had him in a vise when it happened, and it was a tragic thing. It crushed Charles.

Charles left the theatre then. He did not talk later to Fonda. Charles and Herman Wouk made the revisions. I told Henry Fonda that there was a rule with Actors' Equity that said that he either had to perform or be judged by Equity for his bad behavior. I told him, "I expect you to live up to your contract and perform." He performed—though, on opening night in New

York, he mumbled through his performance, and he never spoke to us ever again.

Charles and Henry Fonda played together in Charles' last picture, *Advise and Consent*, but Charles just didn't want to speak to the man. He'd obviously been too hurt by Fonda.

Charles mentioned the incident to me weeks later—though, according to Charles, Fonda used the word *faggot*, and I should think that Charles' version is correct. I believe if a person is crazy with anger, the longer word is too much of a mouthful.

Before *Advise and Consent*, Charles and I were having dinner in a booth for four at Chasen's restaurant, with Burgess Meredith and another member of the cast. Charles asked Burgess who else was cast in *Advise and Consent*, and Burgess said, "so and so . . . and Henry Fonda," and Charles gasped. Charles said, "He's so full of shit and fury signifying nothing—" The sentence was unfinished, because Henry Fonda bobbed up in the seat immediately behind Charles and he said, "You *knew* I was here, you so and so! How are you, Charlie?"

Another year of strained relations passed between Paul and Charles. Then along came *The Night of the Hunter*. It could be that Paul found the book himself, or someone recommended it to him. Paul tended to be magnetized by best sellers (à la Zanuck), and *The Night of the Hunter* was high on his list. I believe it was Davis Grubb's first published novel.

I suppose that Paul had come to have a good deal of confidence in Charles as a director, because when the idea of making the book into a film came up it was naturally Charles who directed it. According to Paul:

I read *The Night of the Hunter* when Charles and I were in New York. I was leaving for Jamaica, so I left him a note with the book that said: "Charlie, this would make a motion picture." We had wanted to find something that we could make that wouldn't cost a million dollars. I'd seen Robert Mitchum as the heavy in this. Charlie called me the next day and just raved and said, "I'm coming down," and Charlie came to Jamaica.

Charles said, "You know, I can't write this screenplay from scratch. I've got to start with somebody, so we've got to think about who could write this." I wanted to bring Charlie into focus as a top director and have him eventually quit performing. The performances were what were killing him; he needed to find something where he could direct one or two things a year and make all the money he needed. That was the goal I had for Charles. With me producing and him directing, and when he didn't direct, we'd be co-producers.

Because Charles was brilliant in directing *The Night of the Hunter*. Utterly brilliant.

Davis Grubb lived in Philadelphia, so Charles went there and worked with him several times on starting the script for *The Night of the Hunter*. I don't remember Davis Grubb ever coming to Hollywood.

To sell a film to distributors, you not only need names of well-known actors but you also need names tried and tested in every technical department. Charles and Paul both knew that distributors would demand an established name for the writer, and Davis Grubb's name was not good enough. And Charles wasn't a tried and tested writer, so according to Paul, Charles thought of writer James Agee to write the script—although he once told me that United Artists unloaded Agee onto him and he didn't really know who he was.

The script James Agee finally wrote for the film was as big as a telephone book. Although he was an experienced screenwriter, it bore no relation to a workable script. Of course, Agee could have been carried away working with Charles, or perhaps he just lost a practical approach. He was ill at the time. I think it was his heart; we didn't exactly know. He would sit out by the pool and look as if he were dying. He was exhausted. He wanted to drink. And we didn't know if he was drinking heavily or was on drugs or what. He didn't sleep in the house —he just came in the mornings and worked all day and every day for months, editing and carving out the story.

Charles finally had very little respect for Agee. And he hated the script, but he was inspired by his hatred. Paul Gregory later said to me that

Charles had terrible disagreements with James Agee on that script, but out of the terrible disagreements with Agee, Charles had a vision and some inspiration to write his own script. While Charles was rewriting, James Agee was lying on the floor of my house in Santa Monica dying, saying that Charles was killing him. He was there for fourteen days, drunk like you cannot imagine. We finally moved him to a motel, but Charlie wouldn't go near him. And it was because Charlie wouldn't see him that Agee was drinking. And we paid him $30,000 for a script that Charles never opened. And James Agee died. But the script that was produced on that screen is no more James Agee's, and no more belongs in the collection of Agee's writing, than I'm Marlene Dietrich.

Charles knew himself well enough to realize that, this being his first venture as a film director, he couldn't direct and act in the picture at the same time. He tried doing both in *Galileo,* and what he found was a "dumb" director—that is, someone whom Charles could dictate to —in Joe Losey. Later, Joe proved to be a successful director on his own.

Davis Grubb had never thought of his book as being a film, so he didn't help in the casting at all. I was involved in it—not officially, but at home. Charles had always thought that I was a marvelous caster. We would sit and talk about casts not only for *The Night of the Hunter* but for other possible productions. Also I always did "off-casting," that is, placing an actor in a role unlike any he had done before.

At one time I think there was some question that I might do the Lillian Gish character, but I didn't want to be around Charles when he was in such a hypersensitive condition and I didn't want to be any-where near Paul Gregory. Anyway, my playing that part was never considered too seriously by Charles or Paul. It was just an idea among many. Charles had merely asked me, "Would you like to do it?" and I said, "No."

I started to ferret around for people who had some relation to myself. I thought of Zasu Pitts, but she was not right because she was associated with fun and humor and audiences would be inclined to giggle. Miss Pitts was in *All Quiet on the Western Front,* and Lewis Mile-stone, its director, had to reshoot the whole thing because the audi-ences screamed with laughter. She would not have been good in *The Night of the Hunter* because the part had to be a touching, delicate thing. It's a great little part, a beautiful part. Then I suggested Lillian Gish.

Lillian Gish had been called the Iron Butterfly—I think it was Hedda Hopper who said it. It's a marvelous name for her. She looks like a gardenia petal. Lillian smells of gardenia and dresses like that, but she is iron, she is a rock. She works hard on parts, and Charles loved having her in the film. It did him good.

But Charles had mixed feelings about Robert Mitchum, who played the preacher, the leading character in *The Night of the Hunter.* He was a sleazy small-town evangelist who went from town to town preaching his own theory of love and hate; his evil charm helped along his tawdry little career. Preacher Harry Powell had the same aura as, say, Billy Graham, but only in the wretched creature's dreams of him-self. A lot of people think that Charles got a truly wonderful perform-ance out of Bob Mitchum as the preacher, and I agree.

Mitchum came to our house a couple of times to talk about his part, and in his anxiety to seem intelligent about it, he talked all through dinner. Charles knew enough to let a person have his head if he wanted to appear to have an intellectual approach. I don't know, maybe Bob Mitchum is very bright, but I never heard such a lot of words—big, long words, one after the other. Perhaps he felt insecure with Charles and he was only trying to impress him. Charles wanted me to mix the salad and make small talk—"Would you care for some more of this, would you like some of that?"—but I really didn't talk at all. I just listened to Bob Mitchum using his long words. But Charles was patient with him because Mitchum was going to be one of his children.

I suppose it was inevitable that Charles and Mitchum would work together. They were kindred spirits, both what you call rebels, with no respect for formal religion or Hollywood society. According to Mitchum, when Charles was first thinking about casting *The Night of the Hunter,* he called up him and the phone conversation went like this:

"Hello, this is Charles Laughton."

"Yes?"

"I have a book I'd like you to read. There's a character in it that I would like you to play in a movie I'm making. The man is a real shit. A dreadful and devout shit!"

"Present!"

Obviously, Mitchum was interested. Then Charles started to lecture Mitchum: "Now, my boy, let's not have a premature discussion on whether you'll play this part or not, because I'd hate to have it announced in the papers that I'm interested in a shit. As you must know, I am a professional non-shit traveling the country reading the Bible and it would be a surprising note in my career if it were known that I was associated with a diabolical shit prematurely."

Mitchum read the novel and called up Paul Gregory and said, "Ready!" Mitchum turned out to be even more of a rebel than Charles could have imagined. For the most part, Charles got along with him, but Mitchum did not get along with Paul. One day, while driving his new Cadillac, Paul almost ran him over. Paul had to buy a new Cadillac after that because Mitchum relieved himself on the radiator, and whenever the radiator heated up it would smell terrible. Finally, late one evening, Charles had to lecture Mitchum on the telephone:

"Charles here."

"Yes."

"My boy, there are skeletons in all our closets, Most of us try to conceal those skeletons or at least to keep the door closed. My dear, you not only fling open the door, you drag forth all your skeletons and swing them in the air. Bob, you simply must stop brandishing your skeletons."

Once they had signed Bob Mitchum, they went after casting Shel-

238

ley Winters. Mitchum's reaction to that was, "My God, the only thing she's going to do convincingly is float in the water with her throat cut" —a part of the plot. But Charles and Gregory cast Shelley anyway, or rather I cast Shelley Winters. Many people saw in Shelley the temperament of an uncontrolled, bitchy, selfish, catty woman. I must say that I have always seen her as a good actress, and Charles not only saw her as a good actress but he penetrated that brash exterior of hers. In those days she was really a vulnerable, fragile woman, a frightened girl. It was all bravado, this other thing. She knew that Charles understood that. Of course Shelley had been one of Charles' students in the Shakespeare class and he was naturally flattered by her adulation, but he also saw her in the part. And Shelley was magnificent and fragile and touching in *The Night of the Hunter*.

I had once worked with Shelley in an unimportant little Western film called *Frenchie*. She had been nasty to me during the filming and I really wasn't comfortable with her because I thought she was a tricky little thing. But in casting, personality doesn't make any difference.

The filming of *Hunter* was a compassionate time for Charles, and he found that he was able to bring out compassion in his performers. Charles was as temperamental during the shooting of that film as he was during his whole life. And he suffered agonies. There was Mitchum to reckon with, not to mention a couple of young children. In spite of Charles' regrets that he was never a father, he had almost no patience with children. More often than not, he just avoided the two young actors on the set, though he admitted to me that he liked the boy but hated the little girl. In several articles Mitchum has been quoted as saying that he found himself directing the two youngsters in several scenes because Charles was ignoring them.

Whatever, Charles certainly got lovely performances from all of them—James Gleason, Evelyn Vardon, Don Beddoe. Some people call parts like those *cameos*. If a part is only a cameo, you can cut it out and it will not be missed. But Charles was so good with actors that *The Night of the Hunter* was a tapestry. If you pulled one thread, it would have taken the whole structure of the story away. He had reached a point in his life when he was getting articulate enough to give form to stories. *The Night of the Hunter* was a great example of this. Although some of the sequences seemed to depart from the theme of the story, all the various threads did come together in the end to create *The Night of the Hunter*, now accepted as one of the finest suspense films ever made.

Perhaps it was before its time, but only a little. Audiences did not understand it. Nor did the critics—then. It is only now—after how long — ten years, fifteen, twenty?—that *The Night of the Hunter* has achieved a cult following and is considered a great and significant film, studied seriously in colleges and universities. Poor Charles. I wish he would have known.

I think that Paul Gregory never really got around to appreciating just what Charles was doing at the time. But Charles certainly knew what he was about, and it was partly the result of some of the paintings he had around him. He actually utilized a Seurat painting, "La Grande Jatte," which shows a Sunday afternoon in the park, the lack of activity, static figures. Charles took the heart of this mood for his picnic scene in *The Night of the Hunter*.

Paul Gregory has said about the film:

> The distribution of it was poor. United Artists, at the time, had a thing called *Not as a Stranger* with Robert Mitchum that they had something like five million dollars in, and they only had four hundred and ninety-seven thousand dollars in our picture and they sloughed it off. It was as simple as that. I don't think Charles felt he'd failed with the picture, but I think he felt that the critics failed to recognize what he'd done. And I think he was right on that score.

You can imagine what a bitter pill it was for Charles when the film was not well received. In the last ten years of his life, Charles developed an aspect of his career to the point where he knew exactly the direction he wished to take, as the editing he did on many of his productions showed. *John Brown's Body* and *Don Juan in Hell*, then *The Caine Mutiny Court Martial*, which was pure form, as was his editing later on of *Major Barbara*, all exemplified Charles' mastery of form.

Charles might have continued to direct films, but *The Night of the Hunter* did not make money. What studio wants to invest in an actor who wants to direct and has an avant-garde failure on his hands? But Charles' readings went on, and these gave him security and almost some relaxation.

28

One gray evening, the light already fading around six o'clock, Charles and I were in the schoolroom having a martini. We were going out to see a play with a buffet beforehand. Obviously, we had to go for some minor business reason, for we never went out, really. Charles was wearing a gray suit and I was in a little gray wool dress. We felt very depressed, for Charles was leaving in the morning by car for another reading tour of four to six months, with a few days' break here and there. He would be with the road man, and a friend to hang out the suits and stack the books for the show. The two fellows would share the driving. Charles and I did not like being together all the time, but we hated parting and loved our reunions.

A tall, slim, very blond man shambled aristocratically into the schoolroom. He said that his name was Leif and that he had been sent by Davis Grubb to meet Charles. We were sorry not to be able to invite him to stay for a drink, but we were just going off, so we both said, "Drop by any day . . . have a swim . . ." And as we talked, Leif let his fingers wander over the piano, playing some dissonant chords and modulating from key to key. He let out a few voh-dee-o-doh sounds and also snapped his fingers. We shooed him out with another, "See you again," and Charles and I dashed off.

The next evening, Leif turned up at dusk and helped himself to a drink and I showed him the pool. He took off his clothes and with a running, flying leap, dove into the pool and shot from one end to the other. I must say he did look more like a goldfish than a person. I cannot recall being surprised or curious.

Ray Henderson came by for a drink later, and Leif and he played the piano together, fighting for musical laughs. Even when a good time is happening, you get hungry, so we went out to dinner. The talk turned to Palos Verdes, with its orchard and five-octave piano. I think Ray and I were going down there, anyway—old friends on a spaghetti-weekend trip; Ray was very good at making spaghetti—and Leif picked up a businessman friend somewhere along the line, the owner of a canned fish business. And all of a sudden, there we were at Palos Verdes. I can only describe proceedings in an abstract way, since energy and laughter and music were so intertwined that no ordering of events is possible. Leif took off in the moonlight with two rolls of toilet paper unwinding behind him as he raced through the orchard. Later, he set fire to his pubic hair but soon brushed it out as if it were a daily trick.

We drove off to our various headquarters at about four in the morning, but in a few hours we met again at the Curson Avenue house for breakfast. There was a little pushing to get into the swimming pool and, afterward, more piano. A friend or two showed up, and no one could leave this strange party. There was some drinking but not much. Very late that day, after more swimming, Leif and I started out on a round of jazz clubs. I was introduced to a world of dusky, moaning rooms of the night. We sat for hours listening to Dizzy Gillespie and Shelley Mann, then headed on to some quiet, dim place and heard Matt Dennis sing "She Wore Violets in Her Fur." We had a short sleep in the car off Wilshire Boulevard, then went on to The Lighthouse in Redondo Beach, and so on to Palos Verdes.

Leif's Boston society mother and father had sent him to Los Angeles for psychiatric treatment with our famous local bigwig psychiatrist and provided him with a car and comfortable, quite elegant places to live. In Boston, Leif had tried a formal life, but it didn't work. He had a wife and two children, who seemed to be among the many things that tilted him. He had been a heart surgeon in Boston.

Charles used to come home for a few days during his tour—a time for extra good cooking and resting. He was delighted that Leif had become a friend, for he had liked their mutual friend Davis Grubb. Leif and Charles didn't have much in common and got on to subjects that made them uncertain of what to discuss. Sometimes it would be politics, but Charles talked like *Time* magazine and Leif talked like Mort Sahl. They both swam in the nude, but the other guests didn't—a friendly link.

Once Charles announced to Leif that he was a homosexual, then asked with a wry smile, "And what do you think of that?" Leif answered, "Not a thing. What do *you* think of *that*?" When Charles left again for his tour, he said to me, "I hope you don't let Leif hurt you."

At that time Ray Henderson was playing the piano at a nightspot, and would bring up performers or friends occasionally after his show.

Leif took off with two of them once—one very famous, the other one black. He wanted the black singer, but she wouldn't take her drawers off. The frizzy blond comic stripped in a flash, but Leif didn't want her. Apparently, a dreary time was had by all. I enjoyed Leif's outrageous tales about people and relationships, for he was a fantastic by nature, the most eccentric raconteur that I had ever encountered. He often said he might finish up with a frontal lobotomy himself, and he had discussed it with his analyst. Leif was a good brain surgeon who needed brain surgery.

I liked absorbing this world of jazz, where even the language was foreign to me—*fuzz, pad, bread, fey, hung up*—strange words at the time; and Leif knew all the origins of such words. He often wrote pieces of complete gibberish, maybe as a result the psychiatrist's treatment:

> From a communications standpoint, it is of signal importance that many of the terms exhibit a vast multipotentiality, including, in many cases, the denotation of exact opposites. This relies upon contextural tone, which of course may be only adumbrated in such a treatment as this. This contextural pliability of meaning not only provides its most fascinating aspect, but perhaps, on closer analysis, may constitute, from a communication basis, its semantic justification to a stable language form . . .

I liked our topographical wanderings—at least, we seemed to have some things in common. He liked me to wear an old fishnet shirt he had. I must say, I rather fancied myself in it. Once, at a small party, he announced that I was "the best lay in Southern California." I said, "Why Southern California?" and he snapped back, "I've never been in Northern California!" Some remarks can be so extreme that they emerge as a form of humor.

During this time, I hosted a memorable TV program called *Words about Music*—memorable because Oscar Levant was my copartner on the stage. It was on every Saturday night for one year. Each week we had three or four famous composers appear as guests, and a special composer-guest's music was played by the Page Cavanaugh Trio. We would talk music and battled with our wits. It was shattering to keep up with Oscar's mind. We all sat back of a long, giant keyboard that crossed the stage—Oscar at one end, and me at the other. Leif helped to give me some very snappy musical answers to use on the air.

One night I stayed with Leif in a fairly elegant pad, where he had a sort of home traction apparatus hanging in the bathroom for stretching the spine—a health gadget, I think, with straps and ropes and pulleys and things. It was not for me. Leif was more or less asleep. I slipped out the door, passed the dewy ferns on the long balcony, passing other flats, down a few steps to the road. Fortunately, we had used my car, so I drove off. And I have not seen Leif since.

Paul's next ambitious project was to get an option on a huge best seller, *The Naked and the Dead* by Norman Mailer. Charles didn't know what hit him. He had told me that he did not feel equipped to handle subjects about the military or the behavior patterns of males at war. His feeling had nothing to do with hatred of war itself. It was that he just didn't understand or *want* to understand the male and his battling instincts. He never could achieve the fighter-soldier side of Macbeth. When he was approached for *Bridge on the River Kwai,* he somehow slid out of it, though he desperately wanted to work with director David Lean again.

For that very reason, Charles fought quite hard not to undertake the direction of *The Caine Mutiny Court Martial.* So when Paul wanted to buy *The Naked and the Dead,* Charles put up a real battle not to adapt or direct it. But Paul became the enforcer, feeling that Charles' genius could now achieve anything.

Herman Wouk had written to Charles, "Best of luck with *The Naked and the Dead,* whatever you decide. I think it's a terribly tough nut to crack, but if it's ever cracked there'll be honor and some money for all." Over months and months of sitting around a table with different writers, Charles tried to carve a screenplay out of the Mailer Monster—that huge World War II story. He would have hope one day and despair the next, and in the end nothing. I was in charge of supplying sandwiches and coffee, and Heidel usually carried in the tray to the writers. Once I had to do it. Charles looked up at me and glowered. "Get out! We're working!"

Paul had borrowed nearly a quarter of a million dollars from an Eastern investor to finance Charles' year of hacking away at *The Naked and the Dead.* So when Charles failed to get a workable script finished, it strained their relationship even more. Paul said:

> I kept having to go and get more money to keep on paying Charles, and my financier in Philadelphia kept saying, "Well, what's the matter, where's the script, Paul?"; and I kept promising, "Look, this is going to be something unbelievable!"
>
> I'm telling the truth, that script with all the people that Charles had to have working on it cost $320,000. Well, finally, after a year, Charles completed a first draft and the script was sent back to Philadelphia. The financier called me and he said, "It's a little thick, isn't it?" And I said, "Yes, it is. It needs editing; everything but the kitchen sink is in it."

So I asked Charles how long did he think it would take him to get a shooting draft out of the script, and Charles said, "Well, at least another year, old boy!" Another year was impossible! And the financier stopped the money. I don't blame him at all for stopping it. I was relieved, to tell the truth.

Then, according to Paul, something "terrible and unexpected" happened, although he admits there was no actual proof. Apparently, the Philadelphia financier's very good friend was producer-director George Sidney, who had directed Charles in *Young Bess* at MGM. Like many directors before him, he had had his troubles with Charles. The financier asked Sidney to read Charles' script of *The Naked and the Dead.* Sidney reported that it would take at least $20 million to make it the way it was written (and this was in the 1950s) and that he thought it was a lousy screenplay. Paul had no defense at all, and he claimed *that* was when the Philadelphia financier stopped the money.

Years later, Paul told me that Charles' script "was absolutely brilliant, absolutely brilliant!" He said he had Marlon Brando interested in the role of Croft, and Montgomery Clift wanted a part in the film, too—according to Paul.

As *The Night of the Hunter* had not been a commercial film, Charles shared that failure with Paul. At the end of another year, the two would part—at Charles' instigation—over a personal matter the size of a gnat.

The matter that brought on their final split involved a young fellow Paul had introduced to Charles—whom we'll call Clyde—a short and stubby man, honest and simple, who became very devoted to Charles. He had no trade and very little education. He had tried being a gas station attendant and then sold enameled watches and bracelets. The initial relationship between Charles and Clyde was close, but in a short time it became more of a friendship. Charles trusted him and poured out his heart to him about our marriage. Clyde was put on the payroll at Gregory Associates as Charles' driver and handyman. He would drive Charles down to Palos Verdes or up to Yosemite to study words, and to Northern California to see flowers. Sometimes Clyde would introduce Charles to other young men, and on rare occasions, I have been told, even supply Charles with marijuana. I can't believe it.

Charles, in turn, was kind and generous with Clyde, exposing the young man to museums and art and literature. They would sit under a great Yosemite tree, I was told, and Charles would read him Shakespeare. I was later to learn, also, through this young man that Paul "was robbing poor Charles blind." They had made perhaps millions at the box office on *The Caine Mutiny Court Martial,* but much of the money was mismanaged. Charles was always careful not to rock the boat.

Perhaps he was afraid of Paul. Anyway, Clyde eventually told Charles that Paul had come to him, asking questions about Charles and actually suggesting to Clyde that Charles would forgive anything, that he could "get anything out of Charles while the going was good." In other words, since Charles had done it for others, why not him? He could even get a car out of Charles, Paul said. This, at last, was the final breaking point between Charles and Paul Gregory.

Clyde told Charles what Paul had said because he was sincerely loyal. Knowing this honest young fellow slightly at the time, I had the feeling that he thought that Paul's remark, after so many years with Charles, was a betrayal. The young man felt a wave of goodness and decency—a tiny St. George to the rescue.

Some years later, Clyde wrote down his feelings about Charles:

> Charles just enjoyed talking with me. He could be particularly relaxed and say whatever he wanted. He knew I didn't judge him and that I was very fond of him. But he had this terrible guilt about his feelings toward men, and he had an unnatural fear of any kind of scandal. . . . His guilts and his drives caused him great pain.
>
> Sometimes when Charles would become especially irritated with his wife, he would call me up to complain. "I'm leaving her," he would say. "I just can't take any more, and I'm through. I'm definitely leaving her." But I knew Charles' mood was only temporary, and that he would never leave Elsa. He needed her, for flowers and scenic beauties, and it was a powerful bond that held them together.

I quite understood this young man. He was never unfair or unkind to Charles, which I appreciated, and afterward he came to dinner now and then.

After Clyde's confidence, Charles simply went to Loyd Wright and said, "End the partnership." I don't think he told Wright the reason. He told me that Loyd Wright said, "I'm very glad." On June 13, 1956, the company was dissolved in Loyd Wright's office in a matter of a few minutes at a "Special Meeting of the Board of Directors of Gregory Associates, Inc." There it was "RESOLVED that the name of Paul Gregory be removed from any and all signature cards . . . in any and all banks where the corporation carries accounts" . . . and that "the office of President of the corporation be . . . declared vacant."

Paul apparently turned white. It was his turn to be amazed and staggered. He said, "I had met Charles and I had noticed that he was very nervous at my office that morning. Charles never said a word to me about the parting."

I would always be sorry, however, that Paul Gregory could have nearly ruined my life when he canceled my tour, but Charles would not have connected that with any break he had with Paul later. At least, though, our marriage was rather better after the company had been dissolved. Maybe the conk on the head with my hairbrush cleared the air a bit, too.

Charles never spoke to Paul again, never saw him again. He felt deeply betrayed and his faith in people was badly shaken. Nothing whatsoever—no letters, nothing—passed between them after that.

Paul Gregory believed that other people had begun to influence Charles. Years before the film version of *Witness for the Prosecution* was made, it was playing on Broadway; and according to Paul, he told Charles then that they should get Tyrone Power and form a company to do the play as a film. But Paul's position with Charles had already slipped. Paul said to me:

The big thing was going to be *Witness for the Prosecution.* And then suddenly I found it was being pulled away from me. Loyd Wright wouldn't talk to me about it. He was in for the big kill on it, too. I think I made the mistake of talking to Tyrone right off about *Witness,* and Tyrone talked to his agent—his agent was M.C.A.— and Arthur Hornblow became producer. I had always thought it funny that I could never get the rights. I think it was a concerted effort to move me out.

According to Paul, Loyd Wright or someone told Charles that his position with Paul was hopeless and that he should get out while he could walk away. So Charles did.

Some time later, in England, Paul met Erich Pommer, who said, according to Paul, that there was "no one worse in the world than Charles Laughton." After Pommer's death, Paul met his son, who said that Charles had practically killed his father. And Paul, of course, also held Charles responsible for James Agee's death:

Charles unequivocally killed James Agee. Charles was diabolical and he couldn't help it. He just couldn't help himself. That's why I don't hold any of it against him. He just couldn't help it. He had to destroy either Elsa or me or someone. He had to destroy to live and create. But I kept popping back up. I realize, as I look back, how he did it to other people. People against people, that was Charles' way. The great divider.

About two years after the split, Paul went ahead and filmed *The Naked and the Dead* on his own. It was a failure.

Sometimes an actor is tempted when he shouldn't be. A script of a play called *The Party*, by Jane Arden, arrived for Charles from producer Oscar Lewenstein in England. At the time, Charles was looking for something *new*. It was the angry young man era, and Charles found it in *The Party*—the angry outpouring of a very pregnant, rather persecuted young woman.

The grim drama was about a daughter's love for her father and vice versa. Charles directed it, and in a few weeks I joined the cast as a chattering neighbor in the first act. Joyce Redman played the wife, who was mystified, cheery, and grizzling, but Miss Redman was very unhappy in the part and every day tried to get out of the play. She did eventually. The young man with a leather jacket, who sniffed sex around the house but could not make head nor tail of it in his profound talks with the father (Charles), was played by Albert Finney. Charles had seen Finney act Macbeth and said that although he was very bad he had the makings of a great actor, so Charles insisted that he join the cast. He was remarkably good.

Jane Arden was Welsh, and the play had a perfume of its own. As director, Charles made the stage drab and suburban. Many of the scenes were almost too moving, but this was not the play for Charles to bring back to his home in England. The relationship between the father and daughter drives the father to drink, and half the critics said: "So Charles came back to England to give us a study of a drunk"— disregarding the complex study of the father and daughter, the true theme. Of all things, Charles hated playing a drunk. This dislike dated back to his youth in the hotel business. I did not have any scenes with Charles, which disappointed the audience because we were, of course, an acting couple and married in private life.

Our play was tried out in Edinburgh and Manchester. Charles was always on the lookout for new painters, and in Manchester a member of the cast, Jacqueline Squire, introduced us to an artist named Alan Lowndes. The young painter lived in one room—and I mean one room—where he slept on newspapers on the floor. Still, he was a happy young man. He painted whatever was in his orbit: suburban streets, factories and their people, and that dismal sky that hangs over industrial districts, a grayish, pea-colored weight; as well as barmaids and Beatles-like basement nightspots. He's now successful, has a family, and I think lives in the real country. I have many of his paintings, but I do not hang them here in California. They disturb any room that they are in, like mysterious ghosts from the black country. But I look at them and I show them to people.

Charles wrote to Taft Schreiber about his new discovery Alan Lowndes, and how his paintings were so far inexpensive—£5, £4, even £2. Taft knew well Charles' eye for modern art—and so cheap!—so he asked Charles to invest in some paintings for him. Wrote Taft: "My wife Rita likes Modigliani." Charles wrote copiously to Taft on the subject of famous painters and new discoveries, and finally Taft sent Charles $18,000, saying, "Buy for me." At this, Loyd Wright turned against Taft and wrote to Charles, "If you've such a talent, buy for yourself and give Taft second best."

When we got back to London, Charles and I took a very small place in a quite elegant block of service flats called Dorset House, just off Baker Street. There I shopped and cooked more than at any time in my life—in a little kitchen that needed ingenuity. I always found that very inspiring. Charles and I also searched the countryside not too far from London for a furnished cottage for the weekends, and we ran into such charming places that we had dreams of coming back to live in England. But then leases were too long for visiting actors.

During the run of *The Party*, Charles and I had a craving to see our old friend Iris Barry.

She had been the earliest actual employee—the Film Library curator—of the official New York Museum of Modern Art. On the very day that Iris was to be the first to receive the modest retirement pension given to the permanent staff, she disappeared. She had already taken away all her personal property, leaving only her inkpot on her desk with a tie-on label saying, "This is the property of Iris Barry."

Charles and I heard from her only occasionally and I think she was on friendly terms with the museum. She did a few lectures for them in Europe and a few interviews. Now she was living in the south of France with an ex-rum runner—a very rough Frenchman named Pierre, from Marseilles, but he turned out to be a nice fellow. They ran a junk shop. After a few telegrams back and forth, Iris and Pierre came over. Charles paid their fare and all expenses to come to London, and we put them in the Paddington Hotel. It is (or was) a damned good hotel, with good food because Charles' brother Tom, who managed the food, had been a major with the Northern Food Command during the war and was overseer for the Northern Railways and the big English Station Hotels.

However much Charles adored Iris, he found her drinking very upsetting. With his early experiences in the family hotels—turning out abusive drunks from the bar—he'd built up this horror of the smell of the saloon, and disgust developed with it. But Iris, in spite of her drinking, was highly original, articulate, quick witted. And Charles and Iris had become very, very good friends. She'd written about films a great deal—and brilliantly. I think her drive to make something of the Film Library of the Museum of Modern Art wasn't only that she was dabbling in history, making history—it was just that she was Iris Barry, a driven film archivist.

We saw Iris and her Pierre for a few weeks and we had a marvelous time. After a drink or two Iris would become very quarrelsome but without being as belligerent as some drinking people. Then she would suffer remorse, and then she would laugh about it. She was very analytical, without any vanity, and she was very forthright. Her delivery of her wisdom wasn't self-conscious at all. She had the great art of making simple statements about things or people or herself that made you collapse with laughter—but she was always very wise.

Charles hated drunkenness in others, yet he became (on and off) a heavy drinker himself. He needed a drink more and more, the last few years, anyway. And Charles suffered remorse, too. But he never laughed about it.

Apart from the depressing play *The Party,* Charles was filling his dressing room at the New Theatre with his newly discovered paintings and showing them off to all and sundry. He had many works by new painters besides Alan Lowndes, and he was always happy to talk about them. Among the many visitors backstage, famous and otherwise, we often saw Tyrone Power with his new wife, Debbie. We went with them many times to a very good Italian restaurant in St. Martin's Lane for an early dinner between matinees and evening shows. We had only to walk across the road. Tyrone Power's favorite dish was osso bucco.

After Iris and Pierre went back to their junk shop, Charles and I heard of the famous "Grease Paint Special," a midnight train that went to Brighton—a fast one-hour trip. Actors and actresses could be seen flying down the platform at Victoria Station and jumping into any carriage as twelve o'clock drew near. Charles and I began to commute most nights, too. We would barely make it after our show, but we usually had time to pick up two cartons of milk. Brighton was a godsend to us. We had "two bed and sit" on the ocean front in the Royal Crescent Hotel, on the elegant George the Third glittering sea front. The beach consisted of nothing but pebbles, and the withdrawing of the waves made a comforting little clatter of its own, unlike the tide on sand. We spent whole days on the South Downs picking wild flowers before heading back to the theatre on the *Brighton Belle,* with dining car.

One trip, driving through that lovely country in a rented car, we passed through a village that was just a decaying little church with a barn or two, and a large house with an old wall all around it. Charles and I gazed through its vast old iron gate at a garden of flowers such as I've never seen—colors tumbling around in ordered disorder. As we stood there, a spruce, past-middle-age gentleman with a white mustache came up and said, *"Do* come in, Mr. Laughton."

We walked through the tumbling rainbow to have drinks with him. We went to dinner at his house on our first night off, a Sunday. There were two or three young men and women at dinner, all relaxed. The house was almost bizarre, overfilled with Italianate furniture—lots of gilt and mirrors and candles and high-backed, red velvet-covered chairs. Our host said to Charles that he knew Enid Bagnold (author of *National Velvet* and *The Chalk Garden*), who lived in the Rottingdean part of Brighton, and insisted Charles and she *must* meet each other. A few days later, a meeting was arranged.

Enid Bagnold had been a beautiful woman and was still handsome, though rather weighed down in front with a bust that had probably always been there. As a matter of fact, she comments on it in her autobiography. Charles told me later she'd twice had her face lifted. She also writes that when she met us at the front door, we were carrying wild flowers. I remember her floating toward us and wafting us into the living room—wearing the rather soft gray and beige chiffon that traditionally sits well on ladies who are getting along in years and have big busts.

I don't remember the name of our host, nor does Enid Bagnold mention him in her autobiography. Since she wrote that she "instantly fell in love with . . . the vitality and power to charm of this ugly man [Charles]," she might have given the old gentleman with the garden some credit. Charles was delighted to be with a playwright who seemed to hang on his every word, and Enid saw him as someone to inspire her to write another good acceptable modern play. Charles went out there a good deal—"He became a total visitor: lunching every day except matinee days," Enid wrote. And she credits me with wisely leaving her alone with Charles. About our first meeting, she wrote: "This was the only time that we three talked together. Or nearly. Why? Did Elsa decide that Charles got on better with women alone? (Or better with writers?)" Her report is not at all correct. She knew that after dropping Charles, I went off to visit my mother in another part of town; naturally I had to spend time with her, and I must add that Charles also saw a lot of Biddy, whom he really liked. I did have a few dinners at Enid's, but she was so active (mentally) getting ideas out of Charles for a play, that I got stuck with her husband, old Sir Roderick Jones, head of Reuter's World News Service, and her thirty-year-old son who didn't talk and only liked old trains and railroad tracks— narrow-gauge.

In her autobiography Enid observed Charles' fame well. When she once drove him to Brighton Station to catch his 5:00 P.M. for that night's performance, she got him there early. According to her, Charles cried, *"Don't* get me to the station so early! *Don't!* I can't bear it! They mob me! Elsa always protects me."

Enid commented:

At first I thought he was putting it on. It was true. People glanced. . . . They clustered and closed in. . . . He was doomed and blest with it. I had never seen a human being unable to lead a private life in public. It was then I tried to write the play . . .

It was to be called *The Monsters.* I don't think she finished it.

Later, Enid wrote to Charles seeking some advice about a nearly completed play:

I have gotten to lean on you so much . . . I am *thankful* you "think about me and the play." It's a help to think so.

And in another letter soon after that:

I miss you so much—the wonderful stimulus of working together —that I've become housewifely and drab and depressed.

But in her autobiography, she concludes: "But it was the theatre I fell in love with. Nevertheless, at sixty-eight, it was very like love . . ."

Glen Byam Shaw, organizer and producer at Stratford-on-Avon, was retiring from the organization after seven years. He had dreamed of making *King Lear* his swan song, and Charles really felt that *this was it* for him—now or never. Charles had always wanted to play *Lear*. His desire had gradually grown since I first met him. *King Lear!* . . . If people asked, "What's your ambition, Mr. Laughton?", he would quietly, not immediately, but eventually get around to Lear. He had some affinity, obviously, with it. Charles' reason for his passion to *be* Lear, to fulfill himself in this part, I do not know.

Glen Byam Shaw later wrote to me about Charles:

> One day during a matinee, the General Manager came to my office and told me that Charles Laughton was in the auditorium. He had been to see all the productions that season . . . "Ask him to come and have a drink with me at the end of the performance," I said.

At the time, Charles was working for director David Lean in *Hobson's Choice*. Charles was playing a drunk again, which he hated. Charles did have his early memory of being a bouncer in his parents' hotel. Anyway, Charles was enjoying working with David Lean. He was a kindred spirit and Charles felt at home with him. Lean was sympathetic to Charles and they wanted to get together for another film. I think Lean was bitterly disappointed that he didn't get to work with Charles again. He offered Charles *The Bridge on the River Kwai*, but Charles could not face the physical discomforts in the part. He found plenty of excuses to turn it down, but actually he could not face the heat of the Ceylon location, the ants, and being cramped in a cage—Charles was not in the mood for degradation in life or even in drama. I'm sure it was a great sorrow to him. I think Charles felt that he wasn't a strong man by then . . . a sort of premonition.

According to Glen Byam Shaw, he said to Charles, "How is it that you come here so often?"

"We've been making a film of *Hobson's Choice* and it has been good to escape whenever I could. Now I have to go back to America, but I shan't forget Stratford."

"Why don't you come and do a season here?"

Charles finished his drink and said he must be going and left. But a couple of minutes later, he poked his head round the door and said, "If you asked me to play *King Lear* here, I should find it hard to refuse." Then he left again.

As 1959 would be the hundredth season, Glen Byam Shaw wanted to make it a memorable one. John Gielgud had already turned down the season but he reminded Glen that Charles had once said he wanted to play Lear. "You should get him," Gielgud said.

Glen Byam Shaw wrote:

Charles and Elsa were in London doing a play at the New Theatre at the time [*The Party*]. I telephoned Charles and asked if we could meet and have lunch together.

"Where?"

"At my club," I suggested.

When he arrived he seemed rather depressed and surly, and I found it tough going talking to him about the possibility of his coming to Stratford. Suddenly he said, "Oh, how I loathe London clubs. Let's get out of here."

We left and went to a restaurant about a mile away. During our walk at least a dozen people greeted him. I was puzzled at first, then suddenly realized that they didn't know him personally but thought they did because they recognized his face.

After a few drinks and some food, I got going and told Charles he had to come to Stratford to play *Lear,* that he owed it to himself, to the British public, the American tourists, and to me. He began to thaw but kept putting up obstacles and I kept knocking them down. Finally he said he would think it over and let me know.

I went back to Stratford and . . . I felt sure I had been wasting my time. The following morning my secretary came into the office to tell me that Mr. Laughton was on the line. So this is it, I thought.

"I've decided that I will come to Stratford next season to play *Lear.*"

"And Bottom in *A Midsummer Night's Dream?*" I asked.

"Yes, if you think it right."

"I do," I said.

"Then I agree."

I had told Charles the day before that it was, from his point of view as well as mine, important that he should come for the whole season and play at least two parts. He had suggested his playing Bottom, which Peter Hall was directing.

Charles said, "But we must meet and talk about *Lear* as soon as possible. There are two things we must do together. One is go to Stonehenge and the other is go to Beachy Head. Could you meet me at Stonehenge next Sunday morning and we could spend the day together and then you could come back to Brighton. I always stay at the Royal Crescent Hotel for the week-ends."

"Alright," I said. "I'll meet you there at 12 o'clock."

It is quite a long drive from Stratford to Wiltshire, but I arrived in good time. As I did so, it started to rain.

"Oh, damnation, this is going to be hell," I said to myself.

Shortly afterwards, Charles arrived in a large hired car. The rain was coming down hard, but he tied a large woolen scarf round his head which made him look like some strange old woman, and we wandered off to look at Stonehenge. There were a few other people there who all stared at Charles. Whether they recognized him or just thought he was mad I don't know . . . after we had been there about an hour we went to a pub in Amesbury and had some strong drinks and lunch. Suddenly Charles said, "I want to read the play to you!"

"*King Lear*?"

"Yes."

"The whole play?"

"Yes. We won't go to Brighton. I'll come in your car and we'll drive to Oxford together and then I'll read the play to you."

Charles dismissed the hired car, squeezed himself into my little two seater and off we went. At the hotel we booked two bedrooms and a sitting room. We sat down, Charles took his copy of *Lear* out of his pocket and started. It was 2 A.M. when he finished. Charles said, "I feel for this scene that I must be seated, up high and very near to the audience, like this," and he clambered on to the upright piano.

"It will be rather difficult to achieve that," I said, looking up at him and realizing how right he was about the position.

"You'll think of something," and he clambered down and went on reading. By the end I was exhausted, but he seemed as fresh as a daisy. I promised to go and stay with him at Brighton in a fortnight's time so that we could visit Beachy Head together.

Glen Byam Shaw met Charles again for lunch and the trip to Beachy Head:

It was a beast of a day. A very high wind and raining. I parked the car and we struggled to the top of the cliff. I hate heights and stopped well short of the edge, but Charles staggered on until he was within a few feet of it.

Standing there alone, battered by the wind and rain, he looked remarkably like King Lear. When he came back to where I was standing my hands were sweating, but Charles was wonderfully gay and excited. On the way back to Brighton . . . Charles said, "I shall, of course, grow a beard. I can't stick on a beard for Lear."

"What about Bottom in the *Dream*," I asked.

"Oh, that will be alright. I shall paint it ginger!"

It was agreed that Margaret Harris of Motley should do the sets and costumes for *Lear*, and Charles and Glen also discussed casting. Glen told Charles, "You realize that the main part of the company is permanent for the season. I can't engage any actors specially for *King Lear.*" Charles said, "Of course, but there is a young man in my play *The Party* who you should get for the season. He will be a great star one day." Charles was talking about Albert Finney, and Finney was engaged and eventually was an outstanding success and—according to Glen—by far the best Edgar he'd ever seen. In the same season, Albert Finney took over for Olivier in *Coriolanus* and made his first huge impression.

 30

The Party over, we returned to California and collected our finances to prepare for our return trip to England and Stratford for the whole season. That summer Charles started studying intensively. We studied at home in the beginning. At first he studied alone. He read *King Lear* in bed at night, but I think he was too disturbed by it really to study something that kept him awake so much. So during this period we often worked on *A Midsummer Night's Dream,* which would be the first production of the season. That work got Charles and me together on a frivolous level. Charles was funny as he showed off the part to me and danced and fooled around. He had always wanted to play Bottom the Weaver, and he really was gloriously antic as Bottom. But his guts were preparing for Lear. Lear was always with him.

Eventually we started to work totally on Lear, with Charles reading it out loud. Charles was always one of the most exhausting people to work with. Many's the time in a film part he would exhaust three or four word hearers in one day. He would say, "I'm going to go through this seven times." And the sixth time you were ready to drop and you would think, "I hope he can't count, I hope he thinks this is the seventh time." You'd think he would breathe between readings, but as he got to the last page, you had to have your finger on the first page because *he* had his finger on the first page and he'd switch from the last word back to the first page and if you didn't switch at once with him, Charles said, "Goddamn it, if you've lost the place . . . !" It made him very angry.

Charles had that infinite capacity for taking pains—said to be one of the symptoms of genius. It's a horrid word, *genius.* Charles got quite sticky about it. It was like a burr or thorn in his side. James Agate, the dean of English critics, said in one of his early reviews, "Charles

Laughton is a genius." Then, about a year later in a review, Agate said, "This so-called genius . . ." And then, some time later he said, "This self-styled genius . . ." The price of fame.

Charles only read his part of Lear. I read all the other parts. Sometimes after breakfast, I started the day by saying to Charles, "This is exciting, but I must be free, to be able to criticize. You're not going to like all the things I say and I may be wrong sometimes, but I cannot go ahead with this huge project unless I speak my mind. I love this project. And I cannot be gentle, I cannot be a hypocrite. I must be able to speak without fear."

I think everyone will remember how when Charles was acting, his eyes would shut as he looked up and the lower lids would quiver. Or he would look like a frightened animal, or squint from side to side like a suspicious animal. All actors have little habits and tricks and I told Charles that he mustn't let them show on the stage. He'd be very silent for a minute but would finally agree. He knew I was right and he was quite glad of it. The freedom to express criticism was the only possible arrangement I could have with him.

By now, as a result of his classes and criticisms since the Old Vic, Charles was sold on blank verse. Iambic pentameter was the law. That's what is so amazing about Shakespeare—he is a dictator. The infallible precision of every line tells the story, and the punctuation is a sort of orchestration. The form is there. The form of the whole play only shifts slightly, according to the generation one is living in. A hundred years ago there might have been a great Lear who would have looked bloody awful today. The contemporary mirror reflects a faster and faster life—the mirror that an actor must hold up to his time when he interprets an old or new writer. Sometimes while Charles and I were working together, I would say, "I wonder what that means?" And perhaps we would find a new interpretation for the present day. One thing I found out—which you don't get in the textbooks—is that the punctuation is often different in the original folio from most of the versions of *King Lear* that you read today.

Then Charles and I went to Hawaii for some solid weeks of work, to get away from the telephone and people and concentrate on Lear. We were entirely inseparable at this time. We allotted ourselves breaks to go into caves and climb rocks and pick flowers again, to fill our place there with strange tropical leaves. That was our relaxation. I drove our rented car to every accessible place and *in*accessible place. We often got stuck in the mud, and Charles' job was then to collect branches and put them under the back wheels.

We made some happy contacts and friends. Our hotel was run by a most knowledgeable and compatible couple, Mr. and Mrs. Butterworth. They could fill us in on most of the superstitions and legends about the islands, and they arranged for Charles to talk to the young islanders at school. We were friendly with two other couples. One of them was soaked in the history of the islands and collected interesting shells and other strange objects—glass balls that had broken away from fishermen's nets and floated over from Japan. The other two friends were Mr. and Mrs. Cordiner of General Electric. They were taking a holiday, I imagine, because Mr. Cordiner's face had been on the cover of *Time* magazine. The man was a charmer, and Charles was utterly relaxed with him. We saw them practically every night for drinks. I would make them laugh, being always good for a few funny, unexpected lines. And, as I liked Mr. Cordiner sufficiently, I wanted to appear gentle, so my jokes were not cutting.

Another visitor to the islands, who played a lot of softball—though he and his family kept to another end of the private beach—was Billy Graham. We were introduced at dinner once by the owners of the hotel. I refrained from making any cracks about God, which was my inclination. Billy Graham said he admired Charles so much, and Charles in turn actually admired Billy Graham. He had said years before that he would be a better Billy Sunday than an actor, and he felt he could have been a second Graham himself.

Wearing a hat that covered me up completely, I used to wander around the rocks in weird places that Charles couldn't reach. God knows what I looked like, but I came back always with shells and bits of seaweed and sorted them out with Charles on the beach. One day we were taking a long walk on the beach and found ourselves trapped by a flash flood. We had crossed a dry riverbed and then we couldn't get back. We were both very frightened. The undertow was terrible, and we nearly drowned. Two small boys pulled us to land with big branches. Earlier, we had seen a white snow line we hadn't noticed before, but it wasn't a line of snow at all. It was water from the flash flood cascading down the mountains, like an image from *King Lear.*

During times of pause or relaxation, I began to discuss with Charles the images I was finding in *Lear.* Very casually, as if I had just noticed, I would say, "By the way, Charles, do you think this means anything?" The thing I found, going through the text—and through it and through it—was the extraordinary connection and repetition of references to water, climaxed by the great storm scene. It was like an outburst of tears, that storm, because there are so many references to water—water animals, rivers, dolphins. It was like a collecting of water behind the eyes and then the storm comes and the tears, and then tears for the terrible death of Cordelia at the end. So we restudied the water theme. We were learning to stretch the water and the tears so that it would be contagious to the audience, a building up of overflowing sorrow, the pressure of tears.

So with the death of King Lear, Shakespeare not only knew life, but also the welcoming of death. It is almost as if such a scene as the death of Lear was written from the other side of the grave when Kent says, "Vex not his ghost, O let him passe, he hates him that would upon the wrack of this tough world stretch him out longer." If there is such a thing as heavenly music, you hear it at this moment.

Charles' performance made its power felt at this moment. Your sympathy reached back and back for his King Lear. I must mark this moment well, for looking back on Charles' own life I am forced to feel the relief at the end of his own self-made burden.

By now Charles had left the book, perhaps dreaming himself as Lear. I still had the book in my hand. The strain had become very heavy but exciting for both of us. He had become Lear. He couldn't sleep at night, not because he was thinking of the words but because he was tortured. I am not quite sure if I became Ariel or Cordelia for him, but Charles was grateful to me. We got on very well and we had a very good time. Charles decided then to stay for another two weeks at Maui.

In the Hawaiian Islands the natives believe in legends and superstitions that are the ruling elements in their lives. Folklore mesmerized Charles. In the afternoon you could hear Hawaiian music gently starting up and various members of the staff would begin to dance by the hotel pool. In a letter to Taft Schreiber, Charles wrote, "I asked (with my eye on Lear) if there were no dances about warriors and Gods and the elements." Among the dancers was a sensitive young man whom Charles tried to help. ("Most sweet savage, dignified and poetic," Charles described him to Taft.) His name was Passio. He was a dancer the like of which I have never seen. His dancing and his gestures were beautiful, but he would rarely come out to be seen. He was too shy. Passio worked at the hotel in a quiet capacity, but no one could persuade him to come out of his shell. Our friends the Butterworths urged Charles to talk to Passio; and Charles, by his kindness and gentleness, reached the boy's spirit and helped Passio to dance for a small group of people. The managers arranged a special luau for us and the chosen few on a moonlight night on the beach.

Passio danced! He used flaming torches that licked around his whole body and seemed to become part of him. He was the moon and he was the moonlight on the sea, and it was just the most extraordinary experience that I've ever known. But the boy was ashamed of what he was—of being homosexual. It was part of his withdrawal from the island and its people. He could not relate to formal education and was subsequently rejected at the school in Waikiki. He had tried to adjust but he was so shy, such a strange person. Passio had escaped home to Maui to become a priest's helper and he wouldn't dance anymore.

There was something mysterious about Passio that nobody could fathom. He lived like a healthy animal. The few facts we learned about Passio came from Mr. and Mrs. Butterworth.

Charles simply tried to help the boy, and in a way Charles was helping himself. Charles wanted and needed someone he understood, too. Charles had been a misfit in his family's business. He felt he was ugly. And Passio was beautiful. The boy was so beautiful that no one would want to touch him, and he became a sort of Ariel to Charles' Prospero. Charles had partly wanted me to be his Ariel, but I think he also thought I was Lady Macbeth.

Some time ago, I had a letter from the Butterworths who wrote that "Passio had gone," and his going was traumatic. On a moonlit night, Passio walked into the reflection of the moon and into the water and drowned. They never found him.

Charles always said that he would never experiment with drugs. In fact, he was vehement in saying that he had no curiosity about them. Yet he said to a close friend of mine, "Can you get me some peyote? I will be seeing many artists and paintings in Paris. I want to see all there is to see . . . what their eyes see. And I want to see as far as I can into the character of Lear. You're a musician and must know people who can get it for me. Here's fifty dollars, and don't talk about it." After protesting too much, Charles again suffered—or enjoyed—this necessary guilt with secrecy.

He had talked to Christopher Isherwood on the subject and had read Huxley's *The Doors of Perception*, and I'm sure he felt that he could enhance his seeing eye through the medium of mescaline or peyote. I do not know what prompted him to make the decision to try drugs. He was very sure of his eye and his taste. His adrenaline was violently stirred by things that he saw, and this excitement was indescribable when sharing his vision with others. I can only think that he sensed somehow that there was little time to reach out and touch some unattainable goal in art. I cannot get away from the thought that he had a premonition of death. My own feeling at the time was fury that Charles should be so selfish and thoughtless of others—that he would put my friend's reputation in jeopardy. Charles used his power to get something he was afraid of, with no thought of endangering others. But it seems now that he was running a race with death that turned out to be punishingly long.

Charles could very well convince a person that his own curiosity was admirable and brave. Such was the persuasive power that he was able to wield, but in this instance, the ending was sad. The peyote was intentionally very mild and came in large capsules. Nobody would take any money, and the fifty dollars was returned to my friend. Charles took the pills and later, rather proudly, reported no effect. He said he could see all the colors and mystic meanings, anyway, so the drug could be of no help to him.

From Hawaii we returned to Los Angeles for a week or two to adjust and pack and line up other things for Charles to do in England. Charles went over to Stratford first. He had to rehearse and open in *A Midsummer Night's Dream* as Bottom. I must have been tied up with something or other—I don't remember what—work of some sort, or I would have gone with him then.

When I did arrive in England, Charles came down to the airport with a young friend called John Beary. Beary was the son of an Irish jockey. He was with us all through *The Party* and had been Albert Finney's understudy. John Beary was a true theatre bug. A theatre bug cannot just breathe air—oxygen isn't air unless it's around the theatre. Anyway, Beary became a good friend and confidant to Charles. But maybe Charles confided in him too much because eventually Charles didn't like him very much.

It was about a two- or three-hour drive from the airport to Stratford. I arrived on a lovely, sunny afternoon. When Charles and I were apart, we talked on the phone a great deal or sent frantic telegrams full of how-are-you's and all that sort of thing. I must admit we seemed happiest when we were apart and then met again. Charles and John Beary were so excited to see me at the airport, and I was equally excited to see them—very affectionate and warm.

In Stratford the visiting star gets allotted a great big house, Avoncliff, about two miles from the theatre, overlooking a tributary of the Avon. I suppose it would be called a late nineteenth-century house—a white painted place with a great conservatory running round two sides of it. We put hanging baskets of flowers round the L-shaped conservatory—petunias, scarlet geraniums, and lobelias. It was a miraculous summer, like California or better, but it was also a time of drought and awful for the English. There hadn't been a rainy day. Instead of the lovely green lawn, there was a brown lawn.

We formed a close friendship with the Dotrice family, who lived in the adapted, modernized staff quarters of Avoncliff. Roy Dotrice was acting small parts then, but Charles really believed in him and helped him to be given a chance. Roy Dotrice is now a successful actor, and his wife and three daughters are now also flourishing in the business. Karen was the lead little girl in Disney's *Mary Poppins*. Charles and I bought huge steaks and introduced the Dotrices to barbecuing. Our feast was set up in the huge glassed terrace that ran along the sides of the Avoncliff house. We did this a few times a week to the happy screams of the little girls.

It was enchanting to me to drive Charles to and from the theatre. Also, I enjoyed driving to the country to bring back our usual armful of flowers. One late summer afternoon we came back from a long drive in the Rover. Later on I couldn't find the car keys. After a long hunt I went into the billiard room—yes, I knew I'd put them there. After a few minutes hunting I saw a large blackbird standing over them, flapping its wings. It was covered in soot. Charles came in and it gave him a loud squawk. Of course, it had been up the chimney, and we decided it might need water. So Charles brought in a huge kitchen bowlful. The blackbird plunged in, picking up the keys and all, and had a tremendous wash. The water and the floor were black. We chatted to the bird until it finally dropped the keys; then it let me pick it up and, with Charles in the lead, we took it into the glass house that ran around Avoncliff. We opened the windows at each end and the bird, flying well and gracefully up and down for several minutes, flew straight off into the evening air—dry and shiny and black.

On another trip we discovered that there were even more primitive Druid circles of stones at a place called Rollright. They were very rough stones, big and small, and in the distance from that circle you could see three great stones leaning against each other. They are called The Three Kings. We went up there two or three times and Charles would just lie around.

Of course, a few tourists were up there, too. Charles had his beard, and fortunately I had my Polaroid camera. I was in a picture-taking phase. You get into waves of taking photographs. I think I could not press a button now, but then I took some really great pictures of Charles lying among the stones, not posing, but merely soaking up the magic of the place in the most spongelike condition that a human can be in. In fact, he just fell asleep there among the stones. He slept and the tourists going by didn't even take any notice of him at all. Nobody worried him.

We had a good old get-together with Biddy during the production of *King Lear*. We had her driven up from Brighton to see all the productions—*A Midsummer Night's Dream*, *Coriolanus*, and *King Lear*. She stayed at the Arden Hotel where she could walk to the shops, the theatre, and also to my brother Waldo and Muriel's puppet theatre and shop. Biddy liked Avoncliff, but was rather at a loss sitting around waiting for our different theatrical timings—supper at 1:00 A.M. and so on.

She also came with us on a few trips into the country. The four-gear Rover (with English left-handed shift) was hard to drive and gave me bursitis—since of course the left arm in English driving does all the work and the silly right arm only has to signal. Up and down the beautiful narrow lanes, we saw some lovely grand houses, pubs, and manicured mansion gardens. Biddy really loved the trip and was treated like minor royalty by the dear lady who owned the Arden Hotel, Mrs. Ash, and by actors that she met.

In repertory theatre, the plays are staggered. So, if Charles had *A Midsummer Night's Dream* on Monday, Tuesday, and Wednesday matinees, for instance, he might have Wednesday night and Thursday night off. I had arrived on one of Charles' afternoons off and got settled in the large house, and we two started studying *King Lear* again. Before Charles began actually rehearsing *Lear*, he had ten days off from the *Dream*, and during this break, Olivier rehearsed, then opened in *Coriolanus*.

So Charles and I went to Portmerion in Wales over the break. I drove, and it was a wonderful, leisurely drive. As you go west, there is more rainfall, so it's very green and wet and streams trickle down all over the place. But in Portmerion it was just more and more hours of *King Lear*. Charles knew the part by then, of course, but he was developing it all the time.

To relax we walked and picnicked in the ruins of Harlech Castle and walked among rhododendron that grew down to the sea at that lovely little town created by Clough Williams-Ellis, rising from the estuary. The weather is warm there because the Gulf Stream from the Atlantic finds its way to Portmerion and certain other places up the coast—even as far as Scotland, where there is a very famous cactus garden, just as though it were California.

Charles' schedule for *Lear* was solid, with costume people and the set designer to be seen, and makeup to be worked out. Charles was very tough. He batted me around—verbally, of course—so I was rather squashed then. Quite different from our days in Hawaii.

The fear of the first night of *Lear*, the costumes that he had insisted on, and the vast sets weighed heavily on Charles. He wrote to Taft Schreiber:

> "Lear" approaches ominously. The further you get into that play the more you feel that never never will you, or any other damned actor, be able to act it fully. From all that I have read of the past, no actor has succeeded, and I am not vain enough to think that I will. One wishes the play wasn't there at all as a challenge, but there it is mocking me and I have just had to try it because it would be sitting on my chest when I took my last breath saying I was a coward.

Charles should have put himself in the hands of other people some-times, but he couldn't—though if he said, "You do it," you did it. At this time he had pictures by the artists Manessier and Soulages around him at Avoncliff. Manessier paints color and form, and Soulages vast blocks in depth, in space. The scene designer was influenced by the paintings. As the curtain went up, Charles was there, a massive figure on massive blocks. Charles really created this massiveness on the set —he had to climb steps as high as his hip, then climb down again— but he had given himself a physical problem in getting around the stage. The set was right. It created the atmosphere, the whole Druidic Stonehenge feeling Charles needed to do the part, but it was physically almost too big for a human frame to cope with. Although he was strong, performing was heavy going, and he weakened himself by working so hard and perspiring so much. He had a great, double-thickness turkish towel robe, dyed bottle green. When the first act was over and he dropped the soaking robe down on the floor, I tried to hang it up. It was so heavy that I simply couldn't lift it.

I went to rehearsals every morning. Charles had told Glen that he wanted me to be at all the rehearsals because he thought, having studied with him, I knew the text almost better than he did. "You don't mind if Elsa's there, do you?" "No," Shaw answered, but later I learned he was a bit worried about it. After the first week I had a little table with the script on it. Charles would keep coming over and whis-pering to me and asking me things. I never said to him in front of the others, "Don't walk this or that way." He'd come over and ask if something was all right, and other actors often asked me about mean-ings and rhythms, too. Among the *King Lear* cast were Mary Ure, Angela Baddeley, Albert Finney, and Zoë Caldwell.

Sometimes it seemed that Charles was forgetting the pentameter and forgetting everything else we had studied. I was frustrated and disappointed when I saw him deteriorating into clichés and manner-isms again. All our work seemed to be going, drifting away.

At dress rehearsal he was dreadful, blinking his eyes and sidling sideways—terrible tricks people would recognize from his films. He looked as if he were paddling a canoe with his hands when he walked. I went to his dressing room and I said, "I don't know what we've been spending this last year doing! You're doing this, this, and this. I've just wasted my time. It was not worth it at all!" I was very, very angry. Charles shouted back to me that I was a killer. He said, "You've ruined it! I'll never do it now, it's hopeless. You've killed everything!"

I wrote to a friend:

The nightmare is on. Sunday night till 4:00 A.M. and back at 9:30 A.M. for two runthroughs on stage (four hours sleep between if anyone can!) I gave my final lecture to Charles at 4:30 A.M. I went through every step of Lear from words to psychology to behavior and personal tricks. (Even Glen B. S. seems to need me around, too), but yesterday Charles was just awful and it was dreadfully disappointing. Anyway, my "brutality"—as it was called—had its effect (it was a terrible gamble) and today Charles turned up with a great performance.

In fact, working instinctively, I hadn't ruined a thing, because the actual performance was the best thing Charles ever did. It was marvelous. No tricks, none at all. And he got wonderful reviews until, I think, later when Paul Scofield did *Lear* and people began to weigh the two performances.

I think Charles avoided reading the reviews because by then he wanted to work on it all over again. He discovered *something,* he found *something,* but he knew he had only touched the surface. Once you've reached a certain point, it's hopeless, and you realize you have twice as far to go as before. Charles died thinking he'd play *Lear* again.

Still, he was almost a different man the day he got this letter:

Dear Mr. Laughton:

All this week my wife and I have spoken to each other and to friends of the memorable performance of "King Lear" a week ago. We can recall nothing comparable to it and we are both still under its spell.

I am more than ever convinced that I have seen the greatest interpretation of a Shakespearean character of my lifetime.

We are both deeply grateful for so wonderful an experience.

Yours sincerely,
Anthony Eden

During *Lear,* Charles began having nightmares. They were fearful and he felt he had to talk to somebody about them, so he rang up his cousin Jack Dewsbery, a psychiatrist. In a letter to me, Jack said:

Charlie rang me up and told me of some nightmares he had been having and asked for my help. I suggested that I go and see him play Lear, as he thought that in some way the nightmares were very much mixed up with that. . . . I went up to Stratford and, for reasons which even now are unknown to me, I was struck by the very first speech he made in the play, in which Lear speaks of his coming death and of the need to dispose of his properties. I told Charlie that was where I thought the trouble lay and we had quite a talk about death and its philosophical acceptance. . . . I can only suppose that in some way his dreams had foretold the future, and that I had unwittingly put my finger on their meaning.

Once *King Lear* had opened, I think Charles was a sick man, with these nightmares and terrors. He had to take glucose to give him strength. I don't think he took pep pills, but he lived on something they drink in England, called glucosade, which appeared during the war to replace sugar. It was a yellow drink with lots of glucose in it. Charles would drink bottles of it and then sweat it out.

Charles played Lear till the end of the season, from spring to late fall. I was lonely, and ambition had not left me, so after a time, I had to leave England for Hollywood to play Mother Goose in the *Shirley Temple's Storybook* show, a TV film.

Leaving Stratford and Charles for America was my own choice. I went back to our house on Curson Avenue, to one or two friends and relationships. I left Charles at Stratford with Bottom and Lear to play, a lovely house, a good cook. By the time I left, Charles was launched. He was set. The whole part was, as it were, framed.

Only a week or less after I left England, Charles met a very good-looking male model, Peter Jones, at a party in London. They took a flat immediately for weekends in Dolphin Square. Every time Charles had a break from the show, he went down to London and stayed with Peter. I also think Charles brought Peter to Stratford, but I never asked him.

When Charles returned to California, he told me, "I met a young man who I think will be a very good actor, who is a model at present." He said that Peter had extraordinary natural sensitivity and seemed to understand everything that Charles had said to him, and that he was hungry to learn about acting. Charles was particularly pleased to start from scratch with Peter because the young man was an orphan, or a foster child. Foster mothers are wonderful people, it seems, because they really bring up nice boys.

I saw photographs of Peter. As a model, Peter had been in a great number of ads in England. He got sent around, as these fellows do, to Germany and Italy to do ads standing on a rock in the Mediterranean smoking a cigarette. He was very good-looking, but a little bit jowly, with deepset eyes that could look quite mean at times. Later, when I met him, I found he didn't laugh very easily. Maybe he was a bit scared of me, though we always got on very well.

Charles had signed for a film in Italy, called *Under Ten Flags*, to start immediately after *King Lear*. He had a small role as a British admiral. He took Peter Jones with him. Charles had been totally exhausted by *Lear*, but now he was in love and floating on air and enjoying once more the role of mentor. He was buying paintings with less judgment than usual, and teaching, teaching—always dictating his opinions to an ambitious, eager younger person.

The more Charles loved somebody, the more devious he seems to have been. Charles had told me he was paid only $10,000 for *Under Ten Flags* and that he needed the money after Stratford. But a business manager told me that Charles had got $75,000, and during probate years later, the report mentioned $100,000. It seems that Charles had to send his student model to drama school and keep him in nice hotels. Charles really didn't have to lie to me. I had always said and felt that he should do everything he wanted with the money he earned. But Charles' guilt about me was eating at him, though I was not aware of it. If only we could have talked with each other.

I think that perhaps one of the reasons Charles felt flattered and touched by Peter Jones' attention was that he felt himself so ugly, and it must have been very appealing to have a young man around who liked him and, in a sense, was the epitome of young manhood.

After all, Charles was odd, different, and unusual-looking, so some called that ugly. Charles often expressed his feelings about his looks. If he was shaving, he was inclined to say something like, "God, what a mug!" Another routine remark was, "I've got a face like an elephant's behind!" In a funny way, I think he expected someone else to say, "Don't say that, Charles." I let Charles know in every way I could how much I liked his face, that it was a wonderful face—but it was difficult to tell him this.

I truly believed that there was a handsomeness in Charles' face, especially when he was acting. I thought he had an exciting visual quality that some might call a kind of "beauty," but I wouldn't have used that word exactly. As Claudius, Charles had that look, a sort of beauty. When he did the murdering businessman in *The Big Clock*, he brought an erotic look to the character, as he did to his Captain Bligh in *Mutiny on the Bounty*—an animal magnetism. I wish Charles had not cared so much about the other kind of beauty, the beauty he sought in others—the physical beauty that gets tangled up in narcissism.

Another thing Charles liked—Peter was not effeminate. Peter was like a child and possessed some of the wonder-struck quality that Charles had. Like Charles, Peter got on well with children, too.

From *Elsa Lanchester, Herself*

**Acting for the press,
but we did have bees**

**On the island of Maui,
during *King Lear* studies**

A seaside portrait

Charles in a pensive mood

Charles as
Bottom the Weaver

I took this shot of Charles at Yosemite

With Charles' brother Frank at Charles' funeral (*The Citizen-News*)

An editorial cartoon by Bert Whitman
from the Stockton *Record*

Jumping (in *Honeymoon Hotel*)

"Miss Mabel" (a dual role)
for NBC television
(NBC photo: Elmer Holloway)

Biddy at 94

TV's "Masquerade Party"
—guess who as guess who?

With Pre-Columbian figures (before the big sale)

Studying a script (photo: Raymond Lieberman)

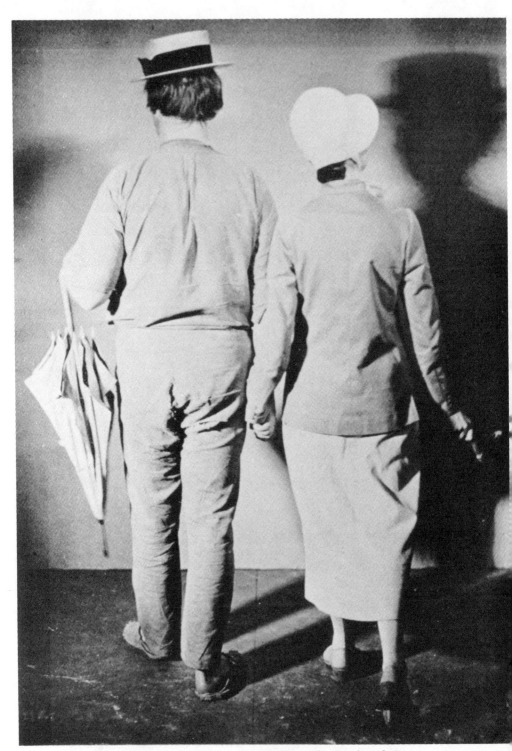

Charles and I (in a scene from *The Beachcomber*)

Charles wanted to thank me for the help I gave him studying for *King Lear.* He had given me presents before, over the long years—a hat for our wedding, a diamond necklace, and a mink coat. But for our months on *Lear,* he bought me a Lincoln Continental in Hollywood. Charles had always said, "I don't drive, you do. You love cars. You must have the biggest and the best." Also, after the Stratford season was over, he wanted to direct a one-woman show for me.

The show would be his own creation—with Charles's structure and sense of form. An autobiographical revue, it was to be called *Elsa Lanchester—Herself,* with two pianos. The first pianist, Ray Henderson, would also be musical director, with Don Dollarhide at the second piano.

Charles had already directed and designed a one-woman show for Agnes Moorehead, and he had directed Anne Baxter and Glynis Johns, Cornelia Otis Skinner and Judith Anderson in various shows, but he had never directed me or done a show for me before. Now that it was my turn, Charles would make use of what I knew how to do well—all the things he'd seen me do at the Turnabout.

In the meantime, in May 1960, a TV acting job came up for Charles. Destiny and fate and inevitability are words that we dismiss for the use of fortune-tellers, but I cannot help recalling that Charles and I dreaded the particular job. I've got to say that I begged him not to do it. It was a *Playhouse 90* television special called "In the Presence of Mine Enemies"—and it was *live.* Charles had never done live TV, though I had. The underrehearsed, vast, tragic virtuoso part of a rabbi was not in his range, mentally or physically. Charles would need at least six months to touch a work like that. On top of everything, the script was medium-miserable writing. Charles got through it, but at what a cost. In my theatrical costume basement room I still have the great heavy coat that he bore the weight of in the part of the old rabbi.

To recover, Charles went to our place in Palos Verdes with his good friend Bill Phipps. While they were down there, Charles fainted, so they rushed back to the city to Taft Schreiber's heart specialist-friend, Dr. Corday. When Charles and Phipps came home, Charles sat in his armchair and said to me, "You must not upset me ever again. It's the old ticker." Corday sent Charles for a full checkup, which proved that the heart condition was caused by his gallbladder. It had to come out, and that meant months of dieting. All of this increased his fears and despondency. Now Charles seemed to develop an inner drive about putting together *Elsa Lanchester—Herself*.

He asked Peter Jones to visit us in California after stopping in New York to attend a few classes with the drama coach Sandy Meisner. On Curson Avenue, Charles would sit at the pool with Peter and they would talk and Charles would read to him. Though Charles himself was on a very strict diet, he enjoyed watching his young friend eat all sorts of sweets—pies and cakes and everything he was forbidden.

I didn't mind Peter's presence. Sometimes, when I joined them at the pool, we would discuss some part of my show and Charles now seemed gentler and less critical of me. Charles always had a more equitable temper when a friend or third party was with us, so naturally I grew to be grateful to these young men. It was not exactly a personal gratefulness to each one, just a sort of happier feeling when they were welcome. I don't think I ever strongly liked or disliked any of them. It's surprising what one can get used to! The friends that Charles did introduce to me were the ones who were inclined to be relatively permanent. This in itself appeared to be safer and the lesser of two evils. The evil I refer to was not the moral aspect, but rather the danger of blackmail from mere acquaintances, leading to more inner guilts for Charles.

Peter later had this to say about Charles:

> I had never known such a person in my whole life; in fact, I didn't know such people existed. His mind overpowered me. I found it almost impossible to grasp the mind within him. . . . I wish it had not taken me so long to grasp the whole magic of the association. Being with Charles, I now realize, was better than attending the best liberal university in the world.

Peter first stayed at the house, but the next time he came to Hollywood, Charles thought it better that he stay at the Roosevelt Hotel. The only thing I resented about that—since Peter spent the whole time out by our pool beside the house anyway—was that Charles got Peter one of the pool rooms at the Roosevelt, which was very expensive. He also bought him a new Thunderbird automobile so Peter could get from the hotel to our house. Peter spent most of his time with us and—since I was buying Peter peach pies and pineapples, which he never seemed to stop eating—the young man became very expensive. With the thrift I had cultivated from my early years, I had a sort of resentment that Peter always had to have the best, which seemed quite unnecessary. We were always buying pâté de fois and cooking on an outdoor spit or barbecue. There was lots of swimming and I was always being asked to run out and buy more peach pies from the Farmers' Market. Peter had a bottomless stomach. But actually there was a jolly insanity about the whole thing.

Peter's visit also made it more difficult for me because the people Charles and I employed didn't like him. They sensed a house divided, I imagine, so they were never very polite to Peter. For instance, Charles' houseman Eddie would say, "Do you know where that Peter is?" He called him "Mr. Peter" or "that Peter." And it's very difficult to ask the cook to prepare something you don't want, but you must say, "Peter would like it very much." Our cook and houseman didn't exactly feel the house was going to fall apart, that I was going to get a divorce or anything like that, but they just didn't like looking after two-and-a-half masters.

When Peter had to return to England for a modeling job, Charles became very depressed again. His remarks to me often seemed quite cruel. He even went so far as to suggest I should go to England and have my face lifted.

When Charles was in Cedars of Lebanon Hospital having the heart checkup, Christopher Isherwood came to visit him several times. Charles told Christopher about the long convalescence he would have ahead of him after the gallbladder operation and that he didn't want to go home and have business going on around him, yet nor did he want to go to a nursing home. He told Christopher and me that he wanted to be among his "own people." And, wonder of wonders, Christopher Isherwood said, "The house next door to me is for sale." The house was in Santa Monica, above and facing the ocean and the Santa Monica Mountains. We bought it.

Houses and places and flowers and trees always played a principal part in our life. Charles and I were held together by them, and later, when Charles died, that's what made me into a seeing-eye person with no one to look after, as it were. Charles and I had some good days and weekends at our then new Santa Monica house—the place where Christopher and Charles planned to work together on a play about Socrates, the place where Charles studied *Advise and Consent*, the place Charles finally managed to reach with a nurse for a few hours a day (I drove) and gaze at the Pacific horizon, at the sunset and the whole Santa Monica range. Then it would be a Dramamine pill from the nurse and home to Curson Avenue, driving very slowly. Charles had about two years in all of rich promise and dreams of lovely years ahead.

We bought the house furnished from two fellows who had their own tastes for an ocean-view house. Charles and I liked the furnishings because they were so utterly different from anything that we would do with a house—very faded dark rose velvet curtains, Persian rugs, so-so antique tables and chairs (mostly comfortable), one faded purple velvet chair (a fringed throne-type of monster, very popular), and paintings on the walls of the two bathrooms a little in the manner of Pompeii (really quite pretty), and a niche in a hall with a "faggot" saint (or else he had a very crooked hip). It was a kick to go there.

Outside was a jungle garden with hydrangeas, fuchsias, and giant honeysuckle. We loved it just as it was, with no thoughts of good taste, bad taste, or our taste. It gave us a new type of restfulness. But in the autumn of 1962, with Charles' illness, I don't think he even thought of our house again in Santa Monica or his upcoming book *The Fabulous Country*, or Peter, or me. For a long, long time I had not expected to be thought of, or even noticed when I came into a room. I was chauffeur, part cook, and complete guard—under the doctors' instructions, of course. I went down to the Santa Monica house alone a few times just for the drive and to look at the sunset over the Pacific. I may have cried a little, but I don't remember. Tears have a habit of sticking somewhere between the throat and the chest.

So the house was neglected for several months. A cleaning lady came once a week and for a short time a gardener twice a week. We had no friends who would use but not abuse the dear place, and so it was broken into and we lost the TV set, of course, and two wonderful religious carved figures from the Warsaw Museum in fallen Poland. Life eventually came back to the beloved house, but later, later.

Charles had the gallbladder operation in August, but later a serious infection set in and he had to return to the hospital. During his stay there, he wrote my mother:

> I got an infected wound and had to be cut open a couple of times—without benefit of anesthetic—most unpleasant! . . .
> The only thing I feel bad about is I am not being as much help as I should for Elsa's show. I just have to lie here doing nothing . . .

> Your crucified son-in-law with a
gash in his side,
Charles

Charles was interested in writing a play with Christopher, based on Socrates, and the two began preliminary work on it. So while recovering from his gallbladder operation, Charles commuted from the Santa Monica house to the Curson Avenue house, at the same time starting to direct my show for its first tryout up in Stockton, California. He was terribly lonely and unhappy now. He wrote to Taft Schreiber:

> I have been disturbed deeply these last months. I have never been sick and have found it hard to hide from you my stupid state of mind. I have not known where to aim myself. For the first time today I have begun to feel myself again and have become sharply conscious of the state I could have got into if it had not been for you . . .

In the letter to Taft, Charles mentioned the tryout in Stockton and how much he wanted to attend the performance, but he felt he might be too weak to make the trip up north.

Then, at the last moment, he decided that he'd make the trip in spite of his health. On the way he wanted to stop to buy fruit at road stands or to pick flowers. When finally we arrived in Stockton, he was so tired he had to spend all of the afternoon resting up in our motel room. But somehow he managed to get to the theatre to see the show.

The audience was very enthusiastic, and I took a number of curtain calls. Charles, out front, suddenly leapt from his seat and ran to the back of the auditorium and pounded on the locked door, trying to get in backstage. Finally someone let him in and Charles rushed through the stage curtains to take a bow, too—but by this time the audience had all left. Standing there before the footlights, he looked lost and a little forlorn. Originally, Charles had refused to put his name in the program, but he finally allowed "Censored by Charles Laughton" to be put in, and now that he saw how successful our show would be, he impulsively wanted recognition for it.

The day before I was to open in UCLA's Royce Hall, which was the beginning of our tour, I suddenly heard screaming at the front of the Curson house and rushed outside. Charles had tried to throw himself down the concrete front steps but was stopped by our longtime friend and former student Bill Phipps. Just before this, Charles had shouted at Phipps that he wanted pills, that he wanted to end his life. Then Charles hurled himself down, as Bill Phipps tried to stop him, and although Charles was still weak from his illness, he had tremendous strength and Phipps could not hold him.

I rushed to the front steps. Suddenly I slapped Charles hard. It was a reflex action because I'd remembered that people can be brought out of such fits with a sudden blow. With the impact of that slap, Charles became silent and said simply, "Thank you."

Then he went out to the garden with me. We were both in shock and shaking. I think I said, "You are trying to kill my show. You want to destroy it and me. How can I possibly stand on that stage now and be light and cheerful as if nothing happened!" Charles said something like "Yes . . . maybe . . . I'm sorry." Then he was taken away by Phipps and a doctor.

I really felt that I could not do the show on Sunday night, that I had no voice at all and all feelings were dead. So I called an old friend, Dr. Hans Fehling, to see if he might give me some sort of leveling drug to help me through the next thirty-six hours. Dr. Fehling said, "You're perfectly all right, Elsa. Drink a glass of water." I did, and gave a very good performance—one almost elevated by the horrifying experience.

Charles was not present at my performance at Royce Hall that Sunday night. His doctor and a psychiatrist came to the Santa Monica house, and they forbade him to see the show or me. Bill Phipps stayed with him, and the psychiatrist told him to tie himself to Charles at night with a piece of string so he'd know if Charles moved at all in the night. Charles was under constant supervision by Phipps and two male nurses.

After Royce Hall my tour continued to Santa Barbara's Lobero Theatre. The reaction to Charles' breakdown hit me then. On stage I could not remember a single line of my songs. Throughout, Ray Henderson and Don Dollarhide were cueing me and feeding my lines, and somehow I got through the show—how I do not know. The Santa Barbara critic, Ronald D. Scofield, wrote that I seemed to be under some sort of sleeping drug. It was a frightening, once-in-a-lifetime experience. Before the following night's performance, Don Dollarhide holed up with me in our motel sitting room and insisted on going over the show, over and over again. That night I was back in my stride and remembered everything.

I returned to Los Angeles, and between show dates Charles' doctor asked me to see his psychiatrist. I met him in the schoolroom—another horrifying experience. In answer to something the psychiatrist said to me, I replied, "Either Charles said that—and he's a goddamned liar if he did—or you just invented it and you're a goddamned liar. And even if Charles did say it, you have no business repeating it to me!" That ended my sessions with the psychiatrist. What exactly it was that caused the explosion I cannot remember. Perhaps hypnosis or some kind of drug could help me recall it. But it was bad enough apparently to force me to forget it totally. I still wonder what could have been so offensive. Something beyond human endurance.

Elsa Lanchester—Herself had a good, solid continuity to it, like a successful conversation, and Charles really was the one who did it. I know I couldn't have tied it all together as he did. Charles had created it, but I nurtured it and made it my own. After almost every single show, people came round and embraced me as if I were an old friend. They really thought they knew me. They'd never met me, they were strangers, but such was the nature of the show that Charles made for me that I was *theirs*—personally *theirs*. The title that Charles gave the show was good. *Elsa Lanchester—Herself.*

In a magazine called *The Diplomat,* I apparently said, "The audiences don't know what I'm going to do when I first come on. They think of me as Mrs. Charles Laughton and expect me to read the Bible. Instead, they get 'Songs for a Shuttered Parlor.' " Charles didn't see the show again until the New York production months later, when he had a break in his reading tour.

The show, his creation but now my responsibility, had grown and matured. Charles was in top form as a director, and I was high and floating on the pleasure of our show, as were Ray Henderson and Don Dollarhide at their two grand pianos. Charles insisted that the stage look warm and welcoming, and even treated us to a dozen kentia palms lining the theatre walls up to the stage.

We opened in New York on February 4, 1961, the night of a big blizzard with seventeen inches of snow. There were no taxis. I got to the theatre in a police car. Amazingly, the theatre was *full.* How did they all get there?

The storm did not stop the critics either. *The New York Times* review on the following Monday, February 6, opened with this sentence: "If there's anyone who can make you forget about 17.4 inches of snow, it's Elsa Lanchester." It went on:

> The program notes that the show has been censored by Charles Laughton. . . . But his heart wasn't in it. In fact, if this is Elsa censored, what is Elsa like uncensored? . . . even if you have to use dog sleds, skis, or bulldozers, drop in on Elsa. She won't let you down.

I felt good about this show because it was nice now having a property of my own. With a property you do control your own career. Besides the salary, I also had my freedom. And I had decided, after New York, to travel with the show. I even got a legitimate offer to take *Elsa Lanchester—Herself* to Saudi Arabia!

It seems incredible, but none of us remembered the bad, bad tryout days in California. Some power that we know nothing about must have given us a draft of nepenthe.

When Charles and I first got to New York in 1931, we thought it was fresh and glittering. And when we first walked down Fifth Avenue it was such fun seeing so many young people walking along at a crisp clip—young girls who all seemed to have hair blowing in the wind, or who wore little hats and little scarves of emerald green and other bright colors blowing behind them. I remember it all like a sort of jewel. But now, years later, I made this tactless statement to a journalist, Mel Heimer:

> This town is beyond rescue. I honestly don't think it ever will rise phoenixlike from the ashes. It's dirtier, noisier, and more non-working than ever. Each time I come here, the windows are harder to open, I get less water out of the tap, I find the traffic more frightening and stagnant than ever—and the smog grows worse. Nobody smiles any more. Everyone is scowling and shoving and jabbing. . . . Whatever New York had, is gone.

I'd probably be mugged now by a publicity agent for saying that. Anyway, the show ran for ten weeks—longer than we expected.

In Hollywood, *Elsa Lanchester—Herself* was to come back three times to the Ivar Theatre, each time for a two-week run, and staying for three. The first run was in 1960, when Charles had been able to redirect us and polish up the whole show—good lighting, a carpet on the floor the same color as my hair.

32

Charles was preparing another reading tour and also working like a fury to get ready for the film *Advise and Consent* for Otto Preminger. Charles' English friend Peter was back again, supposedly helping Charles on both these projects. Charles stayed in bed quite a lot because he had said that his knees hurt. I remember him saying to me once, "You and I are getting older, Elsa. We must find out why our knees hurt." My knees didn't hurt at all. Charles saw a doctor and was told he had gout.

In *Advise and Consent*, Charles played the part of the powerful, aging Senator Seab Cooley, and he gave to this last and inspired performance a superhuman energy. Though he was tired, the company was staggered by his excessive activity toward people on the set and toward the press. During those days, he often stayed down at the Santa Monica house to work on his part or to see Christopher Isherwood. They were still collaborating on their play about Socrates. But this was in 1961—too late.

While Charles was on location in Washington, D.C., he went to visit Robert Mitchum at his farm (or ranch) outside the city. He and Mitchum got on very, very well on this occasion. Mitchum had also invited Shirley MacLaine to visit, and perhaps she and Charles talked about the film version of *Irma la Douce*, which Billy Wilder was going to direct. Miss MacLaine was going to play Irma, and Charles expected also to be in the film in the part of Moustache and, more important, to work with Billy Wilder again. Charles and Wilder had, of course, worked together in *Witness for the Prosecution*, in which I'd played the nurse to Charles' ailing barrister.

Charles never got to do *Irma la Douce*. *Advise and Consent* was the last film Charles did, and he received some of his best reviews for it.

Charles was now preparing for another tour, but he wasn't really fit to go. But such was Charles' love for Peter that he was able to get out of bed and feel well enough to go out on the road again, accompanied by one of his typical road men. That meant someone who could drive a car and remain rigidly awake. I've sat behind these road men often. They're all like bulls at the wheel. Anyway, Peter acted as a second road man and he would look after Charles' clothes.

I remember seeing Charles off on this tour. A high stage moment flashed back when Charles and I had first met and we had seen Sir Gerald DuMaurier in a play with Gertrude Lawrence. DuMaurier was then Charles' idol, and we were both deeply moved in this play when he came in from having seen a doctor to tell his wife, played by Miss Lawrence, that all was well. She knelt by him with her head in his lap. Charles always said afterward that it was one of the most beautiful pieces of acting he'd ever seen—the way DuMaurier very quietly looked at all the things in the room, fireplace, pictures, ceiling, tables, chairs, and silently communicated his feelings to us, the audience. We knew he was saying, "Good-bye, good-bye . . ." The audience knew he had cancer, but the wife did not.

When Charles left on this tour with Peter, as the car drove away, we waved to each other and I felt that shiver of good-bye, remembering Sir Gerald DuMaurier. Sometimes you have a sudden flash that you're not going to see someone in health ever again, and I had the feeling—that I was a free woman. That's a terrible thing to say, in a way. But at that moment, that's how I felt.

Wherever Charles was, we talked every day on the phone. He needed to make decisions and there was no Paul Gregory around anymore to make them. Decisions were always so horrible for Charles, and for me. But just talking together did help. As for running the household, I was the person who handled most decisions. So Charles needed decisions from me, getting my reaction to a new piece he had put into the program, while, I, of course, was interested in the audience's reaction to his new piece, and I wanted to hear how it went. I really tried to help him and tried to share a long-distance interest in his show.

In Flint, Michigan, Charles did not feel too well after a performance, so the road man—Bob Hulter, a family man, went out to dinner with Peter. Charles didn't resent the two men going off without him, and there was something about a married man and his English friend having dinner together that appealed to him. So he stayed in and took a hot bath. As he got in the tub, he slipped and fell. Charles had to wait there in the bath until they got back, which I think was in about an hour. Charles couldn't move all that time and he was in pain. He had broken his collarbone.

When Peter and Bob Hulter found Charles, they carried him out carefully and took him to Flint Hospital, where they gave him drugs. Charles' tour dates were canceled and Burgess Meredith, Charles' longtime friend, took over immediately.

For the ten days Charles was in Flint Hospital, he didn't know what was the matter with him, other than a broken bone. Then he was flown to New York, drugged up to his ears. Both road men—the married man and the English boyfriend—were there with him. They practically had to carry him to the airplane. When they landed an ambulance took him to the New York Hospital. They took him straight there, and they had booked a suite in the St. Moritz.

At the New York Hospital they took many X-rays, and then they operated on Charles. While all this was happening, I was in Hollywood finishing a film. The last three days at Twentieth Century-Fox Studios, Charles called me on the set. He was crying. He said, "I didn't tell you, but they thought it was cancer. The biopsy showed that the bone in the shoulder broke because it's cancerous. But they've cut two inches of bone out and it's completely clean now."

Unfortunately, Charles was a person who could not be told the truth. I mean, he was crying on the telephone, and I was there at the Fox studios waiting for a scene to begin shooting. I was terribly upset and still pleased by his hope, but somehow I just didn't believe it. Throughout my life I had been more curious about cancer than Charles ever was. Charles would always withdraw from any medical conversation. He wouldn't ask questions about a disease for fear he might get it, whereas I was what the English call a Doctor Botz. Amateurs are fascinated by potted knowledge. So I naturally was suspicious that just taking a small piece of bone out of the shoulder would clear cancer from his system, because I knew that cancer could arise in a primary site nowhere near the shoulder. But on the telephone call with Charles, I held back these thoughts and felt tears of relief when he said, "It's completely clean now."

Against Charles' wishes, Jerry Perrencio at M.C.A. booked Ray Henderson and me to replace Charles' dates in Minneapolis and that area. (With Paul Gregory long since out of the picture, Charles and I were now being managed by Perrencio.) Don Dollarhide was no longer with us. Charles in his sickbed was furious that Ray and I had changed the show to a twosome. He said on the phone, "You can't go out with Ray. You must not do that! The show is made for three." He actually said, "I forbid it!" We did the show anyway because M.C.A. had to fill in the dates. Ray Henderson and I had to rehearse like mad, and re-form the show itself.

It took us five days to get everything in order—costumes, rehearsals, and so on. It was a mathematical readjustment of quick changing

—and added bits and pieces for Ray—but we enjoyed the job. And after a lot of telephone calls, we flew out. It is difficult to explain Charles' objections. I suppose he did not want to change the mathematics of his production for me. Charles created with precision, like making a watch. Every show he did was precision-made. As my show was—after all, Charles had created it. He didn't trust Ray and me to keep it a precise show without the second piano.

But Ray and I continued our tour, or, rather, Charles' tour, through Eau Claire, Wisconsin, Moorhead, Minnesota, and so on. We gave lots of shows in school auditoriums and one program in a church. It seemed always fun for the audiences to get my show in place of Charles'. Instead of what they expected—serious readings of the Bible and Shakespeare—they got a clown. The unexpected. A surprise—discovering a clown when you expected Thomas Wolfe or Jack Kerouac.

On the last of that tour, in Eau Claire, the snow was four feet deep and I caught an awful cold, which later developed into ear trouble. Each day I talked to Charles on the phone. He was recovering from the operation and he was still at the New York Hospital. I told him that I would fly into New York, but when he heard that I had a cold, he said, "Don't come near me. Don't come to the hospital yet!"

I flew there, anyway. As soon as I got to the St. Moritz I picked up the phone to speak to poor Charles in the New York Hospital. Ray Henderson took a cheaper room in the same hotel to tide me over this thing. I talked to Charles two or three times a day and sent in unusual branches and arrangements of flowers, but he would not see me for a week in case he might catch my cold. On the phone Charles said to me, "You'll meet the doctor. He's a great fellow." Charles actually had two doctors. One was Otto Preminger's doctor—Charles got the best, thanks to Preminger.

Actually, the doctors called me and I went along to see them. I only half knew—that is, sensed—that this was it. This was a deep illness. One doctor said, or maybe it was the other doctor, who seemed a more gentle person, "Well, Mrs. Laughton, we may as well tell you straightaway that Charles is a dying man. It's cancer. It's bone cancer, osteosarcoma."

I said, "How long?"

He said, "A year." And then, "We think it best you call your lawyer at once."

I called Loyd Wright from their office. Loyd was deeply upset. I suppose I said straight out, "Charles is dying." I learned that *terminal* is a word that becomes of earthquake proportions to the living, so my voice was trembling, I know. The doctor then said to me that Charles was not the kind of person who should or would ever discuss his actual illness. "Some people do and some people can't," he said. So the word *cancer* would never be spoken in front of Charles.

I knew that I was being freed of something. It was really as though I was a kind of Ariel who was being freed from Prospero. I didn't realize then what I would be in for, because a giant gone later becomes a terrible gap in one's life. Whenever a phone rang, I'd at first be thinking, "Is it for Charles or me?" In a way, it is a sort of compliment that Charles would almost still be around the house. And then the truth would be there—not unpleasant. I'd just be alone.

After being told about the cancer I went to the hospital, where I had to be introduced again by Charles to the doctors. Peter was around all the time, and one of the nurses was starting to flirt with him. She was Greek and Charles liked this particular nurse very much. He told me that she was a most wonderful nurse and that Peter and the Greek nurse had become romantic. She started by picking pieces of invisible lint off his suit. The fact that she liked Charles' friend showed Charles that his boyfriend was a man, a masculine man, which was very important to him.

After some weeks in the New York Hospital, Charles went two or three weekends by car to Burgess Meredith's place in New York State about one hour from the city. Peter went with him, and he romped with Burgess' children. They really loved him. Charles had to be helped in and out of the car then, his back was hurting him so badly. The doctors had told him that it was an old back injury, that he had sacroiliac trouble. So Charles accepted that.

Prior to his illness and even during his illness, Charles had worked out a reading program for Burgess; that is why Burgess was ready to fill in some of the dates when Charles was ill. He kept spending weekends at Burgess' place until he could no longer travel and had to go back into the New York Hospital. Now the cancer was in his back and arm. It is a horrible thing to live with the knowledge that a human being is being tortured by specialists. That seems part of the hell of money—that you can afford to go through such modern inventions and devices and drugs to keep you alive. It's almost back to the days of medieval torture, but with painkillers.

After some cobalt treatments, Charles was released and went back to the St. Moritz, where I had lived since my own replacement tour dates had finished. We stayed in a suite that we kept on for six months, through all his ins and outs of hospitals. Bob Hulter and Peter stayed there, too.

Charles never said anything to me like, "This is it, Elsa. I'm resigned," or, "I'm frightened." He now had a strange expression on his face, the staring look of someone who will not live, like a mouse caught in the crush of a trap, with its eyes protruding as if it were staring at you and accusing. You can see that same thing sometimes in people, a dying stare. Charles had it. And, of course, he was getting thinner. I saw suddenly how gray Charles' skin was.

In our suite in the hotel, Charles had full-time nurses—two at first, with eight-hour spells. Then he would be alone at night, with Peter and me looking at the comics. But Charles began to depend on his nurses. Good, bad, or indifferent, they became the important people for him. They became people he just adored. After an absence Althea, the nurse who was so attached to Peter, came back to the hotel and that was good.

Charles had shots every two or three hours now, but he always wanted more. He would cry out for more. It was always a race between pain and drugs, as it is for anyone who's being kept alive that way. Every time Charles started to cry out, the nurses would say, "Not yet, not yet, in half an hour . . ." And every day when Charles tried to get up, one of the nurses would say, "Well, I see you walked a little farther today, Mr. Laughton, and you look much better." And Charles believed it. One of the things I learned about cancer is that it is dangerous for the patient to lack hope, to think he's dying. He gives up. So we and the nurses were creating hope for Charles all the time. We became specialists in hope.

There were old friends also who tried to create hope for Charles. Deanna Durbin, who was now living in France, wrote:

> The last time I heard from you was ten years ago. . . . Now I read that you're sick in a New York hospital—playing Volpone, no doubt—so quit it. Get better at once (that's an order) and recuperate over here and come and see me in Neauphle, I promise not to sing!
> So get going.
> All my love to Elsa and to you, you old poop!

Around this time, our attorney Loyd Wright came to New York to see Charles at the hotel. Wright was planning to run for governor of California, I believe, and he was coming to New York to make political contacts. But he first told me on the phone that he was coming to see Charles to try to persuade him to make out a will. That would mean an acknowledgment by Charles that he was dying. Charles had never made a will prior to his illness, because a will represented death even when he was in the best of health. Charles talked about other people's deaths, but never his own. He didn't even like vaudeville jokes about funerals or anything like that.

In New York, Loyd Wright sat for several two-hour spells, and such was Charles' strength of personality that Loyd Wright never could bring him round to seeing the necessity of a will. So they never did make out a will on those visits.

It's funny. Our lawyer couldn't bring himself to talk about the will, although he had been a lifetime adviser to Charles. Loyd Wright, who was very conservative, would have Charles come down to his office once a year to hear the state of our finances—like a report on the State of the Union—and by the time Charles came home after lunch with Wright, usually at Perino's Restaurant, he would have taken on the color of our lawyer, talking like a Republican. Whenever Loyd Wright visited Charles, it was understood that Peter should not be in the room or even make an appearance. Charles did not want anyone as conservative as Wright to see the young man and told me, "Keep him out of the way."

Loyd Wright was staying at the Plaza in New York, and I walked there from the St. Moritz. He talked to me about our financial status and then, among other things, I told him about how Charles and I had kept Peter out of sight, because at that time it was just too late to pull any punches. Our lawyer was entitled to the truth in order to understand our finances and Charles' behavior better. But I couldn't help being fascinated watching the look on this conservative's face, and at how well Loyd Wright took it. He simply accepted it. He really knew about Charles from the Paul Gregory days, or even before.

I also told Loyd Wright because I needed a little contact with reality on my own. No more games. I had nobody at all to talk to at that time. Ray Henderson was back in California with his wife, and my few New York friends were mostly out of town. So I took advantage of Loyd Wright and the truth poured out. It was a kind of therapy for me.

All the time Charles was ill we kept him believing that he was going to get better. Charles even believed that *Advise and Consent* (the last film he'd done) was going to get the Cannes Film Festival Award, and Otto Preminger, who'd directed it, kept up that belief. Charles suddenly wanted only to go to Cannes, and his motive was to see Iris Barry, who was now living in the south of France on a pension. He insisted, "I've got to see dear, darling Iris." It was a kind of lifelong family feeling, I guess, that made Charles want to see Iris again. Iris *was* like family. I think she was closer to Charles than his brothers or mother could ever be, however much Charles and Iris had their ups and downs. His sudden thoughts of her and his wanting to go to France to see her were the nearest things to acknowledging he was dying.

I was to go along with him. I bought new luggage. I got a white piqué dress to wear for the awards. It was all part of the buildup. I even got myself vaccinated against smallpox. Because of my mother's defiance of the health department, I never had a vaccination before. Later in life, doctors would fake my certificate rather than risk the bad reaction. So when I did finally get a smallpox shot, I got a small case of the disease. I had a high temperature and was as sick as Charles, in a way, for about a week. It was strange thinking of him coming into my room and saying, "How are you today?"—when I knew that it was Charles who was dying.

So I lay in bed reading all of Ian Fleming's James Bond books. In a funny way, I was even glad to be so ill. It was one way to kill time and to kill some of my thinking about Charles. I did some drawings, not very good ones, I thought at the time, on hotel note paper. I drew pictures of nuns in the rain and pictures of traffic, all as seen from the window of our twenty-eighth-floor penthouse, with the park, the pink buildings, maybe a little sun in the foreground. I was occupying myself. It was more therapy.

We had a lot of thunderstorms at this time. The storms made Charles feel uneasy, but they fascinated me. I like any elemental display—thunderstorms, earthquakes, any natural phenomenon. But Charles became fearful and I became extra fearless. I didn't believe in angry gods. At least, I would presume that they liked me. Better to be killed by a thunderbolt than a fellow man's dagger—I wonder why?

33

In our hotel apartment we had a little kitchen, really an adapted closet. Just because it was a large apartment didn't mean it had a real kitchen. New York apartments are like that. Anyway, I cooked everything for Charles because he couldn't stand the hotel food. I'd go across the street to the St. Moritz grocery. I would find fresh strawberries and Peter would come sneaking in and take all the best strawberries from the top of the box. It made me so angry, a little thing like taking the biggest ones off the top and leaving the little scrubby ones for Charles. Of course, if I'd made a fuss, Charles would have misunderstood my anger. So I had to hide the food. I got Charles fois gras, which he loved and shared with Peter, so I'd have to hide some of that, too. I cooked fish in milk, mashed potatoes, almost anything he fancied, on two burners and a carborundum toaster. I was having such a sad time that I actually treated myself sometimes to expensive caviar, which I'd take into my bedroom to eat. That was a compensating thing to help me to keep a cheerful face. Charles hated caviar.

Burgess Meredith came in practically every day and brought branches of dogwood and mountain laurel. He had a great sense of the country and what Charles would like. We would borrow great big cans and buckets from the hotel. We had all day to arrange a branch. From his bed, Charles would say, "A little more this way," and "a little more that way." The result was absolutely beautiful.

Sometimes Burgess and Charles would talk privately. When he went into Charles' room, the nurse left, and I left, and Peter left. I learned later that Burgess and Charles talked about death and what happened afterward. They were both feeling around for something, I suppose. Once, after Burgess had brought Charles a branch of mountain laurel, Charles said, "You know, Buzz, if we could only find the connection between that laurel and the cancer virus, we would have the answer, wouldn't we? The solution to this terrible villain."

Another time, later, when Charles was heavily drugged, he said to Burgess, "Buzzy, I don't think the director knows what he's doing, do you? Do you think I can get out of this picture?" Burgess said, "No, Charlie, the director really is not up to his job. You are too big for him." I have often wondered whether Charles was hallucinating, or whether the director Charles was talking about was God.

Charles would walk in the park as if he were perfectly all right. With his walking stick, he would walk across the road from the St. Moritz and sit on one of those benches you can see from the hotel window. The park bench, the boulevardier with his walking stick. Sometimes we would take Charles down to the Marion Willard Gallery on Fifth Avenue, and I'd walk ahead of him, clearing the way. A male nurse would come along, and occasionally Peter. It was the nurse who held on to Charles' arm, with the road man Bob Hulter taking the other arm. Charles would have to be given a shot before the walk, and the nurse would give him a shot at the gallery to get him back. We always took a taxi back. Charles could never walk far now.

I suppose Charles felt some kind of bravado on these outings. "I'm getting better," he'd say. "I know I'm getting better." But his face was like a mask. Charles wanted to wander through the gallery, to see the works of new painters. We went over to the Willard Gallery two or three times in maybe three or four months.

Eventually Charles had to go into Memorial Sloan-Kettering Cancer Center. This was a new hell for Charles, knowing now that he was going to a cancer hospital. So he turned on it, twisted it, defied it. At the hospital he was X-rayed again, and they found that the primary cancer had spread. Bone cancer creeps all through the body, and if an attendant isn't careful as a patient is turned over, his fingers can crush right through a patient's ribs. You can imagine the amount of drugs it takes to keep the patient from feeling such pain. Charles would go into a deep, drugged sleep. When he first woke up he would be all right, but then there would be a terrible waking phase when the realization came, with the pain.

It had started from a kidney. The cancer circulates through the body and then goes to the brain or the bones or wherever. So now came the question: Should Charles have his kidney out or not? And the doctor thought that there was a chance that that would help.

At first when the doctor had said Charles had one chance in a hundred, Charles started to brood. Then another doctor said maybe one chance in ten. All the same, finally Charles didn't want to have the kidney operation. Otto Preminger wanted him to have it done. Though

I had told Charles to go back to the hospital, I couldn't really say to him, "I think you should have your kidney out." I thought he had had enough pain. The nurses and doctors didn't have the pain. Charles had it.

But when I finally said to the doctor that I didn't think Charles should have the operation if he didn't want it, Otto Preminger shouted at me, "We are trying to save Charles, do you understand? If he should have it out, then he should have it out—even if it's one chance in ten or a hundred or a thousand!" Peter had no opinion on it. But Althea, the Greek nurse, had persuaded a second nurse—a male nurse—and between the two of them talking to Otto Preminger and Preminger's doctor, it was decided that Charles should have it done. So Charles went back to the hospital to prepare for more surgery. But he was only in the cancer hospital for four days.

This being a second trip to the cancer hospital, Charles' illness started to get publicity, so the room was filled with flowers. It was like a great coffin. Why can't hospitals have rooms that are white or brightly colored? But gray walls with gray ceilings and chocolate-colored dado are what you get. Charles' hospital room was just like being in a gray coffin, with little room around the bed. Flowers came in from all kinds of people. I remember we received some from Mrs. Gary Cooper. Cooper had died of cancer about two years before, and although Charles had liked Cooper very much and had wanted to visit him in the hospital, he avoided doing it. He couldn't make himself go, and he never forgave himself for his lack of courage.

The first thing Charles said when he was brought into the cancer hospital was, "I know why you brought me here . . . because I have rectal cancer." He told the doctors that the first thing he wanted was a rectal examination, and around the second day they gave it to him. They reported to Charles that his rectum was perfectly all right, that there was nothing wrong with it at all. Charles made Peter want to sink through the floor when he pointed to him and, in front of us all, said, "We have touched, but never in our house."

I often walked by the stretcher as they wheeled Charles to the examination room. The agony of being moved on that stretcher! The nurses and doctors would try to lift Charles by the four corners of the sheet and then lower him onto a hard X-ray table—with his fragile deteriorating bones, it was cruel beyond belief. You would think someone could invent something that is cushioned or hydraulic or whatever, something that could X-ray only a part of the body at a time without having to move the patient. To X-ray one arm in those days, they had to put Charles' whole tortured body on the rack.

The third day in the hospital, Charles started to make all sorts of confessions. He got the kidney surgeon in to listen. This kidney specialist was a handsome man, and a man with a family. But he didn't talk about his family; he just listened to Charles. He was a masculine man, not pretty but ruggedly handsome. Burgess was there when he came in, and we both looked at each other and said, "James Bond." (Burgess was also a Fleming fan at the time.) We both decided that nobody could ever play James Bond except that kidney specialist. He was a marvelous creature to look at and very sympathetic to Charles' confessions, yet businesslike in his way.

The kidney specialist would take me into the green room where the doctors and nurses go, and I was able to speak freely about the causes for Charles' painful confessions. He was fascinated to listen to a wife who could talk about such things. He had a fiery interest and seemed to find it easy to talk to me about Charles.

I suppose it was quite an experience to sit in that hospital and watch all that was happening. People were wheeled by, half the time with faces full of great pain. The trouble with taking Charles out through the hallways on a stretcher was that he saw these other people. He went out of his mind a little during these four days. He could not accept being one of them.

One specialist told me, looking at the X-rays, that the kidney to be removed was on the right side; the other specialist said it was on the left. So I made a decision and finally said, "We've got to take Charles home. I'm sorry, no operation." Charles immediately became all right. He sat up in bed and miraculously put his own trousers on. We hired a limousine. To Burgess and the road man and the nurses, Charles said, "Isn't New York wonderful? It's marvelous to be out." So he came back to the hotel and got off the elevator and popped right back into bed. There's no pleasure keen as pain's relief. He came back to the hotel really riding on the pleasure of getting out of that hospital and not having to face another operation. It was miracle time—which we have all known, after all. You lose a pain momentarily and spring is waving around you.

But then . . . back at the hotel Charles was again getting worse and worse, with less and less walks and more and more drugs. From shots every two hours it was every hour and a half. Then he would sleep for two or three hours, and it would start all over again, night and day, all the time.

With the expenses of three hospitals and specialists, doctors, and the hotel penthouse, and the road man and Peter, and all the nurses, the finances were cracking. But Charles never once said anything that expressed a worry for others. People don't turn into angels because they are ill, but sometimes there is a glimmer of what another person might be feeling. Yet Charles was as he had always been all through his life. If he said, "How do you do?" I don't think he even knew the real meaning of the words. How do you feel? How are you? I don't think it faintly crossed his mind—not for any of the people who came to see him: the nurses and Loyd Wright and Burgess.

I thought that he might occasionally thank me for something I'd done—even for the fish I'd cooked for him. Maybe he was remembering all the resentments he had for me. Maybe he did have some "How do *you* do" thoughts for his boyfriends. Charles still liked to light the boyfriends' cigarettes, even if he was standing up and the boy was sitting down.

Our finances were now at the breaking point, I was told. Our lawyer and the doctors agreed that we had better return to California. Taft Schreiber's doctor, after all, had been Charles' doctor in Hollywood. He could take over the case. So we took eight places on the plane and made four of the places into a bed. They knocked Charles out completely with drugs to avoid his having any pain on the plane. He was taken in an ambulance to the airport and put on a stretcher bed for the flight. Besides Charles, there was the road man, Bob Hulter, one male nurse, and me; Peter Jones stayed in New York for modeling jobs and stage work. Eight seats, first class, and we got Charles back, still deeply under drugs.

Next thing, Charles woke up in the schoolroom, with the pre-Columbian figures and his paintings all around him. But I believe Charles really didn't know where he was for a day or two. And then he didn't say something like, "I'm glad to be home." A place was a place was a place, and a nurse was a nurse and a drug was a drug.

Long before Charles ever was ill, he had said to me, "I wish I could get over this sex business, so when we're old we can travel together." We had never really been on a planned holiday, except as part of work, and I was glad that at least he thought about that—about this sex thing being something that just got in the way. I thought then that it *would* be kind of nice some day to go abroad with Charles on a pure vacation, to a place like Japan maybe, because Charles wanted so much to go there.

After Charles' gallbladder operation, when I was well away on the road touring, Charles spent the last part of his convalescence fulfilling his life wish of going to Japan. Taft Schreiber saw to it that he had an unimportant TV assignment to cover his expenses. M.C.A. also arranged introductions in Kyoto for Charles to see the gardens and meet priests and visit the temples. But he went with Peter Jones.

I have some photographs of the two of them traveling through

Japan. From descriptions and a few letters and pictures, I see that Charles when in Japan did as the Japanese did. He felt himself akin to people who searched for and found peace. He was such a good actor that I'm sure he convinced them that he was one of them. Even so, Charles seemed delighted when a stranger said to him, "How is Elsa?" Also, he ordered specially made Japanese dishes for our house in Santa Monica.

The Kyoto importers wrote to me that "Charles was so terribly anxious that you be pleased." But Charles never told me that the dishes were made to please me. Maybe he was exploiting the loving husband bit—probably to make the Peter Jones companionship look better.

I hated the dishes. They were too heavy. After all, I did the washing up at Santa Monica where they were used, and they were too large and would not stand on any shelf; you had to tilt them to stack them in the cupboard. We almost got divorced over them. Charles said, "All right, smash them!" I said, "Individually they're beautiful." He said, "All right, we'll give them away separately. Give one to Christopher—*he'd* love it."

Charles had more cobalt treatments in Los Angeles. He knew, of course, that cobalt was for cancer, but he still never mentioned it to me. He never said, "I have cobalt, so I must have cancer." Burgess had talked around it with him, as did Christopher Isherwood.

All through his illness, Charles had been growing a mustache, which had become huge. The mustache was for Billy Wilder—for the film *Irma la Douce*. Billy Wilder had come to the house and sat in the garden with Charles. By this time he knew that Charles had cancer, but Charles was so lively that Wilder was actually hypnotized into thinking that maybe he could still play the part. Or so Billy Wilder said to me afterward.

Hedda Hopper, the gossip columnist, called me and wanted to get the lowdown on Charles, although she already knew, I think. I said to her, "Hedda, please write that Charles walked around the garden with Billy Wilder. And say that Charles is reading a lot. He's reading the papers and scripts and things." It was what had to be told. I was able to leave the newspaper cuttings of Hedda's column by Charles' bed, and when he read them, they became true. Or seemed to.

Shelley Winters sent Charles the following telegram:

DEAR CHARLES IT'S MY BIRTHDAY AGAIN AND I AM
PLAYING EFFECTIVELY TO A PACKED HOUSE AND MY
THOUGHTS ARE WITH YOU ESPECIALLY TODAY ALL YOU

GAVE ME THE DISCIPLINE AND LOVE OF THEATRE THE
RESPECT AND BELIEF IN MYSELF THE UNDERSTANDING
OF THE POETRY THAT CONNECTS ALL MANKIND. MY
FATHER GAVE ME HIS BLOOD BUT YOU GAVE ME A
MARVELOUS PART OF YOURSELF AND THE ABILITY TO
PASS IT ON TO OTHERS I FEEL ESPECIALLY BLESSED
BECAUSE BUT FOR YOU MY FATE MIGHT HAVE BEEN
THE SAME AS POOR MARILYN'S. GET WELL QUICK. I
LOVE YOU
   SHELLEY.

But the cobalt treatments in Los Angeles did no good. Finally Charles'
legs gave out, just like that. He was being kept alive, day by day, in pain,
with drugs—all this with full-time nurses, of course.

One night Charles was taken to the hospital and I had to sign a
consent form for an operation on his spine. Dr. Corday brought in a
spinal specialist, who tested Charles' toes and realized that he had no
feeling below the waist and was paralyzed. They took more X-rays, as
Charles screamed. Then they analyzed the X-rays while Charles lay
there in pain on the stretcher in the basement corridor. The doctors
decided to operate that night. I remember that when Charles was
wheeled into the elevator to be taken to the operating room, his last
words were, "Well, I've still got my voice."

Ray Henderson, Bill Phipps, and I waited in the waiting room. The
operation started about nine o'clock and they wheeled Charles out of
the operating room about three in the morning. It was strange waiting,
because all the time I had really hoped that he wouldn't come round.
After the operation, when they took him to his room, Charles was
moaning. But still, he asked for a smoke. And Bill Phipps was really
the tenderest thing in the world. Bill lighted a cigarette for Charles and
put it to his lips and said, "Pull, Charles."

The doctor came to Charles' room about four o'clock in the morning and again pinched Charles' toes. Charles did feel it, so the doctor,
very happy, said the operation was a success. Afterward, they would get
Charles—for morale more than anything—to walk around the floor.
But his feet never touched the floor. Two interns held Charles up and
merely moved him around. There was a mirror there on the wall, but
whenever Charles passed it, he would not look at himself.

When Charles was in the hospital for the spinal operation, Mrs.
Alfred Hitchcock came there to see him. Then, Charles' brother Tom
arrived from England. Tom was in Hollywood for only two weeks
because of the demands of the Royal Hotel in Scarborough. Frank, the
younger brother, who had never been too strong, had sold the Pavil-

lion Hotel and retired. Anyway, Tom had returned to Catholicism but, to his credit, he did not try to proselytize. Tom may have had talks with Charles—I don't know—about Catholicism, but he talked mostly about things like going fishing with his wife on the lochs of Scotland, and the beauty of the rainbows coming over the lake.

Charles became closer to his brother Tom than he had in his whole life. Sometimes people come back to each other, whatever the past—family people. When Tom left for England, it was understood that Frank would then come to visit. Frank had suffered the same kind of guilts as Charles, for the same reasons, and since Frank had lived with a fellow, his great "sin" returned him to the Catholic Church, too. Jimmy, Frank's fellow, had also died of cancer, and Tom had told me that Frank understood what it was to sit patiently and hold someone's hand who is dying.

So Frank was now here and staying at the Curson Avenue house, and he and I would alternate our times with Charles. Frank would go to see Charles in the morning, I'd go in the afternoon, and evenings we'd both go to say good night. Loyd Wright advised Frank to carry the will on him at all times in case Charles' mind became clear. But under drugs constantly, how could it? The pain always came back, so there were always drugs. Even if Charles appeared cheerful and light-headed, he still wasn't clear, because in this twilight sleep he forgot from second to second. All drugs are forgetfulness.

One day Father Noonan, a Catholic priest, came to visit Charles. Charles had gone on Father Noonan's *The House of St. Francis* radio program to please our housekeeper, Heidel. I liked Father Noonan, but Charles had been so violently anti-Catholic for the thirty-three years of our marriage that I felt any religious pressure from the family might make Charles' depression deeper. All I said to him now was, "Please, can't you take your collar off?" I thought Charles' automatic fear of what he might think was a vision would terrify him. So Father Noonan went away. I suppose he came back some other time.

I didn't work at all during that year, and I wouldn't have worked because I had to be at the hospital every day. I hadn't gone out any-where. I had to cook certain things Charles liked. I began to make peach jellies with tangerine juice. Charles also wanted very thin slices of filet mignon, very rare, on thin pieces of bread and butter, so I took them to the hospital. I would get up early in the morning and be very busy all day.

There were letters, thick bundles of letters that arrived at the hospital. I took these airplane bags full of letters back to the house, two bags a day—sympathy letters hoping that Charles would get better. Of course, after the publicity of Charles' operation had died down, the bundles got smaller. I went through all the letters. I kept a card index listing the people I ought to answer, the people who sent flowers, old friends, and so forth.

Charles had to be turned over every half hour, day and night, because he became sore and it was agonizing for him. By now he was eating practically nothing. He weighed only about ninety pounds.

Under drugs you stop knowing what is real and what isn't. Charles began to believe that the nurses were angels with actual wings, angels of mercy, literally. For a time, he thought they were Hawaiian angels in hula skirts. When Charles came out of a sleep, he'd look through the protective bars—the bars on the bed, like a prison—and he would stare through them most of the time. I suppose he never could tell whether what he saw was real or just a dream.

One day, Charles suddenly turned against me, for he had had a terrible dream. I asked him, "What's the matter, Charles?" Even the nurse asked him what was wrong. Charles said, "How horrible . . . how horrible!" He said that he had been doing a show in San Diego, on this stage, and I was in the audience with Orson Welles. But before the show I had told Charles that I was running away with Welles. Then, during the show—right there on the stage—Charles had a bowel movement in his pants. Though Charles had dreamed it, he didn't say it was a dream, and now in the hospital, he shouted at me, "How dare you! How dare you come to my room! Go away!" For three days, he believed that that dream was the real thing and so he just turned against me.

I suppose one can partly understand and analyze a dream like that. A long time back, Orson Welles had stayed with us in our Pacific Palisades house in order to get away from some problem or other— from some unpleasant publicity about Rita Hayworth. He upset the staff. Anyway, what with Orson Welles staying with us, and also a dreadful telegram he had sent Charles during the *Galileo* tryout days, it seems that Welles became a horrible threat in Charles' dream.

All the time, Frank was around with the will in his pocket. I was in very good health, except I had to have vitamin A shots because my blood pressure had gone up. But it was necessary for me to try to find relief from the continuous hospital routine, so Frank agreed that I should go to the Ballet Folklorico one night. The ballet was playing in Los Angeles and I wanted to see it very much. So several of my friends—I think four of us—went.

Frank wasted no time. While I was gone, he got in a priest who gave Charles the last rites, the last unction, or whatever, and also got him to sign the will at the same time. Charles signed it with an X. During both of those transactions I would say that Charles was not in his right mind. That is, being so drugged, he wasn't what is called legally aware or sane or whatever. To be able to make or sign a will, you have to be "of sound mind and body." But Frank, since he had his own religious foot in the door again, didn't mind this little error or sin on the side of the will and Charles' salvation.

That same night, Frank came to the house very happy and said to me, "Charles has embraced the faith again."

I said, "Oh, well, he hardly knows what he's doing." And then— I'm sure I was probably too frank with him—I said, "You've known Charles all these years and you know that he's always been anti-Catholic. Perhaps, even too anti-Catholic. The church can't do any good now for Charles, but if it relieves him, you're quite right, of course."

And Frank said, very simply, "It helps the soul in heaven."

Charles' great pride was that he had had the strength to question and then give up his Catholic faith. I am of two minds as to whether he enjoyed the guilt of this cardinal sin. I did not know any other side of Charles on this subject, but I see now that he gloried in what he thought of as a winning battle. This pride alone should have caused me to wonder about something that seemed to me was nothing to battle and win about.

I had only read and heard from proselytizers that "Once a Catholic, always a Catholic." Charles had always despised that theory and said so to me and many of his students. Denver Pyle, Jane Wyatt, and Arthur O'Connell, among others who were in Charles' class, had said years before that, like Queen Gertrude, Charles "doth protest too much."

Charles certainly had a large collection of anti-Catholic jokes, but then I knew how truly non-Catholic he had become. Some years before, he and I had been driving past Forest Lawn and he had said, "I suppose we'll both finish up there someday," and I had said that I thought I'd prefer cremation. Then Charles had said, "I did not like the idea once, but now I guess I'd prefer cremation, too." I did not repeat this to Tom and Frank, ever. Why horrify them and make their hearts break and probably actually bleed about something that couldn't matter now, anyway.

Jack Dewsbery, Charles' cousin and a distinguished psychoanalyst, recalled in a letter that

> Charlie and I were both staunch disbelievers in the Catholic religion, and we both went through some considerable travail in fighting ourselves free of it. . . . Charlie told me that there was a particular occasion in the war when the section in which he was a soldier was going into an action in which they were very likely

to be decimated [his own words] and he was offered some sort of religious consolation by the padre, but had no difficulty in refusing it.

Protesting too much to me and others that he had no need for the Catholic faith, Charles had told stories against Catholics and Jesuits that gave the feeling that maybe he had become prejudiced to the point of atheism—in itself another faith, a faith that one *knows* that there is no God. But Charles was hoping—rather than searching, I would say —for something to answer his fears and guilts, and he was ravenously lonely for the comfort of some unknown assurance. Charles said to me, after Frank had got in another priest, "I wish they were more intelligent." Another time, after yet another priest had been in to see him, Charles said, "I guess I've joined the gang." And once he said, "Do you know the Pope has been to see me?"

The bad side of all of this was that Charles also seemed to think he had left his money to the church. The day after I'd been to the Ballet Folklorico, I went to the hospital and Charles half raised up in bed, looked at me, and said, "What have I done?" He looked very agitated.

And I said, "What *have* you done?" And Charles persuaded the doctor, the nurses, and especially Loyd Wright and me that he had made out everything he had to the church.

So Loyd Wright came down to the hospital that same evening, along with the doctors—conference time. We all got in the hospital conference room downstairs and sat at a long table—papers, pencils; big drama and scene. Loyd Wright said, "Keep calm. Charles is not sound of mind." The priest, who was also there, said that of course Charles hadn't done anything like that, and he couldn't have accepted it if Charles had.

It was late at night by then, and we trooped up and stood outside Charles' room. Loyd told the nurse, "I'd like to see Charles. I'd like to see how he looks." Then Loyd Wright went right in, along with the doctor. I didn't go in. It would have been too much. The whole thing suddenly had become slightly sordid. Through the door I heard Charles say, "Am I dying? What's the matter? Am I dying?" It must have worried him to see the doctor, the priest, and our lawyer—all the authorities together.

As it turned out, it was all just another one of Charles' delusions. But the will mixup resulted in a kind of "deal," for in order for Charles to remain blessed and saved by the Catholic Church, it meant that he *must* have been in his right mind when he received the last rites, also when he signed the will. So, regardless of whether Charles was legally in his right mind, Charles got saved and Loyd Wright got the will. This was more important than I knew at the time, because if a person leaves no will, a huge bond has to be posted in the probate court in case the legatee escapes the country with the goods.

With Charles home again in the schoolroom, Rev. Msgr. M. H. Benso, pastor of St. Ambrose Church here in Hollywood, came to the house and later sat and talked to me one evening—after he had seen Charles. Not knowing what to talk about, I had looked up who Saint Ambrose was and what he had done. I found out that Saint Ambrose had introduced the Ambrosian Chant to the church in A.D. 384. His feast day is December 7, and his emblem is a beehive. The legend is that a swarm of bees settled on his mouth when he was a baby, not harming him at all.

Well, I like to be prepared with a conversation bunkhole at all times. It was all unneeded, of course, because Father Benso dropped comforting clichés in rapid succession and, with a parting blessing, said, "How happy you must be that your husband has returned to the church!" I could only be truthful and said, "According to the tenets of your church, I'm afraid he is not my husband. You see, we were married in a registry office." Perhaps I should have stuck to my research about bees.

Maureen O'Hara was calling me a lot around this time to say that she hoped Charles was seeing a priest. She later said:

> When I first heard that Charles was ill, I called up Elsa and she said, yes, it was true. Elsa was terribly against Catholics, which may have influenced Charles. I asked, "Can I see Charles?" and, apparently, I must have been very determined. But Elsa said, "No, the doctor says the less he is roused the better. If roused, he then has to have even more drugs." So I said, "Elsa, I would never do anything that would harm Charles. But I'll pray for him." I knew that Elsa was dead against this.

Swarms of religious people are only too willing to say a neutral person is "against religion" or "terribly anti-the faith," but very few are gracious enough to call a neutral, neutral. Fortunately, Charles' brother Frank was a great comfort to me when all I needed was a little tolerance from others.

34

You cannot say quite why the mind leaps forward and backward unexpectedly, but if there is a reason and you can find it, you can catch the understanding of anyone—like a half-forgotten tune or the smell of autumn leaves and wood smoke. I was sitting in Charles' hospital room one night at Cedars of Lebanon. I had taken him a small but particularly graceful branch of camellia from the garden, and I put it in an ordinary toothbrush glass. Charles was under constant, heavy sedation —if awake, he was in pain, if under drugs, dreaming. I knew from reading about LSD and other drugs that when a drugged person looks at anything, apparently it can become the most superbly beautiful thing he has ever seen in his life. Anyway, Charles woke up for a lucid moment or two and looked at the branch of camellia and said, "You know, that's as beautiful—in fact, more beautiful—than anything you and I saw in Japan."

I said—how badly my honesty now served me—"But I was not in Japan with you, Charles. You were with Peter." Charles' face distorted into a thousand crinkles. He wept the most bitter tears for about twenty seconds, then slept as if nothing had happened.

Eventually, the torture of the cobalt treatments became too much for Charles. Being taken down to the cobalt machine, carried on that narrow stretcher, being lifted down, and being jostled in order to get through doorways and around corners—these treatments every single day, and all the pain and fear that went with them. Charles was always frightened when they were taking him down to that room. One time he thought he was being taken down in a submarine and water was being let in. Then he screamed that *they* were watching him, that there were cameras on him, and how dare they photograph him in the nude for a film. But Charles was left alone with the "camera"—they would all go out of the room because of the rays from the cobalt. Each time he was taken down to that room, he was crying and screaming to have extra drugs to ease the pain. It was terrible. And the treatments did no good.

Christopher Isherwood, who kept a diary, made these entries regarding Charles' illness:

> I got the impression very strongly that this medical solicitude is not the right thing for him, however necessary it may practically be . . .
>
> Charles woke up and we sat together for a while and I held his hand and he said, "Do you think I shall ever get well?" And I asked him, "Well, do you want to?" And he said, "Yes. I don't want to go." And the tears ran down his cheeks.
>
> Charles said once, in his typical abrupt, tragic voice, "You know what's the matter with me, don't you?" . . . He said he was appalled how unprepared he was to die. The only thing that has helped him was thinking about some of the Japanese Temple Gardens he had seen . . .
>
> [Charles] was getting hallucinations. He believed the doctor was practicing witchcraft and was trying to get control of his mind. "Of course," said Charles, "he can only have it for very short periods." And I realized that Charles was mixing up this witchcraft fantasy with show business and this became even more evident when he asked me, "How much do you think I'd be paid as a witch?" "A great deal," I told him, and this seemed to please him.

Albert Finney passed through Los Angeles on his way to Australia and visited Charles. Afterward, I wrote to John Beary, who had understudied Finney in *The Party* and was now a friend of Albie's:

> Albie passed through L.A. a few weeks ago. He crept in to see Charles who was asleep. I made this exception because I felt Albie is a sufficiently brilliant actor to get some good from seeing a giant going.

Albie wrote his reactions to the visit in a letter to Beary dated December 11, 1962, only days before Charles died:

> We went into the room and Charles was at one end of the room on the bed and Elsa and I sat at the other end and talked.

It is terrible, John, as now he has to have injections for everything and blood transfusions, and what is worse, it all seems so futile.

After we talked for about ten minutes . . . Elsa said go and look at him. I walked across the room and looked at the remains of this Big Man. The top half of his body was twisted on to his left side and his face was pushed into the pillow, but even from that extraordinary angle, one could see that all the flesh had left him. All the bones of his face were prominent and on his upper lip he had a white, Wyatt Earp mustache . . .

Elsa had told me that he started to fight death very hard in the last few weeks and somehow that straggly, messy white mustache showed that in his mind, when he was lucid, he was going to get up and act again, but the face and the withered arm, which protruded from the bed clothes, gave me my first look at death.

I then went home with Elsa and talked to her for about an hour. She seems absolutely accustomed to living with the reality of Charles' illness. However, I think when he dies she will break.

I find it difficult to tell with Elsa, really, because she always was so strange, but I think through all the difficulties of their marriage, there has remained a very strong bond between them and when that breaks it will affect her very badly.

With all the cobalt treatments Charles only got worse and worse. Then the doctors tried one more "latest discovery." I think it was developed in Canada and, simultaneously, in the United States. It was evolved from periwinkles and was injected intravenously. I was shown pictures of miraculous cures, and once more had to sign Charles into further fear and pain—and back to the eternal letdown.

So we took Charles back to the house again, and he was once again back in his schoolroom. Since New York we had got a proper hospital bed with all the buttons to lift up and ease up. The day before Charles died, one of the nurses told me that all Charles said to her was, "I wonder what it's like to die." That's all. And Christopher Isherwood also told me that Charles had said to him, "The preoccupation is with death, isn't it?"

Another loyal friend was Bruce Zortman. He had helped Charles with his words and Southern accent during the *Advise and Consent* days, and Otto Preminger even gave him a part in the film, that of a journalist. Today Bruce is a professor at a university.

In 1962 Bruce corrected the galley proofs of Charles' second anthology, the follow-up to *Tell Me a Story*, entitled *The Fabulous Country*. Charles had written very personal introductions to the stories he had collected and read for his tours across America. I consider his writing in these two books the nearest thing to getting to know him, for in them Charles really delved into himself and bared his thoughts and memories as much as it was possible for him to do. When the last book came out, Charles was not aware of it. He probably forgot he ever wrote it, but I always kept it in a drawer by the bed in case he remembered. Like all people, Charles wanted all others to understand him, in a kind of search for comfort. Charles' research and readings and writings are what soothed him the most.

Bruce Zortman had told me that he loved Charles, though he was not *in* love with him. Bruce said he really loved Charles as a person, but his method of showing his love was sometimes painful, too. Unfortunately, if someone was ill, Bruce had to be ill. So every time Charles felt very bad, Bruce felt worse. And finally, when Charles was really dying, Bruce sat by his side because Charles said he wanted to dictate a book, a book about his own life. Charles would go into a dream, and when he came out of it he thought he had written something. If I came around the corner quietly, Charles would say, "Get out, I'm dictating!" And Bruce would signal to me helplessly. Bruce was just sitting there with pencil and pad, and nothing came from Charles.

Charles said to me once, "Today . . . today I wrote something. It's something . . . it's wonderful . . . my mind is working clearly now. It is so profound, so deep. At last, I've seen something very, very clearly and I've written it down." Bruce showed me the work pad. "I was in love with Lillian Gish"—that's all Charles said that day. But in his mind he had written something that was great. Charles was so full of morphine. And Bruce Zortman was so patient.

Then the days and nights were quiet. Patience and impatience became one placid emotion. In the house we had Eddie, the houseman-chauffeur, and a dear, comfortable cook who'd been a nurse and promised to stay to the end. Then there were the three nurses and Frank and I. Frank had been an amazing companion during the last few months—besides getting some sort of sly entertainment out of being a clever businessman in negotiating with that ogre of the Styx, Forest Lawn. Frank had made all the painful arrangements for the funeral, and for his own humor, he did it economically. Everything to be simple and quiet. Frank giving away the name of Laughton—never. Perhaps they guessed a day or so before the funeral, but it was then too late for silver coffin handles and various other trimmings that they offer for sale.

Charles died on a Saturday night, December 15, 1962, almost as if he'd ordered it beforehand. For years, if Charles had a cold or cough or toothache, it had without exception always reached its peak on a

Saturday night. Perhaps because that is a time when it is impossible to get a doctor, perhaps because Sunday is a day of rest. Saturday is the end of nature's working week. So I sat in our little study room—almost like an alcove, there is no door between it and the schoolroom—and I felt this was the time that Charles would choose to go: ten o'clock, Saturday night.

Frank had told me to go and sit in the little room off the schoolroom that was used for theatre books, plays, and art books. Then he came in and told me, "He's gone." He asked me to get a strip of cloth for the nurse and please to go upstairs. We called Dr. Corday from the kitchen phone. For that short time I was a child—all focus had gone. When I got upstairs the TV was on, with no sound, and the screen was filled with Charles' face, cutting from character to character. How did they know so soon? This remained a mystery. There was no priest in the room when Charles died, as several Catholics have stated to each other. The nurse who was on that night, though, was the one out of three who was a Catholic. After forty-five minutes Frank came up to me and said, "You can come down now. Charles has left. The Forest Lawn people came."

Poor Frank died a year after Charles. He died of cancer of the brain. I had become devoted to Frank. I went to England to see him, but he didn't seem to know me.

After Charles' death, Maureen O'Hara later said:

One day, Bronwyn called me and she said, "Mommie, Elsa Lanchester called. She said to tell you that Charles died, but she thought you would like to know that he saw a priest."

I had also called up our former housekeeper, Heidel, who was relieved and grateful as well. I was not trying to be virtuous—it just didn't cost a hill of beans to give a little pleasure to these two.

Maureen concluded:

For me, this gesture makes Elsa the greatest woman in the world. She was dead against all of this, but she just wanted me to know that she did it. It makes her twenty feet tall!

There was the funeral that had to be faced. I wanted it to be nondenominational so no one would be offended, including Charles' brothers. I had a boys' choir sing one of the hymns in Latin to please Tom and Frank, and I knew there had to be a fine eulogy.

I had begun to understand the meaning and depth of Prospero's character in *The Tempest* while Charles was dying. Prospero cleared up in my mind from being a foggy, mysterious memory of the Old Vic to become clear as crystal. In one flash—or perhaps in weeks of flashes—I saw what Prospero's words were all about. *The Tempest* is one of the last plays Shakespeare wrote, and in it I think he is saying good-bye to his art through Prospero. And as Charles was lying there, I saw that it was Charles' farewell to his art, his acting. So I wanted some speeches of Prospero's to be included in the eulogy. I took a pencil and marked the parts of *The Tempest* that I felt appropriate to Charles:

> I'll break my staff,
> Bury it certain fathoms in the earth,
> And deeper than did ever plummet sound
> I'll drown my book . . .

I thought that Burgess Meredith, who had been such a close friend of Charles' and who had even made special trips to Hollywood to see Charles while he was ill, should speak the eulogy. He has a superb speaking voice. But Burgess was busy and would not be able to be there. Then I thought of Christopher Isherwood, who also spoke beautifully. So I did ask Christopher, and I showed him the *Tempest* pieces that I thought were right and that were revelations to me. Christopher's knowledge and experience were beyond my own, but he agreed with the pieces that had floated back to me—and he spoke them with great beauty and power and humanity at the funeral.

The funeral took place on the Wednesday following Charles' death, and I rested upstairs on Tuesday evening. Frank and Ray Henderson were talking downstairs about the programming. Ray was to play the organ, and Christopher was to speak what we had chosen from *The Tempest*. It seemed that somewhere down there someone had dropped a knife or fork or even a pair of scissors—and I broke down. An hour or two later, Frank sat by me and said, "You would not have done that if you hadn't been a nice person. Now, come downstairs and we'll have a cup of tea."

The next morning, as it got light, I walked in the garden and picked a tiny bunch of miniature camellias. I wore a black dress and coat and clutched my camellias. I put on an antique Italian bracelet that Charles had given me years ago—oh, yes—and a small square of black organdy pinned on my hair. Frank thought it best to do so.

I put the camellias on the coffin as a sort of good-bye. I had not thought of doing it beforehand, so my own gesture surprised and upset my heartbeat. I cannot help feeling that the onlookers thought it was calculated, but truly it wasn't. I wish I could forget the poor body to this day.

As part of the service, I asked Reverend John Cantelon please not to use the hymn, "Oh, Death, Where Is Thy Sting?" My father and his fellow atheists used to sing a parody of that hymn:

> Oh, Death, Where Is Thy Sting,
> Oh, Death, Where Is Thy Sting?
> The bells of hell go Ding-a-ling-a-ling,
> For you but not for me . . .

Reverend Cantelon nevertheless *did* use it. Father Cantelon, oh, where is thy gratuity? Also, we all agreed that it would be nice if the Mitchell Boys' Choir sang the hymns with choirboy voices ("head tones"), but instead they sang with what they call "chest tones," more strident. It seems they only do it to annoy because they know it teases!

Although I had not seen much of Jean and Dido Renoir through the years and I had not ever contacted them during Charles' illness, when Charles died I had the awful task of having to pick some pallbearers—and so I asked Jean Renoir. Jean and Dido sat next to me in what is called the family room, where the close friends and relatives sit. Dido looked like a Goya painting in her black lace mantilla.

It was such a release when Charles died that I was rather happy and I could not conceal it. I had been broken by so many months of watching Charles die that, in the family room, I went around and talked to everyone and said, "Please, don't look unhappy. Charles had been in great pain and now it's finished." All of Charles' nurses sat together, and I looked at them and we understood each other. "We all know . . . we cannot help but feel relieved and happy!"

I wasn't giving a performance, I was being quite sincere as I spoke to everyone. Then I said, "I've talked to Burgess Meredith this morning and Burgess said he found himself—this is exactly what he told me —he said, 'When I heard that Charles had died, I had my bath and I was singing and I was wondering why on earth am I singing? and I realized that it is such a relief to Charles and to us that he has died at last.' "

But if you've got to mourn, of course, you've got to mourn. Different people have different inner emotions that pour out in many ways at many times. I think I miss or mourn Charles more now than at the time of the relief.

Three weeks later I had to go and sign the paper confirming the order for the brass plate to be affixed on the square marble door in the Garden of Remembrance. Ray Henderson very kindly went with me to Forest Lawn—past the florist shop and into a wide corridor of beige walls and carpets. After passing several closed doors, we were ushered into a room on the left and gestured to seats. From the first, in the corridor, the vox humana was tremblingly playing its heart out.

The sound seemed to penetrate a thick layer of cotton or, perhaps, I should describe it as an insistent statement that one was going deaf, quite deaf. Ray sat in a beige chair and so did I, by a little beige desk.

At last an aged beige gentleman came in with the papers. "Now," he said, "Mrs. Laughton, would you please sign here?" And as he said it, I read:

1899–1962
CHARLES LAWTON

"No, sir. *Laughton.*"
Ray and I were glad to get out of the joint.

Egham 2465

D̶e̶ Jany 1st

Dearest Elsa,

I wonder what USA weather is like—It has been very cold here   hope it will be better when you come—Do let me have a line to say when—

& I wonder whether I ought to be looking round for some other domicile—I have paid my rent till April 1st & they expect me to pay £160 then in advance for another year; which I don't feel inclined to do. I do not want to bother you, but just think it would be as well to tell you how things stand —Waldo, as you know, has not been helpful—and I have been obliged to ask advice from Tom [Charles' brother] who has been very kind while Charles was here—I know it is not long but are you feeling more settled & happier?

Charles's death must have been an awful upheaval for you & wounds not easily healed—

Perhaps I have "overstayed my welcome"—Apologies! but there—My whole wish has been to see you again with Charles if possible. Now, just yourself—

At the moment I am snowed up at the Bussells

Karlmede
16 Riverside
Egham   Surrey

With much love & my best wishes for '63

Biddy

35

What does a widow of sixty do? I had no offers of acting jobs because there's an unspoken rule not to disturb the bereaved widow too soon. Also there was a second aftermath to Charles' death—a spate of little dinners given by maybe three or four producers or directors and maybe an agent or two; usually a professor or educator was also invited. Then weeks spent answering sympathy letters, flowers, cards.

The full weight of making decisions finally but slowly made itself known to me. How I wish I had invented the lovely line, "The fog comes on little cat feet," for that's how self-responsibility enfolds you. I can see how men and women left alone can mope themselves into another liaison. But the freedom bug got me very quickly and I knew that I must work—at almost anything.

Advisers advised me to go away for a time from the house and its associations. So I went off to England to see my mother in Brighton and to stay with a friend in London. When I at long last got to Brighton —alone after so many years—I really felt a sad kind of ecstasy. The diamondlike air was something that I had breathed before, centuries before, and it gave me a steely strength even at the railway station— really, even before the train the *Brighton Belle* came to a stop. The fading of the familiar smells of the so very-very-first-class Pullman— businessmen, poached eggs, toast and kippers, polished brass, old velvet—into station soot and deafening noise, and into the rattling Brighton taxi.

I went straight up to Biddy at Highcroft Villas. Of course, I'd first been there in the early 1950s when the flat was being got ready and Biddy was staying with a young couple. The 1950s had been an unhappy time for Biddy, Charles, and me, working in separate places, and coughs, colds, and flu. But now, on this trip, it was a new world, with the fears of childhood and the premonition of age that gave me an eerie sort of excitment. Ghosts of autumn and icepicks of spring seemed to be singing away. Poor Biddy. I don't quite know when she felt she first wanted to go back to Brighton, but I do know and I did understand that it was something to do with her roots and going home to the only possible place to die. I feel it myself very strongly. I may be knocked down by a bus anywhere in the world, but I would prefer it to be in Brighton.

The taxi stopped outside 18 Highcroft Villas, and I saw Biddy's long pointed finger holding back the curtain of her living room. She didn't withdraw it, just went on looking at me, adding that extra moment to my visit. The taxi driver helped me out and was so patient waiting for change. Little beads from his breath hung on his walrus mustache. He said a little grumpily, "You're from America, aren't you?" I nodded. The curtain moved a little bit with impatience: Was I going to talk to the taxi driver forever?

I took a deep breath of Brighton air. The sky was navy blue with the last of the long dusk, and I leaped up the flight of cement steps and Biddy was at her front door. The room was warm but somehow smelled fresh as a room does when there is no smoking, drinking, or perfume of any sort from the past. Biddy only liked soaps such as Lifebuoy or Wright's Coal Tar. This day she got out her bottle of (medicinal) Scotch and we had a nip, then a pot of strong tea and chocolate biscuits. Biddy seemed very weak when she talked of the recent sorrow. "Why couldn't I die, an old woman like me, instead of Charles?" she said over and over. I had brought some mixed flowers beautifully packed by Constance Spry, the lovely flower shop in London. Biddy and I found that it was very important to get the flowers in water—the most important thing in the world.

In an hour or two I left in another taxi for my hotel in Brighton, the Royal Crescent. Biddy came down to the curb to say good-bye. "See you tomorrow," she cried out. "Yes, tomorrow," I answered, "I'll pick you up. Shall we drive to the Downs and then eat somewhere?" " 'Op in, young lady," said the taxi driver to me. During the short drive the pleasant feeling that I was on my own and that decisions were suddenly mine, completely mine, gave me a fiery glow. I was not a widow, I was a "young lady" with years ahead. It had taken a few weeks for the feeling to take hold. Well, now I knew that I had become a single person, an alone person, and a re-excited person. I never did like pitiful people and I decided not to be one.

The Royal Crescent Hotel had been my headquarters off and on for so many past visits that it was enough like home to bring back nothing but sparkling associations. Part of the superb George the

Fourth architecture of the Brighton front, the hotel bowed out grace-fully facing the sea. Remembering only good days is sparkling and peaceful, too. Nothing seemed out of place in the recalled picture. The immediate arrival in my rooms of a pot of good, strong tea brought in by a true old retainer with a sweet, familiar face—"I'm sorry to hear about Mr. Laughton, Madame. Would you like some cold ham and chicken and perhaps a little custard and stewed fruit?" "Thank you, yes, that would be very nice, and some milk if possible, and how is your wife?" "As well as can be expected under the circumstances, Madame . . ." "I'm glad to hear it." In England we never ask what "the circumstances" are.

It was too cold to sit on the small ironwork balcony, but the ghosts of wild flowers and grasses Charles and I picked on the South Downs and placed in buckets and jugs were round the room, and those fairly recent days were far from hostile.

Once when I was spending the day with Biddy in Brighton, my cousin Blanche Ward was there, too. I had not seen Blanche for years —not, in fact, since the early 1930s, her Spanish revolutionary days, when she had been quite violent toward anyone who didn't think as she did. Now I would say she was older and angrier, but not about anything I can remember. Perhaps I didn't touch on a cause that drew her into battle.

The big event for the English is, of course, *tea time,* but as the years pass, the event for ladies becomes almost sacred—beer for men, it seems, and tea for women. Biddy, like her kind, lit up at the mention of tea. She said to me, "Why don't you take Blanche into Brighton for tea and give her a treat?" So off we went and had a treat: toasted tea cakes, bread and butter with jam, and sweet cakes and pastries with rather bright icing. Blanche and I talked about Biddy and her still independent spirit, and I recalled her early insistence that she did not have Waldo and me as insurance against her old age. Blanche talked about her mother, Carrie, who had died in 1926. Blanche was quite a strong-willed woman but still appeared to see herself as an orphan. I sensed that she needed to feel that Biddy was almost her mother now. Well, I would say she needed someone to look after, since she had no one to look after her. For her part, Biddy was rather hot and cold about Blanche, sometimes saying that Blanche never stopped talking and then saying that a change of company was nice.

Blanche was critical of me for becoming an American citizen and for being so far away from Biddy. But any such talk was pooh-poohed by Biddy, who with enormous bravado would say, "Oh, I'm all right" —and she was. She really did have a lot of friends and referred con-stantly to people I'd never heard of—comrade this and comrade that, and her talks with the communist group up the road. She never said or admitted that she missed me, but she was very firm about all her friends meeting me when I was in Brighton. I'm afraid I felt like a fraudulent showpiece. She was not at all forthcoming about Waldo and Muriel. Whenever I asked her about my brother and his wife, I got a very chilly answer. I would have liked to have had some contact with them, but that for some reason that has always eluded me, and we stayed distant though not unfriendly. Biddy never had a good word about Muriel, and any little gift from her was shoved out of sight with a sneer. She nailed up a blanket from them both across the kitchen window—"All it's fit for," she said. Once I brought up the subject of Aunt Nancy, whom I had liked so much and who had always been kind to me and witty and gay. Biddy told she was in a nursing home in Brighton and said, "Don't go to see her. She won't know you. She's senile." Now I regret not going. I should have recognized Biddy's same old jealousy. I didn't realize then that such jealousy continued into old age, but I suppose I'll find out for myself in good time.

All this time, of course, the probate court was tootling along beside me with its metaphorical wagging finger saying, "Don't forget, every object is ours until it's yours!" Eventually the question of the big art collection had to be faced. With the overwhelming help of my friends Michael Hall and Bill Mills, who were also collectors, I began approaching art museums that might exhibit Charles' collection all together and then tour the show around the country. I remember that the director of Phoenix's new and prestigious museum suggested the show be called "The Eye of Charles Laughton." But museums argue as to who should have the honor of showing it first, and then who shares the expenses for transport, cataloging, and lighting problems. And time was passing.

Charles' collection had unity, so I made every effort to keep it together, but no one museum or gallery would or could assume the expense and responsibility of touring it. So it was sold at Parke-Bernet Galleries during October, 1966: Pre-Columbian art, Morris Graves, Nicholas de Stael, Alfred Manessier, Sir Matthew Smith, Siqueiros, Pierre Soulages, Vieira da Silva . . . I hoped each buyer was adding the purchase to his own dedicated collection and that in the shattering of this crystal-clear collection into hundreds of pieces, "The Eye of Charles Laughton" would be preserved.

The sale was a lot of work. All art sales are a lot of work unless you're dead. It involved appearing on talk shows and taking a painting or two with me (which they usually showed upside down), having interviews about Charles the collector, and making all kinds of appearances for maneuvering and publicity. The collection sold but not nearly for as much as Charles may have dreamed. He probably turned in his grave at his misjudgments, and Parke-Bernet were definitely disappointed. But they said, "It's a year for comparatively small money on the art market, rather than big money," whatever that means.

In reading some letters from Taft Schreiber, I see that Charles may have been partly the dupe of some dealers and art gallery curators. Receiving flattery, giving flattery—accepting the role of prophet, connoisseur, and mentor, yet preserving some judgment and integrity, too.

With Taft Schreiber as a divine blank artistically, Charles experienced a burst of frenzied teaching that broke the bounds of his real love and sensitive passion for the function of the painter and the art of the collector. I say *art* advisedly. Collecting had always been a rhythmic pursuit of art that drew Charles forward like a will-o'-the-wisp. Every object that drew him on was part of a pattern, and the whole effect of his collection was one of unity.

I can never recall Charles being happier or more gratified, at any time in the years that I knew him, than he was in his role of mentor to Taft Schreiber. He basked in the successful progress of his pupil as Taft became a skilled and successful collector. I shall never forget the proud parental look on Charles' face when, in the early days, Taft spotted and bought an unsigned drawing in London. It turned out to be a Miro.

I could only stand on the sidelines and feel the warmth that reflected from Charles for his achievement, a great pleasure that he was fortunately able to know in his lifetime. Creative artists themselves only see the ocean of imperfections in their own art and the impossibility of capturing their dreams in the short time allotted to them. They are unable to accept praise in the knowledge that they may be found out in their shortcomings, and hate criticism because it opens up the truth.

Here the collector comes in. He can build a structure for perpetuity with his knowledge, his taste, and his eye. If he is faithful to these three attributes he does truly leave something for others, one little step in the selectiveness of another generation; a lesson in the pleasures of learning via somebody else's passion; a lesson also that random collecting simply for the sake of collecting is being no better than a packrat or a magpie.

Taft Schreiber offered to buy from me a large de Stael that didn't sell—that is, it didn't reach Parke-Bernet's high standard. Taft said he had a buyer for twice the amount offered, which made me think of selling. Taft then maneuvered, finagled, intrigued, said the picture could only go down in value, that the buyer had changed his mind. Then Taft said his wife didn't like it and eventually inveigled me into selling it to him for the price reached at the sale—"No percentage, you see, Elsa dear." As Taft left with the painting in his station wagon, he said, "I think perhaps, Elsa, you might let me have the small de Stael collage for what I've done for you." I was so nauseated that I said yes. God knows what the value of the big de Stael became. Anyway, Taft Schreiber died very soon after, having been given a wrong blood-type transfusion at a hospital.

Other visits to England followed between film and television work. In April and May 1964 I took Biddy on several trips to the country round Brighton in a chauffeur-driven car. I got out of the car and walked in the woods and picked flowers, always staying in her full view. She gazed out of the car at me, her little grayish-bluish eyes barely visible over the sill of the window. She was getting very bent and was shrinking; she was so very little and the car was very old and shrunken too. I'd never seen Biddy in a brougham before, after all. In April I picked bunches of primroses and violets and then later bunches of bluebells. She didn't get out of the car for these stops, as she said her "shanks" were too long or the car doors were too short.

But she always leaped out when we stopped at a cottage for tea. The ancient chauffeurs of these ancient cars were always quite used to old people and their strengths and their weaknesses. They knew that too much help caused a severe frown and too little help caused mumbling complaints, and they also had to put up with the savage barking —"Leave me alone!" Brighton chauffeurs are a race apart—such patience, such sympathy. Mostly they referred to me as "the young lady," and it was true, although I was over sixty myself. I never did suspect that they were trying to pay me a compliment—it wouldn't cross the old drivers' minds. I was "the young lady." I was suddenly glad once more to feel how much life I had left.

How Biddy glowed after a true English cottage tea with hot crumpets and probably a jolly little fire in the grate, the windows always drippingly framed with all kinds of vines and sweet flowers, with fruit trees and annual beds beyond. Biddy gazed with steady eyes at all these sights. I believe that old people make a good-bye picture for their inner memory book, but I don't know yet.

When I was once more back in Hollywood, acting parts began turning up, but nothing to turn your grapes sour over—large parts in lousy pictures and small parts in big pictures. I did have two runs of *Elsa Lanchester—Herself* with Ray Henderson at Hollywood's Ivar Theatre, and was content because I was fully aware that I did not like straight acting but preferred performing direct to an audience. You might call what I do *vaudeville*. Making a joke, especially impromptu, and getting a big laugh is just plain heaven. That goes for talk shows too. All the same, I have been in a few rare, well-etched parts in segments of a series that were of quality: *Then Came Bronson, To Catch a Thief*—uh, yes, and *The Lucy Show*.

There were several people who wanted to make a documentary about Charles—among them, Paul Gregory. I didn't want to make one at all at that time, especially with Paul. But a year or so after Charles' death, I met Paul accidentally. He came up to me, suggested dinner, and said that he would still be interested in doing a television special about Charles. I hesitated, but he argued, "After all, you'll only get mixed up with a bunch of crooks, so why not do it with me? Isn't it better to be associated with someone you know is a crook than with someone who's crooked and you don't know it?" I admit we both yelped with laughter.

I was asked by friends, "How on earth can you have dinner or see Paul Gregory after what he did to you and Charles?" Well, quite frankly, I'd rather have dinner and conversation with someone who's got some guts than with a dull person who only enjoys hearing me talk about myself and my career, and who is a total blank as a return conversationalist. Whatever else Paul Gregory was, he used to have a wild, changeable personality, and he could be pretty outrageous. When Charles was ill, Paul sent him a message through Harold Williams, our business manager. I happened to get the message six months before Charles died. It said that Paul bore Charles no ill will!

In the course of business I asked Harold Williams if I could get back a painting that Gregory had borrowed. It was a painting by Matthew Smith, "Woman with a Parrot." Charles had told me he'd only lent it to Paul to help his mental development and discerning eye. Anyway, I got a message back that Paul would rather burn the painting than return it. Loyd Wright told me not to litigate over such a small matter—it would be costly and also it might open up a whole hornet's nest. I have learned not to open up things that would make someone angry, including myself. Maybe Charles gave the goddamn "Woman with a Parrot" to Paul for some practical reason and then told me he'd lent it.

The last I heard, Paul Gregory was a lecturer in various colleges. His subject is Communication! I remember that, when I first met Paul, his daily reading was a book with a title something like *A Word for Every Day*. I remember also how, later, Paul was looking for a title for my first one-woman show. His publicist sent him a telegram: I SUGGEST "ELSA

LANCHESTER'S PRIVATE MUSIC HALL." But the telegram had a misprint. It read: PROVOTE MUSIC HALL. Paul called the publicist back, saying to him what an excellent title it was, and it nearly went to the printers that way! Paul obviously was very impressed with the nonword he'd never heard of.

Nevertheless, I wish Paul Gregory good luck.

Over the years Ray Henderson and I have been working on T. S. Eliot's *Cats (Old Possum's Book of Practical Cats)*—Ray composed the music and orchestrated it and I reading and generally becoming a cat. We have given performances of it, having been invited by orchestras (about twenty-five pieces) that are composed of musicians who like to get together for the pleasure of playing something different.

I've gotten over being angry that T. S. Eliot would not give me permission to record *Cats,* leaving similar instructions behind him. He never heard me do his *Cats* but his publishers had said that they would have liked it recorded—naturally. The story behind the story is that I became a close friend of Eliot's friend, the crippled poet, John Heyward. Since John Heyward couldn't move much, he saw in me the freedom he missed. He talked to me as his Ariel, and then his poor face smiled a lot. I often had dinner with him in his flat in Chelsea, helping him with his food and also changing cans on his wheelchair. This intimacy infuriated T. S. Eliot. John Heyward delighted in this petty jealousy that he created. This part of the story is all so long ago, the late thirties, but when it came to permission to do *Cats* on any record an icy *no* came from *John Heyward.* "Mr. Eliot strongly dislikes his *Cats* being turned into vaudeville acts, far too many people are trying to exploit them now in one way or another." And John Heyward added that I hadn't contacted him in over fifteen years. I only tell this episode now because of the "mild rock" version of *Cats* currently flourishing in the theatre. I hope Ray Henderson's version will survive and some one will perform it—to be known as "T. S. Eliot's True Cats". I finally got permission to speak it from Mrs. Valerie Eliot but *not* record it. I had written this persuasive and true description to her, "I would read from the book and use a microphone, which does tie one physically to one area. Of course, if the audience reacts one breaks the rhythm and picks it up again." Oh yeah!

One day the telephone did ring, and it was for *The John Forsythe Show.* Twenty-six episodes, probably divided into thirteen weeks, then an option for another thirteen weeks, which was picked up. This dreary piece of information is here only because Biddy began to get weaker and weaker during that time. First she had one nurse and finally full-time nurses. I received regular reports on her by mail.

The new Nurse is from the Co-op & is rather expensive, but I said I was sure you would not mind.

Your cousin Blanche Ward is coming to day & is staying a week, but of course Nurse won't leave Biddy to her tender mercies. Last night Biddy had two very bad attacks in the night but rallied round & was quite hearty the next day. . . .

I was both relieved and pleased to be in a series that gave me a regular connection with life again. The scripts were well written. I played the headmistress in a girls' school that John Forsythe seemed to have inherited and supervised the policy, leading to lots of funny situations and misunderstandings. In one episode I was picked to demonstrate what being suspended in space was like, and in another episode I was discovered in the school gymnasium by Mr. Forsythe dressed in a girl's midi, practicing to a scratchy old record of *The Dying Swan*.

But learning words is to me degrading agony—with the exception of the words to a song; that is simple and I never forget them. Doing a series was not all roses, but the safety of a good salary was giving me confidence and it helped me during Biddy's last year. Her last year it was, and I was criticized for not being with her. But my mother would *never* have said or thought, "Elsa, leave your job and come to England." Biddy had never used any tears on me. She had never said, "I am your mother," or "Have you no sense of duty?"

Instead, Cousin Blanche took up the cause:

Dear Elsa,

I have not heard from you anent my last letter, so can only imagine that the Hollywood Circe has worked its usual enchantment! Though I love Biddy very much indeed, and have fortuitously escaped the accustomed Glacification of the normal human instincts so inherent in the Lanchesters, I am not you. Believe me, Elsa, if I had my mother alive, and were in your financial position, even the beckoning finger of fame and fortune would not keep me from her side!

But then I am only a poor relation, and so permitted to indulge in idiosyncrasies of a sentimental nature! . . .

I shall write a book about the House of Lanchester, and just you watch the feathers fly!

I answered Blanche's letter, telling her that "since Charles' death I have been getting an income specified by my lawyers and the probate court. To be able to look after Biddy I am fortunate to be working in a TV series; and by contract, as you must know, it is impossible for me to leave. It is the salary from this series that enables me to provide Biddy with everything she wants."

So in Hollywood I stayed when Biddy faded away in April 1966. I have a very strong feeling that if death cannot be a quiet celebration, then save others the sorrow of waiting and watching. How do any of us know the personality switches that occur in this mysterious transformation to oblivion?

Soon after Biddy died, Cousin Blanche wrote to me again:

Well Elsa,

You have got what you wanted—Biddy's death—and I hope you are thoroughly ashamed of yourself, sacrificing a wonderful person, worth twenty of you, to the mirage of Hollywood respectability! I may not much pride myself on my acting ability, but I fancy I played Cornelia [sic] to your Goneril quite successfully . . . it did not need a modicum of psychology to know she needed affection more than any of the other frost-bitten Lanchesters, of whom you are a fit scion . . .

She wanted to see you before she died, but you found the Medusa of Hollywood to turn you into stone, and preferred the flicker of Television fame to your own mother in the end.

I can only hope, and anticipate *your* own last year of life prove as harassed and unfriended as you caused your mother's to be . . . even if conscience does not gnaw your vitals may the eagles of Prometheus do so!

B. Ward

In the early 1930s, when Charles and I began to work in America, we sent Biddy and Shamus a regular allowance. But Biddy always said then it was too much and that they were very comfortable and kept on thanking me too much. I did my duty in every practical way but I could not pour out the essential attachment that seems innate in many people toward their parents. I seemed to have inherited from Biddy a lack of filial affection—the same lack that she showed her Pater and Mater.

I never understood my father, Shamus. I didn't know him. As I remember him, his fire had gone out. In memory I liked him, but I couldn't ever like Biddy. I tried so hard. Some third party might say I was too much like her, and people have sometimes told me I reminded them of her. Maybe so. We ourselves do not know what we inherit. Perhaps we recognize the same color of hair here and long fingers there, or an alibi for our faulty physique. The voice, speech, style, and mannerisms, we are usually blind to, and in the face itself we cannot see a resemblance. I'm sure that Narcissus, gazing at himself, didn't for a moment think, "Just like good old dad."

Shamus had died in the 1940s, always having sent his love to me in Biddy's letters but never writing himself. When the telegram came saying he'd died, I said to myself over and over again, "Poor little Shamus . . . poor little Shamus." Biddy barely referred to him again. She was a mild atheist and unsentimental, and that was that. With less to criticize now, she was a sad woman with a humourless chuckle. The same allowance that we'd given both of them now went on to Biddy, and she protested again that it was too much. She lived very simply and saved a hundred pounds or so, which she occasionally offered to return.

I don't think that Biddy had much interest in the overall span of her life and its effect on herself or others. Her conversation and her letters never referred to her own past behavior or her parents or the possible repercussions from their or her early actions. Sarcasm, combined with her own form of hollow, almost macabre humor, was aimed at any living relative whose name drifted into the conversation. Her tendency to be "funny" about many simple facts of life quite often cut off communication with a sort of embarrassment on her part and on mine. Birth and babies, old age and death were not ever part of my conversation with her. I never saw Biddy or Shamus hold a baby or go to a funeral or a wedding. I also have never gone to a funeral other than Charles' or a wedding other than my own, and I have never held a baby. No, that is wrong. Once I did hold a baby for a busy mother and I nearly dropped it. I remember that it felt like a live snake in a sack. This emotion—or lack of it—might be called an inherited family trait. Acute undemonstrativeness.

Biddy's overpossessiveness in later years I found mysterious and unnatural and illogical. She had always been self-sufficient, apart from this growing need for me. Fathers dream of immortality through their sons. Biddy saw in me a completion of her tapestry. With this in mind, she thought everything I did was perfect. True, no one should expect logic in mother love.

I often wonder if Biddy felt that her own fight for freedom, when she repelled her own parents' protectiveness, had finally boomeranged back on her through me. But she was not a prober of individual behavior, least of all her own. It is possible that pride cut off self-analysis from the start. She did not indulge in retroactive self-reproach. I really don't think that she had ever said, "I wonder if what I did was right." I think Shamus in his unambitious way wondered about that question all the time.

Biddy may or may not have been aware that she didn't get a widow's pension because she was not a widow. And I question if it crossed her mind that her early fight for freedom had created a binding tie unknown to married people. She was not very kind when talking about Shamus, and I also often wondered if she loved a few other people in her day—but the tie of her enforced loyalty made her stay with him.

Biddy and Shamus seemed to be attached by this unlegal tie but to have less and less in common. Some couples get closer and old age is a sort of reward, but with Biddy and Shamus their *Cause* united them —and time does not reward political enthusiasm. From it all I learned that the cloak of respectability was, paradoxically, one of the keys to freedom. But this cloak involves a degree of hypocrisy, which one is forced to use in daily life to avoid embarrassment and hurting other people. But Biddy and Shamus were never hypocrites.

If my mother and father had met other people they liked, they might have got a divorce—but how could they? They were never married. They were held in a grip by their early strike for freedom. In defying convention they were chained by it. In time they were not even bound together by public opinion. They were forgotten. Nor were they held together by Biddy's hostile family. The family was mostly dead now or nearly dead.

Proud as Biddy's socialist friends were of her and her personal battle in 1895, it was not easy for her to wear the cloak of tradition-breaker. As I see it, after all, she knew that her gesture for women's freedom was only triggered by falling in love with Shamus. She didn't fight for women's rights first and fall in love afterward, so it's no wonder she tended to be modestly withdrawn on the subject. Followers still admired her—followers are born to follow, so they stayed with the only star that had ever shone in their lives. The old guard, Mrs. Gray and the others, kept the flag waving, and some of them were still dropping in for talks in The Kitchen over the later years. The fading aspect of the case was never dwelt on, and any far-reaching results were never dwelt on either—perhaps because there never really were any far-reaching results.

It almost seemed as if the kidnapping never happened as far as Biddy's memory was concerned, although she did keep some cuttings and letters. It was a closed book, and I think that a blank developed about the whole early episode, which was probably as well. Nature's anesthetic.

Biddy remained a professional avant-gardist to her death, insofar as she went on attending political meetings until she could no longer walk to the bus, and she still had communist posters strung up on the

316

railings outside her flat at Highcroft Villas. But Biddy's step for progress did blaze a little trail at the time. The Lanchester case may have affected the lunacy laws, and Biddy was called a brave woman at the time.

Charles and I also each dreamed of a freedom that is rarely achievable, but together we did free each other to some extent. Being successful and fairly prosperous is the nearest a human can get to it. And Charles and I, as actors, enjoyed wearing this "cloak of respectability," but as actors we enjoyed the act—most of the time. "What a wonderful couple!" people said.

When Charles died, his onetime agent Taft Schreiber said to me after the funeral, "Well, Elsa, you've had a satisfactory life, you know, and nothing really to regret. After all, Charles gave you security and freedom, and that's what you wanted, wasn't it?" Charles benefited also from our arrangement. He had the freedom and protection of our marriage.

The Santa Monica house is sold.

That transaction was so smooth. First I rented it because I was asked if I would. I knew fewer and fewer people who could be with me there and exactly at that moment a great performer was in Los Angeles and in desperate need to get away from life in a hotel. He moved in. My tenant loved it so much—thank goodness—that I told him if I sold the house he had the first option. It was as simple as that. We are very close friends now—of course I would never have sold the house to anyone but a genius. Though parting with the house hurt me deep down, it would have been worse in time if I had hung onto it. I don't visit the old place. Everyone has different tastes in furnishings and I would not want the intolerant nitpicking beast in me to be let loose. In the Santa Monica garden, if the show of hydrangea, species fuchsia and giant honeysuckle deteriorates or even dies, finding a good friend is better. A story should have an upward ending, like a retroussé nose.

So I treated myself to a new patio by the pool in the Hollywood house, which is my kingdom. There are a few orange and lemon trees in tubs. This year I had a great crop of tomatoes. I hope to grow herbs.

The schoolroom is still serving.

I rehearse, not for a show, three or four times a week with Ray Henderson, who also teaches and programs singers in the schoolroom. Ray is flourishing playing nights in a top restaurant with a following of admirers. Ray can remember everyone's musical memories, including mine.

So these rehearsals with Ray have become very important. They are therapeutic and wonderful for breathing exercise. I am not exactly a singer. I am, or was, a diseuse who tells a story rather than sings it. In the forties at the Turnabout I taught myself so much about getting to story points on one breath and so holding an audience's attention that the technique is now serving me. And Ray is so technically aware of this phrasing that working with him keeps me forever musically alert.

In the introduction for Charles Higham's book, *Charles Laughton,* I said, "I realise what Charles must have felt from childhood on. No time, no time." And I ended my book *Charles Laughton and I,* published in 1938, with, "the procession of characters in films all have friendly faces now. We look back through rose-colored spectacles." But I cannot tie up this ending with a pretty pink bow. Getting older is, to put it mildly, gruesome. And, having unloaded the past, memory is of course more localized now, though it seems to be a loyal machine willing to serve if forced. So time is now up to its tricks with me—the Bitch! It's suddenly always Christmas again. Oh, I forgot, it's *Father Time*!

Sitting on my patio, I'm enjoying looking at the advance cover for this book. When I sent the picture it is based upon to the publishers I thought it was rather a funny comment on the period. The picture was called "Two Candles and a Star" and was originally published in *The Tatler* in the twenties. And then added to that was the publisher's choice of the title, *Elsa Lanchester, Herself.* I feared for any unwanted stressing of the "I." As an actress I felt a touch of shame, you know, vanity—self-importance. But Hey Ho—"When A Lady Has a Piazza," anything goes.

> And if I should live to be
> The last leaf upon the tree in the Spring,
> Let them smile as I do now,
> At the old forsaken bough where I cling.
>
> Oliver Wendell Holmes

Hold on, I'm still alive—this book is the evidence!

Index